W9-COJ-715

PRAISE FOR *PAYBACK*

"Extraordinarily perceptive . . . a remarkably sensitive story of a generation."

— **Stanley Karnow,** *The New York Times Book Review*

"Klein rescues the grunt from anecdote and restores his dignity. . . . *Payback* is, simply, one of the best accounts of how men respond to combat written about Vietnam or any other war. . . . Klein's reporting is remarkable. . . . He brings each man to life, takes us into the battlefields between men and women, lets us see as we so rarely do the agonies and hard-won victories of growing up in working-class America. . . . He has overcome the many barriers that divided us, and has healed some of the wounds of the war."

— **William Broyles,** *Esquire*

"The most eloquent work of nonfiction to emerge from Vietnam since Michael Herr's *Dispatches* . . . Mr. Klein has a brisk, instinctive talent for illuminating American lives. . . . We come to know the five Marines as intimately as characters in a novel. . . . Indeed, *Payback* has that rare quality in a book—the visceral feel of real life, pinned down and clarified through words."

— **Michiko Kakutani,** *The New York Times*

"Some of the most vivid, harrowing, and emotionally honest writing to come out of Vietnam."

— *The Washington Post Book World*

"It's perhaps good to be reminded just how compassionate the most informed journalism can be. . . . Some of Klein's most interesting reporting concerns the effect on the wives of their husbands' experiences; he shows how supportive some of them could be. . . . Klein's book eloquently demonstrates that what brings these men back into the world is their own efforts: their understanding and their care for one another, their interest in something outside themselves, their brave determination."

—Peter S. Prescott, *Newsweek*

"It's a grim picture, painted in compelling strokes. Klein gets it all—their troubles with women, with employers, with the world—and the book must be a sober look in the mirror for the survivors. For the reader, it's near-hypnotic."

—*New York Daily News*

"A rich and important book that explains a great deal about a lot of people . . . *Payback* is the story of Joe Klein's search for the survivors of Charlie Company, 1st Battalion, 3rd Marine Regiment, vintage 1967. It is a special book because it focuses in depth on the experience of five men . . . who were temporarily thrown together in an unpopular war."

—*Chicago Sun-Times*

"[*Payback*] captures the sort of fine and private detail one ordinarily finds only in fiction."

—*People*

ALSO BY JOE KLEIN

Nonfiction

*Charlie Mike: A True Story of Heroes Who
Brought Their Mission Home*

Woody Guthrie: A Life

The Natural: The Misunderstood Presidency of Bill Clinton

*Politics Lost: How American Democracy Was Trivialized
by People Who Think You're Stupid*

Fiction

Primary Colors

The Running Mate

Payback

FIVE MARINES AFTER VIETNAM

Joe Klein

Schaumburg Township District Library
130 South Roselle Road
Schaumburg, Illinois 60193

Simon & Schuster Paperbacks

New York London Toronto Sydney New Delhi

Simon & Schuster Paperbacks
An Imprint of Simon & Schuster, Inc.
1230 Avenue of the Americas
New York, NY 10020

Copyright © 1984 by Joe Klein
Originally published in 1984 by Alfred A. Knopf, Inc.

All rights reserved, including the right to reproduce this book
or portions thereof in any form whatsoever. For information,
address Simon & Schuster Subsidiary Rights Department,
1230 Avenue of the Americas, New York, NY 10020.

Acknowledgment for permission to reprint previously published
material is on page 399.

First Simon & Schuster trade paperback edition October 2015

SIMON & SCHUSTER PAPERBACKS and colophon are registered
trademarks of Simon & Schuster, Inc.

For information about special discounts for bulk purchases,
please contact Simon & Schuster Special Sales at 1-866-506-1949
or business@simonandschuster.com.

The Simon & Schuster Speakers Bureau can bring authors to your
live event. For more information or to book an event, contact the
Simon & Schuster Speakers Bureau at 1-866-248-3049 or visit our
website at www.simonspeakers.com.

Interior design by Lewelin Polanco

Manufactured in the United States of America

10 9 8 7 6 5 4 3 2 1

Library of Congress Cataloging-in-Publication Data

Klein, Joe, date.
  Payback / Joe Klein.
    pages cm
1. Vietnam War, 1961–1975—Veterans—United States—Biography. 2. United
States. Marine Corps. Marine Division, 3rd. Regiment, 3rd. Battalion, 1st. Charlie
Company. Platoon, 2nd—Biography. 3. Cooper, Gary W., 1946–1981—Friends
and associates—Biography. 4. Vietnam War, 1961–1975—Veterans—Social con-
ditions. 5. Man-woman relationships—United States—History—20th century. 6.
Vietnam War, 1961–1975—Veterans—Mental health—United States. 7. Vietnam
War, 1961–1975—Veterans—Substance use. 8. United States—Social life and cus-
toms—20th century. 9. Vietnam War, 1961–1975—Regimental histories. I. Title.
  DS559.73.U6K57 2015
  959.704'345092273—dc23
                              2015031100

ISBN 978-1-4516-8362-2
ISBN 978-1-4516-8363-9 (ebook)

*Author's Note: The principal characters in this book agreed to the use of their real
names. Some of the other names have been changed.*

For my parents

Payback is

Payback is a motherfucker.

—A MARINE CORPS PROVERB,
POPULAR DURING THE VIETNAM ERA

CONTENTS

Enter the Dragon

PROLOGUE
The Summer of Love

In late January 1981, at the peak of the short-lived national euphoria over the return of the American hostages from Iran, I noticed a brief wire service story in one of the New York tabloids about a Vietnam veteran who had been killed by the police in Hammond, Indiana. The headline was something like: "Viet Vet Goes Berserk over Hostage Welcome."

His name was Gary Cooper and his story was, in its way, as classically American as his name. It was true that he'd been angered by the tumultuous welcome the former hostages received; there had been no parades or visits to the White House when he returned from Vietnam. But it wasn't merely anger over the hostages that pushed Gary Cooper to the brink; indeed, that was only a small part of it. He was far more troubled by his inability to find a job since being laid off by the Pullman Standard Company nine months earlier. On January 20, the safe return of the hostages and Ronald Reagan's inauguration shared the front page of the Hammond *Times* with a story of more immediate interest: Pullman was permanently closing its freight car division, and Cooper's slim hope that he would be called back to work vanished. A week later, he learned that a job he'd hoped to get at Calumet Industries also had eluded him. Two days after that, he was dead. He was thirty-four years old. He had been born in Tennessee, but his family moved North in the great migration of poor Southern whites to the factories of the Midwest during World War II, a migration that now seemed to be reversing itself as steel mills and auto plants along the shores of the Great Lakes closed their gates and the children of the original migrants drifted back to the sun belt. Gary Cooper's tragedy seemed a reflection of several troubling problems—the rising anger of Vietnam veterans, the legacy of the war itself, the dislocations caused by the shriveling of basic industries in the Midwest—and I decided to write a magazine article about his life and death.

I spent two weeks in Hammond interviewing his friends and family. One day Barbara Cooper, Gary's widow, lugged out an old scrapbook filled with photographs and memorabilia from Vietnam. There was a picture of Gary standing proudly at attention in hospital pajamas as he received a Purple Heart for wounds sustained in action on August 16, 1967. There were other pictures—rather touching in their innocence—of Gary and the men in his unit digging foxholes, clowning around and striking various unconvincing (and obviously staged) warlike poses. They were all so very young . . . except for one small, grizzled sergeant standing on a paddy dike, slouched, exhausted, unshaven, eyes glowing feverishly from beneath his helmet, a ninety-year-old man. On the back of the photo, Cooper had written: "S/Sgt. Malloy. Best staff NCO in the Marine Corps. KIA: 7/6/67."

There were names written on the back of several other photos, and I decided to try to locate some of the men in Cooper's unit and find out what had happened to him in Vietnam. It was a decision that led me to write this book.

In a musty, cluttered room in the Navy Annex Building in Arlington, Virginia, I found a faded microfilm roster of Charlie Company, 1st Battalion, 3rd Marine Regiment, for August 1967. Listed there were Gary W. Cooper (service number: 2188001) and several of the other names from the photos, including William V. Taylor (2323311). I also found a casualty list (a partial list, I later learned) for August 16, 1967—with Cooper's name again, as well as four others.

I brought the names and service numbers to Lieutenant Joanne Schilling, a Marine Corps public relations officer. "I don't know if we'll be able to help you much," she said. "I might be able to get you their hometowns—it was all so long ago, you know." So long ago! It was . . . well, fourteen years. After several days, Lieutenant

Schilling called with the information she'd promised and I began to pore over phone books at the New York Public Library, the first of many such excursions.

The first name on the list was William V. Taylor. Hometown: Chicago, Illinois. There were, as might be expected, more than a few William Taylors in Chicago, but no William V. Taylor. I decided to check the suburban directories and found a William V. Taylor in Chicago Heights.

"Jesus Christ," Bill Taylor said when I told him who I was and why I was calling. "The guy that got killed over in Hammond was *Gary Cooper*? I've been living ten miles from him for fifteen years, and I didn't even know it."

I asked if he remembered the day Cooper was wounded.

"Operation Cochise," he said immediately. "I kind of cracked that day."

"Cracked?"

"Yeah, I started firing my rifle into a haystack because I thought the gooks were in there, and then someone grabbed me and I started crying. You see, we were pinned down . . ." And for the next hour, Taylor described—in remarkable detail—the events of August 16, 1967. For another hour after that, he reminisced about Vietnam and the men in his unit, giving me several more names and hometowns. Then he talked about what had happened to him since he came home. "You know, when I got back to California, they spit at me," he said.

"Who did?"

"The hippies, in Anaheim. I was walking along a street. I just couldn't believe it. It made me so goddamn angry . . . and then I couldn't find a decent job for five years. It got so bad I even went down to the welfare office once. But now I've got my own insurance agency and everything's great. Except . . . I got these lumps all over my body. I think it's Agent Orange. We walked through that stuff in the DMZ all the time. When you talk to the other guys, see if they got lumps . . . and, listen, let me know how they are. I haven't seen those guys in fifteen years."

When I talked to the others—and over the next few months I managed to locate twenty of them—I learned that only one had lumps, but almost all of them seemed to explode over the phone as Bill Taylor had, dying to talk about Vietnam, curious about their old friends, shocked and upset by Cooper's death. Several said, "Hey, I never talked about this stuff before." When I asked why not, they'd inevitably say, "No one ever asked," or "I just didn't feel like it," or "They wouldn't understand."

"Why are you talking about it now?" I'd ask.

"I don't know," said Wayne Pilgreen of Wetumpka, Alabama, "but it feels right."

It felt right for me too. After finishing my story about Cooper, I decided to continue interviewing the men of Charlie Company's 2nd Platoon. The treatment of Vietnam veterans—the effects of Agent Orange, post-traumatic stress disorder and even the proposed war memorial in Washington—was more in the news than ever before, but I wasn't interested in the "issues" so much as I was intrigued by the men themselves, and what had happened to them since they'd come home.

I had been a foot soldier in the antiwar movement in the 1960s, attending rallies and marches but never doing anything drastic. Like almost everyone else I knew in college, I managed to escape the draft—my son, Christopher, was born in 1967, and I received a family support deferment. In the years since, I hadn't thought much about the men who fought and died in the war. When I did think about them, two images came to mind: the very moving protest made by Vietnam Veterans Against the War in 1971, when they'd flung their medals on the Capitol steps . . . and, more recently, a vague, media-induced sense that Vietnam veterans were angry loners, teetering on the edge of sanity, people like Gary Cooper. I'd seen some statistics which seemed to bolster that impression: By 1980, more Vietnam veterans had died since they came home than had been killed in the war. They comprised 30 percent of the nation's prison population (about 70,000). *Time* magazine estimated that "something like a quarter of those who served may still be suffering from substantial psychological problems."

More than two million Americans had served in Vietnam, but they seemed to live in a different part of the world from mine. I'd

met a few veterans, pressure-group types, during my years as a political reporter in Washington, but none since. It seems incredible to
me now, but when my research began, I didn't know a single Vietnam veteran; in fact, I'd never spoken at length with anyone who'd
been there. I wasn't at all prepared for the intense reactions my questions would provoke; nor was I prepared for the cascade of feelings—guilt, sadness, anger, fear, envy—the men would arouse in me.

The image of Vietnam veterans as borderline cases, liable to "go
berserk" at the slightest provocation, was, of course, an exaggeration. Most of the men I visited were leading useful, if not always
happy, lives. And yet there *was* something different about them.
They had lived through a horrifying experience, and none was unaf-
fected. Some thought about the war all the time, others only a little
and a few had blotted it completely from their minds. Some were repelled now by the notion of killing; others had spent the years since
they'd come home trying to recapture the exhilaration, the danger
and—especially—the camaraderie of battle. Some had returned violent, angry, aggressive; others were passive, paralyzed emotionally.
Most, though, seemed pretty normal. They were, all of them, quite
willing to share their experiences with me. None seemed to mind
that I'd been "on the other side" in the 1960s—in fact, most thought
I'd been lucky to avoid the whole business. The odd thing was, as
my research progressed, I wasn't so sure that I agreed with them.
The more I learned, the more I wondered about how I might have
reacted to the stress of battle . . . and the more I respected the sacrifices they'd made.

After visiting fifteen members of Cooper's unit, I decided to
concentrate on five of them—not the five worst cases, but five who
reflected a range of reactions to the war and experiences since. Two
would be Cooper and Taylor, the least and the most accessible of the
group, mirror images in a way, with similar backgrounds but vastly
different fates.

Bill Taylor led me to the third: John Steiner, an ecologist working for the Fish and Wildlife Service in California. Steiner was one
of the gentlest people I'd ever met. One day, as we sat talking in
his backyard, he heard a bird cry. "That's a danger signal," he said,

leaping up, and found a mother bird nervously protecting her nest against a cat who clearly had mayhem on his mind; Steiner shooed the cat away. He was a small, almost delicate-looking man, with dark hair and a beard, and vivid blue-green eyes. "You know," he said one day as we drove in his pickup truck to his job at the San Francisco Bay Wildlife Refuge, "I sometimes wonder how I can get so excited about protecting the salt marshes when I was so nonchalant about burning down villages fifteen years ago."

"You burned villages?"

"Well, I didn't set any hooches on fire, but I was there. One time, an old mamasan grabbed me by the sleeve, begging me to help her, patting her hooch, caressing it—it was her *home*, goddamnit—and I just smiled and reassured her, 'Don't worry,' you know, knowing full well that the whole ville was going to be torched. I continued on down the road and I remember looking back, seeing it all in flames . . . I wonder how I could have done that."

Steiner led me to John Wakefield, who had been his squad leader for a time in Vietnam. When I called Wakefield, he sounded tentative, but agreed to let me visit him in Indianapolis. I arrived at his home a week later and found him shaking, nervous, on the brink of tears. "Since you called, I've been very depressed . . . or pensive," he said.

"Very pensive and withdrawn," offered his wife, Elizabeth. "Trying to deny what you're thinking."

"Yeah," he said. "I haven't really talked to *anybody* about what happened in the service. Some of the fun things, yeah. But the bad experiences—I've just completely shut them out."

I told Wakefield that he didn't have to talk about them now either. "If you say, 'Nice meeting you, good luck, there's the door,' I'll say, 'Fine,'" I said, upset with myself for triggering what appeared to be a crisis, and fearful of the consequences.

"On the one hand, I want to do that," he said. "I'll be honest with you. On the other hand, maybe it's time to get it all out."

"It'll come out anyway," Elizabeth said.

"Yeah," he agreed. He was a tall man, with dark hair, trifocals and a recent paunch, who worked in quality control for a huge General Motors subsidiary nearby, and seemed much older than any of

the other men I'd visited; he was, however, only thirty-seven. He
suggested that he go along with me to see Bill Taylor in Chicago,
which was my next stop. "I want someone else who went through it
to be there when I talk about it, because I'm scared to death. There's
a physical bond . . . when you go through something that was hell,
as that day was," he said, referring to August 16, 1967 — Operation
Cochise, the day Cooper was wounded and Taylor cracked. "I've
been through a few of them days. Bill Taylor too . . . I realize I'm
putting you in a bad spot . . ."

"No," I said, "I'm putting *you* in a bad spot."

"No, it's just . . ."

"You're doing me a favor."

"You may be doing *me* a favor," he said, and we began a jour-
ney that would prove surprising and painful for John Wakefield, but
also — as of this writing — worthwhile.

The fifth man was Dale Szuminski, whose name I found on the
casualty list for August 16, 1967. He was easy enough to locate —
there weren't nearly so many Dale Szuminskis in Erie, Pennsylvania,
as there'd been Bill Taylors in Chicago. Szuminski was a postman,
but said over the phone, "I spent the first ten years after I got back
doing nothing. I don't know why."

When I visited Szuminski in Erie, we immediately went to the
Frontier Lounge, where his friend Joey Bruno — "It seems like all
my friends were in the Marines," Szuminski said — was tending bar
and insisted on pouring shot after shot of Jack Daniel's for the visi-
tor from New York. I drove home that night with one eye squinting
at three sets of white dashes dividing the highway. "You ready to
crash?" Szuminski had said when I dragged him from the Frontier
Lounge. "Jeez, I was just getting started."

"It's two in the morning," I said.

"So what? I don't have to be at work till seven."

As inevitable a choice as the five of them — Cooper, Taylor, Steiner,
Wakefield and Szuminski — seemed for my purposes, a fairly serious
question remained: What *were* my purposes?

It was obvious that the five could in no way be construed as a cross section of Vietnam veterans. For one thing, they were all white. There hadn't been many blacks or Hispanics in the 2nd Platoon of Charlie Company in 1967—mostly the luck of the draw, but partly because it was early in the war and the Marines were composed primarily of enlistees, who tended to be white in those days, before the increased pay and perquisites of the all-volunteer armed forces made military life a more attractive path of upward mobility for minorities. That all five had enlisted was, in itself, untypical of most Vietnam veterans. Nor did they represent the geographic, social or intellectual diversity I'd come to expect among American fighting men from the World War II novels and movies. They were—except for Steiner, who came from California and was a bit more affluent—distinctly Midwestern, blue collar, high school graduates. Taylor, Szuminski and Wakefield were Catholic; Steiner and Cooper, Protestant. Although several became sergeants in the field, none was an officer. They were grunts, pure and simple.

This is *not* a book about the plight of Vietnam veterans. Steiner, for one, didn't feel at all mistreated. He'd taken full advantage of the veterans benefits available to him after the war and, he said, "made out like a fat rat." Nor did any of the others want sympathy, although several tended to overstate their woes and attribute all their troubles to Vietnam, figuring (at first, at least) that I was interested in them only because I wanted to write a book about their problems, which wasn't my purpose at all.*

My intention was simply to write about five men who had fought together in Vietnam, and what had happened to them when

---

* My arrival in their lives did cause some disruptions—and, in Wakefield's case, a major change—which I'll deal with in the final section of this book. Obviously, all—except Cooper—were willing subjects, which raised the question of showboating. I tried, wherever possible, to check their stories with other sources, but often had to depend on their version of the events of their lives and my own ability to separate what was likely from what was not.

they came home. They had been through a remarkable experience: not just the war, but returning to a country where all the ground rules had changed, from what a girl might "do" on a first date to basic attitudes about work, family and authority. It would have been a difficult transition even if they hadn't been reviled when they came home, even if they hadn't lost.

Dale Szuminski was the first of the five to join Charlie Company, 1st Battalion, 3rd Marine Regiment, in July 1966; he was nineteen years old. Gary Cooper, also nineteen, arrived in December. Throughout late 1966 and early 1967, they guarded the airstrip being constructed at Khe Sanh, in the far north of South Vietnam. It was cold, rainy and uncomfortable in that mountainous region, but not particularly dangerous. In fact, their unit was distinguished by its complete inability to make contact with the enemy; it was called "Chickenshit Charlie" by the rest of the battalion. Their only fire fight occurred when a patrol was attacked by a bear one day; the bear was blown away, and just about everyone present took credit for the kill. In late February 1967, the 1st Battalion was sent to Okinawa for re-supply—the men were given the new M-16 rifles—and retraining as a Special Landing Force. In the future, Charlie Company would be based on an aircraft carrier off the coast and helicoptered into hot spots.

They were joined in Okinawa by Bill Taylor, who was nineteen years old and green as green could be, and John Wakefield, who was by far the most experienced of the group. He was also the oldest, twenty-two at the time. Wakefield had been a member of an elite Force Reconnaissance unit whose job it often had been to penetrate North Vietnam in small patrols, monitoring the traffic on the Ho Chi Minh Trail and performing "interrogations" of local officials. He had been a sergeant, but was busted to corporal for borrowing a truck and stealing bananas from a private girls' school during a drunken spree in Hue. In December 1966, he wrecked his knee diving from a helicopter into a hot landing zone in Laos, and spent the next few months recuperating on Okinawa. When he recovered, he was told there were no openings in Force Reconnaissance, and was assigned to the 2nd Platoon of Charlie Company, which he considered a more serious demotion than losing a stripe. He wore camouflage fatigues, had an imposing handlebar moustache and carried a K-Bar knife, which distinguished him from everyone else, who wore green fatigues, weren't allowed moustaches and didn't carry knives; less apparent was his quiet but overwhelming arrogance. Wakefield considered himself the best Marine he'd ever met. To the others, though, he was just another new guy.

Wakefield was greeted by Staff Sergeant John J. Malloy, also a newcomer to Charlie Company, but a longtime Marine (it was said that he'd fought in Korea) who had quickly established himself as the most respected man in the unit. Malloy took a look at Wakefield's service record and told him that he could expect a much different war now. "We got a bunch of green kids here," Malloy said. "But we'll get them through."

Wakefield, pleased to be included in the "we'll," said, "You bet we will."

It was a much different war not only for Wakefield but also for the others. They were in almost daily contact with the enemy now. Most of the time it was frustrating, fleeting contact—Viet Cong snipers picking away at them, mines being tripped. Szuminski was wounded slightly in the arm by shrapnel from a mine in June; the wound wasn't nearly so bad as the sight of the man who'd been walking in front of him, whose stomach had been ripped open.

They were based on the USS *Okinawa* but didn't spend much time there. They would be out in the bush for weeks on end, then return to the ship for a day or two, only to be sent out on another operation. There were hot meals on the ship, fresh clothes (their uniforms tended to rot off them after several weeks in the bush) and showers. It was the only place in Vietnam that they felt completely safe.

John Steiner joined them in the field in June. He was the youngest of the five, still just eighteen years old. He had arrived in Vietnam the previous November, but had spent the past five months recuperating on Okinawa after breaking his foot in a rope-climbing drill during retraining exercises.

Cooper, Taylor, Steiner, Wakefield and Szuminski served together in the 2nd Platoon for the next two months, mid-June to mid-August 1967, a time that was being celebrated by certain of their contemporaries back home as the "Summer of Love."

In early July, Charlie Company took part in its first major battle, against North Vietnamese regulars at Con Thien in the Demilitarized Zone. The battle lasted several days, the men endured a horrendous mortar barrage, but there were surprisingly few casualties . . . and only one that would be remembered years later. Staff Sergeant John J. Malloy was killed early in the battle by a recoilless-rifle shell, an anti-tank weapon, while trying to reinforce a squad pinned down by enemy fire. The shell hit him on the left side of his chest. He was knocked six feet in the air, and flipped over. Everyone knew, immediately, that he was dead, but they could not retrieve his body until the North Vietnamese were forced to retreat several days later.

A small party of men were sent out to get the body. Wakefield, Steiner, Cooper and Szuminski were among them. Wakefield remembered someone reaching down to brush the flies from Malloy's face, then pulling his hand back in horror at the touch. No one said anything. No one cried. They wrapped him in a poncho liner and carried him to a medevac helicopter.

Years later, some of the men would be moved to tears by the memory of the little staff sergeant who'd shepherded them through their first months in the bush. They would remember his fairness above all else, which even extended to the way he opened cases of C rations. A case contained twelve meals, each labeled on the top. Most platoon sergeants opened the top of the box and gave the officers first choice. Malloy opened the box upside down, so no one knew which meal they were choosing and a private had as much chance of getting something good, like beef slices, as a lieutenant; when people began to figure out where the best meals were positioned in each case, Malloy went so far as to switch them around. He was replaced by Staff Sergeant Theodore Kochmaruk, who was considered competent enough by the men, but opened cases of C rations from the top and always gave the officers first choice.

There was no memorial service for Sergeant Malloy. There was little discussion afterward, but many had the same thought: If Malloy, who knew what he was doing, could get himself blown away so easily, what chance did *they* have? The effect on morale was shattering, but the only acknowledgment that they had suffered a grievous loss was initiated by Robert Smith, the platoon's best photographer. He asked his parents to make seventeen copies of a picture he'd taken of Malloy several weeks before his death. It was the photo of the sergeant, hunched beneath his pack, that I'd first seen in Cooper's album and would later find, time and again, in musty albums pulled from the top shelves of closets across the country.

Malloy's death was one of two vivid memories that Cooper, Taylor, Steiner, Wakefield and Szuminski would share. The other was the ambush that took place on August 16, 1967, during Operation Cochise . . . and since it was the last day the five would spend together in Vietnam, it is probably where the story of their return from the war should begin.

OPERATION COCHISE

Que Son Valley, August 16, 1967

I was twenty-four when the summer began; by the time it ended, I was much older than I am now. Chronologically, my age had advanced three months, emotionally about three decades. I was somewhere in my middle fifties, that depressing time when a man's friends begin dying off and each death reminds him of the nearness of his own.

—PHILIP CAPUTO, *A RUMOR OF WAR*

"Taylor!"

"What the *hell* do you think you're doing?" Muller screamed.

He was taking pictures. "Oh shit . . . sorry," Taylor said, fumbling to stow the Kodak in his pack.

"Sorry!" Muller went on. "You are one of the *sorriest* motherfuckers . . ."

"Get your rifle at port arms, Taylor," Sergeant Jones, their squad leader, interrupted, "or you lose your stripe."

The squad was crossing the An Son Valley in a wedge, Muller walking point, sweeping toward the tree line. It was a routine enough maneuver, made easier because the paddies were dry and hard, covered with the brown stubble of what must have been last year's crop . . . and Taylor had allowed himself to drift into tourism, lulled by the pristine beauty of the place. It was, he thought, as beautiful as he'd ever seen Vietnam—like a postcard. Off to the right, on the hillside that closed the valley, farmers worked in terraced paddies that were a fresh, brilliant green; closer in, there was a village. He could see old women sitting in front of their hooches and a boy standing atop a water buffalo. There hadn't been many mornings as perfect as this—dry, clear, not too hot. It had been days since they'd had contact with the enemy, and the war seemed far away. Taylor was almost delirious with the absence of discomfort, except for the liquid churning in his intestines (but then, everyone had dysentery—happiness, it was said, was a dry fart—and his was no worse than most), and forgetting momentarily that he was assaulting a tree line, he had reached into his pack for the camera, hoping to capture the scene for the folks back home in Chicago. Not in their wildest dreams, he thought, could they ever imagine anything like this.

"Taylor!" He started, realizing immediately that he had screwed up again. It was the second time that Muller and Jones had caught him doing something wrong that morning. Earlier, as they'd moved into position at the crest of the hill overlooking the valley, he'd stopped at a well next to an abandoned hooch to fill his canteen, and Jones had lit into him. He worshipped Jones, who was widely regarded as the best squad leader in the platoon, but it was impossible to please the man. It was hard to please any of the short-timers. They had spent months together in Khe Sanh, and didn't have much truck with new guys who'd come aboard when the company had been refitted on Okinawa. They especially didn't have much truck with Taylor, who talked too much and laughed too loud and tried too hard to be one of them. He didn't yet understand that the way to prove himself was by not trying.

They were nearing the tree line—it was straight ahead and curved around their right flank—when Muller and Jones caught him with the camera. Taylor was the last man on the right wing of the wedge. Walsted and Pilgreen were diagonally in front of him, then Muller at point. Sergeant Jones was on the left wing, followed by Szuminski, who carried the radio, and Sheoships, an Indian from Oregon who never said much. Hawthorn, the corpsman, was just behind. The squad stopped for a moment as Taylor was chewed out; everyone was staring back at him.

"Taylor, if you don't get your shit together," Muller yelled, still at it, "you're going to find yourself in a world of hurt."

Taylor fought the temptation to argue back, even though he knew he was wrong. He didn't like the way Muller—who was small, well built and bellicose, a real bully—always picked on him.

Obviously, if they were in any danger he wouldn't have been taking pictures. But there *couldn't* be any danger, with the farmers in the fields, the women and children in the village. He looked away from Muller, up toward the terraced paddies where he'd seen the farmers. They were leaving. Closer in, the village was now empty. Quickly, he turned back toward Muller and saw smoke rising from the tree line.

At the same moment, Szuminski—who'd been looking back at Taylor—turned toward the tree line and saw the smoke . . . and heard the *noise*, like a phonograph needle dropping onto the middle of a record and skidding across, full blast, louder than anything he'd ever heard before . . . and he was down, rolling forward to the front wall of the paddy, firing into the tree line—which was very close, maybe sixty feet away—until his rifle jammed. He felt his right leg burning. Then, lifting up on an elbow, trying to eject the jammed shell, he was knocked over by an incredible whiplash force and dazed.

"HELLLLLP!"

Muller was screaming. Everyone was down. Szuminski, flipped back, could see Jones down, not moving; Muller writhing; Pilgreen flat, arms covering his head. There were explosions now, grenades, rocket grenades, dirt kicking up, shrapnel whistling. He could not see Taylor or Walsted, who were in the next paddy over, diagonally back and to the right, where the tree line curved at the valley's end. Then he realized he couldn't feel his left arm. He rolled over onto his stomach, more frightened than he'd been when the fire fight started, and saw it lying there—someone else's arm. He reached across with his right hand and touched it. No feeling. He moved his fingers slowly up the forearm, feeling the warm, sticky blood, touching—but not feeling, the *arm* wasn't feeling—up the biceps to the shoulder, and with a surge of relief, finding that it was still attached. The bullet had entered through the top of his shoulder and he was beginning to feel enormous, throbbing pain there . . . but nothing below. He became conscious again of the noise, still immense, incomprehensible. He saw the rest of the platoon, halfway back across the valley, but *going the other way*, back up the hill. I've still got my arm, he thought, but we're fucked. His leg was burning. He wondered if it was shrapnel. He examined the tear in his trousers, and saw another bullet wound. The round had gone cleanly through his calf.

"Corpsman . . . corpsman," Muller was screaming, and suddenly Hawthorn—the new corpsman from Texas—was there, crouched over him, bandaging his arm (Muller didn't think he had an elbow anymore) and shooting him with morphine. Hawthorn then stood and turned right. He was staring at the bend in the tree line. "Muller," he said, reaching for his service revolver, "we're flanked." Then he was down too, corkscrewed in a heap. Muller felt the morphine oozing through him, his senses dulling. He tried to pull Hawthorn's body close. His rifle was gone and he wanted the corpsman's revolver. He felt bits of shrapnel and dirt stinging his face. Confused and dizzied by the morphine, he couldn't seem to find the revolver; it was an effort to remember what he was looking for. He rested, whimpering—terrified, but the pain fading—and used Hawthorn's body for cover.

Taylor had rolled into the safest possible place, the front right-hand corner of the paddy, shielded in the front and right by dikes. He wasn't quite sure how he'd gotten there. Walsted was to his immediate left, just ahead, in front of the dike but behind the brush and slight rise that began the tree line; further left, diagonally ahead and one paddy over, was the rest of the squad. They had taken the brunt of the initial fire. He could hear a .50-caliber machine gun firing from just beyond where Muller had been yelling at him, but he couldn't see anything. "Wally, can you see anything?" Taylor shouted above the roar.

Walsted turned toward Taylor. His eyes widened immediately and he let out a shriek as he saw the barrel of a second machine gun, implanted in the trees just behind Taylor. Then Taylor saw bullets jitterbugging crazily around Walsted, outlining his body like a knife-thrower at a carnival. Walsted was frozen, staring down the barrel of the machine gun. Then the gun lifted its fire into the next paddy (killing Hawthorn, though Taylor did not know this), and Walsted crawled into a hole between the paddy dike and the brush, which seemed to have a cloth covering over it.

"Taylor!" someone was yelling. "Taylor?"

He couldn't hear what they were saying. There was the machine gun firing above his head, plus the other machine gun in front and to the left, plus small-arms fire and grenades—it was, he realized, a very well-disciplined ambush. He didn't return fire. He was carrying, as always, plenty of grenades—but didn't want to use them. I don't want to get those gooks *angry*, he thought. I don't want them charging out of the tree line at me.

It didn't occur to him—at least, not for several hours—that the North Vietnamese were perfectly content to stay in the tree line; that they were, in fact, using the trapped squad as bait.

On the crest of the hill overlooking the Que Son Valley, Captain G. F. Reczek could see squads from his three platoons crossing the wide, uneven checkerboard of paddies. Stretching off to his left, across the valley, was the An Son village complex, which was Charlie Company's objective. To the right, the valley narrowed and was split by a promontory of trees and brush which, from Captain Reczek's perch, seemed like the tip of an island intruding upon the brown sea of fallow paddies; the promontory curved back into the low brush and foothills at the end of the valley. He could also see the lead squad from the 2nd Platoon nearing the promontory; then he heard the ambush triggered. Immediately, he radioed the other two platoons and ordered them to pull their lead squads back to the crest of the hill. Then he called Battalion and asked for support. Bravo Company, he knew, was deployed to the right and he requested that it be brought up to envelop the enemy force from the right flank. Battalion refused his request, though, and he was forced to radio Lieutenant John Francis, the 2nd Platoon's commander, and tell him there would be no ground support in freeing the trapped squad. "We'll have to do it ourselves," he said.

─────────

Steiner heard the ambush triggered up ahead. He was near the crest of the hill, but had not yet entered the Que Son Valley. Word came back—incorrectly—that White's squad was trapped. The only one he knew well in White's squad was John Wakefield. The night before the operation, Wakefield had gone about the troop quarters on the ship, asking with mock formality, "Will you be coming to the *happening* tomorrow?"—as if it were the senior prom, as if anyone had a choice. Steiner had thought it was pretty funny. Now he thought about the Supremes song that had introduced them all to the word "happening" that summer:

> *ooooh-ooh, and then it happened!*
> *ooooh-ooh, and then it* happened!

Steiner was terrified, and it wasn't very reassuring that his squad leader, Williams, seemed even more so. Williams kept saying, "I don't know what to do. I don't know what to do."

Everyone knew, though, what had to be done. They were going to have to move forward, down into the valley, and try to rescue the trapped squad. The fire from the tree line was fierce, coordinated, unending. This obviously was not a hit-and-run Viet Cong ambush; it had to be North Vietnamese regulars.

"I just don't know what to do," Williams repeated. He was a tall, thin black, a short-timer who, since Sergeant Malloy's death, had become increasingly reluctant and jittery in the bush. The other squad leaders, Jones and White, didn't trust him and had complained to Lieutenant Francis.

And now the lieutenant approached with Staff Sergeant Kochmaruk, and ordered Williams to take his squad and a machine-gun team laterally across the hill to the right, and set up the gun in a position to lay down suppressive fire into the tree line.

Williams refused. He wasn't going, no way.

Francis began to argue with him and Kochmaruk thought: I can't believe this. The man is deserting under fire, disobeying a direct order, and the lieutenant is *arguing* with him—in the old Corps, he would have been shot on sight. Kochmaruk, a lifer, had little faith in Francis, who was a college boy, green and gung-ho, a classic hot dog. He was the kind of commander who would do silly, dangerous things, take unnecessary risks, and yet here he was, wasting precious time arguing with a coward while good men were being chewed up down by the tree line. "Sir, we're wasting time," Kochmaruk finally interrupted. "Let me take the squad and set up the gun."

Kochmaruk led the squad through the low brush at the crest of the hill to an abandoned hooch near the end of the valley, about four hundred yards directly across from the promontory and the trapped squad. Word filtered back that it was Jones's squad, not White's. There were all sorts of rumors about the dead and wounded. Steiner, frightened and depressed, sat down against the hooch while the gun was deployed. A gunner sat next to him, quietly smoking. He wanted to start a conversation, but what was there to say? "Isn't this a horrible fire fight?" or "I feel like crying, don't you?" There was nothing to say. He thought about who might be down there—he knew Taylor and Walsted pretty well; the others were old salts who never spoke to him. Now they were olive dots, hard against the tree line, which, bending around as it did, resembled a whale's mouth about to snap shut.

A line of bullets ripped suddenly through the dirt, moving straight toward the gunner's crotch. They both dived for cover.

"You okay?" Steiner asked.

"Yeah, but *shit* . . . "

There really was nothing to say.

"Charlie two Actual"—Kochmaruk was radioing back to Francis—"this is Charlie two Sierra." He reported that a third enemy machine gun had been located. He estimated it was several hundred yards to the right of his position, in the small ville at the end of the valley. He requested another machine gun be brought up to fire into the ville.

Kochmaruk grew impatient waiting for the second machine gun

to arrive. He was older than any of the grunts, thirty-two at the time, but still smitten by the romance and legend of the Corps (which, unlike the others, he refused to call "the crotch"). This was his second tour in Vietnam. He had volunteered again for combat after his marriage collapsed, and had convinced himself that he didn't care if he lived or died. He didn't want to take unnecessary risks with the men—but as for himself, he didn't care. He had drawn a large bull's-eye in Magic Marker on the back of his helmet.

"Corpsman," he said to Doc Johnson, who'd accompanied the squad to the abandoned hooch, "what say we make our way across and see if we can provide some assistance to the squad out there?" It was a dangerous mission, and he was careful not to order the corpsman to follow him, but Johnson—knowing that Hawthorn was hurt and his presence might mean the difference between life and death for the others—agreed.

Kochmaruk looked out across the valley. About midway across, two hundred yards below his position, there was a deep gully—a dried-out creek bed, it seemed—twisting through the valley. Smaller rivulets extended like veins from the central gully. If he could get down there, he might be able to follow the gully to the left—away from the flanking machine-gun emplacements—then find a rivulet heading toward the tree line. Between him and the gully, though, was several hundred yards of low brush and open paddy which was in easy range of the third machine gun.

Steiner heard him shout, "Here we go! Just like John Wayne!" And then, unable to believe it, saw the sergeant take off—*laughing*—zigzagging through the machine-gun fire, the medic in tow, down safely into the gully. Then he saw a rocket grenade explode a few feet from where they'd disappeared from view.

"Taylor!"
  "Pilgreen?"
  "Yeah. Taylor?"
  "Yeah?"
  "Go get help."

"I *can't* . . . I'm pinned down."

An hour had passed. The fire from the tree line finally slackened. Now there were only occasional bursts—very purposeful bursts, in the direction of any of the remaining members of Jones's squad who tried to move. Taylor, still scrunched down in the corner of the paddy, felt as if he was back in the schoolyard—military school came to mind; he was nine years old—pinned down by the local bully, unable to breathe. He couldn't think clearly. His stomach, his insides were nonexistent. He felt that if he tried to stand or move, his body would simply crumple of its own accord. He remembered cowboy movies, the villain taunting the hero: "You ain't got no backbone." An understatement, obviously. Taylor felt as if he hadn't any bones at all.

"Taylor!"

"Where's Jonesy?"

"He's all fucked up . . . Get help."

Farther in the distance, Taylor could hear someone moaning: "I'm bleeding to death . . . I'm *bleeding* to death."

He felt guilty about not going. He knew something had to be done, but couldn't think it through. He thought about Walsted, still hidden in the little covered hole. "Wally," he said in a loud whisper. "Wally . . . c'mon out, over by me. It's safe here." But Walsted wasn't going anywhere or saying anything, and his frozen terror was heaped upon Taylor's own. If Walsted were okay, he thought, they might be able to figure out something together.

"Taylor!"

"Yeah?"

"Go get help."

When the fire slackened, Szuminski remembered the radio. He had tried it once, in the beginning, and it was dead. Now he decided to get it off his back and find out what was wrong. Slowly, he shrugged off the right shoulder strap. Then, twisting on his side, he used his right hand to remove the strap from his wrecked left shoulder. When it was off, he searched for the bullet hole or shrapnel that had knocked it out. His left arm still felt as if it had been torn out at the shoulder; his right leg still burned. He tried to focus his mind on the radio. There was no obvious damage. Cradling the phone against his good shoulder, he tried to reach Company: "Charlie six Actual . . . this is Charlie two Charlie. Charlie six Actual . . . this is Charlie two Charlie." Nothing. He began to fiddle with the frequency knobs, figuring that if he couldn't reach Captain Reczek, maybe he could find someone else out there. But there was no action on any frequency. He realized the battery might be dead. He carried a spare battery in his pack and, finding it, replaced the old one. Still nothing. He worked at this for nearly an hour as the sun arced higher and whiter, and the dead paddies were bleached with it.

When there was nothing more to be done with the radio, Szuminski once more took stock of the situation. Pilgreen had, somehow, made it back over the rear dike of the paddy and Szuminski could hear him yelling at Taylor. Jones was dead, as was the corpsman, which meant that he and Muller were the only ones left alive in the paddy. Looking back across the valley, he couldn't see anything—no movement, no signs of life. He wondered where the rest of the platoon had gone. The sky, which always seemed vibrating with helicopters, hovering on resupply or darting about in battle faster than he'd ever imagined a helicopter could go, was empty. He considered several possible reasons why no one had come to help: One was that they might not know he was out there, which was ridiculous. They had to know. Another was that they knew, but weren't going to do anything about it—also ridiculous. The Marines *never* left anyone in the field, not even corpses. A third, more likely, was that they hadn't figured out what to do yet. But that didn't explain the absence of helicopters. Without the radio to focus his mind, he drifted from lucidity to numbness to panic, and back again.

"Jesus Christ!" he screamed. "Where *is* everyone? What's going on? I'm bleeding to death out here . . ."

Steiner was running toward the gully through machine-gun fire. He couldn't believe that his left foot, broken six months before on

Okinawa, was still aching. He heard a screech behind him, but didn't stop to look as Sands flipped in the air and, landing, rolled down the slope. Then Steiner was down in the gully, huffing . . . and staring at Sergeant Kochmaruk, who was kneeling, eyes wide as saucers, blood pouring down his face from a piece of shrapnel that had entered through the bridge of his nose and lodged in the roof of his mouth; Doc Johnson was just beyond, with shrapnel from the rocket grenade in his leg.

The gully was deep and safe, with a small stream running through the bottom. White's squad was already there, and Steiner took up a position to the left of Sergeant White. On White's other side, there was a cut in the gully which opened toward the tree line. Wakefield was positioned on the far side of the cut; he and White were chatting back and forth. Raymond Harvey, a black from Chicago, was to the right of Wakefield and there were others stretched out beyond him.

Steiner could see the trapped squad pretty clearly now. They seemed right up against the tree line—someone in the right front was gesturing, he could hear them yelling at each other. He felt hyper-alert, still wired from his run across the paddies, aware of everything, the heat, the sun, the muddy, slightly rancid smell of the stream and the other smells—sweat, gunpowder, diarrhea. He felt as if he were observing everything, aware of everything, and yet his head was spinning and he couldn't quite keep track of the gossip buzzing up and down the gully, which mostly consisted of the names of the dead and wounded: "Jones . . . the medic . . . Szuminski . . . radio's out . . . Sands . . . Muller . . ."

"Sands?"

Steiner was shocked. He hadn't realized that Mel Sands, running just behind him down the hill, had been shot. Sands was one of his best friends. No one seemed to know how badly he was wounded, or where. Steiner wanted to cry, but knew he couldn't. He felt helpless. This was worse even than the mortar barrage at Con Thien after Sergeant Malloy was killed and, he realized, it wasn't going to get any better. Looking across the paddies at the trapped squad, he had no idea how they could free them without losing a lot more men.

To Steiner's left, around several bends in the gully, Lieutenant

Francis had arrived and was orchestrating a nervous attempt to get across the hundred or so yards of open field between the gully and the rear dike of the front paddy. Cooper, Clark and Drust were there — all of whom thought the lieutenant was a gung-ho fool — and, very reluctantly, began to climb the front bank of the gully. Cooper went first, bending low in the scrub at the rim, left leg already up, right leg dangling. Clark followed and, seeing Cooper bobbing his head amidst the twigs and scrubby bushes, asked, "What the hell are you doing, Coop?"

"I'm hiding, man. They ain't gonna get *me*."

Clark, laughing, said, "You crazy bastard, you can't hide there. I'm getting out of here," and as he began to lower himself back into the gully, he heard the tree line open up again and Cooper was flying over his head, landing in the stream at the bottom, blood pouring from a bullet hole through the fleshy part of his left thigh. Cooper was laughing.

"What the fuck . . ." Clark said.

"I'm out of here!" Cooper said, jubilant. "I got me a million-dollar wound! I'm out of here!" He began to splash water from the stream on the wound.

"Hey," Clark said. "Don't do that. You'll get it infected, you crazy bastard."

"Who cares," Cooper said, laughing and splashing. "*I'm . . . out . . . of . . . here!*"

Lieutenant Francis, glaring, marched back toward White's position.

At about noon, the helicopters finally arrived — two Huey gunships, zipping down from the crest of the hill, past the gully, toward the tree line, maybe fifteen feet off the ground. Wakefield watched them firing rockets into the tree line, directly in front of Jones's squad, and decided they weren't going to help very much. The North Vietnamese obviously were dug in well. The only way a rocket could do any real damage was if it landed in a hole and, given the angle of attack, that was next to impossible. It was a difficult situation: the trapped squad was too close to the tree line to call in artillery or fixed-wing jets with napalm or heavy bombs; they also were too close for Charlie Company to try mortars. If the helicopters had any value, it was as a suppressive force—to keep the North Vietnamese down while the rest of the platoon advanced. But no one was moving, no orders had been given; there was no coordination. Wakefield blamed Lieutenant Francis: the man was an incompetent greenhorn. He looked over toward White and saw the lieutenant was next to him, screaming into the radio—his face red, obviously angry—telling the Hueys to hold their rockets until he could put something together. It was too late; they had fired all thirty-six.

The Hueys circled and came in for another run, this time strafing the tree line all the way around with their .50-caliber machine guns . . . and, this time, the suppressive fire had at least one positive result. As the Hueys attacked, Steiner could see Sheoships, the Indian from Jones's squad, hopping back from the front paddy (he had been shot in the foot), across the second paddy and into the gully, safe.

After the helicopters passed, the tree line opened up again, as if the North Vietnamese were saying: *That* didn't accomplish anything . . . and from the corner of his eye, Wakefield saw a tall figure running *forward* into the fire. He turned to his right and saw that Harvey was gone, and heard White yelling at him.

Wakefield figured Harvey was a dead man. He had picked the exact wrong time to make the move. If he had gone when the Hueys were strafing, that would have been smart . . . but this was suicide. "*Damn* him," Wakefield muttered, wondering if even *he* could make it through such withering fire. He liked Harvey. They had pulled the same foxhole many a night during the past few months, and Wakefield believed he was turning Harvey into a half-decent Marine. He was a quiet, sullen inner-city black from Chicago whose natural anger and suspicion were heightened by the facts that there weren't many other blacks in the company and that the 2nd Platoon had a larger than usual allotment of Southern whites who used the word "nigger" loudly and often when talking among themselves. But Harvey, at that moment, was running through heavy fire to join Pilgreen—who was white, from Alabama, and a good old boy if there ever was one—behind the rear wall of the front paddy, and Wakefield wondered about his motivation.

Wakefield distrusted heroism. It was emotional, a loss of control, and he had been trained never to succumb to emotions in the field. When his best friend, Robert McIntyre, had died on a Force Recon patrol in North Vietnam, he had not felt anything. They had been resting in moderately heavy bush, waiting for dusk, when they would proceed to their objective—a nearby village where they would "interrogate" a local official (interrogations were almost always terminal). McIntyre was walking point and, therefore, was the first to move when the time came—and when he moved, he was gone. The bullets had been fired from a distance and it was clear that Mac was dead, and everyone knew the drill was to split up and make their way back to their last control point, about three miles away. Wakefield did not allow himself to even think of Mac while he was doing this. Later, after they'd retrieved the body (it was found castrated) and brought it home, Wakefield finally reflected on his friend's death and realized that, more than anything else, he was angry: Mac had made a mistake. Wakefield wasn't sure what the mistake was, but he firmly believed that you could only get hurt if you made a mistake. He found it hard to believe that Mac, who'd been so good, could have been so stupid.

McIntyre was the closest friend Wakefield had ever had. They had a lot in common: Both were Catholics from the Midwest who preferred walking point on patrol. They played chess in the rec bunker at Khe Sanh—Mac usually won—and talked endlessly about weapons and tactics. There was an art to walking point, but more than that—they both liked being the one who was out there, first, in control. Wakefield felt uncomfortable when anyone else, except McIntyre, did it. He loved the feeling of moving slowly through the jungle, becoming part of it, sensing imperfections—a jigsaw puzzle in which the pieces were constantly changing shape. He'd never done anything so well in his life.

There had been an armory in a double Quonset hut at Khe Sanh, and Wakefield was free to choose any weapon for which he'd been tested and qualified. Walking point, he usually selected an M-79 grenade launcher (the canisters filled with #4 shot) or a 12-gauge pump-action shotgun, depending on the density of the foliage they were expecting. He also carried a Thompson submachine gun, a pistol, several grenades and a K-Bar knife. His theory was that if he sensed trouble, he'd fire the M-79 (or the shotgun) to blow a hole through the ambush, confuse the enemy and, he hoped, buy a few seconds for the other members of his squad. His primary weapon, the Thompson, was carried across his chest on a sling; after firing the M-79 with his left hand, he could reach for the Thompson with his right and, using the sling for balance, put a great many rounds in the general direction of the ambush very quickly—at least, that was the theory; in practice, it was seldom so clear-cut. He carried the pistol for close-in fighting; it was rarely used. The K-Bar knife was good for just about anything, but especially useful during interrogations and for cutting off ears.

Wakefield mutilated his enemies without anger, malice or enthusiasm; it was just part of the drill, a calling card. Aces of spades, supplied in packs of fifty-two by the Bicycle Card Company, were another calling card. The Vietnamese were said to consider the ace a hex sign, and so it was nailed onto a corpse's chest (other Recon units supposedly favored the forehead) with a sharpened bamboo stake. When he joined Charlie Company, Wakefield drew two aces of spades in Magic Marker on his helmet.

There was a strict code of behavior in Force Recon. You didn't brag or gloat, you were as precise and businesslike in the bush as possible, and you didn't talk about a patrol when it was over. There was even a protocol on the taking of ears: They were brought back to the rec bunker and placed in a glass container the size of an overturned water cooler—but only when no one was looking. To be seen dumping ears onto the pile was considered very bad form, an amateurish display of pride. There weren't many flashy or colorful characters in the unit—that too was considered unprofessional. Most were quiet, very calm, entirely unemotional and secure in the knowledge that none of the other elite services—not the Green Berets, not the Rangers, not the Navy Seals—could compare with them.

After he wrecked his knee and was forced to join Charlie Company, Wakefield found that he was becoming frightened in the field at times. The problem was that he was surrounded by inexperienced amateurs who were constantly making mistakes, and one of those mistakes might get him killed. He remained aloof and unemotional, though, as he'd been trained during a year of preparation for Force Recon at Camp LeJeune. When Harvey fell asleep on watch the first night they shared a foxhole, Wakefield had been tempted to chew him out, but controlled himself and said softly, "Y'know Harve, if the gooks come and you're asleep, you're gonna be the first one who gets his ass wasted." To Wakefield's knowledge, Harvey had never fallen asleep on watch again . . . but now, he was doing something far more stupid. Wakefield watched openmouthed—along with everyone else in the gully—as Harvey zigzagged diagonally right, toward the rear dike of the front paddy, where Pilgreen was waiting.

"Jesus," he said as Harvey dived down next to Pilgreen, safe for the moment.

"Hey, Wake," White yelled over from across the cut. "You ain't gonna do nothing stupid like that, are you?"

"You don't see me doin' nothing, do you?" Wakefield replied. Despite his firm intention never to get close to anyone after McIntyre's death, he found that he was getting close to White, who was one of the few in Charlie Company smart enough to respect his expertise. Like McIntyre, White enjoyed talking about weapons and strategy. He wasn't crazy gung-ho, but—like Wakefield—quietly insistent on precision in the field. Neither man cared or thought much about the meaning of the war, but both loved the intellectual challenge of combat: how to sustain the fewest casualties while inflicting the most damage. White, though squad leader, seemed downright deferential toward Wakefield at times, sparing him the more grungy details, asking his advice, following his example. Lieutenant Francis had once caught Wakefield taking an ear and screamed, "We don't fight like that here, Wakefield!" and threatened to bring him up on charges if he caught him doing it again. When the lieutenant moved on, White had quietly taken the other ear—which, to Wakefield, had cemented their bond.

"Hey, Wake," White yelled now across the cut in the gully. "What would you do in Recon in a situation like this?"

"In Recon," Wakefield said, savoring the question. "In a situation like *this*? . . . Well . . . in Recon . . . we'd probably *haul ass.*"

For the next several hours, as the sun stalled in midsky and heat shimmered across the valley, the stalemate continued. There were occasional bursts, back and forth; every movement in the front paddy seemed monitored by the North Vietnamese, unseen but all-knowing, guarding their bait. Staring at the tree line, Steiner felt as if he were fighting foliage. The adrenaline buzz of the first few hours had faded in the heat, giving way to exhaustion and the frustrating realization that it was going to be a very long day.

In the lull, Lieutenant Francis decided that the only way to move a rescue party forward was to go left, down the gully, toward the wider valley past the promontory, and away from the flanking machine-gun emplacements. He chose Sergeant White and several of the men in his immediate vicinity—Clark, Drust, Steiner, among others—and, accompanied by Cravens, his radio operator, they moved down the twisting gully, paralleling the tree line, then forward. The paddy nearest the tree line, where the squad was trapped, was terraced slightly; there was a four- or five-foot drop from its rear wall to the next paddy. The relief team could move in relative safety along the wall. Setting up his command post about two hundred yards to the left of the paddy, near a wide wooden plank which crossed the gully—a crude bridge for wheelbarrows perhaps—the lieutenant sent Sergeant White, Drust and Clark in, along the deep, rear wall of the paddy nearest the tree line, to where Pilgreen and Harvey were positioned.

As the relief team approached, there was more fire from the tree line—Muller was trying to drag himself out, with Pilgreen giving instructions from the rear. With the morphine fading and pain sharpening his senses, Muller had started screaming for help again . . . and Pilgreen, with a laconic, distinctly Southern calm and patience, began talking him out: "You're gonna have to do it yourself, Davey . . . you gotta get to the wall, to the right, Davey . . . to the wall." Muller rolled to the right wall of the paddy, occasioning a burst from the tree line—but now he was protected from flanking machine-gun fire. "Now on your back," Pilgreen said. "Atta boy . . . now *push* . . ."

Harvey raised his head to see what was happening, which invited another burst. "Get down, Harvey," Pilgreen said.

Muller, on his back, staring into the sun, closed his eyes and pushed. He couldn't tell how far he'd have to go. He pushed slowly, bending his knees, digging in his heels, then scraping his back along the stubble, no more than a foot at a time.

"*Push*, Muller . . . atta boy . . . *push*, Muller," Pilgreen called, setting up a rhythm like a coxswain. "Get *down*, Harvey . . . *push*, Muller . . . *push*, Muller . . . you're getting there . . ."

Harvey popped up a third time. "Get *down*, Harvey . . . okay, Muller, *push* . . . keep it comin'." Bullets ripped the paddy just to Muller's left. There were grenades, also off target. Bits of shrapnel and clumps of dirt cut his face. "Keep it comin' . . . *push*, Muller . . . keep it comin' . . . *push*, Muller . . . you got it now . . . *push*, Muller . . ."

Muller heard Pilgreen's voice getting closer, and now it was just behind him. He opened his eyes and saw two pairs of hands, black and white, reaching down from out of the sun to pull him out—then a burst, and the black hands disappeared.

Pilgreen, yanking Muller in, looked for Harvey. He was down, a bullet hole in the middle of his forehead, but little blood. "Get a pack," he shouted at Clark. "Anyone got a first-aid kit?"

"Forget it, man," said Clark, who could see the back of Harvey's head was gone, brains oozing into his helmet.

"Aw shit," Pilgreen said.

Bill Taylor, looking back and to the left, saw Harvey's head popping up . . . two, three times . . . and then he saw him blown back—from where he was crouched, it seemed Harvey's head had been blown off completely. It was the most horrifying thing Taylor had ever seen, and it pushed him past his frozen terror into a confusing swirl of thoughts and emotions. All morning, he had been repeating softly to himself, "You're not going to die. You're going to live and have a son." Now, as it became clear that he was going to have to do *something*, the thought of getting married someday, of having a home and real family, brought tears to his eyes.

He remembered his father, huge, always a bit rusty with coke dust from the ore dock at Republic Steel, screaming at his mother, who, Bill knew, would be going off to her lover—Jimmy, the truck driver—as soon as the old man left for work. They lived in a small apartment in Burnside, surrounded by taverns and railroad tracks on the southwest side of Chicago. His father—William V. Taylor, Sr.—was a precinct captain in Chicago's Democratic Party machine, which entitled him to a succession of cushy government jobs in addition to his regular work as a foreman on the ore dock at Republic. He was always working, either in the taverns or at his real job. He was never home in the evenings, nor was Bill's mother, Pauline, who usually could be found at the Two Cues tavern with Jimmy. Sometimes, after his mother left for her nightly rendezvous, his older sister, Beverly—babysitting for him, supposedly—would sneak out and run with her friends, leaving Bill alone watching television until the test patterns came on. He watched all the old war movies on "The Late Show": *Guadalcanal Diary, Fighting Seabees, The Sands of Iwo Jima* . . . After "The Late Show" came "The Star-Spangled Banner," and he would start to cry.

One day, when he was about six years old, he came home and found the house destroyed. Every bit of furniture was torn up. The television was kicked in. His mother had done it, and left her mark in lipstick on the wall: "Fuck You I'm Gone."

After the divorce, he was sent to military school for two years and hated it. When he was in seventh grade, his father took over again and they lived together in a single room in an apartment hotel in South Shore, which was an affluent neighborhood just south of the Loop, next to Lake Michigan. Bill's father had decided he wanted his son exposed to the best people, the doctors and lawyers and businessmen who belonged to the South Shore Country Club. He would send his son to parochial school at St. Philip Neri, where the best people sent their children. His plan worked, to a certain extent: Bill was a good athlete and won a degree of acceptance at school, although he never felt entirely at ease with the rich kids.

His first real friend was Bobby O'Brien, whose father was a commodities trader. He spent a good deal of time at Bobby's house—Mr. and Mrs. O'Brien were touched by his pride and politeness—and was awed by the quiet, the security, the love there. He vowed that someday he would have a son and give him a home like the O'Briens'—maybe not the affluence, but certainly the security. It wasn't something that preyed on his mind; he rarely thought about it in high school and never since he'd joined the Marines . . . but, for some reason, it had hit him hard during the ambush, scrunched down against the paddy wall.

Gathering his courage, Taylor took off his pack; the camera that had gotten him into so much trouble earlier was forgotten now, along with his food and letters. He unhitched his cartridge belt, checked his ammunition. He carried twenty magazines for his M-16, but had only used three. For all the action that morning, he hadn't fired very much. He took several magazines and stuffed them in his long trouser pocket.

"Pilgreen, I'm going to get help," he offered, unaware that help already had arrived. There was no answer.

"Wally?" No answer.

He began to whisper an Act of Contrition: "O my God, I am heartily sorry for having offended Thee and I detest all my sins because of Thy just punishment, but most of all because I have offended Thee, my God," and saying the words, he remembered all the Acts of Contrition he'd said back at St. Philip Neri. His parents hadn't been very religious, but the O'Briens were. When they went for a drive, Mrs. O'Brien would lead the children in saying the Rosary, to guarantee a safe trip. One night, late, sleeping at Bobby's house, they had vowed together never to commit a mortal sin. Bill couldn't imagine Bobby committing one, but knew he was going to have trouble. Indeed, he broke the vow almost immediately. Two days later, he was back in the confessional—as he was almost every morning. He would say, "Bless me, Father, for I have sinned." And the priest would say, "How long has it been since you've been to confession?" And he, flushed with humiliation: "Yesterday, Father." Yesterday? "Father, I abused myself one time." Each day his penance was the same, three Our Fathers and three Hail Marys . . . and then, alone in the apartment hotel at night, he'd start thinking about one or another of the eighth-grade girls in their little red, white and blue uniforms, the cheerleaders especially . . . and next morning, it would be back to the confessional. It was his first inkling that he might not be able to live up to the O'Briens' moral standards.

He completed the Act of Contrition: "I firmly resolve, with the help of Thy grace, to sin no more and avoid the narrow occasion of sin. Amen."

Then, crawling on his stomach, his rifle in front, pushing himself with his elbows and knees, staying hard against the right wall of the paddy, he began making his way toward the rear wall. Bullets were kicking up dirt to his right and just ahead. He stopped; the bullets stopped. He began to move again. The bullets made pinging noises—this part, at least, was just like in the movies. Harvey's head, though . . . he'd never seen anything like that on "The Late Show." The thought of it kept him going. He reached the rear wall and, with an exultant flip and roll, made it into the second paddy . . . and he kept going. He didn't move over to join Pilgreen and the others; he was, he later realized, fleeing rather than escaping. It felt safer in the second paddy, and he began to run. Then he was in the gully, but no one was there (the others were farther down, around several bends) . . . and so he kept going, following a deep, narrow, dried-out rivulet—it almost seemed a tunnel—which led out to the well where Jones had yelled at him that morning. To his right, he could see men coming down the crest of the hill under heavy fire; some were dropping. He turned left, and saw a haystack. The gooks are in the haystack, he thought, and opened up on full automatic, firing a whole magazine into it; then reloading and again firing . . . and screaming at the little bastards, letting go of the shame and fear and frustration that had been building in him all day.

Someone slapped him in the face. "Stop it . . . stop it." They took away his rifle, and he burst out crying. He couldn't stop. "Okay . . . okay," they were saying, patting him on the back.

"I know where the machine guns are," he said through the tears. No one seemed interested. "I know where the machine guns are," he repeated, but no one seemed to be listening.

Later, he figured he'd blown his credibility with the haystack.

Harvey was making noises—deep, chesty, gurgling, constricted noises—and it was driving Drust crazy.

"If he don't shut up," Drust said, "I'm gonna ki . . ."

"You can't kill him," Clark said. "He's already dead."

"Then why don't he shut up? He's giving me the willies."

Pilgreen threw a towel over Harvey's head, but the noises continued. Szuminski was still in the front paddy, screaming, and that wasn't helping Drust's state of mind much either. Then he saw the jets streaking down from the crest of the hill, rolling in right at them, and he dived, covering his head, thinking: Those bastards are gonna hit the tree line and blow *us* away while they're at it. But the jets continued on, toward the An Son village complex on the far side of the valley, before letting go their napalm, and the ground rumbled from the force of their work.

Harvey was still making noises, his legs and arms twitching. Drust had hated Harvey when he was alive—they'd scuffled briefly a few weeks before—and now it seemed that even in death the damn guy wouldn't leave him alone. "If that nigger don't shut up," Drust said, "I'm gonna finish him off."

"Drust," Sergeant White said. "Get out there and bring in Szuminski."

"Fuck you," Drust said. White was another one. He'd been acting like a big shot ever since he'd been made a squad leader. "I ain't goin', Jack. My momma didn't raise no fool. Anyone who goes out there is gonna get his ass dinged."

"Listen, Drust . . ."

"No, *you* listen," Drust said. He could hear Szuminski screaming. "If you want to help Ski so bad, why don't you go out there your own self?"

"All right," said White, to everyone's surprise, and he heaved himself up, over the dike into the paddy. The tree line erupted, White went down and Pilgreen said, "Aw shit."

Szuminski had seen Harvey blown back and White's head explode up into his helmet as he came over into the paddy, and he knew that he was all alone now that Muller was in, and the shadows were lengthening, and that no one else would be crazy enough to try to come out and get him. For several hours, he'd put most of his energy into listening, hoping for the sound of tanks. He figured tanks were his only salvation. He could picture a line of them pouring over the crest of the hill, across the paddies, then sweeping past him, crushing the tree line . . . but there were no tanks and the sky was empty again, and—with a calm certainty that might have startled him if his brain hadn't been addled by pain and fear—he came to the conclusion that he was dead.

There was no hope. The only question now was how he was going to die; he had, he realized, several options. He could remain where he was and then, when night fell—three or four hours, he estimated—the NVA would come out and either kill him or take him prisoner. He'd heard stories about what they did to prisoners. There was no way he was going to wait around for that. He decided that he would have to try to get out before dark. If he had his legs, he might have gotten up and made a dash for the rear—foolhardy as it was, it would be over quickly—but his right leg was burning, and he doubted if he could even stand. So he would have to crawl. He'd seen Muller go out on his back—although, he realized, he had about twice as far to go as Muller, and he wasn't sure if Muller had made it out alive or been killed in the same burst as Harvey. No matter; it didn't make much difference. He unhooked his cartridge belt with his right hand—the radio was already off and his rifle jammed and useless—and thought for a moment about his parents. He thought about them at his funeral, crying but very proud. He would be buried in the same cemetery, maybe even the same plot, as his uncle Paul Chernicki, who'd been killed at Iwo Jima. His mother would cook something terrific for when everyone went back to the house afterward.

It was a fleeting thought. For most of the day, his mind had been blank. He had lost track of hunger and thirst and time. He felt empty, emotionless. He had even forgotten the one fact that had dominated his life until the moment of the ambush—that he only had ten days left in-country. He had not thought about that all day.

He flipped over, toward the left paddy wall, which was closest, and heard Pilgreen yell, "*No*, Ski, not that way . . . go the long way . . . across the front . . ."

On his back, Szuminski lost all sense of how far he would have to go; nor was he aware that he would have to crawl over the bodies of Hawthorn and White. He knew only that it was "the long way." Lacking the energy to figure it out, he gave himself up to Pilgreen's voice.

"That's it, Ski . . ." Pilgreen yelled, relieved that Szuminski could hear and respond. If he had continued along the left wall, he would have been silhouetted perfectly for the flanking machine gun on the right. In the end, though, it probably wouldn't make much difference: Szuminski would have to crawl the entire width and then the length of the paddy, perhaps two hundred yards in all, and Pilgreen didn't think he would make it. Szuminski was small and frail under the best of circumstances, stumbling along on patrol under the weight of the radio, but never complaining much about it—Pilgreen liked him, as did just about everyone. Exhausted and sad, figuring that he wouldn't be able to pull off the same trick twice, Pilgreen established the rhythm for him: "*Push*, Ski . . . atta boy . . . *push* . . . "

The sky was filled again with Hueys—five of them this time—and jets streaking past the tree line to pulverize the An Son village complex beyond. The Hueys were more effective now, strafing the entire tree line, including the machine-gun emplacements on the right . . . but Steiner still doubted that they'd do much beyond forcing the North Vietnamese to keep their heads down. He had moved, with Lieutenant Francis and the radio operator, along the rear wall of the paddy closer to the trapped squad and, as the Hueys came in—very fast and very low, maybe twelve feet off the ground—he saw Francis giving the helicopters a big thumbs-up sign and thought: What a jerk. We're getting creamed and this guy's pretending it's *The Sands of Iwo Jima*. Then he saw one of the door gunners, leaning precariously out the side of his helicopter, returning Francis' gesture—it seemed half the people in the war were playing John Wayne, and Steiner was revolted by such perversity amidst so much suffering. He saw Muller nearby, wrapped in a poncho liner, face streaked with blood, crying softly, alone and forgotten momentarily while the others played cowboys and Indians.

Two medevac helicopters had followed the Hueys in and were hovering at the crest of the hill, where Sands, Cooper, Sergeant Kochmaruk and Doc Johnson waited to be taken out. As the medevacs approached, the third enemy machine gun opened up again, drawing a bead on the helicopters despite suppressive fire from the Hueys. Windshields shattered and Sands said, "Holy Christmas, they ain't gonna make it."

The medevacs backed off and disappeared quickly, without making an attempt to land, and Cooper said, "Jesus, how they gonna get us out of here?"

Sands liked Cooper. They had been close in the past and were closer now, having suffered similar wounds. Sands had taken a bullet through the arm, and Cooper through the leg, but neither was seriously hurt, their bones and nerves intact. Waiting for the medevac, they shared a secret euphoria, having tested their mortality and proven themselves superior even to bullets, knowing they would be rewarded with a Purple Heart and a ticket to the rear (temporarily, at least) for their trouble.

In his own strange way, Cooper was a model soldier. He certainly wasn't a GAFer; he didn't Give-A-Fuck like Lieutenant Francis and a few of the others who actually believed in the war. Nor was he respected—as Jones and Malloy had been—for his knowledge and precision in the field. He was, rather, a perfect representative of the vast majority of men in Charlie Company, who, after months in the field, didn't care if the war was won or lost, or if they performed well or poorly in battle, as long as they got out of there in one piece. If he had distinguished himself in any way, it was as the guy who, back on Okinawa, had been the most devoted patron of the local whorehouses and, therefore, the most persistently in need of penicillin. His horniness was legend, and the subject of intense debate: Was he actually serious when he offered the withered old mamasan half a fruitcake in return for her favors? The woman, teeth stained betel-nut black, had turned him down. Was his obvious disappointment feigned or real?

From Okinawa, he had written to a high school friend named Philip Bradberry, who had gone on to college: "Son you wouldn't believe this place it is really something . . . I spent the night with this girle the other night. I thought I had had pussy before but this girle man she was reall something. I have been drunk every since I have been here. Rember what Glen Gibbs said about Oriental women it is all true 'there great.' I am going to hate like hell to go back to Viet Nam we are going in about two weeks so that means I am going to get as much pussy as possible and drunk as much as possible . . ."

In the same letter, he wrote: "Viet Nam is a real hell hole if you are in the Infantory and that is what I am in so you know that I am catching hell. But fuck it I guess I will live through It. If I don't fuck that too. If I here you talking about joining the service I will kick your god dam ass. You stay in school."

Bradberry was a bit surprised by the semi-literacy of the letter—although Gary hadn't been much of a student, he wasn't stupid—but otherwise Cooper sounded the same as ever. They had been close friends for two years in Gleason, Tennessee. Gary had been born there, but had gone North to Indiana when his stepfather, Thomas Brummitt, heard there were jobs in the steel mills. Thomas found work at Inland Steel, but never could quite get Tennessee out of his blood. He returned alone once, in 1959, during the long steel strike. Then, in 1963, he packed up the whole family—his wife, Lillian, their daughter, Donna, and Gary—and returned to Gleason, resolved to stay this time. Gary was a junior in high school, and beginning to actively resent that he'd never been more than "Lillian's son" to his stepfather. After Donna was born, especially, he'd been a barely tolerated appendage to the family; Donna always got the spare bedroom in the succession of two-bedroom houses and trailers they'd lived in, and he slept on the couch. Thomas would later allow that he liked Gary well enough, but blood was thicker than water.

Gleason was a small town, well off the beaten path, about halfway between Nashville and Memphis, where nothing of any great significance had ever happened. It was the sort of place where domestic dramas were the prime topics of conversation and Gary Cooper's battles with his stepfather would be remembered years later. Philip Bradberry once saw Thomas slam the door in Gary's face, saying, "Get your ass out, and don't come back." Gary's mother, a scattered, distant woman then in the first stages of multiple sclerosis, always managed to get him back in—but that was the extent of her support.

In a way, Philip Bradberry envied Gary's independence. He never had to be home for dinner, never had a curfew like everyone else, could always be found hanging out at the dairy bar downtown. Philip knew Gary was hurting, but he never talked much about family problems. They did small-town things together—drank beer, drove around town, went swimming at the clay pits, fantasized about girls—but Philip always had the sense that if there had been something more to do in Gleason, something less innocent and more dangerous, Gary would have been ready to do that too. It wasn't that he was *looking* for trouble; he was just available for it.

Gary and Philip usually hung out with Ronnie Taylor and Big Daddy Dillinger. Philip was the only one of the four who wasn't on the high school football team; Gary was the only one who wasn't going to college. Sometimes Gary's real father, Thirby Cooper, would breeze into town from his government job near Memphis in his Buick Riviera and Gary would, very proudly, drive the gang around; usually, though, they went in Ronnie Taylor's car. Ronnie was the best student of the four and the cheapest; when they went for a drive, he would collect fifty cents from each of them for gas. One night Big Daddy, who suffered from a glandular disease and weighed more than three hundred pounds, was riding shotgun and Gary let out the air from the right front tire when no one was looking; Ronnie made Big Daddy pay him three dollars to fix the "flat." Another night, the four of them agreed that if any of them died, the other three would piss on his grave.

Gary didn't seem to have any plans past high school. When armed forces recruiters were allowed to proselytize a school assembly, he was impressed by the man from the Marine Corps, who had the best uniform—dress blues—and seemed more manly than the others. He told Philip that if it ever came to that, he would join the Marines. After graduation, though, he decided to go back North and work in the steel mills, where the pay was much better than anything Gleason had to offer. His stepfather apparently agreed and soon packed up the family once more and joined Gary at Inland Steel.

Philip Bradberry didn't see Cooper for about six months, until Thanksgiving of 1965. Gary had signed up for the Marines by then, and said he was going to be an aviator. One night, he and several others—Philip wasn't there—piled into a friend's car and there was an accident. It was a head-on crash, but didn't seem very serious at first. Ronnie Taylor was the only one hurt; the shift column had hit him in the chest and he was spitting blood. They took him to the clinic in nearby Martin, where the doctors said it wasn't anything to worry about. But Ronnie continued to spit blood and his parents rushed him to Memphis, where he died of a punctured aorta. Philip, Gary and Big Daddy were pallbearers at the funeral. Afterward, Gary called Philip and said it was time to go piss on Ronnie's grave. Philip didn't feel much like doing it, but Gary insisted. "We promised we would, and that's exactly what I'm gonna do." They bought a fifth of whiskey, rounded up Big Daddy and did it.

Philip saw Gary one more time before he left for Vietnam. He had finished boot camp and was strutting about in his uniform. He had washed out of aviation school, but didn't seem to care—the Marines were the best there was, he was going to "kick ass and not take names" in Vietnam. But later, driving around with about a pint of whiskey in him, he admitted to Philip that joining the Marines had been a mistake. He was frightened about going to Vietnam. "I think," he said, "this war is just a bunch of shit."

Nothing in Vietnam had altered his opinion. He did his job and followed orders when they weren't too crazy. He bitched (without whining) about the heat and the food and the shits and the leeches. He skated when he had the chance, but never when someone else would have to pick up his slack. He walked the line between heroism and cowardice, proud but with few illusions.

Sitting there, waiting for the medevacs to return, Mel Sands said to him, "Hey, Coop, one of these years when we get back to the World, I'm gonna have to come down there and look you up. It ain't too far from Michigan to Indiana."

"There you go," Cooper agreed. "We'll have a time."

Soldiers were returning from the valley with jammed rifles (the M-16s were something else, Sands thought; his had jammed the first time he tried to fire it), needing water and ammunition. He and Cooper donated their equipment to the cause, gleefully relieving themselves of the war—rifles, cartridge belts, canteens. "Take it," Cooper said, unhooking his belt. "I ain't gonna be needing it where I'm going."

A good hour had passed, maybe more; Pilgreen had only the setting sun to gauge the time. Szuminski was still working his way back, struggling mightily, his mind blank except for the rhythm of it: knees up, heels in, push back, knees up, heels in, push back . . . inch by inch, dragging along his dead arm, which felt—with each push— as if his shoulder were being bayoneted. He moved through a tunnel of noise, claustrophobic. The Hueys had helped for a while, keeping the North Vietnamese down while he made his way along the front wall, then turned toward home. But they were up again as soon as the helicopters left, and Pilgreen could, from time to time, catch a glimpse through a break in the trees of a little guy in shorts and a pith helmet, shouting orders. He figured it was the North Vietnamese commander and thought: If I could stay up long enough to draw a bead, I'd love to ding that sucker.

The tree line seemed to explode out toward them, a curtain of noise and smoke, machine guns, semiautomatics, rocket grenades, mortars blasting the crest of the hill, and through it all, Szuminski— it was a miracle, the most willful act Pilgreen had ever witnessed, each push as if he were struggling out from quicksand, so much effort for so few inches. "*Push*, Ski . . . keep it comin' . . . c'mon, boy . . . *push*, Ski . . ."

He was getting closer, dragging himself over the medic's corpse, then faltering, almost to a dead stop, but not quite . . . and again, over Sergeant White . . . and Pilgreen was shouting himself hoarse: "*Push*, Ski . . . c'mon, boy, don't stop now . . . *push* . . . you got it . . . you got it . . . *push*, Ski . . ." As Szuminski approached the rear wall and seemed to give out entirely, Pilgreen couldn't stand it any longer and, exposing himself, leaped the wall and—he wasn't sure whether the North Vietnamese had simply, inexplicably, stopped firing or whether, in the sheer terror of the act, he just couldn't hear the bullets—pulled Szuminski back in, over, safe, both of them tumbled in a heap, exhausted.

Szuminski was conscious, but in shock. He wasn't bleeding, but was covered with blood. He couldn't speak. "What're we going to do with him now?" Drust asked. "His arm's all torn up."

"You're gonna carry him out on your back," Pilgreen said.

Drust, happy to have any excuse to get out of there, agreed and lay down on his stomach. "Listen, Ski," Pilgreen was saying. "When you get back to the World, I want you to send me some of that screwdriver mix—you know, the vodka stuff—your folks sent you. Okay, brother?" Szuminski didn't say anything. "All right, now," Pilgreen said. "You *know* it's gonna be all right."

Drust began to crawl, his left arm back holding Szuminski—who didn't have the strength or presence of mind to hold on—and pushing forward with his right arm and knees. And now they were firing at him—he had no idea where the bullets were coming from—and he heard a rocket grenade whistling through the air as if it was going to land directly on his head, which he raised briefly to see if he could spot it coming, then ducked down and felt a cascade of dirt on him, and a noise and pressure that seemed to drive him into the ground. He felt blood running from his nose and ears, and his head was ringing, but he continued on . . . crawling toward the open valley, then over the plank bridge that crossed the gully, depositing Szuminski with a corporal he didn't know.

Then he turned around, head spinning, and went back toward the front paddy.

Steiner, who had pulled back with Lieutenant Francis, saw them leading Walsted out, over the plank bridge. He was stumbling, unsteady, eyes wide open, completely out of it. Then came Muller and Szuminski, carried out in poncho liners. The fire from the tree line had changed, was closer but more sporadic. It sounded as if the North Vietnamese had retrieved M-16s from the corpses in the front paddy and were firing them to taunt the remnants of Charlie Company. Dave McCarthy, carrying one end of Szuminski, screamed—a bullet ripped through his hand—and dropped his end of the poncho liner. Szuminski, jolted back to consciousness, thought: Ain't we out of this *yet*?

The last of them—Pilgreen, Drust, Clark (who was firing his own weapon and Harvey's back toward the tree line)—came out, leaving only the four corpses behind. Lieutenant Francis trailed, and Steiner stepped out to give him covering fire. He popped rounds in the direction of the tree line on semiautomatic, since he didn't have enough ammunition left to go full tilt.

"Thanks, Steiner," Francis said as he went past.

Hey, Steiner thought with mild satisfaction, he knows my name.

"Wakefield," the lieutenant said, "White's been hit. Take over the squad."

Wakefield, who had been pinned down for more than an hour under heavy fire while trying to move back from the gully to the crest of the hill, did not ask how badly hit or when or where. He had lost track of White in early afternoon, when Francis had taken all the men on the left side of the cut in the gully forward; Wakefield, on the right, remained where he was, providing cover fire.

When he learned that White had been shot, Wakefield went numb. He did not want to know what had happened, and went off to find his squad before the lieutenant could explain further.

Wakefield would never be able to recall what he did or how he acted after learning that White was shot. Fifteen years would pass before he found out that White had died attempting one of those heroic, emotional acts that he so scorned. And then, eyes misting, Wakefield would say, "Damn him. He made a mistake."

Captain Reczek had set up a command post on the far side of the hill, and the 1st and 3rd Platoons were digging in, establishing a night perimeter. Medevacs could land safely here, in a clearing near the perimeter. Szuminski, Muller and Walsted were taken off first, to a field hospital. Cooper and Sands were then loaded into a chopper with three Vietnamese prisoners, dressed in camouflage fatigues. Getting aboard, Cooper said, "You know what? It's my birthday. I'm twenty-one. I can drink legal. I can vote . . ."

"What're you voting for?"

"For getting the fuck out of here."

"I was up for R 'n' R tomorrow," Sands said. "I was supposed to go out with resupply, Australia. Now that asshole Francis is probably gonna get it."

"Australia," Cooper said, "Ain't it a bitch."

The helicopter lifted off, then headed northeast toward Danang, nose down as if it were being dragged forward, away from the sunset. The three Vietnamese—neither Sands nor Cooper knew where or how they'd been taken prisoner—were squatting in the doorway;

it was, Sands realized, the closest he'd come to the enemy all day. Cooper, sitting against the wall with his bandaged left leg extended and his right leg drawn up, looked over at the Vietnamese disgustedly, then turned to Sands, who could tell they were both thinking along the same lines. Cooper nodded, smiling slightly, and lashed out his good right leg, planting the boot firmly in the face of one of the squatting Vietnamese, who fell back toward the door with a yelp. Then there was confusion and, before Sands was quite sure what happened or how it was done, two of the Vietnamese were no longer in the helicopter and the third had skittered away, up front to the pilot, and was there, cowering.

"Payback," said Cooper, "is a motherfucker."

Taylor sat alone in the center of the perimeter, crying softly. He could still hear them crying for help, and see the bullets jitterbugging around poor Walsted. He remembered all too clearly how terrified he'd been, and he couldn't stop thinking about the haystack. He was ashamed; everyone probably knew he'd cracked. He heard the mortars crumping on the other side of the hill and thought: I got to get it together. There's still a war going on. He realized that he was starving. He hadn't eaten all day and now his food was gone, left out in the field with his pack. He approached Lieutenant Francis, who told him he'd have to make do—there would be no food until resupply came in the next day. He went around to the others then, asking if they had any extra food . . . and if they'd seen the haystack. "I'm sure the gooks were in the haystack," he said. "They had to be."

Someone flipped him a little tin of C-ration peanut butter, awful stuff, but he opened it quickly and had at it with his fingers and then, despite the jagged edges, with his tongue.

Steiner was sitting with his head between his legs, trying not to cry. He felt completely alone; utterly depressed. The war was hopeless; it was being lost. When the medevacs had gone, it seemed so few remained—only seventeen, in fact, in the 2nd Platoon. There were no squad leaders: Jones and White were dead, and Williams relieved of duty. Two of the three medics were gone: Hawthorn dead and Johnson wounded. Cooper, Sands, Drust, Szuminski, Muller, Walsted, Sheoships, Sergeant Kochmaruk, McCarthy—all wounded and gone. He wondered how many casualties the North Vietnamese had taken. He hadn't even *seen* the North Vietnamese, and the feeling that they were making war against trees and bushes began to rise in him again. It seemed that the Americans never struck first; they always were ambushed. They would be ambushed, then fill the sky with machines, pulverizing the land and occasionally, if they were lucky, the enemy. He had never knowingly fired his rifle at a human being, only at foliage.

He looked up and saw Pilgreen sitting with his head in his hands, disconsolate, and thought: Well, I'm not the only one who feels like this. He saw Lieutenant Francis approach Pilgreen and pat him on the back. "Cheer up," he said.

Steiner had read all the war novels he could find in high school. He read them furtively in study hall and at home when his parents confined him to his room because his grades were so poor. He knew he should have been studying, but school offered nothing that could compare with those sad and glorious books, filled with heroism, best friends dying and cowards redeeming themselves. Mel Sands often joked that Steiner had been bribed into the Marines with a free set of dress blues (it was true that his recruiter had offered him a spare tunic which fit perfectly), but the real reason was those books—especially *Battle Cry* by Leon Uris, which he read early in high school and had mixed feelings about by the time of Operation Cochise. He had seen the movie version on Okinawa and thought: Is *that* how I got mixed up in this? It seemed so hokey. It was nothing like Vietnam. When someone died in *Battle Cry*, there was a sense of sadness and loss—but no inkling of the horrible depression and emptiness he felt after every battle. In the World War II novels, there always was the incredible sense of camaraderie, buddies consoling each other, sharing their grief at a memorial service perhaps. But he had never seen a memorial service in Vietnam, no one even *admitted* his grief, and he could no more go over and console Pilgreen—the lieutenant's pat on the back had seemed so empty—than he could talk about the gooks in the haystack with Taylor. He didn't even know who Pilgreen *was*. He'd only met him a few months earlier on Okinawa and knew little more than that he was one of the old salts who had been at Khe Sanh and who scorned new guys. In *Battle Cry* everyone seemed to know everything about everyone else. But he and Pilgreen had come to Vietnam separately and would rotate separately; their wars had merely intersected for a time. New troops would come with resupply, filling the gaps left by the dead and wounded. There would be more paddies to cross and—inevitably—another tree line. They would assault other village complexes, then leave them to be assaulted, pacified, blown up or burned down by other grunts. There would be more medevacs, and then more fresh troops . . . but never any clear-cut resolutions. Only the land would remain.

At times, though, he wondered about even that. A month earlier, walking through the Trace, a particularly devastated area of the DMZ reeking of defoliants, he had recalled a passage in *All Quiet on the Western Front* where the hero is amazed to hear birds singing in the blasted trees of no-man's-land, between the trench lines. Steiner had searched the barren trees for birds, but couldn't find any sign of life anywhere.

It was dark. The battle was over, except for the ponderous thump of artillery shells landing in the valley beyond the hill. Lieutenant Francis approached Pilgreen again, almost sheepishly, and said, "Pilgreen, you're going to have to go back out there."

"*What?*"

"We have to retrieve the bodies."

"Fuck no, get someone else."

"But you're the only one who knows exactly where each of them is," he said. "We have to get them."

And so a small party was organized to return to the valley. Steiner, Taylor, Burt Wilson, Jim Reynolds and several others, along with Higgenbotham, the remaining medic, were roused for the mission—morose and exhausted, but knowing it had to be done; the Marines never left their dead in the field. A map was drawn in the dirt. They were divided into two-man teams, each assigned to retrieve a specific body. The corpsman said to signal him immediately if any of them were still alive, and he would radio for a medevac. Then they taped down all their loose gear—grenades, dog tags, the swivels on their rifle straps—and started out.

Steiner, terrified, fully expecting another battle, carried about twenty grenades with him. He was teamed with Reynolds, which didn't make him happy. Reynolds was a big, clumsy guy who always seemed to be screwing up—a big baby, Steiner thought. They'd even given him rubber pants when he'd had the shits. "Listen, Reynolds," he said, "we have to be very, very quiet out there, so be very, very careful about every move you make."

It was a clear night, with not much moon. When they reached the crest of the hill, they saw the artillery had been dropping smoke to cover their operation. It lay across the paddies like a great wad of cotton. Crawling down into it, into the gully again, Steiner felt as if he had entered the twilight zone. From the gully, they moved out very, very slowly on their stomachs—Steiner was afraid the North Vietnamese would hear them scraping across the dry, hard paddies. They moved fifty yards in twenty minutes, up to the rear wall of the front paddy. Then he and Reynolds moved forward again, up to where Jones lay . . . and Reynolds tripped—how he could trip while crawling on his belly was beyond Steiner—and fell with a clatter that seemed to echo through the valley. But there was no reaction from the tree line. If anyone was there, Steiner thought, they certainly would have heard *that*, and so he felt safe to whisper, "Reynolds, you dumb shit, how did I ever get stuck with you?"

Taylor was assigned to retrieve Harvey, so he didn't have to go out beyond the rear wall of the paddy. He went around to Harvey's head and grabbed the arms—and, as he began to lift, he heard an empty sloshing sound: the head had moved. He shuddered, nearly becoming sick. The body smelled of urine and feces. He lifted the arms again and the corpse emitted an immense, groaning belch; it was a horrible sound, so very human and yet completely lifeless.

Taylor found that he was as frightened as he'd been in the first moments of the fire fight—*more* frightened, perhaps, since he had more time to think about it now. Around him, he could hear the other corpses being moved and giving off hollow, resonant farts and belches, profoundly undignified in their mortality.

The plan had been to drag the corpses out slowly while crawling, but they were so heavy, so entirely dead, that not much progress was being made and, since it seemed obvious now that the North Vietnamese had abandoned the tree line, the four teams rose and carried the dead back to the gully, where the bodies were inspected and wrapped in poncho liners. They were found to have had their pants pulled down—a final taunt from the North Vietnamese—but all their anatomy intact.

Steiner watched with admiration as Burt Wilson, a rather small man, impatient to get out of there, picked up one of the corpses and threw it over his shoulder, then stomped off, disappearing into a swirl of smoke, heading back toward the perimeter.

The next day they walked, quietly and with a certain reverence, through the tree line. There were no Vietnamese bodies to be found, but shell casings and bandages and blood spattered everywhere, as if the trees—twisted and splintered by the constant punishment— themselves had fought and bled.

Do they matter?—those dreams from the pit? . . .
You can drink and forget and be glad,
And people won't say that you're mad;
For they'll know you've fought for your country
And no one will worry a bit.

—SIEGFRIED SASSOON

1

Within a matter of days—so quickly in fact that he would remember only a blur of airports—Dale Szuminski was rushed from Vietnam to the Philadelphia Naval Hospital, where he remained for the next six months.

He soon found that he was spending much of his time staring out the window near his bed, especially at night. He watched the visitors coming and going, and the traffic heading south on Broad Street toward the new indoor and outdoor stadiums being built on the marshes near the Delaware River. Later, he would remember paying special attention to the traffic on Fridays—date night—wondering where all the cars were going, what the people were doing. Back home in Erie before the war, he often spent Friday night cruising State Street, looking for girls, or crossing the border to the New York bars, where he could drink legally. But staring out the hospital window, he didn't often think about what he'd be doing if he were home; rather, he remembered all the times in the past year—in the bush and on the ship between operations—that he and Dale Walsted had *talked* about what they would be doing if they were back in the World.

They were both saving their money to buy Corvettes. (They agreed that burgundy was the best color.) Their conversations never varied much—engines, options, Friday-night blondes going *crazy* over them because they had such incredible cars—but they never tired of talking. They were going to make up for lost time. Szuminski had kept a little notebook and would write down all the things he was missing. He noted each holiday as it passed: his birthday (he had turned twenty while guarding the airstrip at Khe Sanh the previous October), Marine Corps birthday, Thanksgiving, Christmas, New Year's, St. Patty's Day. He imagined the meal his mother would cook for each holiday, and would write that down too—roast beef with gravy, baked potato, corn on the cob, chocolate pudding. He kept two short-timer's calendars. One, in the notebook, was a simple list of days to be crossed off. The other was a crude drawing of a woman, her body partitioned into one hundred numbered sections to be filled in day by day. Szuminski had finished her hair, her breasts, and was getting pretty close to number one. He had ten days left, a serpentine path from her right hip to the jackpot, when they were ambushed.

The last time he saw Walsted was after the ambush in a field hospital which looked like something out of the Civil War—a confusion of doctors, nurses, blood and screaming. A world of hurt. That was something they often said in Vietnam (Szuminski loved the way the other grunts talked, especially the Southerners, and kept a list of key phrases in his notebook): "If you don't get your shit together, you're going to find yourself in a world of hurt."

He saw Walsted standing there in the field hospital, not physically wounded but white as a sheet, trembling. "Wally," he said, struggling through the morphine, trying to say goodbye. "Hey, Wally . . ." But Walsted didn't even seem to recognize him.

It was strange. For thirteen months, all he could think about was getting home. Now, all he could think about was Vietnam.

They had put him on an amputee ward, even though he still had everything, more or less. His left arm was paralyzed from the bullet that had entered his shoulder and traveled diagonally through his biceps, shattering the bone and severing the nerve; the bullet through his right calf had caused only a flesh wound, and already was feeling better. He was lucky, he realized, compared to some of the others on the ward. There were men with no arms, no legs, an arm and two legs, every possible combination. At night, there would be bursts of hysteria—one or another of the amputees wakening to find something missing and crying out, "Corpsman . . . corpsman," as if it had just happened and he was still back there. Everyone seemed to have nightmares; everyone seemed to wake up startled, ready for battle. Szuminski half expected to hear someone yell "INCOMING!" some night and see them all dive beneath their beds. Inevitably, there were phantom fire fights—some poor devil would lurch into a mad minute, rolling off his bed, flopping around on the floor, tangled in his intravenous tubing and screaming. Szuminski couldn't sleep even when it was quiet. That was strange too. For thirteen months, he had struggled—often unsuccessfully—to stay awake on watch . . . and now he couldn't sleep at all when it was dark. He would nap during the day.

His wounds made sleeping difficult. Lighting cigarettes had become a real adventure. He would have to pinion the matchbook on his thigh with his left hand, and try to twist off the match with his right the way girls used to twist off apple stems in the schoolyard. The match was usually pretty badly mauled by the time he got it off. Then he would take the matchbook and insert it between the fourth finger and pinky of his left hand and, again, pinion it against his thigh. Sometimes he would strike it three, four, five times and nothing would happen; the match would be crumpled, useless, and he'd have to start all over again. The doctors said the chances were that his severed nerve never would heal; his arm would always be paralyzed. He would have to buy a lighter.

When they wheeled him onto the ward the first day, he'd been surprised to see his parents already there. They had dashed across the state, from Erie to Philadelphia, and beat him to the hospital by several hours. His mother was angry and crying. "Didn't they even clean you, Dale?" she asked. She pulled a hanky from her purse, spit on it and began wiping the mud and blood from his hands and feet. Dried blood was caked in the cuticles of his fingers, and his feet were a mess—raw, calluses peeling, filthy. He had been moved from the field hospital to Danang in a morphine haze; from Danang to San Francisco, where he called home; from San Francisco to some air base in New Jersey and then, by bus, stacked with the others in litters, to Philadelphia. It happened so quickly the government hadn't even had time to send his parents the obligatory telegram. They first learned he was wounded when he called them from San Francisco.

His father asked questions. How did it happen? When? Where was he hurt? He gave perfunctory answers: "Ambush . . . three days ago . . . my arm and my leg. The leg's not too bad, but the arm hurts like a bitch up top and I can't feel nothing in my hand." His father wanted to know more, but what was there to say? Szuminski had spent most of his childhood trying to get his uncle Pete Chernicki to talk about what had happened at Iwo Jima, but Pete never would. Dale's mother had been the one who had told him about how Pete had found his brother, Paul, on the troopship the night before the invasion, and Paul had said, "Pete, I got the feeling I ain't gonna make it," and gave Pete his Bible. Sure enough, Paul had been killed in the first wave. It sounded like something from a war movie, the most dramatic thing anyone in the family had ever done, and Dale wanted to know more about it, but he never could get Pete to talk. Now he understood: How could he explain what it was like to his father, who'd worked in a factory all his life and never been in battle? What words could he use, and not sound foolish?

He wanted to ask them about his girlfriend, Patty Hagman, but didn't dare. She hadn't come with them, a clear enough message. Her letters had tailed off toward the end and, when they came, seemed distant—almost formal. He'd never been very serious about Patty until Vietnam, even though they'd gone steady through most of high school. He had treated her badly, often telling her that he was going out with the guys, but heading instead for State Street, cruising, picking up girls . . . but it was Patty he'd thought about at night in Khe Sanh and later, humping the radio through the boondocks; and even, sometimes, when he talked to Walsted about Friday-night blondes. He figured that she had found another guy while he was away, and really couldn't blame her; at least she'd had the class not to Dear John him. There was a guy named Hart, who had been Dear Johnned back in May. He received the letter out in the field, on a resupply. The next day there was a fire fight—their first real action—and Hart just stood up and took several AK-47 rounds in the chest. He was the first in the platoon to go.

His parents tried to cheer him up. His mother told a story about what his sister, Caryl, had said when they found out he was wounded. The phone rang. Walter Szuminski answered; it was Dale—they figured the Marines had let him out a few weeks early. Then there was confusion, and some tears. Walter said that Dale sounded okay, he probably wasn't wounded too badly. Caryl said, "Don't worry about Dale. When those Viet Cong pinned him down, he probably said, 'Now *wait* a minute, can't we talk this thing *over*?'"

His father thought it was pretty funny. "That's Dale all right . . . Now *wait* a minute, let's talk this over."

Dale smiled for them. His mother thought he looked very small and pale and, with his Marine crew cut, very young. He was still just a kid. She began to cry again. Down the ward, a Marine big shot—a general—was making his way from bed to bed. He asked each boy how he was feeling and then said, "Hold on, tiger." Some of them were whimpering; one was screaming uncontrollably. When Dale's turn came, he seemed very proud. He boosted himself up, quickly covering the wince with a smile, and shook the general's hand.

"Hold on, tiger."

"Yessir."

When he stared out the hospital window late at night, the image that came to mind most frequently was the last one in the field: the medevac helicopter lifting him off the LZ, sucked into a deafening vortex of noise and a cool rush of air. In that moment, as the trees fell away and his buddies became faded olive dots on a parched ocher hilltop, he'd had a very unsettling thought: Hey, wait a minute! I'm not ready to go yet. The battle isn't over. I didn't even get a chance to say goodbye . . . He could look down from the helicopter's open side door and see the medics still tending the wounded on the ground. He had wondered who was left down there, waiting for the next bird out. Farther in the distance—he couldn't quite see or hear, but he *knew*—the others were scrunched down behind paddy dikes, putting rounds into the tree line.

He felt that he had abandoned them. He knew that wasn't logical, but there it was. During his first few weeks in the hospital, Szuminski often would wonder where they were now. Still out in the boonies somewhere? Back on ship, getting ready for another operation? He wondered what had happened with Operation Cochise after the ambush. Had they continued sweeping the valley, or pulled out? He felt frustrated, not knowing. At least, his uncle Pete had the chance to *take* his island, see the flag flying over Mount Suribachi.

Dave Muller was several beds down the ward; they had been medevacked out together. But Szuminski had never really been close to Muller, even though they both came from Erie and once, when they were teenagers, had worked in the same McDonald's. There were several others from Erie in the hospital: Don Rogers, who had done boot camp and advanced infantry training with Szuminski, was already there when he and Muller arrived. Rogers had served in the 9th Marines and was wounded in the arm and back. There also was Ken Oberlander, Paul Albert and John Moyack, minus a leg—it seemed half of Erie had wound up in the same naval hospital in Philadelphia.

They hung out together, went to the cafeteria (where Muller and Szuminski were allowed double rations of meat because they had broken bones), watched the bodies being rolled to the morgue and the mental cases raging about in lavender smocks. The hospital was jammed; the wards were full and beds lined some of the hallways. The staff was far too busy to pay them much attention and, for the most part, they were left to their own devices.

Within a few weeks, they were assigned jobs—Szuminski was supposed to clean mirrors and Muller toilets—but since Oberlander was in charge of the work detail, they rarely did them. Szuminski went to physical therapy several times each week and was taught exercises to strengthen his arm, but didn't take it very seriously — the doctors had said the arm wasn't coming back, so why bother? They got drunk as often as it could be arranged, passing quarts of wine back and forth beneath the stalls in the bathroom. Soon they were allowed to leave the grounds on day passes and, soon after that, they were sneaking out. Sometimes they would climb the fence that surrounded the hospital (this wasn't easy for Szuminski, but the others would help); usually they just walked out past the guards, who didn't seem to care.

Muller was the ringleader. He was married, for the time being, and his wife had come to Philadelphia — which was something of an inconvenience, but she *had* brought the car from Erie . . . and he would roar through town with Szuminski, Rogers and the others aboard, screeching around corners, running red lights, daring the police to stop him. He would head for the roughest parts of town, the ghetto, any bar that had a dozen motorcycles out front, his rage perpetual, still fighting his war. His *modus operandi* was rather primitive: he would strut into a bar, chest sucked in, throwing his shoulders about, then seek out the toughest-looking customer and find some way to insult him. He was a small man, with a red, round face, bulldog neck and a weight lifter's body, and could seem flagrantly provocative without ever raising his voice. Szuminski figured that Muller was crazy, but usually was too drunk to worry about it. When a fight started, he would stay out of the line of fire. He seemed able to do this effortlessly, obliviously, without moving a muscle — to the delight of the others, who often weren't so lucky. Later, Don Rogers would consider it a miracle that Muller hadn't gotten them all killed. As it happened, Szuminski was the only real casualty that autumn: one afternoon he fell off a barstool and broke his left arm again.

Even before he joined the Marines, Szuminski had been known in Erie as something of a character, always getting into trouble and then — in his sly, somewhat foggy, low-key way — slipping out from under. He could, it was said, talk his way out of anything.

He had, in fact, talked five of his friends into joining the Marines with him after they graduated from high school in 1965. They were going to be drafted anyway, he argued, so why not go with the best? His campaign was brought to a successful conclusion by a friendly recruiter who plied them with drinks and Marine Corps movies in the basement of his home, and then had the enlistment papers all ready to be signed at the door as they staggered out. They joined on the "buddy" plan, which meant they would have the privilege of suffering boot camp together in San Diego. But there wasn't much time for socializing in boot camp and they didn't really get to see each other until advanced infantry training, when they were allowed off the base for the first time.

Rogers and Szuminski went to Balboa Island, and immediately got into trouble. They missed the last ferry back to San Diego, stole a small boat and were caught in the bay by the Coast Guard—paddling with their hands, since they couldn't get the outboard motor started and there were no oars. Back on shore, they were taken to a police station, and just as they were about to be written up, the interrogating officer's pen ran out of ink (which Rogers regarded as a classic piece of Szuminski luck). The officer went to get another pen, leaving them alone for a moment . . . and Szuminski bolted. Rogers followed him out, over a cyclone fence into a parking lot, and hid under a car. The police, hot on their trail with shotguns and dogs, found him easily enough, but there was no sign of Szuminski . . . and Rogers didn't learn until years later in the hospital that Dale had climbed a tree and was watching the whole thing, scared to death. When they took Rogers away in handcuffs, he climbed down and went back to camp.

Nothing much came of it. Rogers refused to give Szuminski away; he was placed in a holding cell for several days and then released. "Yeah, what *could* they do?" Szuminski would always say when the story was told. "Send you to Vietnam?"

There were other famous Szuminski stories, and Dale enjoyed having a legend of sorts—but the wild times weren't what came to mind when *he* thought about advanced infantry training. He would never forget the speech the instructor had made when they were sent home for a last thirty-day leave: "Kiss your girl goodbye and hug her tight, thank your mom for all she's done, because when you get back here, you're going to Vietnam and a lot of you ain't coming back ... and some of you are coming back in pieces, and you'll wish you hadn't come back at all."

When they returned from leave, the "buddies" were assigned to different companies. Szuminski was given his orders, told to dye his underwear olive green ("So some gook don't spot you taking a shit in the boonies and ding your balls off ..."), then hustled onto a Braniff airplane, complete with stewardesses, and the next thing he knew, he was there.

And now, just as abruptly, he was back. Seeing Rogers again in the hospital and hearing all the old stories, he wondered how the other "buddies" had fared. But he didn't think about them nearly so much as he did the guys he'd left on the ground the day of the ambush.

The burgundy Corvette was sparkling in the driveway when he arrived home in late September, on a three-day pass from the hospital. He couldn't drive it, though; his arm was in a cast, and still paralyzed—although he *was* beginning to feel twinges in several fingers. His parents had rounded up all the aunts and uncles, and there was a big sign in the newly finished basement of the pink house on Candy Lane: WELCOME HOME MARINE. Patty was there too.

The aunts and uncles hovered about, keeping their distance. Nobody wanted to ask any questions, which was just as well; but nobody quite knew what to say either ... and least of all, Szuminski. He felt uncomfortable, trapped: this wasn't what he'd imagined coming home would be. Someone said, "Well, the hero is finally back."

"Bet it feels great."

"Yeah, it sure does."

"What about these goddamn protesters?"

"Yeah."

Szuminski hadn't given much thought to the protesters.

Uncle Pete was there—and he knew immediately that Dale had been through a lot—but what could he say? He couldn't tell Dale anything he didn't already know, so they chatted about places they'd been in the service. He asked Dale if he'd been to Hawaii.

"Hawaii?" Szuminski thought for a moment, trying to remember if Hawaii had been one of the places the plane touched down on the way over or back. "N-no, I don't think so. Maybe."

Gradually, the aunts and uncles forgot about him and began to talk with each other about the usual things—work, vacations, sports, children—and he was able to pull Patty aside for a moment. After some small talk, he decided to put it to her. "So," he said casually, "you been seeing other guys, I guess."

Patty blushed and fumbled. She was too smart to deny it entirely. "Well yes, but nothing serious."

"That's okay," Dale said, knowing she was letting him down easy. "Don't worry about it. It don't matter."

And it didn't, he realized, hurt as bad as he'd expected.

Later, after the guests had gone and his parents were asleep, he sat alone in the basement. His father had done a good job fixing the place up. There was a bar, a pool table, a fireplace and a pinball machine (it was called "Hong Kong," and had pictures of various inscrutable Orientals, the women dolled up like Vietnamese whores). He poured himself a drink and flipped through his stack of old 45s, looking for one in particular that he'd played continually in the days just before he left for boot camp. When he found the record, he put it on . . . Buddy Holly sounded as good as ever:

> *Every day, it's a-gettin' closer*
> *Goin' faster than a roller coaster . . .*

In Vietnam, most of the guys had liked the new, harsh music: the Doors, the Rolling Stones, that sort of thing. It was okay, he thought, but it couldn't touch Buddy Holly.

Being at home, it turned out, wasn't all that different from the hospital. He was still alone, late at night, thinking about Vietnam. He'd never felt so close to anyone as the guys in his platoon. He remembered the cold, rainy nights in Khe Sanh when they slept hugging each other for warmth in the foxholes. At the time, he figured it couldn't get much worse . . . and then it *had* gotten worse, when they began doing helicopter assaults. He thought about Sergeant Malloy, whose corpse was like nothing he had ever seen before . . . and he thought about Operation Cochise—not the battle itself, but afterward: the medevac helicopter lifting off, the wounded scattered on the ground . . .

Szuminski realized he probably would never see those guys again—obviously, there hadn't been time to get their addresses that last day—and he wondered how he could start living the next part of his life if the last part wasn't over yet.

2

Throughout the fall and winter of 1968–69, Szuminski commuted on weekends from the Philadelphia Naval Hospital to his parents' home in Erie, sometimes legally, sometimes not. It was very easy to go AWOL from the hospital, even for several days; someone would answer "present" for him at bed checks, no one minded if he missed physical therapy sessions or neglected his assigned job on the ward. And even if they did, even if they caught him, what then? When his parents expressed concern, he would say, "What can they do to me, send me back to Vietnam?"

In a way, the idea of getting away with something was about the only satisfaction he had during that time. Erie had never been a very lively place—even its most loyal residents sometimes called it "dreary Erie, the mistake on the lake"—and it seemed more hum-drum than ever those first few months, before his friends began returning from the service. He would drive to the pop stand on Twelfth Street, his old high school hangout, and see all new faces. Is *this* what I was counting down the days for? he would wonder, driving through the beautiful fall foliage along the lakefront, which he didn't notice or care about. He drove his new burgundy Cor-vette, even though his arm still was in a sling and very weak; it was, no doubt, dangerous driving around like that, but he didn't worry about accidents. Indeed, the very riskiness made driving—like being AWOL—less stultifying than everything else seemed to be.

His most frequent drinking companion at home was Ross Betti, who'd received a physical deferment from the service. Ross had been a close friend before the war, but was something of a stranger now: he hadn't been there; Dale had no idea how Ross might react under fire or whether he'd fall asleep on watch and, therefore, couldn't trust him entirely. He was, however, a familiar face and a better drinking companion than none at all. Even though they now were old enough to drink in Erie, Dale preferred the bars across the state line in New York, places he knew from the old days, where the women were younger—the drinking age was eighteen—and, perhaps, more susceptible to the stories he loved to spin almost as much as he enjoyed the conquests that sometimes followed.

On one such occasion, at a bar called Anthony's, Dale bumped into a girl named Linda Brown, whom he'd met cruising State Street in Erie before the war and had successfully misled into several dates.

"What happened to your arm?" she asked.

"I fell out of a tree."

"Oh," she said, "I thought I read in the paper that you'd been wounded in Vietnam."

"Oh well, that was before . . ."

"And the name under your picture in the paper," Linda said, enjoying his discomfort, "it wasn't Riesen like you told me, it was Szuminski."

"Well," he said, not very convincingly, "my parents are divorced. My mother's name is Riesen and I like to use that, but my real name is Szuminski."

Apparently vanquished, he offered to buy her a drink. She thought he was cute; his lies seemed innocent and rather charming. He told her that he had a brand-new Corvette.

"Sure you do," she laughed.

"Well, it's not here tonight. I came with friends. But I really do have one, and maybe I can take you for a ride in it sometime."

"Listen," she said, "if you pull into my driveway with a Corvette, I'll go out with you. If you don't, I won't."

Several days later, he pulled into her driveway with a Corvette, and they began to date regularly. It was, she later realized, the first of many times she would think she'd backed Dale into a corner only to be outfoxed by him.

───────

No matter how late at night he came in, Szuminski would always go to the door of his parents' bedroom and whisper, "Mom, I'm home."

Anne Szuminski, who could not sleep until he was in, would put on her bathrobe and offer to fix him something, "a cup of coffee, some french fries?"

She always had done it, but in the months after he returned from Vietnam, she found that he was as interested in her company as he was in the food. They would sit at the kitchen table, chatting over coffee, and she would try to convince him to go to sleep. "It's pretty late, Dale," she'd say. "I have to get up in the morning."

"Can you stay up with me a little longer?" he'd ask. "I can't sleep when it's dark."

She didn't ask him why not, but figured it had something to do with Vietnam. There were other things too. Once, he'd asked her to wake him at a certain hour and when she did, touching his shoulder lightly, he leaped out of bed with a wild look in his eyes. For a moment, he didn't know where he was. Then he said, "Oh God, Mom, don't *ever* do that again."

She was disturbed by this, of course, and wanted to ask him what had happened to make him so frightened of the night and so jumpy when asleep, but figured he would tell her in his own good time. He never did, though; in fact, the only time he spoke about the war was one night when he came home drunk and she began to lecture him about alcohol. "Mom," he said, "after you've been in a foxhole with your buddies, and watched them get blown away and there was nothing you could do about it, what else can you do but get drunk?"

You could try to forget about it, she thought, and live your life. As the months passed, she began to notice that he was more passive and distant, less curious and alive than he'd been before the war. He never expressed the vaguest interest in his future. He never seemed to have any plans.

He'd always been full of questions as a child, and interested in everything. When the family drove across country on vacation one year, he'd asked them to stop the car so he could touch the rocks in the mountains and the dirt in the desert; his sister, Caryl, had slept in the back seat. Sometimes his curiosity was downright embarrassing, as when a relative was killed in an auto accident and Dale was taken to the funeral. He squirmed from his mother's arms, trying to get to the coffin to examine the corpse.

He'd been mischievous, as alert children often are, but never really troublesome. His third-grade teacher, Mrs. Morris, would hold him after school for various misdemeanors—pulling the girls' ponytails, making faces, anything to get attention—but she'd always wind up buying him candy bars and driving him home, completely charmed.

When he was thirteen, he took the family car for a spin one day when his parents were visiting friends. They spotted him driving along, just barely squinting over the steering wheel, on their way home and his father wanted to call the police and teach him a lesson. But his mother said, "Walter, he may panic when he sees them and get into an accident." She went after him in their second car and, when she brought him home, his father yelled a bit, but didn't punish him.

Walter Szuminski was more bark than bite, less gulled than his wife by Dale's antics, but unlikely to do much about it. If Anne was impressed by Dale's industry in taking apart his motorcycle, Walter was quick to note that he hadn't the patience to put it back together again. The Szuminskis were more likely to chuckle over Dale's cleverness—the way he was able to get a girlfriend, Patty Hagman, to carry the picnic basket and blanket when they went to the beach at Presque Isle, while he strolled along unencumbered—than be concerned by the way he continually skirted their rules. They were busy people, both holding regular jobs—Anne at Erie Ceramic Arts and Walter at General Electric—and had neither the time nor the energy to ride herd on him. In any case, he never was involved in trouble so serious that he couldn't talk his way out of it . . . at least, not until his senior year of high school.

He and Patty Hagman had been going steady for three years. He had convinced Patty to rewrite the notes his mother sent in when he stayed home sick; thereafter, Patty would cover for him every time he decided to play hooky. The scam was exposed toward the end of Dale's senior year at McDowell High School when vice-principal Frank Emmons, known as "the Hawk" for obvious reasons, rifled his locker and found notes in both handwritings.

The Hawk had been suspicious of Dale for years and now, having cornered his most elusive prey, would settle for nothing less than his expulsion. He sent registered letters to the Szuminskis, explaining the situation, but they were intercepted and signed by Dale. Finally, there was a disciplinary hearing. Dale did his best to squirm out of it. "I know I did wrong," he said, "but it's not like I hurt anybody. It's not like I stole or did something criminal. There must be some better way to settle this. Can't we talk it over? Isn't there some way you could let me graduate?" But there wasn't. He was expelled, pending a vote of the city school board. His parents were invited to appear before the board, and Dale decided to let that letter go through, figuring he had nothing to lose. "I'm sorry," he told his parents, "but I didn't think I was doing that much wrong. There were other guys doing it too, but the Hawk wants to make me an example. The worst part is, I feel I let you down."

His parents went to the board meeting, and listened as the Hawk offered the forged notes as evidence and listed the dates Dale had been absent (and there were many). His superior, the school principal, then said it was a shame because Dale had the brains to have been an A student if he'd only tried. When the prosecution completed its case, Walter Szuminski rose to his son's defense. "If this here was so important, why didn't you contact us *personally*, instead of by mail. It's not fair to kick him out at the end like this."

But the board voted, four to three, to sustain the expulsion. For the first time in his life, Dale had been caught and made to pay. He didn't seem very upset by it, though. "So what?" he told friends. "It's not like I was going to college. It's not like they ruined my plans."

And within a month after his class had graduated, Dale had

taken a high school equivalency test and received a state diploma. "If I'd known about the test earlier," he bragged, "I would've gotten kicked out earlier."

Thinking back on those days, Anne Szuminski sometimes wondered if they hadn't been too lax with him; more often, though, she blamed the changes in Dale on Vietnam. The curiosity, the freshness that had made his mischief so disarming had disappeared with the war, leaving only the appearance of innocence, which had become a cunning pose tinged with cynicism and a deep sadness.

Szuminski wrecked his first Corvette in the early-morning hours of December 14, 1968. He was AWOL from the hospital, closing out a night on the town with Ross Betti and very drunk. They were crossing the railroad viaduct on Powell Avenue, and it was later said that a car swerved in front of them, sending them over the guardrail . . . but all Dale could remember afterward was the rather pleasant sensation of floating very slowly through the air. They found his shoes in the car and his body forty feet away. He had broken his arm again.

He awakened in the veterans hospital in Erie, and immediately realized he was in trouble. Linda was there, and his parents (Ross had escaped with minor cuts and bruises). His father was telling anyone who'd listen that it was the other guy's fault. A corpsman came around, asking for Szuminski's leave papers and all his other identification.

"I don't know where they are," he said. "I'll have my folks check at home. Why don't you stop by tomorrow?"

He checked out the next morning before the corpsman could find him, and made it safely back to the Philadelphia Naval Hospital. Remarkably, there were no consequences: no criminal or military proceedings, no insurance hearings, the fact that he was dead drunk apparently unnoticed. When the insurance company paid off, he bought a second burgundy Corvette.

He wrecked that one several months later. He'd been drinking at a family get-together, but wasn't as drunk as the first time. He was driving along Twelfth Street with a young cousin when he slammed into a car making a right turn in front of him, and went through the windshield. He was taken to a hospital in an ambulance, barely conscious, and had his head sewn up; the cousin was unharmed, but a child in the other car was injured. Linda went to the hospital with Dale's parents and listened with amazement as his father told everyone—once again—that it wasn't his son's fault. The other driver recently had been released from a hospital and apparently was on medication.

Again, there were no serious consequences. The insurance company paid off, and Dale bought a Chevy Malibu.

In late spring of 1969, the doctors at the Naval Hospital determined they'd done all they could to rehabilitate Szuminski's left arm and decided to release him. A military review board was convened to determine just how serious his disability was. The board consisted of three Navy doctors and two Marine captains; Dale's case was presented by a Navy lieutenant. He went before the board to demonstrate the difficulties he had in tying his shoes and buttoning his shirt. He told them his arm was so weak that he couldn't open a car door, and his fingers so numb that sometimes, when smoking, he would burn them without realizing it. The board voted to give him a temporary 100 percent disability—about $400 per month—and he was retired from the service, rather than discharged, which meant that he could have access to military bases around the world, buy food and liquor cheaply at post exchanges and even travel free on military flights. He never took advantage of these benefits, though; he was more than happy to accept the government's money, but scrounging around military bases for bargains seemed too much of a bother.*

Once home, he moved quickly to set his life in order. Perhaps he

---

* Szuminski's case was reviewed a year later. He had regained most of the feeling in his arm by then, but was granted a permanent disability of 40 percent.

was daunted by the prospect of endless nights alone in the basement with Buddy Holly, perhaps he needed new responsibilities from which to escape with the same furtive pleasure as going AWOL or perhaps, as he would later claim, he was simply doing what society expected of him; but within weeks after he left the hospital, he went to work at the Penn Brass and Copper Company and asked Linda Brown to marry him.

He had spent several impatient months before the war running copper tubes through a die-cutting machine at Penn Brass, which was a small factory near his parents' home. With his crippled arm, he was no longer fit for his old job and so was made a janitor. His occupations included pushing a broom, hiding out in the bathroom for hours on end and tossing rocks at the trains speeding along the tracks behind the factory. He appeared for work with about the same regularity as he'd attended high school, doing just enough to avoid dismissal. He watched the other men in the shop, some of them there for thirty years, married, shoulders slumped, bringing their lunches to work. A bell would ring and they'd unwrap their sandwiches; another bell would ring and they'd go home. He couldn't imagine himself doing that sort of thing for the rest of his life.

His courtship with Linda Brown was roughly as exciting as his job. He proposed to her in the car one night. "Why don't we get married?" he said, not very romantically. She was so surprised, and ecstatic, that she hardly noticed the reluctant quality of the proposal. He bought her a ring, and a wedding date was set for August. His parents were pleased; they liked Linda, and thought she'd be a solid, conventional antidote to Dale's subdued mayhem since the war. His mother was especially happy that Linda had decided to convert to Catholicism and have a church wedding. Dale, though, found it all rather ominous: Why did she have to do something so *permanent* as converting? They were only getting married.

Meanwhile, he continued to compile a remarkable automotive history. Late one night, drunk again, he piled the Chevy Malibu into the rear of a car stopped at a light on Twenty-sixth Street. This time, it appeared he wouldn't escape so easily. The police arrived quickly, arrested him for drunk driving, handcuffed him and threw him in jail overnight. The couple in the other car claimed whiplash and filed suit; there would be a court case to determine the damages. Looking for a way out, Szuminski called a man at the Veterans Administration he'd been dealing with over a seniority dispute at Penn Brass (the company was required to add his years in the military when computing vacation time). "Isn't there anything you can do to help me?" he pleaded.

The man from the VA said the situation was serious, but he understood how it was for "you guys just back from the war" and promised to see what he could do.

It turned out that the man from the VA knew a judge, and the case simply disappeared from the court records. Szuminski never learned just how this was accomplished, and he wasn't about to ask . . . but he never heard another word about the drunk-driving arrest or the whiplash claim. He wasn't particularly surprised by this extraordinary turn of events; he knew he'd figure a way out of it, sooner or later. Escapes were, after all, his specialty . . . though each new one seemed pale and trivial compared to his triumph in the Que Son Valley.

The day he retrieved his Malibu from the repair shop, he was crunched by a truck pulling out of a driveway and the car was declared a total loss. The insurance company paid off once more, but decided it was time to assign him to the high-risk category and raise his premium. It seemed a niggling consequence, given the high-stakes game he was playing. He decided to buy another Corvette, a black one this time.

Having spent so many intimate hours with insurance claims adjusters in recent months, Szuminski decided he might like to become one himself. It seemed an appealing career—he could make his own hours, be out in the fresh air, and he already had a certain expertise in the field. He saw an ad in the newspaper for a correspondence course followed by two weeks of intensive training in Miami. Ninety percent of all graduates supposedly were placed with insurance companies; it sounded like a good deal, especially since the correspondence school was Veterans Approved, so the government would pay his way. He took the course, then went to Miami and stared at wrecks for two weeks with about thirty others, almost all of them veterans. When it was over, the school sent his name to several insurance companies. None of them expressed any interest in hiring him, and Szuminski made no effort to follow up on his own. He simply continued working at Penn Brass.

As the months passed, the "buddies" with whom he'd signed up for the Marines were beginning to return home. There was a round of welcome-home parties, many of them held in the Szuminskis' finished basement, which soon became the buddies' unofficial headquarters. They would gather around the bar, swapping war stories (but never anything serious) and bragging about the times they'd had on R & R, their wives and girlfriends exiled to the other side of the room. It seemed to Linda Brown as if Vietnam were a club to which they all belonged, a secret society with its own obscure language and rituals. They were, at once, little boys and old men, still playing soldier and yet endlessly nostalgic.

One particularly depressing ritual was Dave Horn's boot camp record—"The Making of a Marine"—which seemed to be played every time the buddies strayed into maudlin testimonials or lapsed into nervous silence. They would listen reverently to the Marine Corps Hymn and the announcer's first words: "A Marine is a state of mind, a hard mixture of fitness, tradition, competence and devotion to fellow Marine . . . Membership isn't easy . . . first, there's a twelve-week ordeal called boot camp."

Then the dry, Southern, mannered insanity of a drill instructor's voice: "*Quickly, quickly. Move, move, move . . .*"

Sometimes the buddies would form a line and actually begin a close-order drill.

"*Err, euwrr, herr, hawrr . . . err, euwrr, herr, hawrr . . .*"

"No wonder I fucked up so much," someone would invariably observe. "I couldn't understand a word they were saying."

Announcer: "If discipline is tough, it's also necessary . . ."

Drill instructor, being interviewed: "Discipline? Yeah, it pays off. Always has and always will. This outfit's come a long way . . .

from John Paul Jones to the Boxer Rebellion to the storming of a
fort in Mexico called Chapultepec. If it wasn't for our discipline,
these and a lot of other battles would have come out different. Who
knows? But one thing we do know: When any officer or NCO tells
these guys to fix bayonets, they're not gonna ask why. I saw it work
on a hill named Reno in Korea. Nobody asked why when we fixed
bayonets there . . . and we won that battle. And if there's another
battle, it'll be these kids who win it . . ."

Once, during the drill instructor's speech, Linda noticed that
Dale had drifted off and was sitting quietly alone. She went to him
and asked if something was wrong. "No, no," he said. "Just thinking
about some of the guys I knew."

She wanted to comfort him, but couldn't find the words. She
hoped it would be easier—that she'd be less of an outsider—when
they were married and settled down.

The idea that he might *never* really settle down didn't occur to
her until the week before their wedding, when Joey Bruno—probably Dale's closest friend—came home from the war and there was a
three-day welcome-home party. She didn't see Dale at all during that
stretch. When he finally turned up, late for their rehearsal dinner, it
was with a black eye. She later learned that he'd made a lunge for a
topless dancer in a swing at the Hotel Richford, and had been kicked
in the face.

Linda had been raised on the east side of Erie, in Harborcreek; Dale
on the west side, near the airport. When they married, they settled
in a tiny apartment on neutral turf—downtown, in one of the large,
shambling Victorian homes not yet appreciated for their antiquity
and decaying along with everything else in the fading heart of the
city. Linda expected the apartment would be a temporary stop on
the way to a home of their own, somewhere on the suburban fringe,
but they remained there for three years.

During the first few months, Dale made an effort to seem an
attentive husband. He went to work regularly, banked his disability
checks and limited his nights out with the boys to Wednesdays. He

and Linda would watch television in the evenings or she would read to him, mostly popular histories of World War II. For Christmas, he bought her a bird and a turtle. She wanted to believe they were happy, but had the nagging sense that he was just going through the motions, pretending—for the time being—that he was married. They lived in the same three rooms, saw each other constantly, and yet he seemed more distant, less forthcoming than he had been when they were dating.

Out with the guys, this distance was perceived as urbanity of a sort. He was rarely boisterous even when drunk and had a wry, subtle sense of humor much appreciated by his friends. He never wavered in this, although Linda soon realized that the public Szuminski—and he tried to be the public Szuminski at home as well—covered a vast, subterranean anguish that obviously had something to do with Vietnam. He refused to discuss it with her, even when it slipped from his control—as it often did when he was sleeping—and she was able to glimpse his inner turmoil. Several times a week she'd hear him moaning in his sleep, notice his eyelids fluttering wildly, and then he would begin to scream.

The dream was usually the same, although he never told her that: he was out in the paddy, the North Vietnamese were firing at him and not only was his arm paralyzed, but his entire body . . . and then they would be up, out of the tree line, coming after him, and he would be trying desperately to squirm out; they would come and come . . . but never quite reach him, even though he was paralyzed.

Sometimes, too, he would dream that he was in a defensive perimeter, set in for the night, and then awaken with a jolt and start pummeling her, convinced that she had fallen asleep on watch.

One night, he leaped out of bed and crouched between the mattress and the wall, screaming, "They're coming, they're coming! . . . Get down, get down! The gooks are *in the kitchen!*"

"Dale," she said gently, "you're dreaming."

He looked at her then, desolate, ravaged, unable to hide the pain and fear for once. He crumpled back into bed without a word of explanation, and was quickly asleep.

He was often startled when trucks backfired in the street and once, when they were walking to a friend's house, he hit the dirt when an ambulance sped by. "Get down," he yelled, peering at the sky. "Get *down!*"

"What *is* it, Dale?"

"The siren," he said sheepishly. "They had birds as big as airplanes that made noises like that in Vietnam."

She didn't believe him, but rarely had much success in getting him to open up. The closest he came to admitting his troubles was when he was drunk sometimes, and an almost palpable sadness would overtake him. "Are you thinking about the war?" she'd ask.

"You just can't believe how bad it was over there. *You'd* never be able to understand it," he'd say, as if it were her fault that she couldn't.

"Well, try me," she'd say. "At least, let me try to understand."

"You'd never believe it."

She would let it go at that, afraid that if she pressed, he'd become more reticent and elusive than he already was. She was afraid to press him on anything. She would have loved to ask him what he was saving all that money for: he wasn't interested in buying a house, and seemed terrified by the merest suggestion that they might have children. She didn't want to nag him, but sometimes it would just explode out of her: "Don't you have any goals? Don't you want to *be* anything?"

When she did that, she lost. He was quick to pounce on any excuse to put some distance between them; being asked to explain himself was grounds for escape. If she complained when he came home at two in the morning, he wouldn't come home *at all* the next night. Within a year, their marriage had become the hollow formality she'd feared from the start. She was no more than his valet— cooking, cleaning, preparing his wardrobe—or worse, his mother. She remembered times, when they were dating, that Mrs. Szuminski had fixed a fabulous meal and Dale complained, "I don't want *this* tonight," and his mother had dutifully trooped down to the basement freezer and thawed him a steak; he was, Linda realized, beginning to expect that sort of servility from *her* now. He certainly was much more a spoiled child than a husband. He'd suddenly lost all physical interest in her. They would go for weeks on end without making love. When she'd ask him about it, he would say, *"That's all you ever think about."*

She knew he hadn't precipitously turned celibate. She would watch him primping in the evening, preparing for a night out on the town. He had to look perfect, and demanded that she press his jeans and starch his shirts.

"But, Dale, nobody wears starched shirts anymore."

"I don't care. I want to look sharp."

She would watch him prancing from mirror to mirror, making sure his hair was just right, and wonder: Is he doing all this for Joey Bruno?

Gradually, a perverse thought began to take shape in her mind: He *wanted* her to suspect that he was seeing other women; it was something of a game. He was as titillated by the prospect of narrowly evading her grasp as he was by the extramarital dalliances themselves. On some strange level which she could not quite comprehend, he seemed to need the marriage, hollow though it was. He wasn't at all interested in a divorce; in fact, when she broached the subject, he would turn to jelly and try to sweet-talk her out of it (and always succeed). It was the one way she could guarantee a show of affection from him . . . although later, she knew, he would have his revenge.

One day, she found a gold wedding band on the carpet in the living room, near the sofa. Aha! she thought. I've got him dead to rights. She decided to lie in wait, hoping to catch him looking for it. After two days, though, she couldn't wait any longer. "What is this?" she asked.

"Give me that," he said.

"No, I want to know what it is," she said. "I want it out in the open. There was a woman in this house and she took off this wedding band, and she didn't take it off because her finger was swelling. She probably took it off because she felt guilty going to bed with you."

Dale said nothing, but went to her bedroom and grabbed the baby locket that was Linda's most prized piece of jewelry. "If you don't give me that ring," he said, "I'm going to flush this down the toilet."

"Oh no you won't, you wouldn't . . ."

"Oh yes I would," he said, and went to the bathroom and flushed.

She lost all control then. She ran into the bathroom screaming, pounding him (and wondering: Why doesn't he ever scream or fight back?), and finally gave him the ring. "I don't care about *this*," she said.

He opened his hand and gave her back the locket.

Joey Bruno was short, dark, stocky, gravel-voiced and too obviously sensitive to be a very convincing tough guy, although he often tried. He came home from Vietnam in the same haphazard fashion as Szuminski, marrying quickly and unsuccessfully, going to work with his father in the Marx Toy factory, haunting the bars. He and Dale often talked about how much they had in common; they were very close, and yet Joey soon began to notice that Vietnam had changed his friend in ways he considered rather strange: Dale had always been ready for a good time in high school, but "good times" had now become an obsession. He never knew when to quit. Toward the end of an evening, when Joey would begin to slow down, Dale would speed up, drinking harder and faster. Szuminski was never the one to say it was time to go home; he seemed unable to utter the words—if he had to leave (and this was very rare), he would simply disappear without saying goodbye. He never admitted to being tired or too drunk to stand. He never allowed Joey to throw in the towel without pleading with him, in a tone of amazement tinged with disappointment and disgust, "You're not *leaving*? Aw c'mon, let's have one more." He had the remarkable ability to stay out all night, stop home for a quick change of clothes, then stumble into work and somehow make it through the day.

They would commiserate about their marriages, their jobs, the Marines, the war, and yet Joey had the sense that Dale never really unburdened himself. He would complain about Linda doing this or that—but it seemed more a matter of form than serious conviction, perhaps an oblique way of empathizing with Joey's very real and painful marital problems. Joey hated his job and his marriage, but he took them seriously; Dale seemed to take nothing seriously. He refused to consider his life in any but the most immediate terms; his most serious crisis was what to do each night when the bars closed.

Sometimes Dale would abruptly decide to hit the road and they would take off for points unknown, driving the Interstate at one hundred miles per hour, gone for two or three days at a time (usually over weekends, since Joey didn't like to miss work). They led a charmed life, mostly due to Dale's effortless ability to escape potential dangers; Joey later realized that if he'd spent those first wild, angry years with anyone else, he probably would have wound up in jail, in the hospital or dead. He also came to realize that though Dale was his closest friend, someone he'd defend with his life, he never was sure that Dale would do the same for him.

Joey had fairly strong feelings about Vietnam. He had served proudly but, once home, decided that the war was hopeless and should be stopped before more people were killed. He didn't have much sympathy for the campus radicals, but when he learned—in late April 1971—that Vietnam veterans were gathering in Washington to protest the war, he decided that it was time to make a stand. He asked Dale—who admitted to no strong feelings for or against the war—if he wanted to go along, and Dale, of course, agreed. Later, at the Washington Monument, when a newspaper reporter asked why they had come, Dale said, "We're just here for the party."

On the way out of Erie, they stopped at a bar to tank up for the drive and a strange thing happened—one of the few times Joey ever saw Dale really become angry. The bartender was in a surly mood, and when he learned they were going to Washington for the peace march, he began to rant about how he'd done his duty in World War II, and how they were nothing but cowards and traitors. Dale stormed out, then came back a moment later with his two Purple Hearts and slammed them down on the bar. "There, you asshole," he said, red and steaming. "You want to call me a coward now?"

It was the first time Joey had seen Dale actually ready for a fight. He suspected—correctly—that Dale had retrieved his .22-caliber pistol from the car along with the medals, and decided to hustle him out before there was real trouble. The mood passed quickly; within minutes, Dale was acting as if it had never happened.

The protest by Vietnam Veterans Against the War had begun rather inauspiciously several days before Dale and Joey arrived in Washington. A small contingent—fewer than a thousand—pitched tents on the Capitol Mall. They were a bizarre, wild-looking group, with long hair and beards, dressed in combat fatigues. They staged mock search and destroy missions, attempted to lobby their representatives and marched to Arlington cemetery, a parade led by physically ravaged, sometimes violently truncated men in wheelchairs. They were barred from the cemetery, and Richard Nixon's Justice Department brought suit to evict them from the Mall. But the television cameras—the cameras which had, in the past, shown them burning villages, killing women and children, devastating the Vietnamese countryside—now broadcast their anguish and dignity, and what began as a minor protest quickly became a national catharsis. Around the country, other Vietnam veterans saw the protesters and rushed to join their ranks. Politicians and performers—Senators Kennedy, McGovern and Philip Hart; the cast of *Hair*—visited their campsite to express support and entertain the troops. The Justice Department backed off; the veterans were allowed to remain on the Mall.

By Friday, April 23, when Dale and Joey arrived, the crowds had swelled to the tens of thousands. They gathered on the lower West Terrace of the Capitol and, in probably the most moving protest against a war in American history, they tossed their medals on the Capitol steps in a fury of tears and indignation; some shouted the names of friends who'd been killed as they cast away Purple Hearts, Bronze and Silver Stars, combat ribbons and dogtags.

Dale and Joey were in the rear of the crowd, unwilling to give up their medals—Dale wore his Purple Hearts proudly on his utility jacket—and too excited to be mournful. The tone for their weekend had been set hours earlier, when an obviously befuddled veteran walked into the side of their car as they pulled out of a Georgetown gas station. He was carrying a plastic bag filled with amphetamines and said his name was Mike.

"Wow," Joey said. "You shouldn't be on the street like that."

"I'm going to Washington," he said.

"You're *in* Washington." They decided to see him safely to the demonstration. As they drove through Georgetown, Mike hung out the window yelling, "Hey, I'm in Washington, in *Washington* . . ." and wandered off as soon as they reached the Mall.

They spent the night at the Washington Monument. Dale was in a resolutely festive mood, as were many of the other late-arriving veterans. It was a reunion, a homecoming party they were throwing for themselves. All manner of drugs were circulating through the crowd. Campfires were lit, tents pitched, spectral figures danced in the shadows with toy rifles; perimeters were organized, patrols launched and, as the night wore on, there were casualties. Some took off their clothes and wandered about wearing nothing but their utility jackets; others stumbled through the crowd, tears streaming down their cheeks; still others asked, "Where's my unit? I've lost my unit," and continued on before Dale or Joey could respond. Toward morning, it began to seem as if a phantasmal battle had taken place and been lost. Men were moaning and weeping; some were screaming, "Corpsman . . . corpsman!" A team of medics worked the field.

Joey was shaken by the scene, but Dale seemed untroubled. If the sounds and the uniforms and the night brought back memories, he would never admit to them later.

They marched with hundreds of thousands of others the next day, tossed a Frisbee while the speakers droned and then went home.

3

On a lazy Sunday afternoon in late August 1971, several months after he returned from the Vietnam Veterans Against the War protest in Washington, Szuminski called his wife and announced, "Linda, I'm heading down to Columbus with Davey Horn and Joey Bruno." And then, with a chuckle: "We're going to college."

Linda was surprised, to say the least; not so much by the abruptness of the decision—she had come to expect just about anything

from Dale—as by its apparent sobriety. Was it possible that he finally was planning to do something with his life? Probably not, she
figured when the initial shock had passed; he wasn't even sure which
college he was about to attend—just "someplace in Columbus."
Why Columbus? And *which* Columbus, Ohio or Georgia? Why not
someplace closer to home? No doubt, it was either Dave's or Joey's
idea and Dale had decided to tag along at the last moment.

Indeed, the culprit was Dave Horn, who, having recently driven
his Corvette through the window of a hardware store, had decided
it was time to start living less dramatically. His parents had moved
from Erie to Columbus—Ohio—and he was determined to settle
down and go to college there. "You guys should think about it too,"
he had said. "The government pays your tuition, gives you money
for books and living expenses . . ."

"That's not bad," Szuminski had said.

Thinking quickly—perhaps, she later realized, *too* quickly—
Linda decided to encourage him. It was, after all, the first time he'd
shown any sort of initiative since they'd been married. She would
remain in Erie for the time being; she had a very satisfying job with
a trucking company, and wasn't about to give it up until Dale had
proven he was serious. "If you like it down there," she said, "you
can start looking for a place for us to live."

During the next few months, he called her regularly from Columbus and sometimes came to Erie for weekends, but never suggested that she join him. She thought this suspicious—she *knew* it
was suspicious—but didn't ask him about it, fearing that he might,
for once, answer her.

They enrolled, with surprisingly little fuss, at Franklin University in downtown Columbus. The admissions officer managed to
keep a straight face through Dale's recitation of his academic exploits and then accepted him, having been guaranteed by the Veterans Administration that the government would pay his tuition. "It
was a joke," Joey Bruno later recalled. "We never took it very seriously. How could we? I must have missed thirty days of classes the
first semester and I still got excellent grades. Dale probably missed
twenty-five days—and he made *Dean's List!*"

Consequently, Dale found that academic life suited him very well. There even were one or two business courses he actually enjoyed attending. Since he was married, the government gave him $320 per month in living expenses, plus $100 for books he never bought, plus the $400 per month he already was receiving in disability payments. It was as much as he ever made pushing a broom at Penn Brass.

He and Joey found an apartment in a whitewashed cinder-block complex several miles from the campus. Their furnishings were routine (and quickly lost beneath the debris), except for a large poster of Hitler addressing a mass rally, which Joey tacked on the front door to impress the neighbors. Within months, the landlord was threatening them with eviction, a move heartily endorsed by most of the other tenants . . . with the notable exception of their upstairs neighbors, two young women.

Sandy Davis and Pam Smith had moved in, along with an eight-foot boa constrictor and some gerbils, several months after Dale and Joey. "We've got guys downstairs," Pam had said. "A big one and a little one."

"I'll take the little one," Sandy laughed.

Downstairs, similar negotiations were taking place and it wasn't long before a meeting was arranged. Dale and Sandy paired off immediately. After years of what he considered unfair domestic expectations and nagging from Linda, Dale was happy to be with someone who seemed to enjoy parties as much as he did. They could spend hours together in bed, laughing and talking, enjoying each other without making demands or commitments. Later, Dale would remember one such evening when they talked about how some people became angry and obnoxious when they drank. "That's why I love you," Sandy said. "You're a happy drunk."

He guessed that he loved her too. His ardor was piqued by her elusiveness: she loved him, she said, but she wasn't dependent on him as Linda had been. She didn't seem to mind when he went off on jaunts for several days with Dave or Joey (often to Erie, to visit Linda, whom he didn't tell her about). Indeed, Sandy had plenty of friends of her own. She was small, blond, delicate and very attractive;

she'd never lacked for men. She remained distressingly independent even after Dale and Joey were evicted from their apartment and moved in upstairs; she still insisted on going out nights—alone—with her friends. Dale never was sure if these were men or women, which he found unnerving. As much as he talked about not making demands, he found that he wanted a commitment from her, even if he wasn't ready to make one himself. He was, as always, walking a tightrope, juggling Sandy and Linda, courting danger in the hope of eluding it.

The game ended in March when he, Dave and Joey went off to Fort Lauderdale for the spring rites—the first of many such annual excursions—and Linda called, looking for him. Sandy answered the phone. "Who's this?" she asked.

"Dale's wife."

"Dale's *wife*?"

"Dale's *pregnant* wife."

She couldn't possibly be pregnant, Dale explained when he returned from Florida (indeed she wasn't, just very angry). "We're separated," he said. "But she just won't give up." He talked and talked. Sandy seemed to accept his explanations, but increased her distance all the same, spending more and more nights out with friends, to Dale's utter annoyance.

The spring semester was coming to a close. He begged Sandy for a commitment, but she wasn't buying. Finally, one night when she was out he sat down and wrote her a long letter, proclaiming his undying love and his inability to stand the suspense; then he packed his bags and went home to Linda. He would not see Sandy again for ten years.

"The reason why I got mixed up with that girl," he told Linda, "was that you weren't there. I was lonely. I needed someone. I'm really sorry. I promise I'll never do it again. But you have to come down to Columbus with me in the fall. We'll find a really nice apartment. Everything will be different, I promise."

Linda—still in love, still hoping for a real marriage—believed him. She agreed to quit her job and move to Columbus in the fall. They spent a pleasant summer together, as she tried not to notice that Dale was still very much the same. One day, though, she came home from work and found him sitting at the kitchen table, trying to figure out how few courses he could take and still get a full complement of GI Bill benefits from the government.

"Why are you doing that?" she asked, frustrated; her husband was the military equivalent of a welfare chiseler. "Do you want to be a student for the rest of your life?"

"Why not?" he replied. "Why shouldn't I get all that I can out of them?"

"Okay," she said, "so you went over there and fought and it was hard, but isn't it about time you forget about what the government *owes* you, and get on with your life? You don't give a damn about college. You just want to avoid doing anything. The government owes you—but at least you're walking around on two legs. There are guys who came home with *no* legs and *no* arms, and I'll bet a lot of them are in better shape than you are."

"You just don't understand," he said, and stormed out.

And it was true, she later realized: she didn't understand. If she had, she wouldn't have bothered quitting her job and going to Columbus that fall, where they quickly fell into their old patterns. She mothered him, cleaning his clothes, fixing his meals, waiting patiently for him to come in from his nights on the town. And now she began to do his homework. She realized this was downright perverse, but she was so bored and lonely in Columbus—she knew no one there—that she was willing to do it, just to keep busy.

Meanwhile, Dale continued to find his way into and out of jams. He and Joey were caught doing 115 miles per hour in his new Corvette—a blue one—on the Interstate north of Columbus. They were hauled into court, where the judge turned out to be a distinguished alumnus of Franklin University and let them off with a "boys will be boys." In addition, there were the usual phone calls: "Me and Davey are going down to Florida for a few days." Or Erie. Or New York.

Linda had come to expect such things. In a way, they were

preferable—at least, she knew then that Dale was with Dave or Joey. There were other times, though, when she wasn't so sure. There were nights when he just didn't come home. One night he asked her to iron his suit and his best shirt, which—of course—she did. While he was dressing, she peeked into his wallet (it had become something of a habit) and found two tickets to a concert. It was getting to be too much; he was rubbing her nose in it.

Then, returning to the apartment one day, she found Dale and a girl smooching in his car. Linda went after him, screaming; Dale spotted her, and took off. There was an insane high-speed chase through the streets of Columbus that lasted for nearly an hour. No matter how hard he tried, Dale couldn't shake her (he was, secretly, impressed by Linda's driving ability). Finally, he hit a set of railroad tracks, the car spun out of control and slammed into a pole, crumpling a fender.

"That's it! That's it!" Linda was screaming. "I've had it. I'm going home!"

"Wait a minute," Dale said. "Let me just take a look at the car and . . ."

But she was gone. She went home to Erie, moved in with her mother and did something entirely unconscionable (or so it seemed to Dale). She called the VA and told them she had left him, so he was no longer entitled to a married person's stipend under the GI Bill.

But she hadn't really left him.

Later, she would find her behavior during the next several years difficult to explain. She no longer had any illusions about him. She didn't believe a word he said when he called, and he often called. She was determined to go out and find herself a man who would give her a solid home and children. And yet, she found herself reluctant to divorce him.

He was hardly a constant presence in her life—it only seemed that way in retrospect. Days, weeks, occasionally months would go by with no word from him and then he would appear at her door—pitiful, repentant, pledging reform—and she'd let him in, not believing a word of it but unable to resist. Inevitably, he would exact his price for having abased himself before her: there would be some new humiliation, and she'd kick him out again.

For two or three years he bounced between Erie and Columbus, between Linda and Jeannie Hazelton—the woman Linda had found him with in the car—propelled by forces he never quite understood. He only wanted, he'd later say, to do the right thing . . . but he could never be certain what that was. When he was with Jeannie, he felt that he wasn't living up to his responsibilities toward Linda; when he was with Linda, he felt trapped and—after Jeannie became pregnant—guilty too. Beneath all the guilt and remorse was the sense that the fault was not his, but *theirs*: neither woman understood him, they expected too much. They had trapped him, forced him into a Byzantine muddle requiring constant evasive action.

Both Linda and Jeannie later would wonder how he could have dazzled them for so long, so convincingly. Linda, more bemused than bitter in the end, figured it was a combination of her own gullibility and the fact that Dale actually believed what he said when he said it. He seemed to have no sense of past or future; he told her that he had learned in the Marines to live for the moment. He also told her that he expected to be dead, one way or another, by the time he was thirty. He also told her that his credo came from W. C. Fields: "Anything worth having is worth cheating for."

He was, she realized, entirely forthright about his lack of principle. He as much as announced he would continue to deceive her, and yet she remained an easy mark. And there were times when his effrontery was truly extraordinary. Once, he appeared at her mother's doorstep on a weekend night, begging forgiveness once more. Linda brought him down to the basement, where he produced a pill and invited her to share it. She said no. "It's only speed," he said. "C'mon, that way we can stay up and talk all night." She didn't want to do it, she was afraid of pills . . . but there was a part of her that needed to prove to him that she could still be *fun*. "Okay," she said, "I'll do it."

The pill wasn't speed; it was acid.

She liked it, at first. She felt as if she were rising up from the couch;

the music on the stereo was doing strange, warm things; she was giggling. Then, suddenly: "Dale, I don't want to do this anymore."

He laughed. "We got eight hours left."

She panicked, saw faces in the walls, was certain her mother
would find out, began to cry. "Damn it," he said, "every time I drop
acid with a girl, I wind up taking care of her."

Another time, he found her in a bar with a date and went wild.
He dragged her from the table, slammed her up against a pole—it was
the first time she'd ever seen him violent—and had to be restrained
by the bartender and several others. She went home—she was sharing an apartment with another woman at the time—packed a bag
and left. Apparently he broke into the apartment later that night; her
roommate found him asleep on the floor behind the sofa the next
morning. He tracked her down that evening, and apologized.

"Why'd you do it, Dale?" she asked.

He began to cry. "I don't know," he said. "I don't want to lose
you. We have to talk this over."

He talked her into visiting him in Columbus, where she found—
placed rather conspicuously, she thought—a letter from Jeannie Hazelton to Dale, asking him what he intended to do about the fact that
she was pregnant. "What is *this*?" Linda asked, waving the letter in
his face.

"Oh, that," he said. "It's not important. She's lying. She isn't
important to me."

But it was true: Jeannie was not only pregnant but determined to
have the baby. Her parents came to visit him; he promised he would
do the right thing by her. And then he disappeared, back to Erie.

He seemed contrite to the point of desperation this time. He
convinced Linda to live with him in a trailer park—just a trial, she
could leave whenever she wanted. He was willing to do anything
she asked . . . and, for a time, it seemed as if he actually *had* changed.
He rarely went out drinking with his friends and, when he did, he
came home early. They spent most nights together; he seemed,
for the first time in years, to actually enjoy her company. It lasted
for several months; then he was gone again, back to Columbus.

Jeannie supposed that he was feeling guilty about the baby,

whom she'd named Andy. Dale had disappeared when she was four months pregnant, and reappeared when the baby was four months old; in the interim she hadn't heard a word from him. And now he wanted her to go to Erie and live with him. They would be married, he promised. She agreed to give it a try. Back to Erie . . .

They moved into the same trailer park in which he'd lived so happily, so briefly, with Linda. She stayed there with him for two and a half months. He ignored the baby, he ignored her; he didn't have a job—they were living off his disability check—and didn't seem interested in getting one (or in getting married, for that matter). Every time she pressed him, he disappeared. She didn't know anyone in Erie except Linda, and finally decided to call her.

"Linda, I'm all alone. I don't have anyone to talk to," she said. "Dale's gone. He's left. He's been gone for three days."

"I know," Linda said. "He's here."

"Can I talk to him?"

"He won't talk to you. He knows you're on the phone, but he won't come to it. He's in the other room. I told him to go home to you. I don't want him here. I want him out. Why don't you come over here and get him?"

Instead, Jeannie called her father, who came up from Columbus, packed her belongings and her baby and took her home.

In the end, there was no great cataclysm, no affront so outrageous as to force a complete break: Linda continued to see Dale, but his influence over her waned; she no longer left herself open to serious abuse. Eventually, she found a man who was able to give her the things she'd said she'd always wanted and decided to marry him. Dale meekly consented to the divorce.

He never returned to college in Columbus, but dawdled a few semesters at Edinboro State College, just south of Erie, until his GI benefits were finally exhausted. He slipped into a hibernation of sorts then, living in a small apartment above a favored bar in downtown Erie, getting by on his disability payments, occasionally painting a house with his cousins for extra cash. He spent a good deal of time in the public library just a few blocks from his apartment. He would read the newspaper each day, then find a book about outlaws—bandits like Billy the Kid or Jesse James, Mafiosi (he liked *The Godfather*), Nazis.

His favorite book, though, was Vincent Bugliosi's account of the Manson killings, *Helter Skelter*. He read it at least a dozen times; years later, a battered, dog-eared paperback copy would still occupy a position of honor in his bathroom. He was fascinated by the magic Charlie Manson had worked, the hold he'd had over all those women. He wanted to know more; he read everything he could find about the case and when there was nothing left to read, returned again and again to *Helter Skelter*. He found that the most memorable passage in the book was Susan Atkins' account of killing Sharon Tate: "[I said] Look, bitch, I don't care about you. I don't care if you're going to have a baby. You had better be ready. You're going to die and I don't feel anything about it." Afterward, Atkins said, "I felt so elated; tired, but at peace with myself."

Szuminski understood that. He identified with it. He had often felt the same way in Vietnam after a battle; he'd experienced the same numb elation when he eluded the North Vietnamese at Operation Cochise. And also earlier, at Con Thien, when he'd shot an attacking NVA four times—his only confirmed kill of the war. It wasn't so much the killing that excited him as not being killed; he was Houdini, not Susan Atkins. And now, having spent a half dozen years sidestepping the paltry challenges of civilian life, he found that he had succeeded all too well and had nothing left from which to escape.

4

Years later—it must have been 1979 or 1980—Szuminski called his ex-wife, Linda Brown, and asked if she would have a cup of coffee with him. Linda assumed he was hoping to finagle his way into her heart once more, but agreed to meet him at a diner near her home. She felt secure enough in her new life, in her marriage and her children, to resist any advances. She was curious, too, about how Dale had fared.

It was clear that he hadn't fared very well. They chatted pleasantly enough about old times, but there was a wistful quality to Dale's conversation and he looked awful. When they'd first met in high school, he had seemed so fresh and innocent—blond, crew-cut, All-American, shy and sensitive, especially when he wore his black-rimmed glasses. Now his hair was draped in early-Beatles style, bowl-cut just above his ears and faded to a light brown; his skin was leathery and dull; he wore rose-tinted aviator glasses which reinforced his usual air of fogginess and distance. The total effect was sad and somewhat anachronistic, that of a refugee from the 1960s, a man attempting to seem younger than he was. He had, she remembered, always maintained that he'd be dead by the time he was thirty and now, having muddled on several years past that date, gave the impression of being disappointed by his longevity. He made no advances. "I think he saw," she would recall, "that I didn't want or need him back in my life. I felt sorry for him."

Many of his friends had similar feelings, but their sorrow was tempered by amused resignation. He was considered an amiable drunk, a benign specter haunting the local taverns; no one would have been surprised if he were found one night splattered against a tree in his Pontiac Firebird, although few expected he would exit so dramatically—his ability to avoid danger was, by then, legend. It was said the local police protected him (his sister, Caryl, had married a patrolman). When they found him weaving along a highway late at night, the story went, the police would simply pull him to the side of the road and say, "C'mon, Dale, we'll give you a lift home."

Most of his old drinking buddies were married now, but their wives tolerated his occasional attempts to pry the boys loose for a night on the town. It was difficult to resent Dale; he appeared so harmless, although he was a constant threat to the middle-class domesticity they struggled to maintain. Some of the wives gave him an affectionate nickname: When his Firebird rumbled into the driveway (it seemed always without a muffler), they would say, "Here comes *Rent-A-Party.*"

Indeed, he spent a good deal of his time organizing social events. There was the annual three-day camping trip in late spring, and

Marine Corps Birthday in the fall. There was a flag football team
at the Plymouth Tavern, which he co-captained. He still booked a
room at the Sea Coast Motel in Fort Lauderdale each year for spring
break, even though he was now a decade or so older than most of
the revelers; inevitably, he would cast about for running mates and
usually succeeded in luring away some friend whose marriage was
going badly. Somehow he managed never to go to Florida—or out
on the town—alone. When marriages faltered or disintegrated, he
was always available to celebrate his friends' emancipation.

No one was sure how he survived financially. He still received
government disability checks, and occasionally painted houses with
his cousins. Sometimes he bought and sold a little marijuana—never
more than a few ounces, just enough to cover the cost of his own
supply. Close friends, like Joey Bruno, were surprised by how astute
he was when it came to managing his money. "He played the stock
market," Joey would recall. "His uncle Pete gave him tips, and I think
he did pretty well. But you could never get him to talk about it."

He slept most days; when he roused himself in mid-afternoon,
he'd either walk over to the public library or stay home listening
to records. His taste in music had changed, but still was ten years
behind the times. He had moved from Buddy Holly to the Beatles,
especially side two of the *Abbey Road* album, phrases of which ran
through his mind continually:

Oh, that lonely feeling . . .
Nowhere to go.

And:

Soon we'll be away from here.
Step on the gear and wipe that tear away.
One sweet dream . . . came true . . . today . . .

Gradually, the latter verse came to dominate his thoughts. He decided there wasn't much of a future for him in Erie. The town was
played out; it had never been much of a place for sweet dreams in

any case. If there was such a thing as "the good life," it happened elsewhere. Erie was the row of factories bulked along Eighth Street and the drudgery they promised; it was long winters, and the same forlorn women at the same old bars. It was clear to Szuminski that if he was to start his life over—or, perhaps, finally *begin* it as an adult—it would have to be in some other place; Florida maybe. There seemed an abundant supply of beautiful, unattached women down there . . . and plenty of outdoor jobs, less noisy and dirty and confining than factory work. And then, too, his parents had retired near Fort Lauderdale; he'd have a place to stay until he could get himself established.

So, in the fall of 1978, he loaded all his possessions into the Firebird and left for Florida. His route was circuitous. He figured that as long as he was heading south, he might as well stop in Columbus and visit Dave Horn, yet another old friend who had settled into marriage and was dutifully climbing the executive ladder at a local carpet company. Szuminski couldn't imagine good old Davey Horn wearing a tie to work every day. He figured that somewhere, deep down, Horn would be longing to chuck it all and head south with him, as they had so often in college.

For his part, Dave Horn was amazed—as always—by Dale's unwillingness to acknowledge that he no longer was "good old" Davey Horn. Szuminski would blow into town once or twice a year, expecting him to abandon everything and go off on a bender somewhere. It was sad; they no longer had much in common. Dale was a reminder of that awkward, angry time when they'd just come home from the war—a time Dave wasn't at all nostalgic for; in a way, those years in Erie seemed almost as dangerous as the war itself and Horn was relieved to have survived them in one piece. He still felt a good deal of loyalty and affection for his old friend, and didn't have the heart to confront him with the changed realities of their lives. He would welcome Szuminski each time he materialized in Columbus, go out for a few beers with him, always dreading the inevitable moment when it would be time to go home and Dale would say, "Awww, c'mon, you ain't quitting on me *now*, are you? The night's still young."

By chance, when Szuminski arrived on his way to Florida, Dave and his wife were entertaining an old friend: Pam Smith, who had lived with Sandy Davis in the apartment above Dale and Joey when they'd first arrived in Columbus. Szuminski had seen Pam occasionally over the years, and always asked her how his old girlfriend was doing.

"She's getting divorced," Pam said, when Dale asked. "Why don't you give her a call?"

Sandy Davis would later claim that she'd never quite gotten over Dale. Every time she passed the billboard for Suzuki motorcycles on her way to work, she thought of him. Every time she saw a Corvette on the street, she'd try to get a look at the driver. She never attempted to get in touch with him; she figured that if he wanted to find her, he would.

Actually, even if he *had* tried to pursue her during the eight years since they'd parted, he probably would have found her otherwise occupied. She had been married three times, and lost a baby girl—and nearly her own life—in childbirth; she had suffered a hysterectomy and subsequent bouts of depression for which she'd been hospitalized. Her most recent marriage had foundered when her husband realized that he was still in love with his first wife. Sandy let him go back to her—it was an amicable divorce—but another in the series of false starts and disasters which seemed to plague her. She'd never recovered completely from the death of her daughter; her health was precarious at best, and worse now for the recent trauma. She'd been having severe chest pains. A doctor had diagnosed the problem as a pulmonary embolism—a blood clot in her lungs—and prescribed blood-thinning drugs to dissolve the obstruction, but the pains continued.

Somehow, these indispositions served only to intensify her delicate beauty, but her fragility masked a surprising toughness. She might be frustrated by a man, but never trampled, as Szuminski had found eight years earlier. She was quite intelligent, a shrewd businesswoman chronically underemployed in a series of technical jobs she mastered easily; she had been a pharmacist, a dental assistant and a bookkeeper. Later, she would become an accountant and stockbroker.

In many ways, she was a perfect match for Szuminski: both were deceptively formidable, neither seemed capable of making a sustained effort at anything in life, both were effectively paralyzed by forces they didn't understand—and desperate, now, for the stability that always had eluded them.

He called and invited her to a small birthday party Dave Horn was having for him. "I'm thirty-two," he said. "Getting pretty old."

When he picked her up that night, he seemed unusually shy. He didn't kiss her hello, or even shake her hand. She said, "Dale, are you afraid to touch me?"

He held her hand.

"I want to give you a birthday kiss," she said, and did.

Later, in bed, he said that he loved her and wanted her to go with him to Florida. "I want to settle down," he said. "I'm tired of living like this. I want to get married. Will you come with me?"

"Yes," she said immediately. "But let's not get married just yet. I don't want to make another mistake. There's no harm in just living together for a while."

It took Sandy two weeks to close out her life in Columbus, and she was happy for the breathing space. Despite her quick acceptance, she wanted to be certain that Dale was serious. The next few weeks erased all doubts, though. They enjoyed each other's company as much as ever, spending most nights out drinking—Joey Bruno, then between marriages, had inexplicably arrived in town and joined the party. More important to Sandy was the fact that Dale would talk seriously about the future when they were alone. He actually seemed to have plans and goals. He was thinking about applying for a government job, perhaps in the post office; as a disabled veteran he'd have a ten-point bonus on the civil service exam. They would live with his folks in Florida, and save for a down payment on a house. He was happier than he'd been in years. He figured the Beatles had been prescient: all he'd had to do was leave Erie and his "one sweet dream" came true.

They left for Florida in late October 1978. Both quickly found jobs: Dale as a security guard, Sandy as a dental assistant. They lived modestly, rarely going out. Each week, Sandy would give Dale her paycheck and he'd give her a five-dollar allowance. She didn't mind the austerity; they were saving for the future. Life with Dale's parents was cramped, and a bit strained, but tolerable as long as she knew it was bringing them closer to their goal.

The Szuminskis lived in a barracks-like condominium development of semiattached tan ranch houses, well inland from the ocean. The houses were built close to each other, separated only by slivers of Bermuda grass so green that they seemed polished rather than watered by the silent, ever-present maintenance crew. Inside, the house was cool and dark—it gave the impression of being hermetically sealed—and stiffly furnished with remnants from the Szuminskis' home in Erie, which seemed far too formal for the egregiously casual retirement village atmosphere of enforced leisure. Dale and Sandy had their own bedroom, but not much more. The situation was made more difficult for Sandy because she was, quite clearly, not a favorite of Dale's parents, who had waged a major campaign in recent years to reunite Dale with Jeannie Hazelton. She was, after all, the mother of his child, Andy, their grandson. The Szuminskis often took Andy on vacations and never failed to stop in Columbus to visit the boy when they passed through on their way to Erie, which was a good deal more than could be said for Dale, whose interest was limited to grudging, sporadic Christmas and birthday presents. They could tolerate the confusion and disarray in Dale's life—the war had caused that, they believed—but his failure to be a father was unpardonable. And Sandy was simply the latest evidence that he had no intention of doing his duty.

Still, they all managed to survive the winter in close quarters without any major explosions.

The trouble began in late spring, when Joey Bruno and his new fiancée, Dana Earl, arrived in town for a vacation and Dale joined them for an evening out that soon dissolved into a classic Szuminski bender. Sandy tried to keep up. She'd always enjoyed going out with Dale, and knew her presence was important to him (she didn't want to be considered a stick-in-the-mud, like all the other women in his life), but soon found herself falling behind, exhausted, ill and more than a little frightened. They stayed out all night. She called in sick at work the next day, something she'd never done before. She said she'd been in a car wreck, which was technically true (it was a minor collision); Dale used the same excuse for his job and the party continued. After another night on the town, he advised Sandy to call in sick again, but she refused. "I can't do it," she said. "They might fire me." He scoffed at this and seemed generally disappointed with her, then took off for a third night out with Joey and Dana. He called her at four in the morning, incoherent. She was furious—it was their first real argument since arriving in Florida—and more frightened than ever. There was a frenzied, obsessive quality to his carousing that she'd never noticed before and couldn't understand; he was, clearly, out of control.

Later, he was unapproachable on the subject. She sensed that a wedge had been driven between them; he was cool toward her, distant. He began to complain about Florida. The houses were too expensive, they'd never be able to afford one. There was too much competition—everyone was coming down from the North and it was impossible to find a decent job (he'd taken the post office exam, but hadn't yet received the results). Finally, he admitted it wasn't so much *Florida* as that he wanted to go home to Erie and be with his friends. She balked at this. "If you really love me, you'll go wherever I ask you," he said, "and I want to be with my friends in Erie."

She went, reluctantly. They left for Erie in early June 1979.

Sandy's health hadn't improved in Florida. Her chest pains continued. The blood-thinning drugs caused her to bruise easily; she was always black and blue. Once, at a party, she'd banged her ankle and it had ballooned alarmingly; Dale had been forced to carry her to the car. She then visited a doctor, who added pain-killers to her regimen of blood-thinners. The chest pains continued, nonetheless.

Soon after they arrived in Erie, she began to feel much worse. Her heart seemed to be pounding in her chest; she often became dizzy when she climbed the three flights to the apartment they'd sublet, sometimes she grew faint when she simply stood up. Then, on a Monday night two weeks after they'd arrived in town, after

another weekend of nonstop welcome-home celebrations, she began
to vomit blood. Her stomach felt as if it were going to explode. "I'm
taking you to the hospital," Dale said, scooping her up and carrying
her down the three flights.

She was rushed to intensive care. The doctors said she was hem-
orrhaging. They gave her blood transfusions and took her off all
the pills she'd been taking; it was the combination of pain-killers
and blood-thinners, they said, that had caused the bleeding. They
weren't sure why she'd been having chest pains, but it certainly
wasn't a pulmonary embolism; indeed, they couldn't find anything
wrong with her. It was suggested that she go to the Cleveland Clinic
for more elaborate tests if the pains continued.

Dale was very solicitous throughout, spending hours on end at
her bedside, holding her hand. He was furious with the doctors in
Columbus and Florida who had bungled the diagnosis, and wanted
to sue. Sandy was touched by his concern; it was clear, for the first
time since their argument in Florida, that he still loved her.

The chest pains returned soon after she was released from the
hospital; she felt, at times, as if she could hardly breathe. In late June,
Dale drove her to the Cleveland Clinic, where a battery of tests were
run and, once again, the results were negative. A doctor suggested
that perhaps *anxiety* was her problem.

Sandy had mixed feelings about the news. It was, she realized,
probably true—the mere knowledge that her chest pains were caused
by anxiety seemed to lessen their intensity, which was a relief. At the
same time, though, she was embarrassed. She had put Dale through
an ordeal, and feared she'd lost some credibility with him. He wasn't
the sort to acknowledge emotional problems; they were a sign of
weakness. She didn't want him to think her weak—she was afraid
he would stop loving her (or, at the very least, consider her a less
plausible drinking buddy). She wanted reassurance.

Dale *was* a bit puzzled by all that had happened. In some ways,
Sandy was the most competent—and confident—woman he'd ever
known. Despite her physical woes, she had found a very impressive
job, as billing supervisor for the Buffalo Molded Plastics Company;
meanwhile, he continued to muddle along, waiting for the results of

the post office test, which he had taken again in Erie. In traditional economic terms, she was far more successful than he . . . but at home she seemed very unsure of herself. She pestered him with questions: "Do you think I'm pretty?" and "Do you still love me?" and "Why don't we get married?" He had been impressed by her initial reluctance to be married—it was another indication that she was different from the others. Now she said she wanted to be married so they could establish themselves as a stable couple and adopt children; she also claimed she wanted to please his parents, who thought they were living in sin. Szuminski didn't *mind* getting married now, but wondered about the reasons for her change of heart.

Their wedding—performed on September 12, 1979, by a justice of the peace in Erie—seemed to Sandy more perfunctory than joyous; she had an uneasy sense that Dale had, somehow, gained the upper hand in their emotional life. But her misgivings vanished in the excitement of the next few weeks: Dale finally landed his post office job and, within days, they bought a nice suburban ranch-style house just west of the city. It was brown-shingled with yellow trim, bright and airy and modern—and easily affordable with their two salaries.

Szuminski entered the 1980s a happy man. He had a steady job, a wife, a mortgage and a lawn to be mowed. He was in danger, for the first time in his life, of becoming a solid citizen and didn't mind it a bit. He no longer felt trapped, as he had with Linda; he no longer felt the urge to go off drinking by himself or hit the road—he and Sandy went out drinking together, with other couples: Joey and Dana, George and Teka Choklas. Sometimes at night, when they were alone together, he would dream with Sandy about going to Europe, seeing the world, buying another Corvette. But those were dreams, nothing he really needed. "I've *got* everything I need," he told himself, "and I'm gonna make it work."

He liked his job. He liked being out in the fresh air, on his own, delivering the mail (and didn't mind the holidays, paid vacations, health and pension plans that came with government work). In the

beginning, he worked as a substitute mailman and would get to
see parts of the city he'd never noticed before. He found that he
liked being in uniform again too; Sandy tailored his shirts so that he
would look trim and sharp. The uniform brought back memories of
the Marines, not all of them unpleasant, although sometimes when
he was walking his route he would imagine he was back on patrol.
This was especially true when the weather was bad, when it was
raining hard and he'd be slogging along in his poncho, with no shelter from the storm—he'd remember the incessant rains and cold at
Khe Sanh. Sometimes, on particularly hot, muggy days in midsummer with the sun white in the sky and the sweat trickling down his
back, he would—for an instant, a millisecond—be back in the Que
Son Valley, pinned down. He'd shake his head to clear it, feel a shiver
down his spine and the goose bumps rising.

The summers weren't easy, he found. For some reason, the tensions with Sandy seemed to increase when the weather grew warm.
Part of it, no doubt, was that his parents would come up from
Florida for July and August, camping out in the spare bedroom,
his mother taking charge of the cooking and gardening, his father
grumpily doing the chores and carpentry Dale never found time to
do. Part of it, too, was that the summer was a more *social* time of
year—and Sandy had grown increasingly reluctant to socialize, especially on weeknights.

"You used to like to go out drinking," he would complain.

"I did it to please you," she'd say.

She still did it to please him, from time to time. One weeknight
in early August 1980, they were out drinking with Joey and Dana,
who were about to be married. Sandy was exhausted after a hard
day at work; Dale apparently was tired too, because he passed out.
Sandy called a cab to take them home, then went back to rouse him.
She tapped him on the arm, he opened his eyes . . . and punched her
in the mouth. It was the first time he'd ever hit her; she was shocked,
and then furious—the whole bar had seen it. She smashed him over
the head with a drink glass. Joey drove them home.

The next day, she asked Dale, "Why did you hit me?"

"I was dreaming about Vietnam, and you startled me."

She wasn't sure about this. He had looked her directly in the eye before throwing the punch. "What were you dreaming?" she asked.

"I don't know," he said. "Anyway, you wouldn't understand."

"I won't unless you tell me," she said. "I've never been in a war, but I've lost people I loved. I lost my daughter."

They had been through this several times before. Sandy had found he was unlikely to be candid when questioned directly about Vietnam; he would talk about it at times, but only on his terms, when *he* chose to. He was more likely to deflect her probing with a series of homilies he had learned in the Marines: "They taught you to forget your father, your mother, your girlfriend back home. In the bush, nobody loves you but your buddy," he would say. "Don't worry about tomorrow. You might not be alive tomorrow, so enjoy it while you can."

He told Sandy that *she* should be more like that. "You worry too much," he said. She spent so much time worrying about getting to work the next day that she never had fun when they were out. "You might as well enjoy it," he'd say. "You don't know what's going to happen tomorrow. You might get killed in a car wreck."

Sandy wanted to be more like that; she wanted to please him. But she also was angry with the Marines: "They trained him to forget all about his home life," she would later say. "But they never had a boot camp when he came home to drum all that nonsense *out* of his head."

Vietnam and the Marines were very much on her mind several days later when Joey and Dana were married. All the old "buddies" were gathered together, and seemed—as they often did on such occasions—to revert to Camp Pendleton. Joey, of course, would not be satisfied by a mere reception: close friends were invited to continue the party at Cedar Point in Ohio, where the Brunos would be honeymooning. Dale, somewhat chastened by the scene in the tavern, had told Sandy he would skip the Ohio part; he had work the next day. But driving home after the reception—they'd both had quite a lot to drink—he decided to go on to Ohio after all.

"You can't *do* that," she pleaded. "Please, Dale, don't do that. If you don't go to work tomorrow and call in sick, they're going to *fire* you . . . and don't expect me to call in for you. I don't want any part of this."

She was growing angrier by the minute, screaming at him in the car, crying. She had no control over him, no way to reason with him. He wouldn't even discuss it. He was going.

When they arrived home, she grabbed the keys from the ignition and jumped out of the car. "Please, Dale," she said. "Please, don't go . . ."

He lunged at her, and had her by the throat. She dropped the keys, and he was gone.

Later, Szuminski would claim that he didn't remember choking her, but he knew that they had fought, and the damage might be irreparable. He still loved her, and wanted to stay married; he still hoped to live a normal life. But he couldn't understand why her attitude toward socializing had changed so completely—it was the same way she had been about marriage. He figured she was insecure, jealous of the attention he gave his friends. He knew he had acted badly, but she had pushed him to the brink. She had to give him some leeway, if the marriage was to work at all.

When Dale returned home after three days, Sandy took him back in. He seemed repentant. The marriage settled into a sullen truce. They continued to see friends on weekends, but Sandy refused to go out during the week. She was attending night school in accounting, and didn't have the time to carouse. Szuminski made a real effort to domesticate himself, but couldn't manage more than two or three nights straight around the house. She allowed him his nights out, grudgingly—she had come to the conclusion that his drinking was an illness. It wasn't so much the frequency as the way he drank, the need to keep on drinking once he started, to drink harder and faster as the evening wore on. There were times when he would stay out all night, stopping home at six in the morning to change into his post office uniform. "Where *were* you?" she'd ask.

"None of your business. Get off my back."

Joey Bruno, then tending bar at a place called the Frontier Lounge, began to notice a change in Dale. He wasn't holding his liquor. He would have two or three beers and become sick; instead of going home then, he'd sit back down at the bar and keep on drinking. One night he vomited all over the jukebox. Joey knew something was wrong, but figured it would be bad form to mention it—and, anyway, if Dale was still getting to work every day, paying his bills and meeting his obligations, it couldn't be *that* serious.

His supervisor at the post office had noticed the change too. Dale was careful not to violate his quota of sick days, but he'd often come to work groggy, reeking of alcohol. The supervisor pulled him aside several times and said, "Look, this isn't official, but you better straighten up, or you might be in some trouble."

The sullen peace with Sandy continued. There was a grim, lifeless quality to their house—it seemed furnished, rather than lived in, a motel suite. Except for Dale's Purple Hearts, framed and hung on the bedroom wall, there weren't many family artifacts. They spent most of their time in the kitchen and the den, the latter shag-carpeted, plywood-paneled, with an imposing color television set in a dark, Mediterranean-style cabinet. Some of Dale's old college books and Sandy's accounting texts relieved the emptiness of the built-in bookcases. The couches, chairs, tables and lamps were recent purchases and were comfortable, but not distinctive. A sliding glass door opened onto a cement patio that seemed to have been forgotten as soon as it was poured. The back lawn was bare as well, joyless and unused.

They spent a quiet winter there, and then it was summer again, 1981. Dale's parents returned from Florida. Sandy sensed that the truce was fraying, that another explosion was imminent. She vowed it would be the last.

It happened one night in July, when a cousin of Dale's from Atlanta stopped by with his wife and a case of beer. By eleven the beer was gone and the cousins departed. "Hey, it's still early," Dale said hopefully. "Why don't we go down to the Frontier, have a couple of beers, shoot a game of pool and be back by midnight?"

"I've got work tomorrow," Sandy said, "and you're drunk already."

"The hell with you," he said. "I'm going."

Perhaps it was his tone of voice, perhaps she had simply reached her limit, but Sandy lost control then; she chased after him, screaming and cursing, trying to snatch the car keys again. Dale's parents were astonished by the vehemence of her attack. They heard more screaming and what sounded like a struggle in the garage, and raced out there. Dale and Sandy were grappling awkwardly, pushing a folded lawn chair at each other—it was difficult to tell who was pushing and who was fending off—and then Sandy was punching and scratching him. "Dale, stop!" his mother screamed as he pushed Sandy away and she fell down, then started back at him, and he tried to kick her away; she grabbed hold of his leg. "Sandy, leave him alone! Let him go!" The neighbors were out now, watching. Dale kicked at her, trying to shake her off. "Why don't you just *kill* me?" she screamed. Finally, he broke free and went away.

There was a good deal of confusion and melodrama in the next few days. Sandy was a mess; she couldn't stop crying. She went to the family doctor, who treated her for bruised ribs and diagnosed her hysteria as "emotional exhaustion." She spent three days in the hospital, recovering, and fuming. She wanted to teach Dale a lesson; as soon as she got out, she hired a lawyer, went to court and won an injunction barring him from the house. It was a drastic step, made more awkward by the fact that his parents were still living there and siding with Dale. "He may be violent," Walter Szuminski said, "but he's not *that* violent."

Mrs. Szuminski's strategy was more soothing, but no less partial: "Sandy dear, I know you're upset," she said. "But I don't think you're going about this the right way. You're taking everything from him."

"I'm not *taking* anything," Sandy said. She wasn't sure what she *wanted* yet, except time to think. Dale received notice of the court injunction at work, but refused to acknowledge it. He lurked around outside the house; she called the police, and he ran away. He phoned her then, begging forgiveness. "What do I have to do to get us back together?" he asked. "I'll do anything."

She wasn't sure, she said. He called again and again. She was surprised by his persistence—the marriage hadn't seemed to mean that much to him when they were living together—and by his desperation. The pendulum was swinging; for the first time since their wedding, she was beginning to regain emotional control. It was up to him, now, to meet *her* expectations. From time to time she had met with a counselor at the Family Crisis Unit in Erie and now she decided not to allow Dale back unless he agreed to visit the counselor with her.

Szuminski always had considered therapy rather ridiculous. He believed—again, it was something he had learned in the Marines—that if you couldn't solve your own problems, there wasn't much chance someone else would be able to solve them for you. Still, the cataclysm had made him aware how badly he wanted the marriage to work. Sandy was never so attractive to him as when she was bold and, though he resented her kicking him out of the house, the challenge of winning her back was the most interesting test of his wiliness in years.

The family crisis counselor turned out not to be the man Sandy had seen in the past, but a young black who questioned Dale closely about his drinking.

"I've been doing it for twenty years and it's never been a problem," he said. "I don't think it's a problem now."

"Do you drink every night?"

"No. I don't *need* to drink, I just enjoy it."

"Do you have more than three beers frequently—once a week, twice a week?"

"Yes, but . . . if that's being an alcoholic, everyone I know is an alcoholic."

The counselor then said that he didn't think Dale and Sandy should get back together. "Not until you face your problem," he said to Dale, "and decide to do something about it."

"I can stop drinking anytime I want."

Sandy was crying now. It was clear the message wasn't getting through to Dale. She wanted to get back together with him, but agreed with the counselor: it would be hopeless until Dale admitted he had a problem, and *that* hardly seemed likely. She couldn't stop crying, and the counselor recommended that she go back to the hospital. Dale drove her home to pack some things; she seemed calmer to him, and he said, "Why don't we just forget about the hospital? Why don't we just go to bed, I'll go to work in the morning and everything will be all right."

She became hysterical again. He simply didn't understand. There was no hope. He took her to the hospital.

When she was released three days later, there were more anguished phone calls. Again, Dale asked, "What do I have to do to get us back together again?"

"You have to do something about your problem," she said.

"I'll stop drinking."

But she wanted more than that. She had learned about a treatment program for alcoholics and drug abusers at St. Vincent's Hospital—two weeks of isolation and therapy. "You'll be a new man," she assured him.

"I don't know," he said. It seemed a major escalation. He didn't mind humiliating himself before her, but this would be public humiliation; all his friends would know. "Well, if that's what it'll take," he said to her, "I'll do it."

He entered the program in early August 1981. The rules were very strict: he wasn't allowed to talk with Sandy or anyone else in the outside world; he wasn't allowed to read newspapers or magazines, or watch television. Brochures provided by Alcoholics Anonymous were the only acceptable reading material. There wasn't much individual therapy (for which he was thankful), but three times a day he would be ushered into AA meetings, all of which sounded the same to him. A businessman would confess that he'd lost his job, his wife and all his money because of alcohol, but now—because of AA—he hadn't taken a drink in four years and was happy as a clam. The only AA lecture Szuminski found at all interesting was from a young woman who described how alcoholism had led her to be gang-raped and forced to perform sodomy. He decided that most of the speakers had been leading more exciting lives before they took the cure.

There were about fifteen others in the program; he had little in common with any of them. There was a ten-year-old boy who'd been caught siphoning the gasoline from his father's car and drinking

it, and a nun who was hooked on downers, and the predictable array
of old winos—male and female—who'd been ordered into the program by the courts. He thought: I'm going to have to keep my wits
about me, or this place is going to drive me crazy.

He wrote long, remorseful, passionate letters to Sandy. He told
her how sorry he was. He said that he knew now that he was an
alcoholic, and that he'd been to blame for all their troubles. He admitted he had lied and cheated to get his way. He hoped that would
do the trick.

After two weeks, he was given a supply of Antabuse pills, which
would cause him to be violently ill if he took a drink, and set loose
upon the world. Sandy, quite moved by his letters, allowed him to
come home, with certain stipulations. If he fell off the wagon, it was
all over. There would be no more contact with his old drinking buddies, not even phone calls. She was in control now, and set about
establishing a new, wholesome social life for them. They went to
the movies, and had a picnic at Presque Isle. She took him to play
Bingo. He thought: Am I going to spend the rest of my life like this,
listening to some clown say "B-7, N-23 . . ."?

Sandy noticed he wasn't very happy. She was at him continually
about it: "There's something wrong. You want to go out for a drink,
don't you?"

"I don't see how one lousy beer would hurt," he said. "A glass
of wine with dinner . . ."

And then she'd get angry, tell him he hadn't changed at all, that
he was still a liar and a cheater. And she soon found some hard evidence for the latter: She had taken to counting his Antabuse pills
secretly and, within weeks, discovered that he was skipping days.

"I don't need them," he said. "I'm not drinking."

She threw a fit. She said that if he didn't take the pills every day,
it was all over. After that, he began to flush them down the toilet.

One day, he bumped into Joey Bruno in the grocery store.
"Jesus Christ, Dale, where you been keeping yourself?" Joey asked.
"I heard you were in the hospital."

"Just tests," he said. "Nothing serious."

That's not what Joey had heard. The rumor around town was

that Dale had cracked up and been sent to the mental unit. Of course, he wasn't about to bring that up; but then, he didn't have to—Dale seemed more depressed and troubled than Joey had ever seen him. "Are you okay?" he asked.

"Yeah, sure. Fine."

But Sandy knew he wasn't fine. She also knew that he wasn't going to remain on the wagon much longer. The hospital, the letters, the remorse, had just been another con job. Her rage over this ultimate deception caused her to ride herd on him more closely than ever ... and still, she felt the marriage slipping away. She had tried so *hard*—not only because she loved him (and she did love him, though it was increasingly difficult for her to explain why), but also because she saw it as her last chance. If it failed, she would be a four-time loser, damaged goods in the eyes of any decent man (and certainly, unlikely as a prospective parent in the eyes of any adoption agency). She'd wind up a childless, bitter old maid. The alternative—waiting for Dale to let her down—wasn't much more attractive.

His eventual tumble from the wagon was almost anti-climactic. He simply came home drunk one Thursday evening in early October. She made no scene. He went to work as always the next day, and that night was surprised to find his clothes, neatly packed, in the car, along with a copy of the never-vacated court order barring him from the house. He raced home, but couldn't get in the door; she had changed the locks. He tried to call, but the number had been changed; the new one was unlisted.

Eventually, she let him have the house—for a price—and returned home to Columbus. For the next year, he continued trying to win her back, and sometimes nearly succeeded. Even when they divorced in early 1982, Dale was hopeful the formal separation would clear the way for a fresh start. He reread *Helter Skelter*, and wondered again about the amazing magic Charlie Manson had marshaled to keep his girls in line.

When she thought about Dale later, Sandy would remember the oddest things—the way he dressed, for example. He dressed like a kid. She would buy him grown-up slacks and shirts and shoes, and he'd wear them to please her (and look great too, she thought), but when left to his own devices, he'd always choose his old bell-bottom dungarees and a cowboy shirt, and his clunky, old, square-toed *mod* shoes, with the elevator heels. It was as if the 1960s never had ended for him, as if he were trapped back there, still a twenty-year-old boy. His notion of what a "good time" was, the way he treated women, the way he related to his parents—all were adolescent. He had simply stopped growing at some point, she decided.

But *when* had he stopped, and what had stopped him?

She thought perhaps it had something to do with the day he'd been ambushed and trapped in the Que Son Valley; perhaps when he'd given up hope that day, when he'd said to himself, "I'm dead," he actually *had* died in some obscure psychological way.

It was an eerie thought, one that never failed to raise a shudder, but she could not dismiss it.

STEINER

And it's been proved that soldiers don't go mad
Unless they lose control of ugly thoughts
That drive them out to jabber among the trees.

—SIEGFRIED SASSOON

1

The first touch of civilization John Steiner encountered when he left
Vietnam in December 1967 was a beautiful blond surfer girl on television. He was in the waiting room at Hickam Air Force Base in
Hawaii. It was a huge open space filled with soldiers, sailors and
Marines bustling about with their seabags, talking, laughing, on
their way home—as he was—for Christmas. A group of men clus-
tered near the television, which hung from the wall at one end of the
room. The images on the screen were a dream vision of the World,
everyone's jungle fantasy—surfers, palm trees, rock bands, beautiful, healthy boys and girls cavorting in bathing suits.

It was some sort of teenage beach party. The host—a perfect
specimen—was standing in the surf, talking about how wonderful
it all was. Standing next to him was the beautiful blonde—also a
perfect specimen, tanned, wholesome, spilling out of her bikini. The
host asked a question, and Steiner heard her say the words "Vietnam" and "downer."

"Downer?" said a weathered little grunt next to him, who looked
as if he'd just stepped out of a paddy. "What does *that* mean?"

Steiner had never heard the word before, but he knew what it
meant. The men standing around the television fell silent. Everyone

was listening now. The girl was saying, "The people I really admire are the guys with a conscience, the guys who are fighting against the war and going to Canada. They're the real heroes." She said this easily, with enthusiasm, as if she were talking about her favorite rock band. "The guys in the Army are just a bunch of baby-killers, burning villages, killing innocent people . . ."

No one said anything. If she had been a radical antiwar type (Steiner had a definite idea what *those* people looked like), there might have been an explosion of epithets—but this was the sort of girl whose picture could be found in wallets throughout Vietnam, who sent letters on pink stationery doused with Tabu or White Shoulders. She was the girl everyone dreamed would be waiting at home. Steiner put his head in his hands and felt the same emptiness he had after every battle. He was angry—What does *she* know? he thought—but mostly depressed. Another ambush.

He arrived at the San Francisco airport in the middle of the night. He called his parents, who said they would come pick him up. It would take them about an hour to cross the bay from Lafayette and, in that time, he smoked nearly a pack of cigarettes. His parents didn't know he'd started smoking, and he wanted to get rid of the evidence before they came. When they arrived—his mother and father and older brother, Bob, on leave from the Air Force—Steiner began to giggle. He couldn't stop. They asked questions and he would try to answer, but every time he opened his mouth, he would dissolve. He laughed until his stomach hurt and tears rolled down his face.

His room was exactly as he'd left it. There was a neon Budweiser sign in the window and a surfing poster on the wall, along with a skunk skin and his shotgun. There was a big sign which said "High Voltage," two large sandstone rocks filled with fossils, his books (which included the James Bond series, *Born Free* and *Living Free*, and *Brave Men* by Ernie Pyle) and his collection of deer bones. It all seemed rather childish, a boy's room. He remembered the person who had lived there with a mixture of embarrassment and disgust.

Steiner had thirty days before he would have to report back to Camp Pendleton, and he spent most of them wandering alone through the woods near his parents' house. They lived in Hunsaker Canyon, a wild, beautiful place, well above the town of Lafayette, where his father managed the Pacific Gas and Electric Company office. The house was set deep in the canyon, next to a pleasant stream and surrounded by majestic live oaks. The air was soft and fresh there; the woods languid and benign. Climbing the hills, collecting more deer bones, throwing sticks for Jiggs, his parents' German longhair, Steiner occasionally could forget that he was a corporal in the Marines and experience the same calm, the same reassuring solace in nature that had been his only escape from the constant anxiety of high school. He'd never felt awkward, stupid or frightened in the woods; the only limit to his contentment had been the knowledge that he'd eventually have to go home for dinner and, probably, another argument with his parents about school.

Seth and Jane Steiner were affable, easygoing people—except when it came to education and politics. They had moved to California from Aurora, Illinois, after World War II, and had remained bedrock Midwestern conservatives. Friends who were liberal knew better than to discuss politics with the Steiners, especially Seth, whose corny jokes and informality would turn abruptly to cold steel at the slightest disagreement. The Steiners demanded hard work in school from the children, and were alternately outraged and perplexed by John's poor grades. The guidance counselors said his aptitude and IQ test scores were high and insisted on putting him in advanced classes, where he would always struggle. His teachers said he didn't pay attention, and wouldn't do his homework. When confronted with this, John would produce a handful of smudged and tattered assignments, and say he'd simply forgotten to turn them in. When pressed further, he could grow as cold and quiet as his father. He was a distant, dreamy boy, small, not very athletic, with a squeaky, high-pitched voice that never quite changed; he always seemed young for his age.

He wasn't lazy. He would dive into anything that interested him, especially nature and art, with a naïve, infectious enthusiasm that could—for a time, at least—dissolve his parents' fears and make them feel proud. But there was more to it than that. His older brother, Bob, was brilliant. He had a flashy, precocious intelligence, the sort of mind that excelled when put on public display. In elementary school, Bob—who was twenty months older than John—was starring in regional spelling bees. By the time he reached high school, he was traveling to national math competitions. One of John's clearest memories was of Bob sitting in front of the television on Sunday afternoons while their parents fixed dinner, answering questions on "College Bowl" before the contestants could. He was as "serious" as John was spacey, and regarded his younger brothers (Tom was the youngest, five years and light-years behind Bob) with condescension. Friends of the family say that Bob was under a great deal of pressure from his father (whose own academic career was a bit more like John's). Seth doted on Bob, relished his triumphs, and when the boy was in junior high, would even interrupt work each day to drive him to the high school for special math classes.

John was jealous of the attention his father paid Bob, and daunted by his older brother's successes. He grew to hate the words "potential" and "expectations," which were constantly being thrown in his face. At first, his parents reacted angrily—punishing him for bad report cards, forcing him to quit the high school swim team (which he'd joined only to please his father), confining him to his room after dinner to study. The worst punishment was when his father volunteered to help with his math homework. John would freeze, unable to think, a moron. The harder Seth pushed, the more distant John became; it would end in screaming and sullenness.

Sometimes when John brought home his report card, his mother would start to cry.

"Do you *like* doing this to your mother?" his father would yell.

Once, anticipating particularly disastrous results in seventh grade, he ran away from home. He spent several lonely hours on a hill, watching the sun go down and munching a salami, then returned home, defeated, in time for bed.

In high school, he began to have dizzy spells. He could always feel them coming—a strange light-headedness, an intense feeling of déjà vu, and then he would lose track of everything. His parents, fearing epilepsy, took him to several doctors, who ran batteries of tests but couldn't find anything wrong. Finally, a doctor asked if the spells occurred with any regularity. They weren't sure. For the next few months, Jane Steiner monitored the attacks—John would always tell her when he had one—and soon realized there was a definite pattern: he blacked out only during the two weeks before a report card was due. She never told John this, but decided to ease up on him a bit.

He was, apparently, too panic-stricken to notice. The idea that he was a disappointment to his parents remained the central fact of his life, and not even Bob's surprising failure at Berkeley—where he concentrated the full force of his intellect on bowling and, in effect, flunked out—could ease the pressure.

So John spent the afternoons wandering through the woods and the evenings surreptitiously reading the books he wanted to read, instead of studying. He remained very much a boy, filled with fantasies of doing heroic, dangerous things. He was at a loss in the fast, relatively sophisticated, upper-middle-class world of Del Valle High School. He tended to hang out with the losers, the kids not destined for college, passing the time with childish pranks—pelting the dean's car with water balloons, indulging in various automotive lunacies, shoplifting skin magazines, a half-hearted outcast. He lacked the confidence or eccentricity to pursue the things he really loved, like collecting butterflies, with any real conviction. Being caught with a butterfly net would have meant instant ostracism; he was more likely to be found carrying a shotgun when the gang trudged through the forest together, wasting much ammunition on uncooperative birds and squirrels. Women also proved rather elusive. He was most definitely interested—but girls seemed to have the same effect on him as English class, freezing his brain and tying his tongue.

The few times he managed to get past his academic paralysis and actually become interested in school, the results were not encouraging. He fell in love with *Beowulf*—a saga filled with heroes battling monsters and winning fair maidens was more to his taste than the moral complexities of *The Great Gatsby*, which he was forced to read in English class and loathed. He pounced on an assignment to summarize *Beowulf* in German, spending weeks at it, poring over German-English dictionaries, using grammar and vocabulary that hadn't been covered in class, typing it out with careful margins and turning it in proudly. His teacher was certain it was plagiarized. "I can't prove it," she said, "so I'll give you a C."

After that, all he cared about was getting away. When two recent graduates—erstwhile losers, like him—returned to Del Valle ramrod straight and proud in their Marine uniforms, and were immediately surrounded by adoring women, his course seemed clear. He'd been thinking about the Marines since reading *Battle Cry*; that his father had tried to join during World War II and failed was further incentive. The prospect of college was horrifying. If Bob—now a computer specialist in the Air Force—couldn't get through, what chance did he have?

The local recruiter's name was Buchanan. He gave John a Marine Corps poster and later, when he signed the enlistment papers, the snappy dress-blue tunic that Mel Sands and the other grunts would never let him forget. His parents seemed happy with his decision, although his mother would rather have seen him go to college. He was the only member of Del Valle High School's Class of 1966 to join the Marines, which made him more of an outcast than ever, but John didn't care: he had visions of himself in some far-off, exotic place, resting after combat, helmet tilted rakishly, a cigarette dangling . . . a hero, finally.

There was, however, one last problem. The Marines, checking his records, discovered that he'd been arrested several years earlier in Walnut Creek for shoplifting. He'd been caught taking a skin magazine from a drugstore, hauled down to the police station and released to the custody of his mother. It was a minor humiliation, and he'd forgotten it completely when he filled out his enlistment papers. That made him technically guilty of perjury.

He was told to report to the Federal Building in downtown San Francisco, and was grilled there by a stern captain who asked such questions as "Do you bite your nails?" and "What if you can't take it in boot camp and start crying?" and "Why don't you join some other branch of the service?"

Steiner said he didn't bite his nails, he wouldn't cry in boot camp and he'd always wanted to be a Marine. He had, in fact, signed up for a four-year hitch to atone for his misdemeanor and convince the Corps of his ardor. Sitting outside the office with several other perjurers waiting for the verdict, he wondered: Is it possible that I've screwed *this* up too? The thought of going home and telling his father that he hadn't made it was unbearable. At that moment, the Marines seemed his only chance, his last hope for self-respect; he would have done anything they asked. As it happened, all they asked was that he raise his right hand and take the oath.

He entered boot camp in San Diego four days after graduating high school. It was a rigorous eight weeks, but he'd seen *The D.I.*, with Jack Webb, and was prepared for the worst. He never cried, or bit his fingernails. And, to be absolutely certain the Marines wouldn't have any unnatural expectations, he purposely answered a number of questions wrong on the multiple-choice aptitude tests they gave him. He did not want to be singled out for anything except combat.

Eighteen months later, he was home again and a hero—in his parents' eyes, if not his own. He did not tell them much about the war, and they respected his privacy. He didn't call any of his old friends, or go out on dates. He wore his uniform in public only once, for his grandparents' fiftieth wedding anniversary. He felt uncomfortable when he ventured into the World, certain that people were staring at his haircut—his scalp all too visible, sickly white, like stomach fat protruding through an unbuttoned shirt. He wasn't so much ashamed as overwhelmed, afraid that he would be forced into a confrontation and have to explain his position; he could barely comprehend what he'd just been through, much less defend it. The doubts about the war that he'd felt so strongly in the bush were still there, but submerged beneath a quiet defiance. He felt incompetent to make moral judgments about Vietnam; it seemed obscene that others, who knew far less than he, could dare to. He would not give them the satisfaction of hearing his doubts.

In a way, Steiner's private turmoil reflected the country's at that moment. Recent polls showed that nearly half the people now believed that getting involved in Vietnam had been a mistake, but only a small minority favored immediate withdrawal. At about that time, in an essay titled "Why Are We in Vietnam?," *Newsweek* wrote: "The cost of fighting the war is far smaller than the long-range cost we would incur by a retreat." There were no longer any illusions about fighting to preserve democracy in South Vietnam; it was now a war to save face.

This was a far cry from the romantic crusade Steiner had envisioned when he left for boot camp. But he didn't want to think about that. Nor did he have much curiosity about the strange developments across the bay, in the Haight-Ashbury section of San Francisco. The "Summer of Love" was over, buried in a mock funeral by the hippies themselves, but there still were hundreds of kids wandering into town each week from across the country. They were not so different from what John had been a few years earlier—spacey, romantic and alienated—and, under other circumstances, he might have been tempted to explore. But now they were the enemy, and he stayed away. The only hippie he would remember meeting during his month at home was his younger brother, Tom.

He was nonplussed by Tom, who had hair down to his shoulders and wore ratty, disheveled clothes. He was no longer living at home, but in an abandoned bus in the nearby town of Canyon. He would drop by occasionally to irritate his parents. Once, when asked by a friend of the family what his philosophy of life was, Tom said, "Drop out of society. Let it collapse of its own weight." John couldn't believe it; he'd been much closer to Tom than to Bob, and now he barely recognized his younger brother. They never discussed the war. John was particularly vigilant when Tom visited, skittering away whenever a confrontation seemed likely.

Tom could be dismissed as a mixed-up kid; the hippies and the protesters, John believed, were all mixed-up kids. The girl in the bikini was mixed up too, just following the latest fad. The peace movement was childish; responsible people knew that you supported your country. But then his parents' close friends St. John and Betty Smith came over for dinner one night and Betty promptly announced: "You know, we're against this war. What do you think of it, John, now that you've been over there?"

It was, of course, the very question he'd been trying to avoid since arriving home, and it caught him completely off guard. The Smiths were the first respectable, middle-class people he'd met who were against the war. He didn't know what to say.

John was beginning to look forward to getting back to Camp Pendleton. He hadn't spoken with anyone remotely resembling a peer in weeks.

Pendleton wasn't much better. The dreary rows of Quonset huts and dusty parade grounds were filled with tired, cynical grunts returned from the war who had little patience with the pointless ceremonies of barracks life—rifle inspection, close-order drill, filling out forms, standing in line, being processed. Steiner was assigned to an MP company composed almost entirely of Vietnam veterans; it was widely assumed that the Marines had no intention of actually using them as military police, but couldn't think of anything better for them to do. He was happy, though, to hook up with some old friends from infantry training school—Joe Raymond, Bob Southwick and Ed Skaronek. They had been thrown together in ITR by alphabetical coincidence and now had the common experience of a tour in Vietnam to bind them.

But Steiner soon found that he had little in common with them either. They smoked marijuana, he didn't—it was *illegal.* They told incessant stories about the women they'd ravaged on thirty-day leave; he had no stories, only frustrations, and wasn't about to share those. He decided to keep his distance, making excuses when the others would go off to Oceanside on passes, often hanging back in the barracks, reading *The Love Machine* and *Valley of the Dolls*, which didn't do much for his frustrations. When Jacqueline Susann proved inadequate, he attempted the local porn movies in Oceanside. He longed for a non-pecuniary romance.

Lacking anything better to do—and, in truth, hoping for some moral support and inspiration—he went to see *The Green Berets*, and was outraged. It was nothing like the Vietnam he had known. In the climactic battle scene, rows of Viet Cong marched forward like the British at Yorktown and were mowed down by John Wayne, with the help of several convenient and ridiculously effective helicopters. The movie did bring back some memories, though, and he found—to his surprise—that he missed Charlie Company. In the aimless boredom and stupid bureaucracy of Camp Pendleton, he was beginning to romanticize combat again. As horrible as it had been, at least it had a point. He'd been alone, but never really lonely, especially toward the end, when he'd made close friends and enjoyed a certain status as a short-timer, respected by the new guys. He had never overcome his fear in battle or discomfort in the field, but fear and discomfort were appropriate there; it seemed as though nothing since was really "appropriate." Combat, in its way, was easier to deal with than the amorphous *weirdness* he'd been feeling here in the World, which apparently wasn't shared by any of his old friends from ITR.

And then Mel Sands, his old hole-mate, showed up. Sands was assigned to an infantry company down the road at Pendleton, and Steiner was overjoyed to see someone who was—after a fashion— family. They went to Oceanside, had a couple of beers, told the old stories, reminisced about this guy and that, the exotic pleasures of Okinawa . . . and then, suddenly, there was nothing left to say. Steiner had admired Sands in the bush—he was one of the few who seemed to know what he was doing—but here he was a laconic, painfully unsophisticated farm boy from northern Michigan. They saw each other, rather dutifully, several more times and then lost touch.

Steiner's MP company was being trained for cold-weather duty. It seemed a pointless exercise, but not unpleasant. There were movies about how to survive in the Arctic, lectures and books to read, many of which he found fairly interesting. They were issued nifty thermal parkas, and other convincing gear. Then, in mid-January, the entire unit was loaded—trucks and all—onto a single, huge C-141 airplane (Steiner thought this was one of the most amazing things he'd ever seen) and plopped down in the Nevada desert for a week of cold-weather exercises. A tent city, complete with field kitchens and all sorts of conveniences he'd never seen in Vietnam, sprouted within hours. The grunts—mostly new recruits—had to pull long stretches out in the freezing desert, but the MPs spent most of their time relaxing in heated tents. It was more fun than Steiner had had in quite some time.

One night he had a nightmare. He could not remember what the dream was—he rarely remembered his dreams, and never the bad ones—but apparently he'd been screaming. He awakened to find one of the new recruits staring at him, shocked.

"You had a nightmare," the kid said.

Joe Raymond, seeing the recruit was in worse shape than Steiner, threw an arm around him and explained, "Don't worry, kid. This guy's a Nam boy . . . You'll understand what *that's* all about some-day."

When they returned to Pendleton, they discovered that there might have been some point to the cold-weather training. The North Koreans had seized the *Pueblo*, an American spy ship patrolling the Sea of Japan, and imprisoned its eighty-three-member crew. There was outrage in Washington, and talk of punitive action against the Koreans. The President activated 90,000 reservists.

And then, on January 31, just as the country was beginning to assimilate the *Pueblo* humiliation, the North Vietnamese and Viet Cong launched the Tet offensive. Viet Cong sappers penetrated the U.S. Embassy in Saigon, North Vietnamese regulars stormed and held the Citadel at Hue, there was fighting in every provincial capital throughout the country, even in Danang, the Marine Corps' headquarters (which seemed, to Steiner, as brazen and unbelievable as the attack on the embassy).

The reaction at Camp Pendleton was shock, and then a flurry of rumors. Within days, a formation was called and the company commander announced that it was true, they were going over—but he didn't say where. The word was that it would be Korea, especially after the cold-weather training. Everyone would go except those who'd already been overseas and hadn't yet been home for six months. The CO made it clear, though, that those men were needed badly and he hoped they would volunteer.

Steiner agonized, but not for long. He figured that unless something drastic happened and the war in Vietnam ended quickly, he would be going overseas for another tour anyway (after all, he still had two and a half years left). If he went back now, it would be as an MP—easy duty. He also felt that he had skated through half his first tour with a broken foot, and *owed* the Marines a full shot—half a tour with the grunts and a full one with the MPs would just about do it.

"I'm volunteering," he announced in the barracks.

"You're crazy," Southwick said.

"No, I can't stand it here anymore. This place is driving me nuts."

"You're still crazy."

But Joe Raymond, listening quietly, finally said, "You know, I'm thinking about doing it too."

Steiner went to call his parents, and found that he was all choked up. "I'm going back," he said, fighting the tears.

His father asked where. He didn't know, probably Korea. "It's an emergency," he explained. "They need us."

Several days later, the unit boarded a C-141, just as it had for cold-weather training. The men still had no idea where they were heading, but they had been issued field jackets, hardly appropriate for tropical duty. Steiner took his place in a webbed jump seat overlooking the vast cargo bay. When the plane was in the air, a gunnery sergeant came down the row, reading an announcement. The noise was so loud that he could read it to only two or three men at a time. As the gunney approached, Steiner caught the word, passed down the line: *Danang.*

"Danang," he said. "Oh shit."

He had been home exactly two months. He felt now as if it had all been an elaborate illusion, not really home, but a place that re-sembled it superficially. He remembered the last weeks he'd spent in Charlie Company, counting down the days. He didn't even have *that* now—it would be months before he could begin the count-down again.

2

One day, near the end of his second tour in Vietnam, Steiner saw two pigs in a small clearing in the jungle. They were pink, fat, doc-ile—food for the North Vietnamese, he figured. He asked his radio operator to "call the six"—the platoon lieutenant—for instructions. The word came back: "One bullet, one pig; two bullets, two pigs." Steiner understood. Any more firing might draw attention to their position. They were in the Ashau Valley, and had been in contact with the enemy nearly every day.

Steiner had spent six very pleasant months as an MP in Danang. He investigated traffic accidents, and sometimes would roar about town in a jeep, siren blaring. It was so much fun that he suspected the fates would have a payback waiting for him somewhere down the line, and he was right. In late summer of 1968, his MP company was ordered back to the States—but since he had volunteered for a second tour overseas, the Marines saw no reason to disappoint him and he was transferred into a grunt unit. It was a startling turn of events, but he didn't protest. He was still feeling guilty about not having served a full combat tour. He knew these feelings were irra-tional, but couldn't shake them. And though the war proved as frus-trating, elusive and senseless as ever, his second hitch with the grunts did turn out to be more gratifying than the first. He became a squad leader, a sergeant, well respected—admired, even—and more sure of himself than he'd ever been in his life. He'd become, at the age of twenty-one, the tough old salt—helmet tilted rakishly, cigarette dangling—of his high school fantasies. He still didn't enjoy being out in the bush (that would be crazy), but there was a real satisfaction in knowing that he performed his job well. He had never made a mistake that caused one of his men to be killed.

His pride was dimmed, though, by the fact that the war was so obviously a disaster. They had spent months in the thick, mountainous jungles of the Ashau Valley without accomplishing anything. There were no decisive battles, just ambushes, as always. It was still a war against foliage, the enemy invisible; there were times after a fire fight when he would pass through an area the enemy had occupied, and it would seem as if someone had taken a power hose and sprayed the trees and bushes with blood and bits of flesh; there were rarely any bodies. When he drew a bead on the pigs that day, it was the first time he had ever taken aim at a living enemy target.

He didn't want to kill the pigs. It seemed ridiculous. But he had reported them to the lieutenant out of some obscure sense of duty— they *were* food for the enemy—and now he had no choice. They were about ten yards away, across a small stream. He aimed, fired once, then again. The pigs dropped, but didn't die—they struggled, blood pouring, squealing, convulsive. He couldn't stand it. He fired again at the first pig, and put it out of its misery. Three bullets, two pigs . . . he had disobeyed orders. He thought about the fourth bullet. The third had been reflexive, but the fourth would be deliberate. He hesitated a moment, then moved on, the squeals reverberating through the jungle.

"Steiner," asked K.P.—Kevin Patrick Kelty—his radio operator and a close friend, "did you really have to do that?"

"Yeah."

But they both knew he didn't, and he was disgusted with himself.

Later that day they were mortared. They were settling in for the night when they heard the first dull thunks, and dived for cover. It was unexpected, but not uncommon; one way or another they were attacked almost every night. This time the enemy was more

successful than usual. Staff Sergeant Clark, a large, obnoxious former drill instructor known as "Big Daddy," had his stomach ripped
open by shrapnel. When the barrage ended, Steiner went over to him
and held his hand; the big man was scared and starting to blubber.

"Cool it, Big Daddy," Steiner said. "Everyone's watching you."

It was true. The platoon recently had been replenished with
green troops and Steiner didn't want them spooked by the sight of
the biggest, toughest man in the unit freaking out over a wound.
They might panic, make mistakes, get themselves killed. Wounded
or not, Big Daddy had a responsibility to the others; pigs might
squeal, but Marines didn't. As he was tending to the sergeant, Steiner
noticed one of the medics on the ground nearby, his eye dangling by
a thread from his cheek. He asked, "Are you okay?"

"Yes," the medic said calmly.

"Hey, Steiner," Big Daddy said, struggling to hold himself together, "you're all right."

All right? He was sick of the whole business. Why should pigs
have the luxury of honest unrestrained suffering and not men?

Medevacs arrived. Big Daddy and the wounded medic were
taken off. The lieutenant came over and told Steiner that, as the senior squad leader, he was next in line for Big Daddy's job. He was
now platoon sergeant.

He was shot the next day. It happened in early evening, just after
they had established a perimeter in thick cane on the side of a hill.
Steiner's job was to position the squads—they were nicknamed
Linus, Snoopy and Pigpen—around the perimeter. He did it slowly,
carefully, not wanting to make a mistake his first time out. Then, as
the men began to dig in, he used a machete to hack out a command
post toward the rear of the perimeter. George Roe, the radio operator from Linus, came over and said, "Steiner, I'll dig a larger hole—if
you need it, jump in."

He found that he was enjoying his new status. He surveyed the
lines for a moment, then remembered he had left his pack outside the
perimeter and went to get it.

The pack was leaning against a fence post, at the edge of a field. It was a beautiful place, an absurdity in the midst of the jungle, peaceful, bucolic, not all that different from the pastures in Hunsaker Canyon, near his parents' home. For a moment he imagined he was back there . . . alone in the woods, at peace. He leaned his rifle against the post and sat down. The sun was setting, the air soft and fragrant. He allowed himself to drift for about ten minutes, then realized with a start that he was absolutely crazy to be outside the lines at dusk, and headed back.

A machine gun opened fire just after he reached the perimeter. There were screams from down the hill, where men had been cutting a field of fire. He ran down to see what the trouble was—one of the new guys, a well-built Chicano admired by the others, had been shot in the arm and wasn't acting at all like a Marine. The wound wasn't serious, but the man wouldn't stop screaming. It was a bad scene; he was scaring everyone. Steiner left a medic to tend to the kid and headed back toward the perimeter, promising to return when they were ready to move him.

He jumped into George Roe's hole and radioed the CP. A medevac seemed out of the question. They were in thick, canopied jungle and would have to blast out a landing zone. Even then, a helicopter would have a rough time finding them in the dark, landing through what was sure to be heavy enemy fire. After a few minutes, he heard the medic calling him and started back down the hill, zigzagging—rifle fire was interspersed with the machine gun now—and then he was in the air, tumbling forward, his legs flying out from under him, landing flat on his back . . . a searing, scorching pain in his left thigh near the hip, the bone vibrating in there like a tuning fork, the whole leg shuddering. I've been shot, he thought, *very* clearly. It hurts more than I thought it would.

The first thing that came to mind after that was the last paragraph in *All Quiet on the Western Front*: the hero, dead in a trench, staring into space with a slight smile. Steiner did not believe he was going to die, but the pain was enormous, excruciating, flowing out from his leg in waves. He did not cry, or make a scene. The medic was there and others, surrounding him. He looked down and saw his left trouser leg, tucked into his boot as always, but ballooning; the medic slit the trousers, and blood—an unbelievable amount of blood—poured out. The medic called for an *emergency* medevac. Steiner figured he had called in "emergency" because he was afraid they wouldn't come in the darkness and thick canopy. He refused to believe that he had been wounded seriously.

But they were apparently having trouble stanching the flow of blood. The bullet—probably an AK-47 round—had entered through the top of his thigh, about three inches to the left of his testicles. It was a difficult spot to tourniquet.

The lieutenant was there now, freaking out; Steiner wanted to tell him to cool it, but his tongue felt as if someone had clamped it with a clothespin. He thought back to his first tour, when he and Bill Taylor had carried a wounded man, his body just riddled with bullets, back to the command post. They asked his name and he said, "Corporal Penny," thick-tongued, just as Steiner was now. Corporal Penny died.

Steiner tried to stay coherent. K.P., his radioman, was holding his hand. He remembered the scene in *Battle Cry* where Levin, the Jew, died at Tarawa and Speedy, an anti-Semite and Levin's tormentor, sat holding his hand. Levin's last request to Speedy was that he make sure they put a Star of David, not a cross, on his grave. Steiner had no intention of making a last request. Instead, he decided to reorganize the platoon, concentrating on giving instructions and not the pain, slurring the words half coherently: he made Miller, the next senior squad leader, his replacement as platoon sergeant, combined two depleted squads and made K.P. a squad leader. Then he asked K.P. to take his watch and wallet and send them to his parents; there were stories that the orderlies in field hospitals were stealing things. He looked at his skin and it seemed as white as his scalp. No one, he thought, has ever experienced this much pain.

He heard them blasting out a landing zone. K.P. was still holding his hand. The fire fight was continuing, more intensely now. He heard the sound of a helicopter and then, looking up, could see it landing through what appeared to be a chimney in the jungle. It was the most amazing thing he had ever seen. The downdraft felt good, cool, clean.

There were palm fronds when he awakened. He figured he was lying beneath a banana tree somewhere. Gradually, as he became conscious of the pain, the palm fronds became the dark gaps between the fluorescent lights in the ceiling. He was in a hospital. There were tubes attached to both his arms, tubes and wires everywhere.

When he awakened again, a medic formerly attached to his unit was sitting next to his bed. "Jesus, Steiner," he said, "they had you in surgery all night."

"Where am I?"

The medic told him that he was in an underground field hospital in Quang Tri. This worried him. He'd heard that the North Vietnamese had attacked an underground field hospital somewhere, and gone down the wards shooting patients.

He drifted in and out. It seemed as if they were shooting him up with morphine every two minutes. A medic told him that his femur—his thigh bone—had been shattered and the femoral artery destroyed. The doctors had taken a vein from his right leg to replace the artery in his left. If the graft didn't hold, they would have to amputate.

"*Really?*" Steiner asked, more impressed by the idea of the vein graft than the possibility that he might lose his leg.

A doctor visited him. "Hey, Doc," he said, "I only have twenty-one days left in-country. You don't think they're going to send me out there again, do you? It'd be a waste. I'd just rotate a few days after they sent me out . . ."

The doctor was smiling. "Don't worry," he said. "You're through."

"I am?" Steiner was giddy, buoyant, his whole body seemed to relax, even the pain lessened for a moment. He was not going to die in Vietnam. He would never have to spend another day in the bush. He didn't remember to ask the doctor what the chances were of keeping his leg. He didn't care—a leg was nothing. He had made it through.

The pain returned. It wasn't a throbbing or stinging pain, but deep, profound, shuddering, constant, burrowing down through his innards. He felt an urge to leap up, shake it off—but they had told him not to move, it might endanger the vein graft. They came with morphine, and he drifted off again.

He was on another LZ, and freezing. He was wearing only a full body cast, ice-cold blood still seeping into him through tubes in his arms. They had given him twenty-two pints, he later learned. He was shivering on the LZ, and someone gave him a blanket. He was still freezing. It was odd that after all the days and hours of stifling heat, his last moments in Vietnam would be so cold.

They took him to the hospital ship *Repose* in Danang harbor for several days. Then he went to a hospital in Yokohama, Japan.

Jane Steiner was heading down the canyon to meet Seth in town for dinner when she saw the U.S. government car coming up the road. She remembered how a similar car had come to her parents' home in Aurora, Illinois, twenty-five years earlier, with the news that her brother had been killed in World War II. She slammed the brakes, and turned around. Sure enough, the car pulled into her driveway. She began to cry.

The Marine was kind, but not very helpful. He handed her a telegram which said that John had been very seriously wounded. He didn't know anything more than that. She found herself thinking about John as an infant, five months old—he'd had diarrhea and then began vomiting violently. The doctors said there was something wrong with his intestines. They put him in an oxygen tent with tubes coming out his head and feet. They operated on him six times;

at one point, they left the intestine exposed, on his stomach, to see if the blood would start circulating. A doctor said, "Quite frankly, I don't know how he will be able to survive this." But he had. John was so damned stubborn. She thought: He'll survive this too—and felt better.

He spent a month in Yokohama in an amputee ward. There were several other men who'd had the exact same operation and, every so often, a nurse would notice that a vein graft had broken and there would be a flurry of activity: six orderlies would dash in from all directions, and the man would be rushed to surgery. Sometimes they were able to repatch the graft; sometimes the man would return without a leg.

Steiner didn't worry about losing his. For one thing, he simply didn't believe it was going to happen. For another, he felt better—despite the pain, which was intense—than he had in a long time. An immense, claustrophobic pressure had lifted; the war was over for him. He exulted in every detail of hospital life—the hot meals, the clean, crisp white sheets that were changed every morning, the daily newspaper (even if it was *Stars and Stripes*). He could sleep without worrying about getting up to stand watch. He could see the snow falling outside his window and know that he was *indoors*, finally, safe and warm and dry. Each day, candy-stripers came around, chirpy, pleasant girls handing out books and magazines. He spent much of the time reading, which helped to keep his mind off the pain. He read magazines mostly, and once a war novel about a commando who was captured by the enemy and tortured. Between tortures, he would try to think about pleasant things. A good idea, Steiner thought, and he would try to think about pleasant things too, rather than the constant temptation to move his left leg, to react somehow to the pain. He tried reacting with his *right* leg, jiggling it around, but it wasn't nearly so effective as reading or thinking about something else. He thought about home, the woods, scuba diving, the candy-stripers, the future. Nothing, not even an amputation, would ever be as difficult as what he'd just lived through.

He would talk about Vietnam with the Army lifer, a master sergeant, in the bed to his right—nothing very serious, just war stories. Sometimes they speculated about who would be the next on the ward to have his leg chopped off . . . but never about their own pain, even though they had identical wounds. They would hoard Darvon, saving one of the two pills in the dose, then take four or five at once and zone out.

After a month in Japan, he was loaded on a plane and taken home, to Oak Knoll Naval Hospital in Oakland; by then, he knew the graft had held and he would not lose his leg. The doctors said that he would have to wear a leg brace for the rest of his life. He didn't believe that either.

3

Steiner spent nine months—from April 1969 to January 1970—at Oak Knoll. His physical recovery was slow, painful, frustrating; it was months before he could put the slightest pressure on his left leg, standing tentatively on crutches, the leg held firm by a steel brace. That he could stand at all seemed a miracle, though. When he saw the X-rays, Steiner was shocked to find that his thigh bone no longer ran in an uninterrupted line from his pelvis to his knee, but was two shards overlapping slightly, welded together side by side, like a bayonet protruding from the barrel of a rifle. It appeared a precarious and unlikely solution, and his awareness of its makeshift quality was continually reinforced by the throbbing pain, which seemed more plausible now that he'd seen its source. The healing proceeded so slowly as to be unnoticeable from day to day; it was only when he took a longer view and thought of how he'd been a month or two months earlier that he realized his progress had been steady and—given the nature of the wound— remarkable.

His attempts to come to terms with the war and his role in it were not nearly so methodical as the physical healing, but they also pointed in an obvious direction. He began to read everything he could find about Vietnam, and Asia in general. He read a history of the French involvement in Indochina. He read *Street Without Joy* by Bernard Fall, Gandhi's autobiography, Mao Zedong's Little Red Book, a biography of Ho Chi Minh and *The Making of a Quagmire* by David Halberstam. The Halberstam book finally convinced him beyond any doubt that the war had been wrong. Reading the firsthand account of the misguided, corrupt attempts to "pacify" the villagers in the Mekong Delta, Steiner remembered—with anger and embarrassment—the brutality his comrades, his *friends*, in Charlie Company had visited upon helpless villagers during his first tour. They would go from hooch to hooch terrorizing people, beating old men and women, knocking over baskets of food. He remembered families cowering in the corners of hooches, shaking with fear, their eyes rolled back in their heads, and Sergeant Albertson—a man Steiner otherwise respected—dragging the papasan by his hair to the middle of the floor, slapping him across the face, humiliating him for no apparent reason. Sometimes, Steiner would hang back after the others had left and whisper, *"Sin loi, sin loi"*—"I'm sorry, I'm sorry"—and give the people C rations or cigarettes. Usually, they were too terrified to notice. He would be terrified too, afraid that if his friends ever caught him showing sympathy for the gooks, he would be ostracized. He lived in constant fear of this—the other grunts might behave monstrously at times, but they were the only allies he had in a very dangerous place. If his compassion was discovered, they might no longer trust him . . . or worse, find some way to get rid of him.

Thinking back on those days, he began to despise his comrades. Some were intelligent and not all were brutal—he'd never forget the time Bill Taylor retrieved an orphaned Vietnamese infant from a tunnel and carried it with him all day, gently cradling the baby until a medevac arrived—but far too many were fools, bullies pretending to be heroes, taking full advantage of the lawlessness of the place. Many of them actually seemed to believe the villagers when they said, "GI numbah one, VC numbah ten," as they swaggered past; half of them fell in love with the whores they had on R & R; some of them excelled in the bush on animal instinct, but they had no idea at all what they were doing there. And neither did he.

His parents noticed that John was quietly disgusted with many of the other patients at Oak Knoll (especially those who gave in to their pain, but also those who listened to country music, which he hated) and that he joked sarcastically about what a bunch of heroes they were. Although John never said so, Seth and Jane sensed that he was sick of the Marines. "I want to go to college," he said one day.

"Really?" his father said. "You were always so dead set against it. Why the change?"

"Well, look," John said, "how much does the average meter reader make at Pacific Gas and Electric? Ninety dollars a week? That's only two-seventy a month . . ."

"Actually," Seth interrupted, "it's more like four hundred a month, four and a half weeks, you know."

"See," John laughed sheepishly, "that's why I need to go to college."

But even if he was now ready to rejoin the middle class, even if he believed what he read in the books about Vietnam, he was not yet ready to admit his new feelings about the war publicly. Later, he would be unable to remember when he became able to distinguish between the war and his role in it; the two were still hopelessly tangled during those first few months in the hospital. When he watched the huge antiwar demonstrations in Washington on television, he reacted much as he had to the girl in the bikini in Hawaii: What do *they* know? At such times, he would remember his comrades in an entirely different way—as courageous, frightened, innocent, essentially decent men placed in an untenable position. The demonstrations seemed a direct attack on them; the speakers were angry at *him*, were accusing *him* of atrocities.

He could not help but feel proud of his own accomplishments in Vietnam, nor could he erase the years he'd spent convincing himself that he was doing the right thing. When he listened to Peter, Paul and Mary sing "Blowing in the Wind" and heard the line "How many years can some people exist before they're allowed to be free?" he would think about the South Vietnamese struggling for freedom from Communism—even though he now knew that struggle was illusory and the lyrics weren't referring to it in any case. He'd always twisted the words of popular songs to suit his own feelings; it had been difficult loving the Beatles and knowing where they stood on Vietnam, for example, but if he could believe that he was fighting for "peace" and "freedom," he could pretend that they were on the same side. Now that he'd made his private, intellectual decision against the war, it should have been easier to appreciate their music . . . but then he saw John Lennon on television saying that Lieutenant Calley had been a scapegoat for My Lai. How could Lennon be against the war and defend a man who had perpetrated a massacre? The antiwar people apparently could twist the lyrics to suit their own devices too.

The utter absurdity of it all was no farther away than the black sergeant in the next bed. He had been shot fourteen times by one of his own men, a racist on a drunken spree. *Both* his femurs were busted, he was in constant pain, and he certainly had more than enough reason to hate all white people, and yet he was one of the kindest, most decent men Steiner had ever met. Sometimes, when wondering why anyone would shoot such a man, his thoughts would drift back to Ben Hollins, who'd been his closest friend when he first joined Charlie Company in the field.

Hollins was very smart, a college graduate (Steiner had no idea how he'd gotten stuck in the boonies), a husband, a father, and completely cynical about the war. When they walked through the villages and the little kids would approach, begging for "chop-chop"—food—Hollins would say, "C'mon, kid, don't you realize we're making this place safe for democracy? Isn't that *enough*?"

Hollins was obsessed with the idea of getting out of there, especially after Operation Cochise. He would roll up his sleeves to make his arms more available to mosquitoes, hoping for malaria; sometimes, during a fire fight, he would wave his hand in the air, trying to get shot. He often said, "I'd shoot myself if I had the nerve," and sometimes asked Steiner, "Would you do it for me?" Steiner would laugh, but Hollins persisted and—for reasons Steiner never would understand—he finally agreed. They planned it carefully, consulting a friendly medic about the best location for the wound: A foot wouldn't do—they'd just patch him up and send him back to the boonies. The medic recommended the shin. Steiner had just received a whole canned chicken from his father, and it was decided that when Hollins was ready, they would have a going-away feast and then Steiner would send him home.

Steiner carried the chicken around in his pack for nearly a month before Hollins said, "Let's eat the damn thing."

They arranged to share a foxhole that night. After the meal they covered themselves with a poncho, Hollins pulled his trouser leg tight over his shin and Steiner fired. There was an enormous sound, much louder than a normal rifle shot. Hollins jolted back, writhing. Steiner was shaking.

"Are you okay?"

"I don't know."

"Are you sorry we did it?"

"Yeah."

The medic came quickly, soon followed by the CO, who asked what had happened. "Accidental discharge," the medic said, but no one in Charlie Company believed him. Hollins was medevacked out and never heard from again.

Steiner had fired his rifle thousands upon thousands of times during two tours in Vietnam, but had taken aim at actual targets only twice: when he shot Hollins and when he killed the pigs on the day before he was wounded.

Early in his second tour, Steiner had received a letter from a girl he'd never met. She'd been given his name by a friend of a friend, and wrote to let him know he wasn't forgotten, that there were people back in the States who appreciated what he was doing and hoped he was safe. He replied, thanking her for the letter, and a correspondence ensued. As the months passed, John began to think of her as *his* girl; he fell in love with her handwriting, her stationery with the little flowers . . .

Soon after he arrived at Oak Knoll, the girl visited him. She was absolutely gorgeous, a clean, fresh California beauty. He felt moldy, disheveled, awkward. He figured that she was expecting John Wayne and there *he* was—weighing little more than ninety pounds, in traction, his left leg raised so the bottom of his foot was all too visible, the calluses there an inch thick and beginning to dry and peel like old tile from a floor. He knew immediately he'd blown her innocent letters out of proportion; she'd only been doing her duty. She made a nervous but valiant attempt at small talk and then, after an appropriate interval, went home. He was completely embarrassed.

There was a steady stream of cheerful, patriotic, innocent and maddeningly voluptuous girls passing through the hospital on missions of mercy, bearing fruit, candy, magazines and wheelchair shawls; it was as if every cheerleader in the state of California had decided to converge on the place. They played checkers, fluffed pillows and drove Steiner wild with lust. His frustration increased as the pain in his leg diminished and he moved from traction to a wheelchair and, eventually, to his feet. Toward the end of his stay in the hospital, a group of girls came to visit from the Central Valley town of Loomis and he noticed one of them staring intently at him. He dared not hope, but a letter soon arrived from Loomis with the postscript: "Write back! Write back! Write back!" He wrote back. Her name was Peggy Swenson, and she was very impressed with the fact that he was a sergeant.

He was, by then, able to leave the hospital on weekends and soon was spending most of them in Loomis, double-dating with a friend from the hospital named Tex. The town seemed a figment of Norman Rockwell's imagination, and so did Peggy. She was still in high school, blond, beautiful and somewhat purer than the driven snow, certainly too naïve to be very interesting; Steiner was twenty-two, an ancient, lecherous cripple. They went to the movies, listened to records, hung out at the malt shop and necked in the car. Her father glared at John every time he brought her home.

It was perfect America, right down to the aggrieved father. It was the place Steiner had dreamed about through two tours in Vietnam, a wonderful respite from the real world—the sixties seemed to have passed it by—but a dream nonetheless. He couldn't bring himself to deflower the girl. It would have been unfair. After a time, his visits to Loomis only served to intensify his loneliness and her expectations, and he stopped going.

Even though he no longer felt very much like a Marine, Steiner still owed the Corps six months of his four-year hitch when he was released from the hospital in January 1970, and the Marines were determined that he should serve it out. He expected it would be a hollow exercise, since he couldn't march on his wounded leg or do many other Marine-like things, and it was. He was sent to Treasure Island for reassignment and waited four weeks there before the Marines decided he would complete his service behind a desk at Camp Pendleton, processing training forms.

Before reporting to Pendleton, Steiner decided to take some of the leave time owed him. He bought a Volkswagen and headed off to the Southwest. His trips to Loomis had always been fairly predictable, and this was the first time in years he'd traveled without an itinerary, on his own, outside the strictures of a hospital, a military base or a war zone, and the complete freedom of it was rather daunting. He felt aimless, floundering, not quite a Marine and not quite a civilian; it almost seemed a long-range recon patrol, and he was scouting the enemy through binoculars.

He especially felt that way in Las Vegas, which was his first stop. Although he wasn't much of a gambler, he'd always wanted to see the place—it was a city devoted to the pursuit of pleasure, and that was the nominal purpose of his trip. He wandered through the casinos feeling very *obvious* in his crew cut and leg brace as distracted crowds of gamblers swirled around him. It was all so disorganized, so extravagant and absurd. The cards at the blackjack tables and the craps moved too quickly for him to understand the games; the men wore fancy suits, the women were bedecked in furs and jewels. He felt like a malingerer, unsavory in some obscure way, and imagined that the casino guards were staring at him. He donated some money to a slot machine. He went to see Frank Gorshin, the comedian, perform at the Sahara and shared a booth with an elderly couple, who, he was certain, felt sorry for him. It was strange having to pay for dinner—fifteen dollars plus tip—after eating free for so many years. When the show was over, he found his car and went in search of a campsite.

It was winter, and cold in the desert. He spent several frigid nights camping at Hoover Dam, the Painted Desert and the Grand Canyon, where it snowed. His leg ached in the cold, but—once again—he found that he was more comfortable in the natural world than he'd been in civilization. He could spend hours watching the lizards basking in the weak winter sun; he was fascinated by the shapes and colors of the rock formations.

He went to Phoenix, where it was warmer, and decided to look up Ed Kalwara, who had been a machine gunner with Charlie Company. Kalwara was married, had a new baby and was overjoyed to see him. He jumped up and down, slapped him on the back and helped him unload the car. "What's this V for?" he asked, spotting a Navy Achievement Medal with a V for valor on the uniform Steiner had stowed in the trunk.

"Vanilla," John said.

They didn't talk at all about Vietnam. Kalwara mostly went on about his marriage—he loved the baby, but felt trapped and misunderstood by his wife. "I'm going stir crazy," he said.

They made plans to go out on the town, but Kalwara had some work to do first and Steiner decided to take a nap. He slept for more than a day. He vaguely remembered being moved from a couch to a bed, and Kalwara asking if he was all right. He wasn't sure. He didn't feel ill or weak, just tired and strange.

The atmosphere at Camp Pendleton was much different from the last time he'd been there, two years earlier. Perhaps it was only that Steiner's attitude toward the war and the service had changed, but a sense of defeat seemed to haunt the place. Troops were gradually being withdrawn from Vietnam and, despite the government's insistence that the war was being "Vietnamized," no one had any illusions about what the withdrawals really meant. The Marines were in the process of losing their first war, and were understandably demoralized. Beneath the rigid façade of discipline and order, there was a lax cynicism; only the most stubborn lifers continued to take the rituals of camp life seriously. The major topic of conversation was not the war, but the hippies, who were perversely fascinating to the Marines: They were the enemy, the American wing of the Viet Cong, camouflaged in weird clothes, winning the war at home as surely as their counterparts were in Vietnam. They had overwhelmed Camp Pendleton's social bastion, the town of Oceanside, and the Marines—confused, disheartened and envious—would watch them parading along the beach. One day Steiner and a friend were sitting on the hood of their car, watching the parade, pretending that the occasional taunts and sneers didn't bother them; they went off to a restaurant and, when they returned, found the air had been let out of their tires. Steiner couldn't help being curious about hippies and sometimes stopped to give them rides, enjoying their surprise when they realized they'd been picked up by the enemy. "Hey, man," one said, "a lot of Marines are becoming hippies."

"Well," he lamely replied, "a lot of hippies are becoming Marines. A lot more, I'll bet."

He was looking for a way to admit that he had changed his mind about the war without feeling like a traitor; in his heart he was still a grunt and stubbornly loyal to those he perceived as comrades. When the Ohio National Guard killed four students at Kent State University that spring, Steiner found that he identified with the guardsmen. He felt sorrier for them, being pelted with rocks and ordered to fire at unarmed targets, than for the students.

Nowhere was the disarray at Camp Pendleton more evident than in the office where Steiner glumly shuffled papers. His co-workers were obvious misfits: one was being hounded by creditors and would hide each time a civilian approached; another was always depressed and tried to commit suicide with an overdose of sleeping pills. Steiner couldn't wait to get out of there. He was looking forward to college—his mother had registered him at Diablo Valley College for the fall—and anxious to get on with his life. After several months at his desk job, he spotted a flier on a bulletin board for

Project Transition, which was a six-month job-training program for infantrymen who were leaving the service. All sorts of menial work were available; the Marines paid the salaries, and local employers were happy to get free labor. Steiner decided to learn how to cook. He figured it was a skill he could use to make money on the side in college; it certainly was better than hanging around the office.

He started in the pantry at the El Camino Country Club in Oceanside, making salads, but soon began to work his way up. The chef was an old Englishman named Harold Callaghan, who'd obviously seen better days. He was in his sixties, emaciated, with gray, greasy hair, but once he'd been head chef at one of Queen Elizabeth's more obscure castles. Even though he was constantly aquiver, he could be remarkably deft when the pressure was on. If a party of fifty suddenly arrived for dinner, Callaghan would bellow, "Stand aside!" and in a flurry of pots and pans, mixing, fussing, adding a pinch here and a pinch there, he'd fix all fifty meals and have everything come out perfectly. Steiner loved to watch him working breakfast, moving along a line of egg pans, holding two in each hand and flipping four eggs at once. He could make hollandaise sauce—a delicate operation—by dipping the ingredients in a stainless-steel bowl into the deep-fat fryer and cranking away with a wire whisk; he was magic. Callaghan took a liking to Steiner, taught him how to flip eggs and make perfect omelets and told him long, sometimes only vaguely coherent stories about cooking for the Queen. Steiner spent almost all his time at the country club, and earned some extra money working as a janitor there in the evenings; he returned to Pendleton only to sleep. He found that he truly enjoyed cooking— each meal was a challenge, it could be slapped together (usually the patrons didn't notice) or made perfect; he loved watching Callaghan nonchalantly creating perfection and, though he wasn't at all sorry to leave when September came, he decided that being a chef might not be a bad life if college didn't work out.

Before leaving the Marines, he was summoned to a review board to determine the size of his disability pension. The length of his scars was measured, and the length of his left leg (it was now an inch shorter than his right); he was told to flex his knee and walk about wearing his brace. When they asked about the pain, he said it was troublesome only on days when the barometric pressure was low. The board voted to retire him from the service with a 40 percent disability. Steiner felt cheated—the going rate for similar wounds seemed to be 50 or 60 percent—and decided to challenge the ruling. The board took its time considering his appeal and, apparently riled by his effrontery, eventually decided to *reduce* his disability to 30 percent. Later, realizing that he wasn't at all disabled in any practical sense, he was embarrassed that he had caused a fuss.

Diablo Valley College looked more like a shopping mall than an institution of higher learning. It was a cluster of modern buildings, surrounded by sloping acres of parking lots and populated by a bizarre assortment of academic dabblers, many of them attending school for form's sake, the dregs of their high school classes, refugees from the four-year colleges, earnest part-timers, underachievers like Steiner and countercultural flotsam. Marching up from the parking areas in the mornings, they looked like the cast for a summer stock production of *Oklahoma!*—lots of blue jeans, boots and bib overalls; the men wearing their hair long (ponytails were popular), with flamboyant sideburns and moustaches; the women in granny dresses and granny glasses, sometimes barefoot, often braless . . . and Steiner in his crew cut, which was growing out ever so slowly, wearing his clunky black military shoes because they were specially constructed to accommodate his leg brace. He often felt as if he had "Disabled Veteran" tattooed on his forehead. There were other veterans at DVC, but they tended to be older, beer-bellied, defiant squares, and Steiner, hoping to ingratiate himself with the young women, stayed clear of them. He didn't socialize very much at first, but studied hard, taking it all very seriously. His parents noticed the change immediately. Having spent his childhood dreading his father's interventions with math homework, John now sought Seth's help. When his mother praised him for getting a B on an English test, he scowled and said, "I want A's."

In addition to math (which, in his case, was remedial, high school algebra) and English, he took courses in biology, history (taught by a former Army officer who spent the semester knocking the war) and psychology. The latter was titled Fundamental Aspects of Psychology 121, but might better have been called Introduction to California 1970; it provided Steiner with a baptism into civilian life as unexpected as his first fire fight.

The professor insisted the class call him by his first name, which was James. (Steiner noticed that the use of surnames had pretty much disappeared in his absence; this was the exact opposite of the Marines, where first names were never used.) There was a reading list which included some Freud and lots of pop psychology books like *Games People Play*, but none of them were required. In fact, *nothing* was required. There were no tests or papers; classes were free-form, ersatz group therapy sessions. After years of living by the Marine code and keeping a tight rein on his emotions—he'd never been very demonstrative in any case—Steiner was nonplussed by the ability of many in the class to pour out their deepest feelings at the slightest provocation. Personal accusations—"You're not being honest about your feelings!"—flew back and forth like shrapnel. There was a strong subtext of sexual politics in all this, the men— usually more aggressive and accusatory—vying for the attention of the women. Sometimes James would have them play a version of musical chairs: they would wander through the classroom until he gave a signal, then sit down and have a heart-to-heart with the person closest. Steiner, in desperate need of a mate, would try to position himself near one or another of the more attractive women in the class, but his efforts to woo them usually proved frustrating. They spoke a different language; the rules of the game had changed drastically since he'd last been a civilian.

He spent most of his time in class trying to be inconspicuous until one day when the topic was "What's Wrong with This Class?" he decided to make his presence felt. Nervously, he stood and admitted, "Actually, I'm a little disappointed. When I signed up, I thought we were going to get into what the mind is all about. You know, what the ego and the id are . . ."

Earlier, Steiner had made a tentative move on one of the semi-attached women in the class and now he was interrupted by her would-be mate. "You're stupid," announced the aggrieved suitor. "You shouldn't have stayed in the class if it wasn't what you wanted. It's your own goddamn fault, and I don't want to hear anything more about it. You're wasting our time."

The gentleman had a point. Steiner's reasons for staying with the course had been prurient and vicarious; it was something like giving rides to hippies. He was learning the language and mores of his contemporaries, and didn't mind listening to pretty girls spill out their frustrations either. But he wasn't about to admit any of that, and so he defended himself: "Don't *you* tell me to shut up. He wants us to tell him what we think," he said, pointing to James.

"What do you think about this, James?" one of the other students asked.

"Well, I tend to agree with John," the teacher said, in what Steiner thought was a typically flaccid display of egregious sensitivity. "I'm particularly pleased with his willingness to say what he really believes. There are those who are looking for a more intellectual academic experience, and we should respect their views . . ."

To Steiner's astonishment, others in the class rose to his defense. "I . . . I think John was really *brave*," said one of the more emotional women. She seemed to be trembling on the brink of tears. It was unbelievable. "I thought it took a lot of courage for him to say that," she said softly, hiding her face, unable to look at him. "I wish he would share his feelings with us more often . . ."

The enemy routed, he began to feel more confident. He never quite lost the sense that he was on patrol in hostile territory, though; booby traps and ambushes abounded. One day he came to class and James said, "Today, I'd like each of you to tell us what you were doing a year ago."

For a moment, Steiner debated whether or not to startle them: "A year ago, I was a platoon sergeant, shooting gooks in the DMZ." Actually, a year earlier he'd been in the hospital, but he'd never admitted to the class that he was a veteran—he thought it was obvious to everyone—and was tempted now to shake them out of their smug, pseudo-therapeutic reverie. He wanted to tell them about Big Daddy with his guts hanging out struggling not to cry; about the woman begging him not to burn her hooch; about Sergeant Malloy's mangled body and Operation Cochise, all of it . . .

But then, a narcissistic hippie named Mark, very handsome and confident, with long, flowing blond hair, stood up and started talking about how, a year earlier, he'd been in an antiwar riot at Berkeley. Everyone in the class seemed impressed. He was a hero. When he finished his account with a ringing denunciation of the war—the *immorality* of it—he turned and gave John a long, meaningful look, as if to say, "Okay, defend yourself . . ."

John froze. He couldn't talk. He lost track of what was happening in the room, but realized they were debating his silence . . . and gradually became aware that, once again, people were defending him. The teacher said, "Well, not everyone is going to want to share their past and we should respect that."

A bronzed Adonis type then went after Mark the hippie: "You say you believe in peace and love, but you're always attacking everyone . . ."

Steiner realized that he was becoming an innocent bystander. All this was madness, all the true confessions, all the sharing of secret feelings . . . everyone had ulterior motives. At the end of the semester, James suggested they grade themselves.

Steiner gave himself an A.

After living with his parents for a brief time, he found an apartment near the college, in the town of Concord. It was a clean, modern and empty place, in a standard square, two-story building with a swimming pool in the inner courtyard. With little else but school to occupy him and feeling rather lonely in the apartment, Steiner decided to buy a fish for company. He borrowed an old tank from his parents and bought an angelfish, since it didn't need much more than the tank, water and some food to survive.

One fish led to another. The angelfish wasn't much of a challenge, and Steiner became interested in more exotic species. He read books about tropical fish and hung out in pet stores, asking the salesmen questions. He spent twenty dollars on a rudimentary filtration system and a heater, then decided it might be nice to have another tank. He bought several varieties of tetras, discuses, silver dollars, redfin sharks and shrimp.

The process really began to accelerate when one of the pet stores—Frank's Feed and Farm Supply—offered him a part-time job. He had money saved from the service, plus his disability benefits, and didn't really need the work, but it seemed an interesting job and, most important, he would get a 40 percent discount on all fish and accessories. He bought more tanks—hexagonal, long and narrow, tall and skinny, a huge seventy-five-gallon model he propped on bricks and redwood planks—and more sophisticated filtration systems. He decided it might be fun to try some saltwater species, and spent thirty dollars on a single coral-reef fish. He bought a lionfish, butterfly fish, puff-fish, blue-tangs and an anglerfish with a wormlike projectile that shot out of its snout.

Several of the more sensitive species died of nicotine poisoning—he was smoking two packs of cigarettes a day—but most of them thrived. Soon he had between eighty and a hundred fish, and his apartment was filled with tanks of all shapes and sizes. The air was muggy, positively tropical, because of the evaporation from the tanks. He would sit watching them glide placidly through the undulating plants, luminous shards of brilliant color, and listen to the water bubbling gently in the air compressors; sometimes, watching them, he would put on his favorite record album, *Sounds of Silence*, by Simon and Garfunkel.

When he was asked to do a biology project on animal behavior during his second semester at DVC, it seemed logical that he do something about fish, but he was at a loss for a topic. His fish didn't *behave* very much; they just hung out. But he'd read about a species that exhibited dramatic behavior—Siamese fighting fish, also known as bettas—and decided to buy a half dozen and study them. This meant buying more tanks as well; the males had to be kept apart or they'd kill each other. His project was to establish a pecking order, then see if he could reverse it by starving the more dominant fish. He set up a neutral tank for jousts and would drop the bettas in, two at a time, and watch them have at each other. He stopped the fights when the result was clear—one of the fish would cower in a low corner of the tank—and before any real damage could be done. It wasn't the most profound study, he later realized, but it worked—he was able to reverse the alpha and omega males (he called the paper "Alpha Betta")—and it was fun. He received another A for it.

He had registered as a history major, but was finding that he was far more interested in biology. High school biology had been boring—the only things he remembered were dissecting frogs and pricking his finger to determine his blood type—but the courses at DVC were a revelation. His second-semester class spent a good deal of time in the field, watching the behavior patterns of ducks, studying the tide pools in Mendocino, collecting butterflies, insects and wildflowers. It was the sort of thing he'd always loved but had been too embarrassed to pursue, and now he began to wonder if he might, in some way, make a career of it. He decided to switch majors, and try some serious biology courses.

His interest in biology had another lucky side effect: it provided an unexpectedly congenial way for him to make his peace with the antiwar movement. Environmentalism suddenly had become as hot an issue as Vietnam among campus radicals; hundreds of thousands across the country had protested on Earth Day. And though Steiner considered much of the "ecology" movement trendy and superficial—symbolized, he believed, by the unconscious irony of antipollution bumper stickers on *cars*—he found that he was impressed by its basic validity. He read *Silent Spring* by Rachel Carson, heard Dr. Barry Commoner speak, and slowly realized that everything fit together: the population explosion, the use of pesticides, the various industrial depredations. His enlightenment wasn't dramatic—there was no one moment when he decided to devote his life to the cause—but it proceeded inexorably, and was blissfully free of the mixed feelings and confusion that had plagued him about Vietnam: when he saw petroleum-covered ducks struggling to survive after the great Santa Barbara oil spill, he could be unreservedly outraged. He wasn't the sort to protest noisily, and was still too self-conscious to involve himself in environmental circles at DVC, but, for once, he felt the satisfaction of having some common ground with his contemporaries.

Meanwhile, he was becoming something of a celebrity in his apartment building. Word of his fish had spread, and the neighbors were curious. The Siamese fighting fish were especially popular, but Steiner—not wanting to turn his aquarium into a circus—kept their jousts private, and only allowed his guests the vicarious thrill of feeding time. One of his more frequent guests was Buddy Sanderson, who had served in the Navy and was now working in a factory. Buddy, in turn, brought his cousin Stan to visit, and Stan went wild over the fish. He peppered Steiner with questions—"Where does that one come from?" "Is that one easy to keep?"—and listened with real interest as John held forth on the lifestyle of bettas and the feeding habits of anglerfish. Stan loved animals, and said that he was thinking about raising rabbits.

"Really?" Steiner said. "I'd like to do that too."

"Then let's do it together," Stan said.

Stan had also been in the Navy, and was now working on a construction job. He was talkative, intelligent and constantly surrounded by women. He quickly pulled Steiner into his social circle, taking him to parties, introducing him grandly: "This is John Steiner. He's a *Marine*, and he just got back from Vietnam."

Steiner was embarrassed by such effusions, and often with good cause. More than one woman responded by saying, "That's *his* problem," or grimacing to similar effect. But Sanderson, ever jovial, didn't seem to notice negative reactions. Steiner soon realized that the secret of Stan's success with women was that he approached almost all of them on the theory that a certain percentage would always accept, although those who did tended not to be the sort of women Steiner would bring home to meet his parents. They were more obvious than sleazy, often young divorcées saddled with incongruous children, afraid they were no longer alluring to men and desperate to prove otherwise. Sanderson flattered them, teased them, mocked them (he called them names like Rhoda Rooter and Nita What), but it didn't seem to make much difference. Two or three always seemed to be hanging around Stan's apartment and, if he was otherwise occupied, they had few qualms about attaching themselves to whoever was available. At first, Steiner was reluctant to join in—one night, a woman who worked in a sausage factory chased him around Stan's apartment, trying to undress him—but, gradually, he became less diffident and rationalized that if it wasn't perfect, it was the only social life available at the moment.

Steiner didn't care for the way Sanderson treated women. He thought he drank too much and lacked responsibility, but liked him anyway. Stan was always good for a laugh, always interested in the things Steiner was doing—interested in *him*—the only real friend he had in those lonely postwar years. And when Stan suggested that they share a house together, Steiner agreed. It was a bargain—the rent was only $195—a standard tract house in Concord which soon became a neighborhood curiosity, filled as it was with Steiner's fish, Sanderson's women, their rabbits, four dogs and a Siamese cat; there also were chickens, a goat grazing in the backyard, a boa constrictor and, briefly, a python in the kitchen (the python bit Steiner and was returned to the pet store), as well as a supply of white rats to feed the snakes. Sanderson was an easygoing housemate. Responsibilities were shared: both cooked—though Stan's repertoire was limited to macaroni and cheese—and neither cleaned. Occasionally, a hasty effort would be made to put the house in order when guests were expected. Snake feeding was a popular ritual with their friends, especially after two rattlesnakes were added to the menagerie.

The rattlesnakes were caught in the desert by a truck driver friend of Stan's, and Steiner decided to use them for his next biology project. He had a special, somewhat inexplicable affinity for snakes; he liked the way they looked and moved, was intrigued by their primordial nature and imagined them a direct link to the dinosaurs. Watching them coil and strike, seeing the rats convulse and die, he wondered if it was possible to immunize a rat to rattlesnake venom. He learned how to milk the snakes, stretching Saran Wrap over a sterilized jar—when the fangs pierced the membrane, the venom flowed. He would then take a drop of the venom and inject it into a white rat. He killed several immediately, trying to determine a lethal dose, but eventually was able to find a level where the rats went into convulsions but lived. He gradually increased the dosage and, finally, when the paper was due, gave one of the rats an injection that should have been lethal; the rat went into a coma. Steiner kept a cage-side vigil and, when the rat did not revive, concluded his paper: "At the time of this writing, the rat is still unconscious but will probably recover."

The rat eventually pulled through, but his paper was only a marginal success. He was a biology major now, in a class of serious students, and the professor was critical of his imprecise methodology. How much, for example, was a "drop" of venom? He received a B for the paper and realized he'd have to be far more scientific in the future, but doubted that he'd ever have the patience for serious biological research. What's more, with the ecology movement so popular, biology had become a "hot" field; a great many people would be competing for very few jobs, and he was beginning to wonder if there was any practical future in it for him.

He kept at it, though. Trying to make up for lost time, he decided not to break for the summer and took a course in anatomy. He found, somewhat to his surprise, that he was bothered by the cadavers they studied. The dead bodies brought back painful memories, which were intensified when the instructor—who had long hair, a beard, and made no secret of his politics—found Steiner's cigarette lighter in the cadaver room. He had bought the lighter in Phu Bai, during his first tour. It was inscribed: "John Steiner, Charlie Company, First Battalion, Third Marines," and had a list of the company's operations and a Marine Corps insignia. "*Who* is this John Steiner?" the instructor asked—rather sarcastically, Steiner thought—and when John identified himself, the instructor gave him a long, disgusted look that could not be misinterpreted. He had to work especially hard for his B that semester.

Despite that incident, he no longer felt so obvious on campus. He had pretty much discarded his steel brace by then, his leg was stronger and his hair longer. Days, sometimes weeks would go by without him thinking about the war, but it was never far from his consciousness, and would surface at the oddest times.

He and Sanderson had raised their rabbits with the intention of eating some eventually. It was something he'd often done with his father before the war, but he found it rather more difficult now. The killing didn't bother him—he would simply snap the rabbit's neck, a quick, painless cervical dislocation—but the butchering was something else again. Each time he stuck his knife into a rabbit's stomach and smelled the warm, sticky sweet blood, he would remember the stench of dead bodies in the field. Rabbit blood and human blood smelled the same. His reaction to the smell wasn't very dramatic; he wasn't overwhelmed by horrific visions or emotional memories of Vietnam. He did feel queasy and nauseated. He didn't want to admit his discomfort to Sanderson and, for a time, continued to slaughter the rabbits, hoping that he'd grow accustomed to it. He didn't, and eventually decided that he just couldn't do it anymore.

4

Steiner worked hard at Diablo Valley College. It was as if he was hoping not only to recapture the years he'd given the Marines but also to erase the war itself from his memory. Vietnam was always there, on television and in the newspapers, a waning clangor that still could bring him up short when a familiar place was mentioned. It was there on cold, damp days when his leg ached; he still used the steel brace when he had to stand for more than a few hours. It was there, less obviously, in the discomfort he felt when dealing with much of the World. He kept his distance; not exactly withdrawn, but cool and clipped even when he was trying to be friendly. He found relaxation difficult—he might be caught off guard, ambushed again—and so he worked.

Steiner's only real friend remained Sanderson, his housemate, who was able to pierce John's protective shell simply by refusing to acknowledge it. Stan continued to drag him into conversation and off to parties; his careless good humor was the perfect antidote to John's terse vigilance. And then, in the spring of 1972, Sanderson simply disappeared. John didn't take it personally; it was bound to happen sooner or later, given Stan's mercurial nature. He was left with a wad of unpaid bills and the menagerie—the dogs, cats, chickens, rabbits, rats, snakes and goat—to care for. He decided to take a second part-time job (he continued to work at the pet store) as a short-order cook, to pay the bills and fill the empty hours. He also began to look for someone else to share the house.

One possibility was Joe Raymond, his old friend from infantry training school and Camp Pendleton, who'd recently entered DVC as a business major. Like Steiner, Raymond had returned to Vietnam for a second tour after the Tet offensive, and—like Steiner—he'd been seriously wounded. He had tripped a booby trap filled with white phosphorus, which scorched most of his body. Only his face was spared. He was in constant pain, often returning to Oak Knoll Naval Hospital for skin grafts. He had tried to escape the agony through pain-killers and marriage, both of which proved disastrous. Steiner felt sorry for him; but he also found that it was easier to spend time with Raymond than with most of his classmates. There was no danger of being asked, "What was it *like* over there?" Or "Did you ever kill anyone?" Or "How come you couldn't get out of it?" Not that people often asked those things; it was just that they might.

So he invited Joe Raymond to share the house, and soon discovered that it was much harder to live with a woeful relic of the war than with the threat of civilians invading his privacy. Joe was a mess, his charred body a constant reminder of things best forgotten. He lived in darkness; most of his sweat glands had been destroyed, and the California sun caused him to overheat. He seemed to have given up, and spent most of his time watching television. He loved the show "Kung Fu," a peculiar artifact of the early 1970s, with its commercially astute combination of violence and ersatz Eastern philosophy; Steiner thought it was stupid. Despite his best intentions, he was repelled by Raymond and sought ways to get rid of him, especially after he began to complain about the animals.

"You didn't tell me there were going to be all these animals here," Joe would say.

"You *saw* them here when I showed you the place."

"Yeah, but I don't like eating with a bunch of rats in the kitchen. It bums me out."

"The rats were here before you were," Steiner said. "Back off."

Raymond stayed for only a few months. Eventually, he went back to the hospital for another skin graft and then decided to move north, where he wouldn't have to worry so much about overheating.

That summer, Steiner was undone by exhaustion and trigonometry. The exhaustion was the inevitable result of going to school in the mornings, working afternoons at the pet store and cooking evenings at Carrows, one of a chain of moderate-priced "family" restaurants. The trigonometry was a requirement of his biology major, and not nearly as much fun as watching rattlesnakes eat rats . . . or restaurant work, for that matter. He would pop Benzedrines and try to study trig functions between orders for late-night hamburgers and omelets, only to forget everything he'd crammed by the time he arrived at school the next morning.

He had gone to college for six semesters without a break, and was beginning to tire of it. He wondered if a degree in biology would be worth anything in the real world; it sometimes seemed half the college students in California wanted to earn a living saving the earth. How could he compete for jobs against hotshots from schools like Stanford or Berkeley?

His future in the restaurant business appeared far more promising. Having been trained by a master, he was far superior to the standard run of hash slingers who darkened the kitchens of Carrows, and he soon attracted the attention of Ian McConnaughy, the district manager. In late summer of 1972, McConnaughy offered him a spot in a management training program, with the promise of a restaurant of his own after six months. "It could be worth a lot of money to you," McConnaughy said. "Maybe as much as fifty thousand dollars a year."

Steiner was impressed. Biologists didn't make near that much, and his future as a biologist was far from certain. He told his parents about the offer, expecting the worst. But his mother said, "John, we never demanded that our kids go to college. If it's what you want to do, do it."

He became assistant manager of the Carrows in Santa Clara that September, and was determined to impress the higher-ups by working as hard as he could. He worked the cash register, learned how to schedule employees and do the billing; he cooked when they were short-handed and even waited tables when there was an unexpected rush. He worked seven days a week, abandoning any pretense of a life outside his job and eventually moving into a small room upstairs at the restaurant that was fitted out with a cot and a shower. He imagined himself an eccentric of sorts, the phantom of the restaurant, a character out of Steinbeck's *Cannery Row*; there were times he didn't leave the premises for days on end.

His immediate superior, the restaurant manager, was more than happy to take advantage of an assistant who not only was eager to please but was accessible twenty-four hours a day. Steiner's putative hours were from seven in the morning till seven at night, but the manager felt free to summon him down from his room whenever a crisis arose, and there were crises nearly every day. Soon John was working more than one hundred hours per week, and was as tired as he'd ever been on patrol in Vietnam. His eyes burned; he couldn't think straight. Months passed this way. It was, he later realized, a kind of madness.

After five months and no word from McConnaughy, he became convinced that he'd been lured into a trap. They were just using him; there would be no restaurant to manage when the training was over. He was sure they would try to find a way to continue to exploit him. Unless he did something dramatic, he might spend the rest of his life a galley slave. His mother had been pressing him to take a vacation. "You've been working too hard," she said. "You need a rest. Why not take a military flight to Hawaii?" The more he thought about it, the better it sounded. He had thousands of dollars in the bank and, having been retired from the service, the promise of free travel on military aircraft anywhere in the world. He needn't stop at Hawaii, he realized; he could go on to Australia, and scuba-dive along the Great Barrier Reef.

He found it inexplicably hard to leave Carrows. He delayed confronting the restaurant manager with his decision, and finally left a note on his desk. Years later, he would remember the exact words: "On careful consideration, I have decided that this is not the life for me. Sincerely, John Steiner." The manager didn't seem very upset. He asked John when he planned to leave.

"Well, I'll stick around until you find a replacement," he volunteered.

McConnaughy, having learned of his decision, suddenly arrived and was outraged that John had been allowed to live upstairs and made to work so hard. He promised a transfer to a restaurant in the Los Angeles area.

"No, no, you don't understand," Steiner said, surprised by how distraught he felt. His voice was quivering; for some reason, he was on the brink of tears. "I've made a *decision.* I'm *leaving.*"

His flight to Hawaii was eerie. He took off from Travis Air Force Base in a C-141, the very same sort of plane in which he had flown back to Danang after the Tet offensive. He sat in a webbed jump seat like a paratrooper, looking out at the huge open cargo bay; he felt strange not being in uniform. When he landed at Hickam Air Force Base, he felt the same old hot, sticky tropical air—it was all too familiar. Then he was walking through the terminal, the very same waiting room where, five years earlier, he had watched the blonde in the bikini on television say that grunts were just a bunch of baby-killers.

In December 1968, the terminal had been bustling with soldiers and sailors, spiffy and purposeful, heading home to the States or west to the war, but now something very strange had happened. The place was filled with *hippies.* They were lounging on sleeping bags and playing guitars, drawing angry looks from the military brass passing through. At first, Steiner couldn't imagine why Hickam Air Force Base had been overrun by hippies, and then he realized that they were former grunts. On closer inspection, he noticed that many were missing arms and legs, ears and fingers; they had plastic noses, glass eyes, skin patched together like an old afghan; some had bodies that were whole, but were betrayed by their eyes—that blasted, haunted look they had called the "thousand-yard stare" in Vietnam. All of them had been wounded grievously enough to receive disabilities and be retired from the service, and were taking advantage of their free travel privileges, just as he was. Many were in their old combat fatigues and field jackets; many had long, flowing hair and wore beads. They had the battered, scruffy yet defiant look of a defeated army, which was—Steiner realized with a start—exactly what they were. They welcomed him as a brother.

Hickam AFB was the hub of the Military Airlift Command (MAC) in the Pacific. There were flights to all sorts of exotic places. The flight to Australia stopped at Wake Island, American Samoa and New Zealand, all of which sounded magical to Steiner. But there was a problem: there were only two such flights each week, and a long waiting list. He realized that that was the reason for the ghost army in the terminal. They were waiting for flights.

There were two classes of MAC passengers: active-duty personnel on orders and everyone else. The latter category was called Space Available (or Space A) and was divided into four subgroups—active duty on emergency leave, active duty on regular leave, dependents of those on active duty and, finally, retirees. As a retiree, Steiner was lowest-priority; it might be weeks before he'd catch a flight to Australia. He decided to sign up for Japan as well, figuring he'd take whichever came first.

The intricacies of Space A flying was the prime topic of conversation among those who waited in the terminal at Hickam, and also at the nearby transit barracks where they could sleep for just $2.80 per night. Some had been using the system for years and knew it inside out: flight schedules, military bases where the waiting lists were relatively short, the quickest way to get from place to place. The system afforded room to maneuver, and creativity was prized. Inevitably, someone would brag: "Hey, see that guy over there? He just got in. He was seventy-five names *ahead* of me on the list at Clark [AFB, in the Philippines], and *I* got here three days ago." And then everyone would want to know how he'd done it. The secret usually involved hopscotching from base to base in search of a short waiting list.

There were some legendary Space A fliers. One was Steve Thomas, a former Army surveyor who'd lost an eye to a sniper in Vietnam, and he soon became Steiner's mentor. He had been using the system for years, but was proudest of the time he finessed a trip from Guam to Hawaii via Thailand, where a military coup had discouraged other travelers. Thomas and the other Space A veterans could talk endlessly about the places they'd been and the things they'd seen. They would compare passports, which usually bulged with additional sections to accommodate customs stamps from the hundreds of places they'd visited. They talked of Saudi Arabia as if it were the next town over, compared the relative merits of Karachi and Katmandu, argued whether the best route to Africa was to fly east or west. The one place in the world they never mentioned was Vietnam. Steiner could understand how Space A might easily become addictive.

He relaxed for about a week in Hawaii, swimming, sunbathing, learning the ropes from the experts. He felt more comfortable, more at peace with himself and the world, than at any time he could remember. He did not stop to consider how ironic it was that he'd only found peace by returning to the shelter of the military. Space A promised all the camaraderie of the grunts, and none of the pain. It was a phantom branch of the service, where the only orders were for R & R.

5

Two years later, Steiner watched the fall of Saigon on television. The North Vietnamese Army, finally emerging from the foliage, entered the city in a traditional column of tanks. Days earlier, Danang had fallen (or been liberated—he wasn't sure which). He remembered roaring through those streets in his jeep, hailed by the locals: "GI numbah one!"—the same people probably would rip him to shreds now, if given the chance. South Vietnam, the illusion for which he'd fought and nearly died, disappeared like cellophane set afire.

He followed these events from the relative tranquility of Chico State University in California, where he had resumed his career as a biology student, having learned that travel—when overdone—can be more flattening than broadening. He had been to Australia, Japan, Thailand, Taiwan, Samoa, Guam, even Ethiopia, all of which were memorable, but unrelievedly exotic after a while. He made the decision to return to college during a four-month stay at Heron Island on the Great Barrier Reef in Australia. It was an easy, restful time and he passed much of it on the beach, reading—Charles Darwin on coral reefs, among others—and thinking. He collected shells, quit smoking, hung out with the biologists from the local marine research station and cooked part-time at the island's resort hotel when his money ran low. Each afternoon, he'd strap on his scuba gear and explore the reef, which seemed an immense tropical fish tank, filled with the most beautiful plants and animals he'd ever seen. He realized that he'd given up too quickly on biology; even if the hotshots from Stanford and Berkeley were destined to get the best jobs, there had to be a place in the field for him—*if* he worked up to his "potential." It was time, he realized, to exorcise that demon.

Chico State was a four-year school located at the northern tip of the Sacramento Valley, near the rugged foothills of the Sierras in California gold rush country. He lived in a dormitory, a twenty-seven-year-old junior, surrounded by students seven to ten years younger. He didn't have much in common with them under the best of circumstances, but was dumbfounded by their indifference to the fall of Saigon. They simply didn't care about Vietnam; it was history. The enormity of the events that glued him to the television each night in late April and early May barely touched their consciousness. He thought about Sergeant Malloy, and Szuminski crawling out of the paddy to safety, and Big Daddy struggling not to cry, the wounded and the dead . . . There wasn't even the requisite bull session in the dorm about what a waste it had been. It was gone, and no one cared. It was May, and they talked about summer.

Steiner had, by then, established himself as a favorite of the biology faculty at Chico. The professors tended to be much more his peers than the kids in the dorm. Many of them were young and hip in an unthreatening, botanical way. They had distilled the upheavals of the 1960s into a lifestyle grounded in whole grains, herbal tea, polished oak and measured humanitarian concern. It was a style that appealed to Steiner, and the rigor of his commitment to biology appealed to them in turn.

Late one night his faculty adviser, Robert Ettiger, had found John organizing a collection of pressed plants in the cafeteria. He had commandeered most of the table space in the room, and was preparing labels for each of his specimens. Ettiger stopped to admire the neatness and quality of the work, then said, "John, are you planning to go on with this? Are you thinking about graduate school?"

"I don't know," Steiner said. "It's pretty hard to get a job in biology."

"*You* won't have any trouble," Ettiger said.

That summer, Ettiger showed him how easy it could be with the right connections. The Biology Department ran a month-long field research program at Eagle Lake, near Lassen Peak in northern California. It was required for all biology majors and just the sort of work Steiner loved—outdoor seminars in ornithology, field botany and aquatic ecology, as well as an independent research project (his was a census of the garter snake population at a nearby lake). The month was almost over when Ettiger learned that late funding had come through for a summer job with the rangers at Lassen Volcanic National Park. He thought Steiner would be just right for the position.

He sent John to be interviewed by the chief park naturalist, a casual, friendly man named Dick Vance, who explained the opening was for someone who'd entertain the tourists with slide shows and nature walks. "You'll have to lead people through the wilderness," he said. "Think you can handle that?"

"Well, I used to do it all the time," Steiner said. "I was a platoon sergeant in Vietnam." Vance laughed and gave him the job.

He was quartered, rather undramatically, in a mobile home in the park's trailer camp, which he shared with another novice ranger named Bill Jong. They each had been asked to prepare a slide show about wildlife at Lassen, and Steiner was worried. He had visions of himself, wooden and foolish in his Smokey the Bear hat, droning: "This is a picture of a muskrat . . ." while kids fidgeted and parents snored. He didn't want to be just another tediously edifying park ranger, and so he decided to take some chances. He would tell jokes, keep the kids involved by asking them questions, make it seem as spontaneous as possible. He labored at this spontaneity for more than a week, selecting slides from the library at park headquarters, organizing them, practicing alone in the darkness until very late each night.

His first presentation was at a nearby resort hotel, and he was amazed to find two hundred people—mostly families, wall-to-wall wholesomeness, decked out rather officially in denim and plaid and hiking boots—waiting to hear him. He had organized his show from the smallest animals in the park to the largest, and he nervously started in on the insects. He sensed their interest when he talked about garter snakes, his specialty (he could get very excited over garter snakes), and when he told a joke about a skunk—not a very good joke either—there were giggles from the kids, and appreciative groans from the adults. He *had* them now; he found that he could sense their involvement, and when it flagged he would ask a question or tell a joke or change the pace of the slides. His high, squeaky voice seemed constitutionally incapable of droning; his genuine enthusiasm about nature proved contagious. At the end, he said, "Now, what do you suppose the *largest* animal is at Lassen Park?"

The kids shouted various possibilities: grizzly bears, mountain lions . . . and Steiner flashed a slide of Bigfoot. There was laughter and applause and, afterwards, congratulations from his roommate, Bill Jong, who had come along for moral support. "Steiner," he said, "that was an A-plus."

He was even better at nature walks. It was odd at first, being back in uniform, leading patrols through the forest, but it didn't bother him. In fact, he played off his memories of Vietnam, enjoying the contrasts . . . the enormous luxury of not having to worry that his next step might be his last. He was exhilarated by the absence of terror, and improvised wildly along the trail. Each new trek became an adventure. Sometimes he would play squad leader, holding up a hand and shushing his chaotic line of flannel-shirted irregulars, in the hope of ambushing some natural wonder or other. More often, Steiner burbled uncontrollably as he walked point: "Hey! Wow! Look at that!" as a family of deer danced off into the shadowy pine forest. And "Hey, look at this. This is a really *amazing* flower. It's called a monkshood . . . can you figure out why?"

One day, near the end of summer, he led a group to the edge of a clearing near a placid lake and saw a golden eagle swoop down from the sky and snatch up a fawn in its talons. The magnificent bird tried to rise, flapping its wings in a furious attempt to carry off the fawn, lifting it three feet off the ground . . . then dropping it back, stunned and bleeding. The mother deer came to the rescue then and, pushing the fawn with her head, nudged it up and into the safety of the forest.

Steiner was awestruck, and ecstatic. He couldn't believe his good fortune: the United States government was actually *paying* him to do the one thing in life he enjoyed most.

When he returned to Chico that September, Steiner fell in love. It was an experience as unexpected and breathtaking as his interlude with the eagle and the fawn. He was twenty-eight years old and had never been in love before. He could recall infatuations, dalliances, yearnings, but nothing resembling a serious romance. He had almost given up hope, by then, of finding a cure for the loneliness that had been part of his life for as long as he could remember. Over the years, he had lowered his expectations, tending to befriend women who attracted him rather than make passes at them, women like Eve Holguin, who had lived across the hall from him in the dorm the year before.

Eve was a junior, an accounting major from Los Angeles. She was a Mexican-American, and Steiner was intrigued by the contrast between her looks, which were exotic—long dark hair, dark eyes and olive skin—and her personality, which was unpretentious, friendly, funny and kind. She had a boyfriend, of course. His name was Steve, and he would visit her occasionally from Los Angeles; they were considered a unit: "Eve 'n' Steve."

Eve Holguin's initial impression of Steiner was that he was strange. She first noticed him in the dorm cafeteria, his dark hair plastered down—he had just taken a shower—a weird-looking guy, very quiet, a campus eccentric. They bumped into each other frequently after that, and Eve found that she enjoyed his company. He was filled with all sorts of facts about animals and nature, history and politics. He could explain the importance of the Bay of Pigs or the fall of Saigon in a way that was interesting to her, though she cared little about politics. When his hair dried, he looked much better, although he did have a dark, bushy moustache that seemed borrowed from some nineteenth-century outlaw. His eyes could be startling at times, a brilliant blue-green, with long, delicate lashes; they conveyed a certain innocence and fragility. She could hardly believe he'd been a soldier. He was very friendly, but distant in an odd way, and tightly clenched—impersonal more than shy. He never gossiped about other people or complained. He was resolutely cheerful. On the whole, his kindnesses outweighed his constrictions: he was intelligent, faithful, unthreatening—a human porpoise—and she never doubted that his intentions were honorable.

Steiner assumed that "Eve 'n' Steve" was an immutable fact, and kept his distance until, returning to school in September, he learned that Eve had jettisoned Steve. She was no longer living in the dorm, but in an apartment with three other women. Steiner found every possible excuse to hang out there, his motives obvious to everyone. Finally, he gathered his courage and made what was, for him, a rather brazen move.

"I'm going to Paradise to buy a rat," he announced to Eve one afternoon. Paradise was the town west of Chico. The rat was for a biology project. "You want to come?"

"Sure," she said.

Several miles west of Chico on the road to Paradise, the earth falls away precipitously into an enormous canyon, miles wide and thousands of feet deep. Steiner pulled his Volkswagen off to the side of the road, and they stopped to admire the scenery—the alluvial

strata of pale rose and olive, the jagged erosions casting violent afternoon shadows, hawks wheeling a thousand feet down in the hazy
sun and, below them, the silver thread of Big Chico Creek. Steiner
explained that layers of silt and mud had been covered over by a
cap of solid basaltic lava; the mud eroded away beneath the lava,
which eventually collapsed, leaving the sheer cliffs. Eve nodded,
standing at the edge, staring down. "I'm scared, I'm scared," she
said playfully. He reached out, pretending to save her. They scuffled, giggling. There was, for the first time, a hint of sexual electric-
ity between them.

Several days later, Eve and her roommates had a party. Em-
boldened by the rat-buying expedition, Steiner cornered her in the
kitchen late in the evening and kissed her; much to his relief, she
didn't object. Within a few weeks, they were inseparable. By the end
of the semester, they were living together.

They lived together happily, if tentatively. They were good at the
day-to-day things—cooking, cuddling, studying together, chatting—but when the level of discourse threatened to become more
serious, there were problems. John's commitment to Eve was as
complete as it was sudden; he was ready to spend the rest of his life
with her, but he was uncomfortable discussing anything so personal.
Eve was quite the opposite: she needed to rummage through her
feelings and she wanted John to talk about his. She was reluctant to
do anything final; she couldn't even admit they actually were living
together. She never stopped paying the rent on her old apartment,
though her presence there had been reduced to a box of belongings hidden away in a closet. She claimed that she'd made a financial
commitment to her roommates and that she didn't want her father
to know she was living in sin. At the same time she knew there was
more to it than that.

Eve had been one of seven children, an awkward, spindly girl—
hopelessly ugly, she was convinced—very shy, and very close to her
mother; her father was more remote, a quiet man who concentrated
his energies on building his small construction company into a larger

one. When Eve was in the eighth grade, her mother died of cancer. She was gone before Eve quite understood what was happening. In an instant, it seemed, she had lost her best friend, protector and only confidante.

Later, she became convinced that the sudden loss of her mother had made her frightened of forming close attachments. She'd had several boyfriends, none of whom had been able to penetrate her defenses. John Steiner had taken her by surprise. He'd been a friend, and then a *close* friend, and then something more than that.

One night, they were cuddling on the couch and John blurted, "I love you."

"Oh, Johhhhn," she said. "Don't start that."

He retreated immediately, without asking "Why not?" or getting angry, or even sulking. He just let it drop. Eve was perplexed by this. She wanted the conversation, but not necessarily the commitment; he wanted the commitment, but not the conversation. It was their usual impasse.

But she didn't want to disappoint him either. She could see it in his eyes, feel it in his silences. She had come to depend on his stability, somewhat to her dismay. She was beginning to have job interviews with various accounting firms, a terrible ordeal; she felt gawkier than at any time since eighth grade. John was always there when she came home from an interview addled by all the stupid things she had said; he was always there to reassure her, and cheer her up with some obscure fact about his beloved garter snakes. Finally, grudgingly, she admitted she loved him.

Which only raised the stakes. She knew he wanted to get married. He never came out and said so, but she knew it. The unasked question clouded their lives, along with other, more immediate uncertainties: What were they going to do when she graduated? He would be staying on at Chico for at least another two years, working toward his master's degree. But she had no idea where she was headed. She wanted to land a job with one of the Big Eight accounting firms. The tension—interviews, waiting for calls for second interviews, then waiting again—was unbearable. She suffered migraine headaches and cried a lot. John would hold her in his arms, rock her, stroke her hair. Occasionally, he would say, "Wouldn't it be nice if we could always be together like this?" Usually, she could manage little more than a grunt in response to this oblique proposal.

Meanwhile, he was doing quite well in graduate school. He had taken an exam to become a teaching assistant, and placed second out of fifty-five applicants. He was given human anatomy and zoology to teach, the latter a real plum—only the best graduate students taught zoology. He was frightened at first, but his experiences at Lassen Park had served him well—teaching was not that different from giving a nature talk; he could make zoology exciting for undergraduates. Word of his talent began to spread through the department.

One day, Donald Wooton, the department chairman, caught John as he was cleaning up after a zoology lab. "Steiner," he asked, "what was your undergraduate grade point average?"

"Three point nine."

"Keep that up," he said, "and I might be able to get you into the doctoral program in agricultural entomology at Kansas State."

"Are you kidding?" Steiner asked. Agricultural entomology—pest control, essentially—was Dr. Wooton's specialty, and Kansas State was said to have the world's best program in the field. Steiner's area of interest was the physical ecology of cold-blooded animals, but Dr. Wooton knew he liked bugs almost as much as garter snakes; in his spare time John had been using an electron micrograph to construct a detailed picture of a beetle's face and Wooton had admired his work.

"I don't know," Steiner said, flattered the department chairman would consider him so talented, but dubious. "Kansas State is really high-pressure, and I can hardly stand the pressure here."

"You don't seem to be suffering all that much."

"Yeah, but that's *here*," Steiner said, lamely.

"Well, think about it."

"Okay," Steiner said, but he couldn't take the offer very seriously. It seemed that even when he worked up to his "potential" people wanted to push him further. He decided not to worry about it. There was plenty of time yet, he still had a master's thesis to finish, and the situation with Eve to resolve.

She had decided to go home to Los Angeles after graduation.

None of the Big Eight wanted her; she'd also been unable to find work with any of the better accounting firms in San Francisco or Sacramento. There were several possibilities in Los Angeles, and she intended to pursue them.

Steiner accepted his fate with equanimity. He knew they would be separated for at least the next two years. There was nothing he could do to hold her, nor did he dare to try—that would be as unproductive as it was unfair. He did hope for some commitment from her before she left; he needed to believe their separation would only be temporary.

There is some doubt as to whether he ever actually uttered the words "Will you marry me?" Steiner thinks he did; Eve isn't so sure. She remembers him hinting more pointedly than usual. The actual proposal, she believes, was still something on the order of "Wouldn't it be nice if we could always be together like this?" In any case, instead of her usual noncommittal shrug she offered a muffled assent. He immediately insisted they call his parents and tell them they were going to be married.

Eve thought he was rushing things, but she was reassured by the fact that it would obviously have to be a long engagement, two years at least.

Steiner had other ideas. He pushed ahead with plans. A wedding date was set, a family ring refurbished. The Holguins were invited north to meet the Steiners, at which time John surprised Eve with the diamond over breakfast. "Here you go," he said, slipping the ring on her finger. She was embarrassed. Her grandmother said it was beautiful.

Eve found work in a Beverly Hills accounting firm, and started studying seriously for her CPA exam. Her life was crowded with these things, and she had little time—and less inclination—to get into a confrontation with John over the wedding. It rankled, though; he was pushing too hard.

His monthly visits to Eve's home in Santa Monica were another source of tension between them. Her brothers and sisters were always around, talking about cars and fashion and football. The sisters called him "Smokey the Bear." The brothers tried to be friendly, attempting to lure him into arguments over the 49ers' chances that year. He knew the 49ers were a football team, but not much more than that. His relations with Eve's father consisted of uncomfortable silences, interrupted occasionally by strangled attempts to find some common ground. When he was alone with Eve, he talked about the wedding—hoping to wrest a confirmation of continued interest from her. He knew he was pushing too hard. He pretended not to notice Eve's reluctance, but he was very worried about it—and pushing was his way of asking, "Are you *sure* you still want to get married?"

They had been living apart for nearly a year and the wedding date was fast approaching when the inevitable explosion occurred. It was Christmas 1977. John drove down to Los Angeles to spend the holidays with Eve's family. He could sense there was trouble brewing; Eve was tense and withdrawn. Finally, she said, "John, I just can't get married," and gave him back the ring.

He left immediately, without a word, and drove home in shock.

Eve cried when he left. She hadn't intended to go that far; she simply wanted to have the rational discussion they'd never had about the marriage. As always, he refused to negotiate. She tried to call him in Chico, but he hung up on her.

She wrote him a letter, saying that she'd only intended to break the engagement, not the relationship. She said she still loved him, but felt that he'd been rushing things—their futures were still so uncertain. She wanted to continue seeing him; she didn't want it to end. When she called again several days later, he didn't hang up, but he didn't say much either. It would be quite some time before he'd be able to trust her again. He spent New Year's Eve in Chico, alone.

Steiner had staked his academic future on garter snakes. He found them by the hundreds at Mahogany Lake near Lassen Park, and used them as the subjects for all his term papers—a population census in one class, a feeding behavior study in another, and so on. His *pièce de résistance* was to be his master's thesis, a complicated analysis of how garter snakes used the food they ate. From his census studies, he knew the snakes were dying out—they fed on tree frogs, which were disappearing from Mahogany Lake. It was a gradual process, though, and he figured he'd have more than enough snakes to finish his work. But a severe drought hit California in 1978, and wiped out the remaining garter snakes at the lake; by midsummer, there were none to be found.

"What are you going to do?" asked Dr. Kenneth Evans, his thesis adviser.

"Well, I was thinking about newts," Steiner said.

He didn't like newts nearly so much as garter snakes, but at least they were plentiful. There had been something very pure about the snakes: they were reptiles, spiritual descendants of the dinosaurs. Working with them had been romantic and mysterious—almost archaeological, in a way. Newts were amphibians, a muddled, transitional class of vertebrates, neither fish nor reptiles. He couldn't empathize with newts; there was no rapport. Still, he figured they were similar enough physiologically to serve his purposes.

He spent the next year weighing worms, then feeding them to newts, then weighing their feces. If he could determine the amount of calories the newts ate (which was easy enough), then find out how many calories they expelled (also not very difficult), he'd have a rough estimate of the calories they were using to stay alive. The next question was more difficult: What, specifically, were they using those calories for? To find that out, he first had to measure the amount of oxygen they used . . . and that's where the newts had their revenge. He spent two semesters running reluctant amphibians through an oxygen chamber before he realized that he was in real trouble. He simply could not get the newts to breathe normally; they were just too skittish. Any disturbance—if someone walked into the room and asked Steiner if he wanted to go out for a sandwich—would set them off. The results were scrambled, meaningless. He couldn't even prove one of the basic facts of nature, that animals used more oxygen when the temperature was warmer. Nearly two years of work had been wasted. He realized that in his haste to find a replacement for the garter snakes—who were much more placid creatures—he had made a stupid mistake. He was sick to death of newts, their feces, the slow pace of laboratory work and school in general.

His parents tried to comfort him with the old saw: "No results are results too." But Steiner knew there was a difference between meaningless results and inconclusive ones.

"You can't produce trash," he said, "and expect to live with it."

Still, he could have salvaged his degree. All he had to do was prove that he'd done the best he could, and that he'd learned something about research methods. But he was too embarrassed, and proud, and disgusted with himself. He was one of the stars of the department, and was expected to come up with something more than an elaborate apology for choosing the wrong animal to study.

With conclusive evidence of his essential mediocrity in hand (or so he thought), he decided to quit school and become a full-time park ranger. It was a drastic act; his teachers tried to talk him out of it, to no avail. It was odd that the work that once had seemed the fulfillment of a dream—being paid to walk in the forest—now became an admission of defeat, but he refused to entertain any illusions about it. The Park Service offered momentary satisfactions, but not much of a future. He had, by then, spent three summers working at Lassen Park, and he knew how the system operated. The most interesting jobs were the low-level ones. Promotion meant becoming a nature bureaucrat, shuffling papers, supervising budgets. It was administrative work, not much different from running a refrigerator factory. He was a teacher, an explainer of nature, not an administrator. He would have been quite happy teaching zoology at some junior college and spending his summers as a park ranger. It wasn't an unreasonable goal—all he had to do was submit his jumbled findings, get his master's, and the rest would fall into place easily enough. But he refused to submit the thesis and sought refuge instead in the Park Service.

In order to get a full-time job, he had to take a civil service exam. He scored 98 out of 100 and, when his ten veteran's preference bonus points were added, he had the second-highest score in the San Francisco area. He accepted a position at Marin Headlands State Park, across the Golden Gate from San Francisco.

Three years had passed since he and Eve lived together in Chico. Two years had passed since she'd broken the engagement. After a brief period of wariness and embarrassment, they had resumed their old routine—two weekends a month, the Christmas holidays, a summer vacation together. John still hoped they would marry. But he never raised the subject, or even hinted at it. If anything was going to happen, it would have to be at Eve's initiative.

Eve was now working for the Internal Revenue Service in Los Angeles. She'd quit her job with the Beverly Hills firm after a dispute with her boss; once again, John had helped her through a rough time. He'd been very patient, calming her, helping her to figure out what to do next. Having passed her CPA exam, and with the anxiety over work resolved, she found that she had a lot of time on her hands, and that she was lonely. She began to think that perhaps it was time to settle the business with John, one way or another. She loved him—there was no doubt about that now—their weekends together were wonderful, but she still had misgivings about living with him. He remained relentlessly cheerful, and never confided in her. He hadn't expressed anything beyond a mild annoyance over the collapse of his academic dreams. She knew he had to be suffering inside; she knew he felt humiliated. It was very disconcerting: at times, he was a total stranger. Perhaps if they lived together, he would loosen up and talk, and learn to trust her. She decided to apply for a transfer to an IRS office in the San Francisco area. It was promptly granted.

Steiner, elated, assumed the move meant that Eve finally was ready to settle down, get married, have children, buy a house. He was sharing a tract house in Mill Valley with three other rangers—he slept on the back porch—and, at the age of thirty-two, was tired of impermanence; he couldn't even plant a garden without the landlady's permission. He wanted a home of his own.

Eve moved to Mill Valley in January 1980. Their first few months together were as their weekends had been, wonderful, low-key, no pressure. Gradually, though, John began to buffet her—as always, in his oblique way—with hints about marriage and, especially, buying a house.

"Let's wait a little, John," she said. "I just *got* here."

But he continued to push. One night, Eve would recall, they had a confrontation that actually resembled a fight. "You'd better make up your mind about these things," he screamed at her, "or you might as well move out." Within minutes, though, he was back to his usual self. "I'm sorry," he said. "I didn't mean that about moving out."

This was progress of a sort, she figured. He had, for a moment at least, been something other than cheerful or silent. She agreed to start looking for a house.

Once again John seized upon her concession. He began a furious search for a house, even summoning his parents to help. The results were disappointing; real estate prices were very high. The only way they could afford a house, John realized, was to get a 7 percent mortgage loan from CalVet, the state veterans agency, and to be eligible for that, they had to be married. Eve had another alternative. One of her old roommates from Chico, Julie Williams, wanted to buy a place. They could share a house with her. John didn't like the idea at all. He had imagined that owning a home with Eve would represent a de facto marriage; having a roommate—even a nice, quiet, clean one like Julie—would make it all seem less formal, more transitory. It wouldn't be a *real* home. But it was better than remaining on the back porch in Mill Valley, so he agreed.

They soon found a place in the hills above the city of Richmond, just north of Berkeley: three bedrooms, a view, a basement for John's collections of bugs, butterflies and fossils, a sloping backyard perfect for a garden. They decided to rent out the third bedroom—to another woman, as it happened, a college student. There were jokes, then, about John's harem, but he wasn't amused. His old Marine buddies would, no doubt, have found the situation tantalizing, but Steiner often felt as if he were living in a women's dorm, constrained, his privacy with Eve violated, the odd man out.

After two years at Marin Headlands, he transferred to a higher-level job at the San Francisco Bay Wildlife Refuge, which was run by the U.S. Fish and Wildlife Service. It was a promotion of sorts, and brought with it the expected—and dreaded—administrative duties. He was now, officially, an "interpretive specialist," with a staff of two "interpretive technicians," as well as fifteen volunteers to supervise. There was all sorts of paperwork to be done, jobs to assign, schedules to plan. He figured that if he were really efficient, he might be able to free half his time for the work he enjoyed—leading nature walks, giving slide shows at the local schools, running programs for kids.

The refuge headquarters was a modern structure of weathered redwood siding and plate glass, perched atop a hill near the southwestern corner of the bay, commanding a bleak panorama of paddy-like salt marshes and industrial offenses. Steiner's domain was enclosed by chemical factories, salt-mining and gravel operations, a most unlikely wilderness. And yet the tidal flats were crammed with life—flowers, butterflies, lizards, fish spawning grounds and more than two hundred species of birds. The marshes had, for Steiner, much the same sort of primordial attraction as garter snakes; they were where life began. He saw himself as a missionary, bringing enlightenment to the uninformed—the remaining salt marshes had to be preserved. When reporters from the local papers appeared on slow news days to write features about the refuge, Steiner held forth passionately.

He would ride the rapid transit to work each day from Richmond to Fremont, along the eastern shore of the bay. He stored a bicycle at Fremont, and pedaled the eight miles from the BART station to the refuge. Considering what had happened to his leg, it was something of a miracle that he was able to ride a bike at all; the leg had regained much of its strength and flexibility, although it still ached at times. But days would pass when he wasn't even conscious of it. Sometimes he'd think of the hospital and his old Marine self, and he'd find himself giggling over how *weird* he'd become in the past ten years—he had a full beard now, he baked his own bread, he collected butterflies; politically, he was the next thing to a pacifist. He figured his old Marine buddies wouldn't consider him much of a "man" anymore; but then, he no longer thought much of the Corps' notion of manliness. When the newspaper reporters asked him about his background, he never mentioned the marines. On the rare occasions when Vietnam came up as a topic of conversation with friends, he'd softly admit, "I think they're better off there now."

He was, however, thinking about the war more often than he had in years. Part of it was the constant stream of stories in the papers and on television about Vietnam veterans flipping out, flashing back, having gun battles with the police. He found these stories hard to comprehend. He didn't have nightmares or flashbacks. He wasn't angry at the government—how could he be? The government had put him through college, and allowed him to fly around the world for free on Space A. The government still sent him monthly checks for a "disability" that was practically nonexistent.

And yet, reading the Vietnam veteran horror stories, he couldn't help but wonder whether the war had affected him in some strange way that he couldn't grasp. His combat experiences seemed unreal now, like a horror movie he'd once seen; he could remember being scared to death, but he no longer could *feel* the fear. But, despite his new guise as a super-environmentalist, he was still a Marine in many ways. His Fish and Wildlife Service uniforms had to be starched and pressed perfectly; when he saw any of his subordinates sloppily dressed, he'd get angry. There had been a confrontation with a woman ranger who insisted on wearing her own blue jacket instead of the regulation khaki one; even after he'd upbraided her, she continued to wear what she wanted. He shuddered at such . . . *insubordination.* He was outraged when people didn't defer to their superiors.

Besides, there was his reluctance to express his feelings, especially negative ones. He wasn't sure if this was a result of his Marine training or his upbringing. His parents never had been the sort of people who talked about personal feelings; but the Marines certainly had reinforced that tendency in him. He had fought so hard not to cry, he had wanted so badly to prove that he could do *something* right, that he had allowed a significant part of his personality to be cauterized. The result was the peremptory cheerfulness that Eve found so frustrating, which masked his fear and anger much as the bouncy walk he'd adopted after the war masked the slight limp that was the one enduring consequence of his mangled thigh. His emotional constraints were so ingrained that he only became conscious of them when Eve complained. And then, he tended to dismiss her criticism as California psychobabble. He knew things weren't going so well between them. There were times they didn't speak to each other for days on end. He was at a loss to explain why their relations were so strained; perhaps if she'd been willing to get married . . .

Eve had given up all hope by then of achieving a breakthrough with John on her own. His style had proven dominant; their extended silences were *his* form of guerrilla warfare, not hers, and she'd been entirely unable to draw him out. For a long time, she had believed the only possible answer for them was therapy, but she was reluctant to mention it because she knew what John's reaction would be. Finally, in the summer of 1981, after they'd been living together for more than a year, she broached the subject. "I don't need that," he said brusquely, without hesitation.

She tried again several weeks later. "I'd really like you to come to couples counseling with me," she said.

"I don't want to."

"I know that," she pressed. "But *will* you? I think it's really important."

They went to a man named Oscar, whom Eve knew. He was a pleasant, grandfatherly sort who lived in a quietly expensive home in the Berkeley Hills with a spectacular view. They sat in his mahogany-paneled living room, and Eve immediately began to unburden herself. She said John was unwilling to be intimate with her, and it was killing their relationship. She said he made her feel as if their problems were all *her* fault. *He* never had problems, at least none he'd admit. He refused to share his fears and uncertainties with her; he wouldn't let her get close to him. She went on like that for quite a while.

He was stunned, more by the vehemence than the accusations. He felt numb, almost dizzy, and couldn't speak. He knew she'd been upset with him, but . . .

"John," Oscar said, "how do you feel about all this?"

"Weird," he said. "Really strange. Really, really strange."

They saw Oscar each week after that, and it was always pretty much the same. Eve did most of the talking. John sat catatonic, as if someone had hit him over the head with a sledgehammer. He saw the truth in what Eve said, but couldn't believe he was as bad as all that until, several months into the counseling, something happened at work that gave Eve's accusations a lot more credibility.

He was called in for a talk one day by his immediate superior, the assistant refuge manager. "John," the manager said, "there have been some complaints about you from the staff. They say you are cold, insensitive and militaristic . . ."

Again, Steiner was struck dumb. He couldn't believe it. Militaristic? Why was everyone suddenly ganging up on him? He sat dazed as his boss went on, saying that Steiner was trying to run his staff as if it were a Marine platoon; they often felt as if he were drilling and inspecting rather than supervising them. "You have to go a little easier," he said. "Try to be more friendly."

"Yeah, okay," Steiner said, pretending to agree. He figured the only thing to do now was to quit the Fish and Wildlife Service. He thought about becoming a carpenter, or maybe going back to school. His natural inclination was not to tell Eve any of this—he wanted her to think of him as successful at work, and not the utter failure he apparently was. On the way home that night, he tried to plot his strategy: he could just announce to her that he was quitting, that he was tired of being a bureaucrat . . . he *could* do that, but after months of being banged on the head by Eve and Oscar, he knew it would be wrong. He decided to tell her the truth.

"Eve," he said finally, after procrastinating a while that night, "there was some trouble at work today."

She took the news well. She didn't seem to think any less of him, which he found surprising. She assured him that he was very good at what he did; it was just a communication problem, easily handled. She suggested he tell Oscar about it.

"I don't know," he said. "You think so?"

As soon as they sat down with Oscar several nights later, Eve spilled the beans. "Oscar," she said, "John has something to tell you."

He told him. Oscar, as always, asked, "Well, John, how do you feel about this?"

"I'm still in shock," John said. "It happened three days ago, and I'm still wiped out by it. I can't think, I can't function . . ."

Oscar said it might be a good idea if John went into group therapy. "Sometimes, John, you speak very quickly . . . and sometimes that may come across as cold and insensitive."

"But I'm *not* insensitive."

"Of course not. But we're concerned with appearances here. You'll get feedback in a group—people will be able to tell you if you're seeming cold and insensitive. You'll learn what works, and what doesn't."

So now he would be going to therapy twice a week. The group also met in Oscar's living room; there was a co-leader named Penelope, who was very Eastern. She had a red dot painted on her forehead, and opened each session by suggesting that everyone should meditate for a moment. Then she'd say, "Okay," and everyone would compete to spill out his or her most intimate feelings—except Steiner, who thought the whole thing was pretty ridiculous. It reminded him of that psychology class at Diablo Valley College. A few of the people, like the woman who'd been molested by her father, obviously had serious problems; others just seemed lonely. He couldn't understand their compulsion to *talk* so much . . . or how they could do it so easily. He had difficulty keeping up with the Niagara of emotions; he'd find himself ruminating on some startling confession or other, and then realize the group had moved on to some other startling confession. With all the others competing for attention, it was easy for him to get lost in the shuffle . . . although Oscar occasionally would remember he was there and try to draw him in: "John, what do you think about what Susan just said?"

"Oh yeah," he'd reply. "I agree completely."

One time, Oscar zeroed in on him about Vietnam. "Were you involved in killing people over there?"

"Yeah."

"How did you feel about that?"

"I didn't like it too much," he said, sensing that everyone in the room was waiting with bated breath for him to break down and cry, or freak out like the Vietnam veterans on television. He wouldn't give them that satisfaction. He wouldn't give an inch.

Finally, after much unsuccessful prodding, Oscar said, "Well,

John, I don't know what exactly happened during your military experience . . . but I suspect you're going to have to get it out or you'll never be able to establish an intimate relationship with Eve."

Steiner's reaction was much the same as it had been to the girl in the bikini who'd called him a baby-killer fourteen years earlier: How did *he* know? These people were so free with words. They regurgitated feelings and emotions so easily they couldn't help but be phony. He didn't really trust Oscar.

And yet, he found it easier to speak to him when it was just the two of them, talking man to man, as it were. They did this several times, when Eve was unable to make a session because of work. She was furious when she learned that John had been more forthcoming in her absence. "Why will he talk to you and not to me?" she asked Oscar.

"He has nothing to lose by talking to me," he said. "He might if he talked to you."

Eve didn't think there was very much left for them to lose in any case. "There's no future in this," she said. "I think we should separate."

"All right," said Oscar. "What do you think, John?"

"If that's what she wants . . ."

The truth was, he didn't believe it really was happening. It seemed about as real as the emotions people disgorged in group. And his disbelief was reinforced when Oscar proceeded to negotiate a formal "dissolution" of their relationship. There were, he said, serious questions to resolve: Should John move out of the house immediately? Should he move to the basement? Should they sell the house? The holidays—Christmas 1981—were approaching, an awkward time for a dissolution. Should they wait until January? Neither John nor Eve volunteered any answers.

"Well," Oscar said, "even though your relationship is over, do you still intend to remain good friends?"

John and Eve agreed that they did.

"Sometimes," Oscar continued, "good friends live in the same house. Do you think you can handle that for the time being, until the situation sorts itself out?"

John and Eve said they could.

"Occasionally," Oscar suggested, "good friends even sleep in the same bedroom. Are you going to do that?"

There were no objections.

"They even sleep in the same bed . . ."

"Fine with me," Steiner said.

Eve agreed that it would be okay for a while.

Their relationship thus dissolved, living together became much easier for them.

At work, too, Steiner found a deft solution to his problems. He announced that he would resign sometime in the future — maybe in six months. Having convinced himself that he no longer cared how the refuge was run, he eased up on his staff . . . and immediately became a much more successful administrator. He came to work smiling, said "good morning" to everyone and sometimes shot the breeze with his "interpretive technicians" over a cup of coffee. He never withdrew his offer to resign, but he never mentioned it again either.

Christmas passed. Eve didn't say anything about a change in their provisional non-relationship . . . and if she wasn't going to mention it, he certainly wasn't. Since they were no longer officially a couple, there was no need for "couples counseling." Oscar had done his job.

They lived together tentatively, and often happily.

Happy are men who yet before they are killed
Can let their veins run cold.
Whom no compassion fleers
Or makes their feet
Sore on the alleys cobbled with their brothers.
The front line withers.
But they are troops who fade, not flowers,
For poets' tearful fooling:
Men, gaps for filling:
Losses, who might have fought
Longer; but no one bothers.

—WILFRED OWEN

1

John Wakefield planned his exit from the Marine Corps as carefully as he might have prepared for a Force Recon patrol. He did not want to spend a single day doing left-faces at Camp LeJeune or Pendleton after leaving Vietnam. He extended his combat tour six months to be sure that he would walk directly from the bush into the World, his four-year hitch complete. And, when the time came, the plan was executed perfectly. He arrived in San Francisco on December 7, 1967, and was a civilian three days later. There was, however, a serious flaw in all this: once out, he had absolutely no idea what to do next.

It was as if his mental discipline—his proudest possession, so carefully cultivated through years of training and combat—had been just another piece of equipment, to be handed over with his rifle and helmet when he was processed out. It simply disappeared. He could not plan anything. He slipped into a lassitude that extended well beyond the understandable need to relax and blow off steam. He could not even bring himself to think about going home to Indianapolis, although he knew he should get back there for Christmas. He neither dreaded nor relished the idea of going home; he had no feelings either way. So he gave himself up to San Francisco—specifically, to a stewardess he'd met on the charter flight from Okinawa. There was little pleasure in their liaison after the initial conquest, but he couldn't think of anything else to do.

He had won her easily enough, late at night while the others on the plane were sleeping. She was the first Caucasian woman he had spoken with in a long time and, to break the ice, he gave her a little test that had been common in Vietnam. It was a list of words with vowels missing, unexplained numbers and several crude drawings—a game short-timers played with new guys, a way of teaching them the language and ground rules of the place. There were words like "KLLZN" (kill zone) and "CNCRTN WR" (concertina wire) and pictures of a house on stilts ("hooch") and a stick figure with a conical hat ("gook"). One of the numbers was sixty-nine.

She laughed and asked—suggestively, he thought: "Does that mean the same thing over there as it does back home?"

"Uh-huh," he said, then asked for her telephone number. She gave it without hesitation.

The plane landed in the middle of the night. He was taken by bus to the naval base at Treasure Island, and billeted in a near-empty barracks. The next morning he was awakened by a new recruit who tapped him on the shoulder. Wakefield came up swinging, knocked the kid down and pounced on him, his K-Bar knife at the ready.

"Hey, *easy* . . ." said the recruit, his nose bloodied. Obviously, he'd had little experience waking Vietnam veterans.

"Sorry," Wakefield said. "But you ought to know better."

He spent the next few days filling out forms, being examined by doctors and dentists, debriefed by a psychiatrist and drawing his last pay. The doctors were intrigued by a bullet still lodged in his right arm. He'd been wounded on the operation following Cochise, when a rookie stupidly tripped a mine—Wakefield had warned him to watch where he was walking moments earlier—which sprayed shrapnel and bullets, and confirmed his worst fears about the relative safety of Charlie Company. After that, he abandoned the last, lingering thoughts of a career in the Marine Corps—a real possibility when he'd been in Force Recon, but less so after he joined the grunts—and decided to exercise the quick-exit alternative he had prepared months before. He returned to the field after several weeks' recuperation, and began counting his days along with everyone else.

The doctors at Treasure Island, like the doctors at Danang, decided to leave the bullet where it was. He would trigger metal detectors at airports for the rest of his life.

The psychological debriefing was a joke. The word "debriefing" had a certain resonance for Wakefield; he remembered the careful questioning after each Force Recon patrol in Hue, but this was nothing like that. It was merely a lecture given by a Navy psychiatrist on the perils of re-entry. Wakefield noted, with mild disdain, that the man wasn't very precise in his dress—hair a bit too long, tie tucked haphazardly, shirt loose with laundry folds still visible. His very first sentence confirmed Wakefield's doubts: "Well, I hope you all *got some* over there," the psychiatrist said, attempting to ingratiate himself with in-country slang, "or else what I say won't mean much to you."

It didn't mean anything at all to Wakefield. He refused to consider the perils—or any other aspect—of re-entry, and promptly tuned out. When it was over, he called the stewardess and arranged a date.

He was familiar with San Francisco. He had spent time there after boot camp and sea school, attached to the USS *Ranger*, an aircraft carrier loaded with nuclear bombs. He hated the duty, always fearful that one of the bomb teams would make a mistake and blow them all through the bottom of the ocean (later, even walking point in enemy territory would seem less dangerous; there, at least, he had the illusion of control). Hoping to mask his anxiety with bravado, he requested a transfer to Force Recon—but when weeks passed and it didn't come through, he staged a wild-cat strike of sorts and went

AWOL for several days in San Francisco. Remarkably, the powers-that-were seemed to respond to this and, after a brief stint in the brig, he won his transfer. In the meantime, he had got to know San Francisco well enough to have established several favorite haunts. One was Henry's Pub, an Irish saloon near the USO on Market Street, where he would drink Irish coffee, eat roast beef from the steam table (his favorite dish) and pass the time with USO staffers. Another was the Rose and Thistle, a Scottish pub—when it came to socializing, Wakefield's taste ran to Celtic nostalgia—where he drank ale, played darts and listened to the bagpipes. He arranged to meet the stewardess at the Rose and Thistle.

After some hasty preliminaries, they went back to her apartment, where, he'd later confess with embarrassment, he made love like a Marine—storming the beach, taking it, then growing bored with the mop-up operation. The stewardess apparently expected little more, but no less—an expectation that became problematical over the next few days as his interest flagged and hers didn't. The liaison ended after a week of perfunctory bliss when the stewardess went off again to Asia. He accompanied her to the airport and, once there, had little choice but to go home.

Years later, recalling his return to Indianapolis, Wakefield would say that no one met him at the airport, that he took a bus downtown and a cab home, was greeted by a handshake from his father, tears from his mother, and then went to bed. But that is not what happened.

His parents met him at the airport with as many relatives as they could muster. Afterward, there was a party at home.

When reminded of this, Wakefield acknowledged that it probably was true—he had, no doubt, confused that homecoming with some other during his four years in the service. An innocent mistake, perhaps, but typical enough: his version of the events of his life would differ, time and again, from theirs. The discrepancies more often involved emotions and interpretations than bare facts; the "Johnny" Wakefield his parents described—childish, petulant and mercurial—was far different from the precise, rational sort he made himself out to be (or, for that matter, the cool professional remembered by Charlie Company). The gap between the two versions was formidable, but eerily bridged at times when Wakefield talked about his family and that other *Johnny* would sneak out, despite his best efforts. As a child he'd always felt as if he were misplaced somehow, plopped down in the wrong family; he was certain he'd been adopted. When he was thirteen, he ran away to Boys Town in Nebraska and declared himself an orphan. He was sent home, unrepentant, when school officials checked with the Indianapolis police and discovered his identity. His mother was crying and angry when he returned; his father, not one to show his emotions, morose. They didn't seem to care *why* he'd gone, just that he'd done something flagrantly wrong again; but then, John didn't seem to care that his father had spent days searching for him, combing the foundations of a half-completed tract house development nearby for his body.

Watching his son at the homecoming party that evening in December 1967, Ed Wakefield thought: same old Johnny. He was still the life of the party, backslapping, joke-telling, everybody's best friend even if he didn't know them all that well . . . just the sort of person he most distrusted. He had always been rather appalled by John's emotional extravagance. He couldn't understand how someone who looked so much like him—the owlish, thin-lipped facial resemblance was striking—could be so different. His wife, Dorothy, and daughter, Cathy, were emotional people, ever teary, but quietly so—and, anyway, they were women. John was always so *extreme*, flinging himself at people without quite befriending them, taking offense at the merest slight, real or imagined, raging, sulking, prancing . . .

The most routine disappointment could become a major crisis. In sixth grade, Dorothy told John he was too young to go out for the school football team. He was upset, but accepted it. The next year she relented, but also let his younger brother Steve—then in sixth grade—join the team. John was outraged. He hadn't played in sixth grade, why should Steve? Older brothers traditionally endure such travesties of justice, but John couldn't seem to let it go. In fact, he *never* got over it; it festered and, over the years, became a mortal affront, a turning point in his life—the moment he realized that Steve was favored. The "football incident," as it was called, would be revived time and again when grievances were aired, even after he returned home from Vietnam.

Such behavior was incomprehensible to the Wakefields. They were even-tempered people, as modest in their expectations as they were in their lifestyle. They wanted only a modicum of comfort and a certain righteous anonymity that they defined as "respectability." John, though, seemed to need melodrama. His noisy thrashings about for something important to do or feel disrupted the determined placidity of their home, which was a small white bungalow on the corner of their block, surrounded by a low-slung chain link fence, protected in later years by aluminum siding and in no way distinguishable from the other homes in their working-class neighborhood. Ed Wakefield, who disdained grand gestures as thoroughly as John seemed to crave them, believed that life was a deceptively simple proposition: if you worked hard, played by the rules, kept your mouth shut and weren't unlucky, you'd get along. He had spent his adult life patiently climbing the ladder at Detroit Diesel Allison, the huge General Motors subsidiary that sprawled across southwestern Indianapolis, working his way up from machine operator to supervisor, from labor to management. His success was modest, but satisfying. He hoped his sons would take the next step—college—then start as management and go on from there.

Steve was never a problem. He was an average student, but a splendid athlete. When he was in fifth grade and John in sixth, Mr. Wakefield bought them tennis rackets with a book and a quarter of green stamps. It was, he would later say, the best investment he ever made: Steve eventually won a tennis scholarship to Middle Tennessee State University.

John—always tall for his age, and thin, and a bit gawky—was an acceptable athlete, but not in Steve's class. He might have competed more successfully against his brother in the classroom—the family consensus was that John was smarter—but didn't seem to have any interest in school. Instead, he spent his youth chasing in vain after the same sort of approval Steve routinely received from their father. When Ed Wakefield coached the Catholic Youth Organization basketball team, Steve was a starter and John a reserve, smoldering quietly, convinced that his father was once again playing favorites. He was certain he was just as good as Steve, and tried to win his father's praise through aggressiveness—sometimes going too far, but occasionally earning the ultimate Ed Wakefield compliment, "Nice game, son." Of necessity, he became an expert in the rules and strategies of the games they played. He worked the angles, made the most of his ability by learning how to frustrate his opponents, if not defeat them; he loved harassing them physically and with little-known rules, an obnoxious but sometimes effective tactic that came to dominate his style, on and off the playing field. He was continually provoking arguments, and then arguing fine points rather than substance, which drove Steve—his most frequent opponent, at home and on the tennis court—to distraction. His father noticed John's caginess and admired it on those rare occasions when it was appropriate. But he wasn't the sort to say so, and John, living for each "Nice game, son," hoping against hope for some evidence of his father's regard, watched every nuance of Ed's quiet admiration for Steve's skill with the same obsessed acuity he would later bring to walking point in the jungle.

If there was any respite for John from this constant vigil, it was in the Catholic Youth Organization, where he became a leader of sorts, establishing himself—in his own mind, at least—as a behind-the-scenes type, a mediator and manipulator. By 1962, when he began his last year of high school, he had become vice-president of the CYO on the deanery (area-wide) level. He was more John than "Johnny" in the CYO—but then, he was playing to a different audience.

Bill Sahm, the CYO director, seemed everything his father could never be. He was an enormous man—six feet, 275 pounds—with a right leg crippled by polio. The boldness and ease with which he overcame the physical awkwardness was an object lesson to the socially awkward adolescents in his charge, who idolized him. They called him Hoss, after the character in the "Bonanza" series on television; his tiny office, in the dull cinder-block building at the CYO football field, was known as the Ponderosa. He was kindly, disheveled, informal and yet formidable. More important, he was the one adult John Wakefield knew who was able to talk, with a sensitivity that seemed all the more remarkable for his size, about personal feelings—love, friendship, disappointment, devotion and pain, the very things Ed Wakefield found so hard to express. John sought Bill Sahm's approval as fervently as his father's, and found it more easily—or, perhaps, more obviously—won. They worked together closely during John's year as deanery vice-president . . . and later, when he began to think about joining the Marines, he went to Bill Sahm, not his parents, for advice.

Father John Elfred, another CYO adviser, was a teacher at nearby Marion College and had told John that he might be able to sneak him in on probation, despite his bad grades. "But I'm sick of school," John said, sitting in the Ponderosa one afternoon. "I'm tired of the regimentation."

"Won't there be regimentation in the service too?" Sahm asked gently.

"Yes, but . . ." He found it hard to admit to Sahm that some of his reasons for wanting to enlist were basically trivial—the desire for action, adventure, romance—and others decidedly vengeful—to get away from his parents, to *show* them. It was early in the summer of 1963. He knew there was a country in Asia called South Vietnam where American advisers were teaching the local government to fight Communists—it sounded exotic and alluring, just the sort of thing he wanted to do.

The decision was deferred for a time. John didn't want to do anything drastic until after October, when the CYO National Convention would be held in New York. He was planning to attend as a last hurrah. He graduated from high school in June, and took a job welding bread boxes in a small factory. It was a temporary move, but depressing all the same. The factory was dark, grimy, a sweatshop; he couldn't imagine doing that sort of thing for the rest of his life. The Marines seemed fresh and exhilarating by comparison. He visited the recruiter downtown and found that he could join on a delayed-entry plan, go to the CYO Convention in October and then to boot camp a month later. Still, he put it off.

His parents, especially his mother, would always believe that John's decision to join the Marines was a spiteful, spur-of-the-moment reaction to an event that soon took its place in the family mythology alongside the "football incident." His brother Steve would remember it, too, as a classic case of John being John, always looking for trouble, never knowing when to stop.

One evening that August, John and Steve were coming home from the tennis courts at Garfield Park with two other boys in their cousin's 1955 Chevy. They noticed the streets were lined with garbage cans, to be picked up the next morning. It is not known whose idea it was—John seems a likely suspect—but they decided to swerve from side to side of the street, picking up garbage cans, then taking off and letting them fly. Steve was a willing conspirator—it was a kick watching the cans go off like depth charges from a destroyer—but he soon grew wary and asked to be let off at home before they were caught. "You coming, Johnny?" he asked.

"No, let's do some more," John said, and went off down *their* street with the other boys, emptying cans from the Chevy . . . and was, of course, immediately spotted by one of the neighbors.

Ed Wakefield was furious and humiliated; Dorothy was in tears. It seemed impossible that John could be eighteen years old, a high school graduate, and still so infantile. He and the others were told to clean up the mess, and then he was grounded for two weeks. It wasn't exactly brutal punishment, but Steve got off scot-free—and John, as always, considered himself to have been victimized.

Within a week or so, he came home one afternoon and announced with a flourish: "I just joined the Marines."

His mother cried. He expected she would. His father said nothing for a moment and then, softly: "Are you sure you know what you're getting into?"

John, expecting something on the order of "Nice game, son," felt as if he'd been slapped. "Of course I'm sure," he said.

"Well, okay then," Ed Wakefield said, and that was all he said.

On the final evening of the CYO's National Convention in New York that October, President John F. Kennedy appeared—distant, tiny, but *glowing*—on a balcony overlooking the formal dance that concluded the proceedings, and received the loudest ovation John Wakefield had ever heard. No announcement was made when the President arrived, just scattered gasps and then the eruption. Kennedy waved at the crowd in that distinctive, almost shy way of his, and Wakefield—momentarily forgetting his cool, competent, behind-the-scenes pose—found himself cheering wildly along with everyone else.

He had admired Kennedy since the first time he'd seen him on television, debating Richard Nixon, in 1960. He was tickled by the Boston accent, as was most everyone he knew in Indianapolis. The day after the first debate, his classmates at Cathedral High School were giddy with "vigah" and "Cuber" and "ahsk," and all the rest. When the election was over and Kennedy had won, John found that he was more aware of the presidency, of politics and world issues in general, than he'd ever been before (though, in truth, those things still weren't very important to him). Part of it, no doubt, was that Kennedy was a Catholic; each Sunday at St. Catherine's, the priest would close the mass with a prayer for *our* President. But it was more than that: Kennedy's style and idealism seemed to permeate everything. It was especially true at CYO meetings, where "Ask not what your country can do for you . . ." became the dominant rhetorical style, and members were constantly being asked to cross new thresholds, meet new challenges and explore new frontiers during debates over the plans for the next CYO dance or bake sale. Some of the boys tried to look and act like the President, brushing their hair back, left hands stuffed in jacket pockets, right forefingers jabbing as they said things like "Well, let me say this about that . . ." just as *he* did at press conferences; many of the girls, too, began to emulate the First Lady, sprouting stiff bouffant hairdos. Indeed, that night in the Sheraton ballroom, Wakefield was surrounded by a sea of nascent Kennedys—the boys in narrow ties, belts and lapels; the girls in bouffants and formal dresses the color of Valentine's Day candies—pink, chartreuse, tangerine and baby blue.

Wakefield, tall and gangly in an English-cut, double-breasted suit that he'd worn to his high school graduation in June and not since, wasn't much of a sartorial New Frontiersman, nor did he consciously ape the President's style. He admired Kennedy, but politics didn't mean a lot to him, at least until that day. In fact, when he'd been told earlier that he would be one of sixteen CYO members who'd actually meet with the President and ask questions, he wasn't particularly excited; he was too busy with his "inside" work, managing an Indiana girl's campaign for the national vice-presidency, serving on this committee and that. So much already had happened during his week in New York; meeting the President was just another unscheduled event, an unexpected bonus. It seemed just the sort of routinely remarkable thing that happened all the time to people in New York.

But then, in the early evening, when John had walked over to the New York Hilton and taken an escalator to a second-floor meeting room, there *he* was, standing at the podium behind what seemed to be Plexiglas shields, flanked by secret service agents, just a few feet away from the CYO panelists seated at three tables facing him. Their questions were more adoring than substantive—about his role in the Newman Society, and whether he'd been active in the CYO, and whether he kept in touch with the other men from PT-109. The President was relaxed, informal . . . and awesome. John figured this must be what the newscasters meant by "charisma." When he mumbled his question and the President answered him by name, "Well, John," he was so overwhelmed that he immediately forgot what the question had been as well as the President's answer. They'd been asked to take notes, but he forgot about that too; he was transfixed by the man at the podium. Kennedy stayed for half an hour, then shook everyone's hand. When he left, the room changed, shrinking—or, perhaps, expanding—back to normality, the spell broken.

Wakefield felt as if he had a stake in the presidency now, as if in some small way he'd become a part of it. He felt a surge of patriotism and importance, and these feelings became entwined with the others—more complicated, less pure—that had propelled him into the Marine Corps.

By the time he entered boot camp in December, the President was dead, but Wakefield's fervor had not diminished. The Marines seemed the military arm of the Peace Corps, expanding muscular Kennedy-style democracy throughout the world, bringing civilization and progress to far-off lands. His commitment was immediate and total. He was, finally, part of something *big*.

When he returned home on leave after boot camp, he made a grand entrance, striding into the room he shared with Steve and announcing proudly, before even saying hello: "I know seventeen different ways to kill a man with my bare hands."

Steve, nonplussed, slowly realized that this madman was indeed his brother John, condemned to a lifetime of diving off the deep end.

He rarely wrote his parents from overseas. He was off doing important, mysterious things and it seemed better to keep them in the dark. They never learned of his exploits in Force Recon. They did, however, know that he'd gone AWOL in San Francisco, that he'd been busted from sergeant to corporal twice (once for stealing bananas in Hue and a previous time for killing an MP's dog during a drunken brawl on Marine Corps Birthday in Japan) and that he'd called them once, from Hawaii, to ask for money . . . all of which seemed typically John.

At the homecoming party and in the days after, they saw no evidence that the Marines had changed him at all. He wobbled between frantic sociability—especially in the presence of strangers—and sullen torpor. He spent his days lolling about the house, watching television. In the evenings, he would go out and be everyone's friend at the Grog Shop, the bar at the Stouffer's Inn downtown, where he would sip anisette at the piano and smoke Benson and Hedges Deluxe cigarettes—if he was to be dissolute, it would be done distinctively—while Red Kern played old-time, sing-along music, the words flashed on a screen on the wall. When John came in each night, Red would stop what he was doing and swing into "Hail, Hail, the Gang's All Here." The gang was mostly older than he, but John felt more comfortable amidst their manufactured gaiety than with people his own age. He had few friends outside the Grog Shop, none of them close; his occasional romances were measured in hours, and as quickly forgotten.

He had some money saved from the Marines, and devoted himself to working his way through it. When his father asked what he was going to do with himself, he'd say, "Dunno." After a few months, his money dwindling, he took a job as a short-order cook.

Occasionally, he would visit Bill Sahm at the Ponderosa. They would have a cup of coffee, chat about CYO activities . . . and then Bill would ask what John was doing with himself.

"Cooking," he'd say in a way that made it clear that he didn't care to pursue the conversation (but also, that he was expecting some sympathy). They never talked about his plans for the future. Father Elfred, his link to Marion College, had moved to Terre Haute and John figured that even if he wanted to go to school—which he didn't—the chance had disappeared. He made it a point not to complain about his life, but made an obvious show of pissing it away.

He never mentioned the war, and his parents never asked. But there was one remaining piece of business left over from Vietnam that he thought about from time to time. It didn't exactly gnaw at him, but it was there to be done and one day he jumped into the car, drove to Lorain, Ohio, and did it.

He stopped in front of a small green tract house, not much different from his parents' home. When he rang the doorbell, a heavy-set, defeated woman appeared.

"Mrs. McIntyre?" he asked. "I knew your son."

He went inside. She offered him a Coke, which he accepted. Mr. McIntyre was there—tall, thin, quiet, rather old. They sat in the living room. He told them Mac had died without suffering. They didn't have any questions, and he stayed no more than ten minutes.

Driving away, Wakefield lost himself in memories of McIntyre, who had been one of the first people he'd met when he came in-country after a brutal year of Force Reconnaissance training at Camp LeJeune. Mac had walked point on his first patrol; it was a short one, only a few days, within South Vietnam. Wakefield didn't realize that the objective had been to reconnoiter *him*, to see how he reacted in the jungle, until they returned to Hue for debriefing and he saw the others laughing. Mac said, "Well, you passed." They showed him their rifles, which were empty; the area they'd covered, though re-mote, had been completely safe. Wakefield fumed, humiliated. That night, when they returned to their base at Khe Sanh, he was nursing a beer in the rec bunker and Mac pulled up a chair. "Hey, Wake, don't be paranoid," he said. "It's standard procedure—toy patrol. Don't worry, the next one will be real . . . bullets and everything."

They became very close after that. Wakefield soon learned there were two basic Force Recon types: those who were obsessed with finesse in the field and those who got their kicks from violence; both he and Mac were finesse men, though they participated in "interro-gations" along with everyone else when they went on patrol. The distinctions were not based on performance in the bush so much as on what people liked to talk about back in Khe Sanh. The hammers, as Wakefield called them, were as understated in their way as the fi-nesse men; they were technicians, not sadists (when a trooper named the Hippo went a little crazy on one patrol, slicing out the eyes of his victims, it was considered showboating and frowned upon). The hammers placed a good deal of emphasis on cutlery and physiol-ogy; their discussions revolved around knives, and the best places to insert them. Wakefield and McIntyre talked about more abstract things: tactics, strategy, the relative merits of different weapons for different purposes, grenade launchers versus shotguns and so forth. They talked very little about themselves. Wakefield didn't know how many brothers or sisters Mac had, or whether he had a girl-friend. They played chess, and Mac taught him a few things about strategy.

When McIntyre was killed, Wakefield declined the offer to ac-company the body back to Ohio. He was still too angry at Mac for letting himself get blown away (at least, that was how he rationalized it at the time). He wasn't sure what the fatal mistake had been; he spent hours reconstructing the moments before the fusillade. Why hadn't Mac sensed the enemy presence? Why hadn't *he*? He did not think about the results of the skirmish, about the mutilation they found when they returned to retrieve the body.

For some reason, Mac's bunk was left empty for weeks afterward; his presence lingered in the Quonset hut, which made Wakefield nervous and queasy, plagued by visions of gooks lurking around every corner. He felt much more comfortable out in the bush, and so, after Mac's death, he volunteered for patrol after patrol, never resting. He was part of an eight-man ambush team that chopped up a North Vietnamese unit on the Ho Chi Minh Trail one night. There were other patrols, less clean, less successful—it was all the same to him. He didn't have to think so much in the bush, just respond. There was enormous power in walking point; he controlled the fate of the three men behind him. It was mesmerizing, hallucinogenic. At times, he would cease to be conscious of his body and become the jungle; he imagined he could hear snakes slithering, branches bending slightly under the weight of a settling bird. He was certain that he could *sense* the enemy before seeing, hearing or smelling him. He was beyond any sort of emotion then—except, perhaps, an ethereal contentment. Eventually, after several months of patrols, the higher-ups began to notice his subdued ardor, and worry about it. "Why don't you lay back a bit," the CO suggested. "Take it easy. You're going to get burnt out."

He could not imagine such a thing, but followed orders—a little too well, as it happened. He was caught one evening on a drunken spree in Hue, having hijacked a truck and broken into a girls' school. He said he'd only wanted to get some bananas—the school was a former plantation—but they busted him from sergeant to corporal anyway. The demotion didn't make much difference to him, although it may have been a bad omen: soon after, he wrecked his knee diving from a helicopter in Laos, the injury which led to his being reassigned to the grunts.

He had visited McIntyre's parents because he felt he owed Mac that, especially after he'd refused to accompany the body home. But if he had hoped to find some loose thread of his past there, some hint of recognition or appreciation, he was disappointed. There was nothing about the house or the people that reminded him of Mac; they didn't seem to know who *he* was either. It was as if Vietnam never had existed. He was perplexed that he could have gone over there, been so *good*, and then returned home so anonymous, so unimportant, a short-order cook, the "same old Johnny" to his parents. He was not looking for brass bands or even a "Nice game, son," but *some* tacit recognition, some respect. In Force Recon, when they had surreptitiously dropped severed ears into the glass jar in the rec bunker, no one watched but everyone knew. In the World everyone always seemed to be watching, but no one knew anything or seemed to care very much about what they saw. Even outright disapproval—he knew there were protesters, though he hadn't met any—would have been preferable. He did not believe that he was groveling for acknowledgment and perhaps he wasn't, but he did seem intent on debasing himself until someone bothered to notice.

2

Wakefield celebrated his twenty-fourth birthday on January 13, 1969, by drinking an entire bottle of anisette at the Grog Shop. He then tried to drive home but was stopped by the police, who admonished him gently and called a cab. When he reached his parents' house, he vomited all over the bathroom. His mother, awakened by the racket, cleaned up after him.

"Johnny," she said, "*you* didn't have to grow up seeing and hearing things like this, and your sisters shouldn't have to either."

He ignored her, and went to sleep.

He was awakened at dawn by his father, who was steaming. "Where's my car?" Ed Wakefield asked.

"I left it by the side of the road."

"Well, it's snowing. There's a snow emergency," his father said. "We better go out and find it. I don't want to have it towed."

On the way to the car, his father said, "Johnny, isn't it about time you started doing something with your life?"

John decided it was about time he moved out. He had been home for a year, a sullen encumbrance on the family. He slept there, took some meals and, while never quite causing a scene, made everyone very much aware of his extravagant indifference to his own fate.

During that year he had worked in a series of restaurants. At first, he was the assistant manager of a waffle house but, finding that insufficiently demeaning, decided he would rather cook than manage; he could cook drunk. He worked afternoons and evenings, arrived home when everyone was asleep, awakened in late morning and started drinking in early afternoon. He would buy a pint of vodka or some wine on the way to work and, if he began to feel drowsy, would take speed to keep his eyes propped open. He closed down the Grog Shop every night, drinking anisette and water at Red Kern's piano, bellowing out the old songs. His favorite joke, repeated endlessly to newcomers, was: "My voice is somewhere between a baritone and a bass—it's a bare-ass." Sometimes, on the way home, he would pull the car to the side of the road, stick a finger down his throat and vomit. He did not want to run the risk of being sick at home, of giving his parents an excuse to deliver the lecture he knew he deserved. He pursued a subtle strategy—wanting to provoke them, but not through any overt act. If and when the confrontation came, he wanted to be able to say, "I haven't *done* anything."

He lived that way for a year, watching the tension build, waiting for some reaction. His parents were, by turns, angry, disappointed and distraught, but they refused to rise to his bait. During that time, John slipped only once to ask them for help: One night, when he still was managing the waffle house, he misplaced the receipts from the cash register—several hundred dollars—and was forced to borrow the money from his father. John later claimed he was dead drunk and had no idea what happened to the money, but suspected that it was stolen from his car while he was drinking in the Grog Shop, before he could drop it in the night slot at the bank on his way home, as he usually did. Ed Wakefield figured that it had been gambled away, but extended the loan without much fuss. John was too humiliated to be very appreciative, and somewhat disappointed as well. No matter what he did—or didn't do—the man wouldn't react.

And so, when his father finally did ask—quietly, but with obvious disgust—what he intended to do with his life, John leaped at the opportunity to take offense, and announced he was leaving home. He moved into an apartment with an older, alcoholic cook in a rotting section of town and allowed his deterioration to accelerate. Except for the few hours of neon conviviality at the Grog Shop each night, he spent most of his time in muddled bitterness, alone.

Occasionally, he would be roused by a clean, sharp gust of anger. It was not an unpleasant sensation, more visceral than emotional, and not unfamiliar; it was the same cool rage he'd experienced when "interrogating" Vietnamese suspects. He would allow himself to be swept along by it, knowing that it could only be purged violently—usually in a bar where he was not well known. He wasn't subtle about choosing his targets. He might shoot pool and accuse his opponent of cheating; or he might spot a happy young couple, and make a move on the woman or humiliate the man. The fights were one-punch, two-punch affairs, quickly smothered by patrons and bartenders, but in that instant of action, feeling his one punch connect, he was euphoric . . . and afterward, completely serene.

One afternoon, he was sitting in a topless bar called the Rat Fink. A noisy group came in from the training school at Fort Benjamin Harrison; one of them, he noticed, was in the Chaplain Corps, with a red Conscientious Objector patch on his sleeve. Wakefield hated him on sight. The CO was silly drunk, noisy and obnoxious; he went up to the stage and started fooling with the dancers, pretending to sniff their panties. Wakefield, gliding easily, came up behind him, grabbed the back of his collar, spun him, slammed him against the wall, slapped him back and forth across the face, then turned very purposefully, inviting an attack from the rear, and walked back to the bar. The CO hesitated for a moment, then decided to leave.

His parents came to visit his apartment once and were suitably horrified by the filth and decay, but said nothing. Soon after, he decided to leave Indianapolis. There was an employment agency for restaurant personnel in town, which sent cooks and waiters to resort hotels throughout the Midwest. He landed a summer job at the Grand Hotel on Mackinac Island in northern Michigan.

The hotel was an immense, gorgeous remnant of Victorian elegance, white-pillared, with a three-hundred-foot porch, surrounded by perfect sloping lawns and gardens, tended by eighty gardeners, but Wakefield didn't get much of a chance to enjoy it. The dining room sat 1,500 and was patrolled by one hundred waiters, all of whom seemed to scream their breakfast orders in his ear at once. He was the egg cook, a position of no small responsibility, with two assistants and eighteen frying pans arrayed in front of him in rows of nine (half cooking and half warming). There were no written orders, just screaming waiters, and he would have to be listening, remembering and cooking at the same time; it was enormous pressure for about an hour each morning, which he would relieve by immediately heading for a small bar just outside the hotel compound and drinking—Boone's Farm apple wine was very popular that summer—until it was time to stumble back to the kitchen for the evening meal (for which he prepared the vegetables, a much easier job). Inevitably, he was hung over when he awakened at four-thirty each morning, and soon was in the habit of popping a Benzedrine to get himself started.

Most of the waiters and busboys were college kids on summer vacation. Sometimes he smoked marijuana with them, and found that it produced a happy numbness when used in tandem with alcohol. The waiters were the flower of Midwestern youth, innocent, optimistic and preoccupied with Vietnam, which they saw as a dark cloud impinging on their brilliant futures. When they asked him how he'd managed to escape the war, he'd say, "I didn't," curtly, in a way that made it clear he didn't care to discuss it. He watched Vietnam on the evening news, but was unmoved by it; the battlefield reports triggered no strong memories or emotions.

He met a woman whose name he'd later be unable to recall. She was a college student from a well-to-do family, working that summer as a maid in the hotel. She was quiet, rather plain, and had had a child when she was fifteen; the baby lived with her parents. She and John coordinated their days off, and every two weeks would drive to Traverse City, where her folks had a summer cottage on a lake. They didn't approve of him, which—he later realized—may well have been her purpose in the desultory affair. His own purpose was shrouded by alcohol and drugs. None of it seemed very real. In midsummer, he called his parents and told them he probably was going to be married; they rushed to Traverse City. The excuse was that his brother Steve was home from the Air Force, and it would be nice to see all the children together. They found John in one of his relentlessly convivial moods, apparently oblivious to the seriousness of the step he was about to take; the woman made no lasting impression on them at all. His mother said, "This isn't much of a life that you're leading. How are you going to provide for her and the child? All you're going to do is hurt them, and yourself."

Having successfully appalled both sets of parents, John and the woman drifted apart. His superiors in the kitchen had given him several warnings about his drinking; he decided to quit before they fired him, and moved on.

He spent the next few years drifting from resort to resort, living out of a suitcase, spiraling downward. He worked in ski lodges in Michigan and Wisconsin, a kosher hotel on a lakefront . . . and other places, which blurred together after a time. He enjoyed the ski lodges—cooking in the morning, skiing in the afternoon, taking nips from a flask on the chair lift, then plunging wildly downhill; his stay at the kosher hotel was acrimonious and brief, as he had trouble remembering the intricacies of the dietary laws. He never was fired from any of these places, but often was forced to quit. Inevitably, he would return to Indianapolis and stay with his parents while waiting for the employment agency to find him another job. He'd arrive home without warning, usually broke, sometimes with just the clothes on his back. If his parents asked what had happened to his money or clothes, he'd say, "I don't know." He'd stay a few weeks, then disappear without saying goodbye or telling them where he was headed. They wouldn't hear from him for months at a time, and then he'd appear on their doorstep once more. Sometimes there'd be a phone call asking for help. He had an emergency appendectomy in Wisconsin, and they rushed there to care for him and pay the hospital bill. Another time, the police called from Chicago and said that his car had been sitting in the parking lot at O'Hare International Airport for a very long time. Did they know where he was? They didn't.

He was in San Francisco. He had flown there on a whim; it was a place he'd once enjoyed. He was, by then, doing a pretty fair imitation of a skid row bum, lolling all day in a bayside park just west of Fisherman's Wharf, drinking cheap wine by the half gallon. The park was shared by leftover hippies who played conga drums and smoked marijuana, more traditional hoboes and winos and elderly Italians from the adjacent neighborhood who played bocce. Wakefield moved easily among all three groups, playing bocce, drinking wine, smoking marijuana. He kept his hair short, but had thick muttonchop whiskers; he dressed in flannel shirts over turtlenecks and wore a knitted watch cap, which became his trademark.

One day, John bumped into an old friend in the park, a former USO volunteer named Jim O'Neill. Jim was about ten years older than he, with a leg crippled from childhood polio, a lonely man who didn't seem to be doing much with his life. They had been drinking companions in the days when John was stationed on the aircraft carrier, and now they became drinking companions again, often playing sodden games of chess in the park. Jim was staying in a fleabag hotel in the Embarcadero section and John took a room there too, a tiny cubicle with a bed, a dresser without drawers, a hot plate, a tea kettle, two pans. Sheets cost two dollars per week. The bathroom was down a moldy corridor strung with bare light bulbs. John earned some money cooking nights in a nearby diner, where he also ate most of his meals. After work, he would return to the hotel and stare at the acoustical tile ceiling, drinking his wine and trying to make maps out of the patterns of dots in the tile until he passed out. In the morning he'd find Jim, buy a half gallon of Thunderbird for $1.35 and head over to the park.

Later, he'd be uncertain how long he allowed himself to live like that. Perhaps it was a year. He never quite reached the point where his degeneracy became involuntary; he never craved the cheap wine, but drank it by choice. His disgrace was deliberate, conscious and, he liked to believe, controlled. It was as if he was pretending to be a wino. He was not at all introspective about this, hadn't the vaguest idea why he was doing it to himself, and after a time the satisfactions of self-abasement began to wear thin. Seeking salvation rather than help, he began to sample the carnival of pseudo-psychiatric faith healers that had sprouted in San Francisco to service the distressed casualties of the 1960s. They advertised their cults, cures and halfway houses on the radio, sent emissaries into the streets and parks, plastered handbills on light poles and the sides of buildings. Wakefield tried several, but he couldn't take them seriously. Then he heard an ad on the radio for an open house at Synanon, the famous drug-treatment program. He stumbled drunk to the meeting, was told that he was weak, sick and pathetic, an observation he'd apparently been looking for, and decided to join.

Synanon had been founded in 1958 by a reformed alcoholic from Toledo, Ohio, named Charles E. Dederich. His second wife had sent him off to Alcoholics Anonymous in Los Angeles on pain of divorce and, like many before him, he soon became addicted to giving inspirational accounts of his struggle toward sobriety. Later, he would tell *People* magazine, "I was a salesman and a fair-to-middling stand-up comic for AA." But Dederich apparently was a man with ambitions as well, and the germ of an idea: instead of the predictable testimonials, sympathy and mutual support of AA, he envisioned a more direct, dramatic cure. A group called "Dederich's Faction" began meeting in his Santa Monica apartment for confrontational, no-holds-barred bull sessions. The sessions were given a name by Dederich, who had a positive genius for such things—he called them "the Game." In July 1958, he opened a Santa Monica storefront, called the Tender Loving Care Club, for alcoholics and drug addicts. When the original group of renegades from AA protested that the addicts were overrunning their club, Dederich said, "It's *my* club," and told them to leave. Several months later, he incorporated

Synanon—the name allegedly inspired by an addict who tangled the words "seminar" and "symposium"—as a full-time therapeutic community for addicts and alcoholics (the emphasis was on the former) with about forty residents. The numbers grew rapidly. Dederich claimed a success rate for heroin addicts of 80 percent (as opposed to 10 percent in more traditional programs). His figures were disputed later by various experts, but he was lionized in the early years for the apparent rigor of the program. Addicts weren't coddled in Synanon. They confronted each other in the Game, tearing down defenses, ridiculing excuses, forcing themselves to accept responsibility for their own weaknesses. Discipline was strict; those who broke the house rules had their heads shaved. When the first newspaper and magazine articles appeared, public response was predictably favorable. Courts began to give addicts the option of Synanon or jail. Books were written about the miracles performed there.

Meanwhile, Dederich was very cleverly building an empire. He bought valuable real estate for Synanon centers in Santa Monica and Oakland, and a huge tract of land in western Marin County, north of San Francisco. He established a business which employed addicts in the manufacture of ballpoint pens and other doodads with corporate logos, and soon counted General Motors, IBM, Control Data and other giants among its clients. He also realized that heroin addicts weren't the only ones who might benefit from having their egos ripped apart; group therapy was becoming a growth industry in California and, in 1966, he organized "Game" clubs for non-addicts. By 1968, an estimated 3,400 were playing. The next step was to expand Synanon to include non-addicts—indeed, anyone who was looking for an "alternative lifestyle"—and this began to happen in the late 1960s. By the time John Wakefield appeared at the open house, Synanon had de-emphasized drug treatment and was well on its way to becoming a cult. In 1971, Dederich told an interviewer: "We once had the idea of 'graduating.' This was a sop to social workers and professionals who wanted me to say we were producing 'graduates.' I have always wanted to say to them, 'A person with this fatal disease will have to live here all his life.' I know if they go out of Synanon, they are dead."

Wakefield spent his first few weeks in the program ill, sweating the cheap wine out of his system. He was thirsty all the time, and barely able to move from the couch where he'd fallen asleep when he'd first arrived. Synanon members took turns sitting with him; he was never left alone. When he finally regained his strength, he was moved from San Francisco to the huge Synanon center in Oakland, formerly the Clay Hotel, and it was there that he was introduced to the Game. It was odd at first, having people who'd previously been understanding and supportive screaming at him, but he tended to agree with them. The basic message was that he was weak and destructive, unable to function in the real world. One by one, they pounded it into his head: "I know I'm going to be here for the rest of my life. You haven't come to that conclusion yet, but you better get there in a hurry . . . because you're just fooling yourself if you think you can make it in the world. You'll only wind up drinking again and miserable, hurting everyone you love."

After about a month of this, he sat down and wrote his parents a letter:

Hi Mom and Dad

I guess that by now I know a little about myself and maybe I can be a little honest with you and me. I'm kind of finding out who I am and what I am. I know I'm not what I think I am. I'm kind of a messed up person who messed up everything he touched or had anything to do with.

I also know that I'll have to stay here for the rest of my life. And to do that I am going to have to cut loose all outside ties. Maybe once in a while I can write a letter or something, but most of the time I won't be able to. I would like to have all of my clothes sent and my radio, if you don't need it. I guess you still think I'm taking from you but I'm not. It's just that right now in my life I'll have to almost forget that I have anything outside of Synanon. I hope that you understand why I am asking for this.

Love,
Johnny.

P.S. Don't buy anything new. Just send what I have, if you would please.

For some reason, though, he never mailed the letter. Instead, he sent a postcard telling them where he was and asking them not to try to get in touch with him.

Life in Synanon certainly was easier than the real world. He never had to worry about getting fired, or where his next meal was coming from. He lived in a two-bedroom suite with seven other men, which was part of a platoon-sized housing group called a "tribe." There were all sorts of rules and regulations, but the regimentation wasn't nearly so strict as the Marines and Wakefield found that he was relieved to have some limits imposed on his behavior. He was given a job in the transportation department, shuttling people in a van between Oakland and Santa Monica. There were precise instructions for each trip, the route, the restaurant where he was to stop along the way, the money allotted for food and gas. In Santa Monica, waiting to make the trip back north, he would drive a van taking workers to the various Synanon-owned factories and warehouses. When he wasn't driving, he was assigned to the Synanon gas station; several times he decided he'd rather hang out at the Santa Monica beach than at the gas station and had his head shaved for the misdemeanor. But he abided by all the important rules and never was tempted to take a drink. After six months, he was given a weekly allowance of $2.50 and a pair of bib overalls, which, along with a white shirt, constituted the unofficial Synanon uniform.

He made no close friends, although he had a girlfriend for a time. Cohabitation between unmarried people was allowed, but strictly regulated. Reservations had to be made for a "couples" room, and conjugal visits were limited to two a week. His girlfriend was an indifferent young woman, a former heroin addict who said, "Okay, if you want to," when he first asked her if she'd like to visit the couples room. She seemed to have no will of her own; he'd ask and she'd acquiesce. There was no passion involved and, after a while, he stopped asking.

On Saturday nights in Oakland, the Game would be played in a large room at the hotel, ringed with bleachers and open to the public. Wakefield lacked the seniority to participate in these showcase sessions, but he enjoyed watching them. Several times he saw Dederich running the Game, and was very impressed. Dederich was the ultimate Gamesman, able to pick up on the most innocent remarks, twist them around and use them as a bludgeon to peel away defenses. Most of the regular group leaders weren't nearly so acute. After Wakefield's first few Games, when he allowed himself to be convinced that he needed to make a lifetime commitment to Synanon, he began to gain confidence and actually look forward to the twice-weekly sessions. If it was indeed a game, he was resolved to win it. He defined "winning" as successfully fending off the efforts to pry him open. He did this through a rather juvenile form of passive resistance. The group leaders and members changed from week to week, which made it easier for him to avoid being trapped. Usually, they would try to get at him by asking why he'd been drinking so much before he came to Synanon. "Because I felt like it," he'd say.

But didn't you realize you were becoming addicted to it?

"Yeah, but so what? I'm not now, so what's the worry?"

You might start drinking again.

"Or I might not."

When they attacked him for not cooperating, he would lean back in his chair triumphantly, sometimes cupping an ear as they screamed and saying, "What's that? I can't hear you." At other times, he'd take the offensive and call them "a bunch of junior psychologists," which never failed to get a rise.

He refused to talk about Vietnam. He refused to even acknowledge that he'd been there. When asked about the bullet wound in his arm and his collection of shrapnel scars, he'd invent stories—he'd been shot by a farmer while stealing watermelons, he'd injured his knee playing football, he'd been slashed in a knife fight . . . He found that he enjoyed misleading them.

Meanwhile, back in Indianapolis, his parents had rushed to the library after receiving his postcard and read everything they could find about Synanon. They had mixed feelings as they read the glowing accounts of the program's success with drug addicts—they were happy that John finally was getting some sort of help, but shocked that he was finding it in such a place. They'd never had the slightest inkling that he was involved with drugs or even—aside from his birthday night—that he was a heavy drinker. On the pretext of visiting Steve, then stationed at Travis Air Force Base, they decided to go to California and, despite John's instructions, visit him.

Dorothy Wakefield had written to Synanon, asking for more information about her son, and received the name of someone who was described as John's "tribe leader." When they arrived in San Francisco, they immediately called the Synanon center in Oakland and found that John had been moved to Santa Monica. They called Santa Monica and eventually spoke with the man who said he was John's "tribe leader." He said that he'd check to see if John wanted to talk with them, and suggested they call back the next day. When they did, he said that John wanted to be left alone. "Well, maybe you can help us," Dorothy Wakefield said. "Is Johnny a drug addict?"

"No, that's not his problem."

"What *is* his problem?"

"His problem," the tribe leader said, "is that he's a chronic liar."

It wasn't easy hearing this from a stranger—a *tribe leader*, of all things—and their inclination was not to believe it . . . but, at the same time, it was more plausible than being told that he was a heroin addict. They knew all about his evasiveness, his caginess, his tendency to embroider stories in a self-aggrandizing way. They considered it chronic immaturity more than anything else, but quietly acknowledged that there was a germ of truth to what the tribe leader said. They made no further efforts to contact John, and returned home disheartened.

He called them soon after that. He wanted to leave Synanon, and needed money to get home. He claimed that he'd never been told they had come to visit him, that he would have been happy to see them. By this time, though, Ed Wakefield didn't know what to believe, but he had a very strong feeling that if he agreed to send

John the money now, he would be doing it again and again for the rest of his life. He told John that he was glad that he wanted to come home, but he'd have to figure out a way to get there on his own. "Your mother and I have decided we just can't do this anymore," he said. John took the news quietly. Ed put down the phone, then went to the bedroom, shut the door and cried.

Years later, Wakefield would offer several reasons for leaving Synanon. He'd say that he gradually became aware that it was more a cult than a treatment program, although, by his own admission, he had joined for rather cultish reasons: not so much for treatment as escape from the depressing reality of his life. More to the point, he'd say that he simply had grown tired of the place, that he was bored with the rules and restraints . . . and, sheepishly, that perhaps his act in the Game was beginning to wear thin and the group leaders were closing in on him. When told that his tribe leader had described him as a chronic liar, he didn't grow angry or uncomfortable. "I guess," he said, "I wasn't fooling them as much as I thought."

In any case, he walked out of Synanon one day and never returned. He went back to San Francisco, back to cooking, but not—apparently—to drinking. He drifted to a ski lodge in the Donner Pass and then to Salt Lake City, where he worked in the restaurant of a small hotel. For the first time in several years, he began to feel surges of the old, cool anger and was arrested twice in Salt Lake City for bar fights. He went before the same judge both times. The first time, he was made to pay a small fine and replace the pool cue he had used on his opponent. The second time, the judge suggested that he leave town before he got into any real trouble. He agreed to go.

After nearly four years on the road, he was finally growing tired of drifting, tired of smelly kitchens and fleabag hotels. He still had no idea what he wanted to do with his life, but decided that it was time he figured out something. The first thing was to get back to Indianapolis. He noticed an ad in the newspaper: a man with two Corvettes was looking for someone to drive one of them back to Indiana. He quickly made arrangements to make the trip.

On the day he was to leave, a strange thing happened. He began to feel very frightened, sweaty and sick. He rushed to the bathroom and vomited.

It was a nice piece of symmetry—his years on the road had started and ended the same way—but also the first of many such nervous attacks.

3

Wakefield lived with his parents again, but less obstreperously than before. He took a job managing the lunch counter at the McCrory's five-and-dime store downtown. He had lost his taste for melodramatic dissipation; his rebellion collapsed into a lobotomized imitation of normality. He had never been very introspective, and now that ability vanished entirely . . . as did all conscious memory of Vietnam, his travels, his dreams at night. Thus benumbed, he went through the motions of settling down.

To his parents, he remained the "same old Johnny." They saw only the forced joviality he affected in the presence of strangers—a near-universal category of acquaintances, since he had no friends. Occasionally, they would visit him at McCrory's, where he presided over the lunch counter as a bartender might, sharing the latest corny jokes, chatting with the regulars, teasing and flirting with the women.

One of the regulars was a woman named Elizabeth Wilson, a legal secretary in one of the offices upstairs. Wakefield flirted with her too, but in a more subdued way. He was drawn to her more for her composure than for her looks, although she was not unattractive. She always carried a book with her when she came down for lunch, and had a sardonic sense of humor. She seemed dignified, independent, mature.

Elizabeth Wilson had been working on her composure for ten years, since escaping a very bad marriage. She had raised three children alone, achieved a measure of financial security, bought a house and learned how to make do on her own after many years of struggle. She was thirty-seven years old, ten years older than Wakefield, and had reached a moment of comfortable self-sufficiency in her life; the last of her children, a daughter named Cathy, was about to graduate from high school and leave her—and Elizabeth found, to her great satisfaction, that she wasn't daunted by the prospect of an empty house. She'd had several affairs in the years since her divorce, mostly with older men who seemed perennially in need of someone to mother them; only once had she allowed herself to fall in love, and then the fellow had abandoned her literally on the steps of the church. She wasn't opposed to the idea of getting involved again, but she wasn't desperate for it either . . . and, after so many years alone, didn't think it very likely in any case. Wakefield's obvious interest was intriguing; she was flattered to be found attractive by a younger man, even if it seemed likely that he'd turn out to be another one who wanted to be mothered. She began to sense that his intentions were quite serious; later she would claim that he had proposed marriage through his manner long before he ever asked her out on a date.

So she wasn't very surprised when John Wakefield did, eventually, ask her out. He seemed confident, casual, if a bit vague. He asked, she accepted, but the details were unclear. She assumed he'd call her at home that night to set a date, but he didn't. She went down to lunch as always the next day, carrying a copy of *The French Connection.*

"I've never been stood up by *The French Connection* before," he said, and she laughed. Apparently, he'd expected her to meet him after work.

"You've got to be more specific, John."

"How about tonight, then?"

He took her to dinner at a restaurant called Jackie's. They ordered drinks, which made her a little high. She was pleased that he didn't make a fuss when she refused a refill; he wasn't trying to get her drunk. She noticed that he nursed his drink along, and when she didn't order a second, he didn't either. He was very thoughtful, in fact; softer, more sensitive than he appeared behind the lunch counter. Elizabeth believed she was a very observant person, and enjoyed that trait in others. It was clear that John Wakefield was quite perceptive too, especially when he said to her, "You're very careful, aren't you? You never let down your shield."

"My shield?"

"You never let down your guard."

She was stunned by this, and began to talk about why she had constructed her "shield." She talked about her marriage, her hysterectomy (she figured she'd better take care of all the bad news right away), her years of loneliness and uncertainty. At one point, as she was discussing a particularly painful incident involving her ex-husband, he patted her hand and said, "I wish I could have been there for you then."

It was very impressive. He wasn't at all like the other men she had known, who talked incessantly about themselves; he seemed more interested in listening to her problems than in strutting or bragging. In fact, she realized much later, he revealed practically nothing of himself.

They went out again the next night, and the night after. She was thrilled by his willingness to listen—perhaps she'd been lonelier than she'd thought—and relieved that he appeared not very interested in being mothered; indeed, it was quite the reverse. He seemed intent on taking care of *her*. He was very much a gentleman and never took liberties, though she found herself hoping he would. He began to spend evenings at her house, a small cottage on a cul-de-sac near the Indianapolis Speedway, overstuffed with her books—mysteries and romances, mostly; they watched television together. They were both avid baseball fans and he would laugh at the intensity of her hatred for the Oakland Athletics, especially Reggie Jackson, who she thought was too full of himself. A few weeks after the Athletics won the World Series, John proposed.

She said, "You realize we won't be able to have any children."

"That's okay," he said. "If we find we want some, we can adopt."

"We-ell, if you're sure . . ."

"I'm sure."

But not entirely sure, especially after she accepted. At first, he wanted to get married right away—two weeks, he said; but she couldn't pin him down on a date. He remained as thoughtful and outwardly pleasant as before, but was different somehow—distant, skittish. Elizabeth thought it might have something to do with his reluctance to tell his parents about their plans, especially his mother. "She won't like me marrying someone who isn't Catholic," he said.

"Well, if you're *going* to marry someone who isn't Catholic," Elizabeth said, "you'd better tell her, before she hears it from someone else."

He told his parents. Their reaction was restrained. Privately, they believed it was another case of Johnny being Johnny: he couldn't just get married, he had to marry a woman who was ten years older, had three kids and couldn't have any more; that she wasn't Catholic was merely icing on the cake. But they gave their blessings, taking solace in the fact that Johnny finally seemed interested in settling down.

That hurdle cleared, he continued to procrastinate about setting a date. As the weeks passed, Elizabeth Wilson noticed other curious things about her fiancé. When her son, Billy, came home for the holidays, John was very nervous about meeting him. He vomited a few hours before Billy arrived, then proceeded to handle the situation deftly. But that wasn't nearly so strange as his attitude toward sex. He had, by then, moved some of his clothes into her house and was spending most nights there—on the couch; their courtship remained resolutely chaste. Rather than wonder what all this said about John, Elizabeth worried continually about getting jilted at the last moment again. Finally, she confronted him: "Are you or aren't you going to marry me . . . and if so, when?"

They were married on February 24, 1973, at St. Andrew's Presbyterian Church. He vomited an hour before the ceremony. There was no honeymoon.

Several weeks after the marriage, Wakefield swallowed what remained of his pride and asked his father to help find him a job at the Detroit Diesel Allison factory. When he joined the anonymous army of 10,000 hourly workers at the General Motors subsidiary that August, it was the last thing he'd expected ever to do, a final capitulation. The war had been a momentary turbulence, lifting him up and away from Indianapolis, spinning him about, then allowing him to float back to where he started, still somewhat dizzy and exhausted from the whirl.

There were, of course, practical reasons for going to work at Allison's. His job at McCrory's had paid a flat $150 per week, with no health plan or pension. He would now average $400, depending on overtime, and enjoy the cornucopia of fringe benefits—health and pension plans, cost-of-living adjustments, vacations, personal holidays, work rules—won by the United Auto Workers union. He was assigned to a chucker machine at Allison's plant no. 5, on the south side of town. The chucker was a large, noisy, greasy automatic lathe, which cut pieces of raw metal into rough approximations of transmission parts for heavy diesel engines. Wakefield worked in a room with hundreds of such machines, fluorescent-lit and clangorous. Thus ensconced, the reality of his choice—thirty years of hard labor, feeding metal to metal, with no time off for good behavior—struck home, and some of his adolescent contentiousness revived.

He was a miserable employee from the start. He studied the union work rules and used them to his advantage whenever he could, filing grievances about as often as he punched his time card. Once, for example, on a Saturday-night shift, a foreman accused him of "running bad parts all night long." This was something of an exaggeration, and Wakefield responded with a tantrum, screaming, throwing tools about, finally calling for the union committeeman. He filed nine separate grievances, which took seven hours to resolve, and he was paid overtime for all of it. When he returned to work the next Monday—triumphantly, for news of such events traveled fast—he went straight to the foreman's office and said, "If you say one goddamn word, I'll do it again tonight."

He enjoyed pushing the system to its limits, finding and testing the most obscure, absurd clauses in the union contract, flaying management with technicalities. His father had always said the UAW had gone too far, and now he was proving the old man's case. The two of them argued continually about labor and management at family gatherings, both unbending, the father taking the game far more seriously than his son. Ed Wakefield had seen others like Johnny at Allison's; he knew the type. Even before he became a supervisor, when he'd been a union man himself, he'd been appalled by them. The brief satisfaction and hope he'd allowed himself when John had asked to be put on at Allison's soured into mortification. Over the next few years, his oldest child would prove a constant source of embarrassment.

It wasn't long before John's reputation for petulance spread through the chucker room, and his supervisors searched for some way to get rid of him before his attitude infected too many others. One night, after he'd been on the job for about a year, he filed a productivity report claiming that he'd turned out 125 pieces during his shift: three layers of forty, plus five. His supervisor claimed that he had exaggerated by a layer, and fired him for falsification of records. It wasn't a very strong case (some of the missing pieces were eventually found), and no doubt would have been overlooked if Wakefield's attitude had been different. He challenged the firing, of course, and missed about a month of work while the union fought for his reinstatement. He won back his job, but returned only partially vindicated. The company refused to pay him for most of the time he'd been out. He decided to watch his step for a while, having learned that management could make his life miserable too.

He was afraid that he would now be subject to reverse harassment, that the slightest mistake might lead to another dismissal, and the pressure began to take its toll. He suffered physically. At least twice a week he came home with searing headaches; his intestines had never quite recovered from Vietnam, and he was plagued by chronic gastritis; he had an excruciating anal abscess, which required surgery. He put on a good deal of weight despite these travails, more than fifty pounds over several years, and his body sagged with it. In settling down, he appeared to decompose. In outward appearance, he seemed ten years older than he actually was—as old, in fact, as his wife.

On the face of it, their marriage was placid and comfortable. John rarely complained and was never angry with Elizabeth; he remained protective as ever. She tried to be a source of comfort to him too, listening patiently to his accounts of the battles at work, taking his side in all disputes with the outside world. Sometimes, however, despite her best intentions, she grew peevish, angered by the sight of him perennially anchored to the couch in front of the television, wondering why he was such a live wire at work and so depleted at home. He wasn't very romantic or charming anymore; the expectations raised by their courtship faded into a bland mutual acceptance. They lived together, and that was all. She worried about him. When the headaches began, she assumed they were a sign of stress and suggested there might be some other, less pressured and noisy job for him to do at Allison's.

"I could go into general maintenance," he said. "It would be less money . . ."

"I don't care about the money," she said.

Ed Wakefield cared, but not about the money. He was dismayed by his son's downward mobility. It was the final indignity: Johnny was going to be a *janitor*. The janitors at Allison's were, in his opinion, the very worst—chronic slackers and goof-offs, malcontents, drunks and gamblers. What would he say when one of his colleagues asked, "How's Johnny doing?" or worse, "Heard Johnny went to maintenance, that so?"

Wakefield didn't make it any easier on his father, bragging as he did at family dinners that he could goof off all day, get all the overtime he wanted and still make almost as much as he had before.

At one such dinner, Wakefield's brother, Steve—now a tennis pro at a local country club—jumped in on their father's side. "You can't have much respect for yourself, doing a job like that," he said.

"That's fine for you to say," John replied. "But I make ten dollars an hour. That's more than you make, and you went to college."

"But you're a *janitor*. Don't you have any pride?"

"I don't need pride," John said, leaning back in his chair, smiling, puffing smugly on a Benson and Hedges Deluxe, pretending detachment. "I just need the money."

He became, in his usual fashion, a pre-eminent slacker. He was as lugubrious now as he had been contentious before, and again made the most of his knowledge of the union work rules. He often could be found playing cards in the cafeteria—blackjack or showdown, a dollar per hand. For all his caginess, he was a lousy card player, an easy mark for the cafeteria sharks, and soon was more than a thousand dollars in the hole. He didn't care. He was putting something over on the management. As long as there was no money on the table, there was nothing illegal about playing cards. If a supervisor came by, he'd claim to be on a break; if the same supervisor came by again and told him to get back to work, he'd agree immediately, and then continue to sit there—knowing how hard, given the work rules, it would be for them to fire him for *agreeing* to an order. Later, he would assess this period of his life succinctly: "I was a complete asshole."

It was during this time, too, that he became involved in Little League.

If Wakefield had a dream in life, it was to manage a team all the way to the Little League World Series. He knew just how he would do it: The players would be handpicked—not the best athletes, but hard workers who'd follow his instructions to the letter. He would teach them not to make mistakes; he would teach them that winning was more fun than losing, and winning meant making fewer mistakes than the other guy. They would win through persistence and perfection; they would always be underdogs, beating more talented teams all the way to the championship game in Williamsport, Pennsylvania. And when they won it all (and this was the part of the fantasy Wakefield enjoyed most, running the scene through his mind time and again in slow motion), when they won it all, they wouldn't showboat or be *childish*; they would be poised, far more poised than professional athletes, more like Force Recon rangers after a successful patrol, calmly congratulating their vanquished opponents, not at all surprised by their success, as if they believed that victory had been assured all along. He might even schedule a practice the day after the championship, just for form's sake, just so they didn't grow too smug, a reminder that the championship would be there to be won again the next year . . .

For four years in the late 1970s, Little League baseball was Wakefield's consuming passion, though he never got the chance to manage his own team. He served merely as a coach, the second-in-command to a young supermarket stock clerk named Kevin Stanton, who was the son of one of Elizabeth's friends. Their team was called the Panthers. It was composed of children between the ages of eight and ten, most of whom successfully resisted being transformed into a pre-pubescent version of the New York Yankees. Though the Panthers played only two games per week, Wakefield found reason to haunt the Little League complex—five fields imposed on farmland several miles north of the city—every weekday evening, from April to August. He was a volunteer groundskeeper, manicuring the fields, and an occasional umpire for games involving the older kids. Most of the time, though, he scouted the opposition. There were six teams in their division, and Wakefield soon learned the strengths and weaknesses of each, the predilections of their managers . . . and, of course, he knew the rule book cold.

At first, Kevin Stanton valued his help. They worked well together. Neither had children in the league, both had boring jobs and Kevin, at least, tried to keep a sense of proportion about it all. They were a janitor and a stock clerk getting vicarious kicks out of other people's kids. He was every bit as obsessed with the team as Wakefield, but tried not to impose his fantasies on the kids; he was a fierce competitor, but his opponents were the other adults—the managers—not their players. He wasn't so sure about his assistant.

Wakefield was, for the most part, an excellent coach. He had a consummate knowledge of the game, and knew how to communicate it to the kids. He taught them the fundamentals and also some tricks, like how to slide into second base in a way that would obscure the umpire's view of the play. He lectured them on good sportsmanship, and insisted they stand at attention when "The Star-Spangled Banner" was played. He was patient with them and never yelled—not even when they made the sort of mindless mistakes that lost ball games and sent him and Kevin up the dugout walls, chewing their caps in frustration.

The kids seemed to love him too. They especially liked the way he stood up for them during games. Since he knew the rules so well (and also because Kevin didn't have much stomach for arguing), Wakefield dealt with the umpires. In the beginning, even Kevin enjoyed his stylized posturing. It was obvious that the guy was living out a Billy Martin fantasy—trotting confidently onto the field after a close play, calmly suggesting that perhaps the umpire was out of position on that play ("Are you *sure* about that call? . . . I know it's hard to get to the right place every time"), planting a seed of doubt in the umpire's mind, playing for a break next time: Wakefield, the master strategist, playing mind games with the umpires. Sometimes, though, the master strategist would turn juvenile—flinging his cap on the ground, stamping about, screaming, convinced the umpires were persecuting *him*. "They're out to get me," he'd say. "The clique that runs this league just doesn't like me."

Kevin was perplexed by John's need to build elaborate conspiracy theories out of a bad call at second base. He knew *he* took the games far more seriously than was healthy, but Wakefield—his whole *life* seemed to be on the line twice a week. The kids loved it, but Kevin wasn't sure about the example his assistant was setting. Sometimes he was embarrassed for him.

Elizabeth didn't help matters much. She'd often come to games and support her husband in his rows with the umpires, booing from the bleachers. She wanted to show John she was behind him, even if it seemed he wasn't much interested in her anymore. She figured there was a message implicit in his fanatic devotion to Little League. Perhaps he spent so much time with other people's kids because he resented not being able to have any of his own; perhaps he'd simply tired of her. She wasn't sure. She looked forward to the end of the season, when he wouldn't have an excuse for staying away all the time and finally would be forced to deal with the deathly silence that had fallen between them. But when the season ended, he found a new passion—union politics. He ran for union office several times, a hopeless cause since his UAW brethren knew full well that to elect Wakefield to any responsible position would be a clear-cut message to management that war had been declared. No doubt he knew this, but hanging around the union hall kept him busy most of the winter. And then it would be time for Little League again.

Elizabeth's sense that he was avoiding her was substantially correct. He was paralyzed by a quiet hysteria over his marriage. On the one hand, he felt smothered by Elizabeth's love and concern, and did everything he could to push her away—not only Little League and union politics, but also gambling, losing money, refusing to go to work some days, walking out of the house and not telling her where he was going, ignoring her—zoning out—when he was home; he even became physically repellent, shaving and showering less frequently, dressing sloppily. At the same time, he was terrified she would leave him. None of this was ever discussed. It wasn't even discussed when John called her from work one day and announced he was leaving.

"Why?" she asked.

"It's the way it should be."

"Don't you still love me?"

"Yes."

"Then shouldn't we talk about it?"

He came home, but didn't talk about it. She never learned why he'd almost left her (and, years later, he would be at a loss to explain it himself). Soon after, he suggested they build a major addition onto the house—a family room. Elizabeth thought this curious, but had to admit it was a good idea; the house was cramped. Maybe with more space, John would loosen up too. He had, in fact, proposed the room as a reaffirmation of his devotion to her . . . but he'd also calculated that the construction loan would add $450 to their monthly house payments of $110, an amount Elizabeth would never be able to raise on her own. Since the house was still in her name, she would be stuck with him, needing his salary; she'd never be able to get rid of him.

The new room was completed in 1979, and their life seemed to improve for a time. In his janitorial wanderings about the factory, Wakefield had stumbled onto a job he really enjoyed—analyzing and correcting the computer tapes that controlled the milling machines. Instead of playing cards in the cafeteria, he spent his spare time learning to read the tapes, mastering the computer code easily. He loved looking for mistakes; it was like walking point. Soon, he was being *consulted* when the milling machines went awry; he was the most patient and tenacious tape reader in the factory. And then they spoiled his fun by offering him a job supervising the computer tapes. It was a management job, the pay was quite good and, given the growing importance of computers, the future bright. He refused it peremptorily. He didn't want to lose his union seniority, he said. What would happen if he worked at the job for fifteen years and then they fired him? He'd have nothing.

He returned to Little League each spring with a vengeance, having declared war on everyone in authority. He was constantly pestering them, questioning every decision the higher-ups made, from the starting time of games to the way the teams were chosen. He involved himself in disputes that were none of his business, like the selection of a coach for the girls' softball team. At one point, he tried to get himself elected to the league's board of directors and was decisively defeated. Tom Wagner, the league president and an executive at Allison's, asked Kevin Stanton, "Is Wakefield one of those union guys?"

Kevin, reluctant to speak ill of Wakefield (but growing tired of him too), said, "Yeah, I think he ran for office over at Allison's."

"Well, that explains it," Wagner said. "I've seen these guys a thousand times."

Each year Kevin would hope for the best, but Wakefield became steadily worse, especially after it became apparent that the league fathers weren't about to give him his own team. Kevin found himself embarrassed to be seen with Wakefield, embarrassed that people thought he was his friend. Sometimes he'd be hanging out with a group of managers and coaches at the field and they'd see Wakefield approaching and someone would say, *"Oh, God,"* and they would all nod their heads in agreement.

Kevin felt guilty about this. His mother had told him that Wakefield often said that Kevin was his best friend. He knew John would do anything for him. Sometimes he would see him alone in the bleachers, the setting sun reflecting off his glasses, accentuating the blankness, the forlorn, thin-lipped self-pity in his face. The guy seemed in very bad shape, unshaven most of the time, slovenly. He might easily have been mistaken for a skid row bum.

Several times, Kevin tried to talk to Wakefield about his behavior, but John would have none of it. It was, Kevin thought, like trying to get through to one of the worst kids. "I think," Kevin would later say, "the classic way to describe John is that he was a jerk."

His behavior at games became truly outrageous. He began to use his knowledge of the rules against opposing teams, as well as the umpires, rattling the kids with technicalities. Once, he insisted the opposing pitcher not be allowed to play because he was wearing a T-shirt that was a different color from his uniform, which violated league rules.

It came to a head during a game near the end of his fourth year as a coach. The umpire was Tom Wagner, the league president. He wasn't doing a very good job, and Wakefield was on him from the start, questioning every close call, jumping out of the dugout, chasing him around the field. Kevin told him to cool it, but John continued to fume—in the dugout now, flinging his cap against the chain link fence, stomping back and forth, kicking the fence, knocking the equipment around. He was inciting the kids on the team, and the crowd. The kids were banging their bats on the aluminum dugout roof, the crowd was booing every unfavorable call. Kevin was afraid there was going to be a violent confrontation—especially after the game was lost and Wakefield raced out again to scream at Wagner, completely out of control. The two were separated before any punches were thrown, but it was an awful scene. Afterward, Wagner said to Kevin, "How can you stand it?"

He couldn't. He decided not to ask Wakefield back again the next year, a decision made easier by the fact that his brother was coming home from the Navy and would help with the team. He told John, "I promised Kit years ago that he could be my assistant when he came back."

"I know," Wakefield said, without emotion. "Anyway, I don't know that I could have done it next year. I'm going to be pretty busy, working nights."

Kevin felt guilty, though. He knew he was taking something very important away from Wakefield. He thought about how *he* would feel if someone took Little League away from him. He shuddered at the thought: the supermarket would seem a prison, he would have no escape from the dour reality of his life.

Wakefield watched television. He would recline on the threadbare couch in the new room, a frosted-glass ashtray on his stomach, a pack of Benson and Hedges Deluxe and a sixteen-ounce bottle of Pepsi on the end table near his head, the remote control switch in his hand. Each time he changed a channel, a box would appear in the corner of the screen giving the time of day and number of the new channel; the remote control was his favorite toy. Usually he would turn on the television as soon as he came home from Allison's in the afternoon, and watch until bedtime. At four o'clock, a repeat of "Charlie's Angels" would come on; at five, a repeat of "Hawaii Five-O"; at six, the news; at seven, a repeat of "Little House on the Prairie"—Elizabeth's favorite show, she had most of the episodes memorized; at eight, prime time began. Sometime during "Charlie's Angels" And "Hawaii Five-O," dinner would be served on a plastic tray table. The routine wasn't exactly the same every night—on Wednesdays in winter, he bowled; on Thursdays, he played cards at his brother Steve's house—but for far too many nights it was. His favorite programs were sports and movies, especially war movies, but anything would do. Sometimes, late in the evening or on lazy weekend afternoons, he would drift off into a light sleep, always semiconscious of the television, never conscious of his dreams.

Elizabeth would sit in the Barcalounger, crocheting and smoking Salem 100s, watching the television and her husband. The Barcalounger was ragged with age, the vinyl upholstery patched together with silver electrical tape. The new room had quickly become a cluttered bunker of domesticity. There was a fireplace on the far wall amidst bookcases sagging with Elizabeth's paperback mysteries and romances. The television, a color portable, sat in a corner to the left; tucked behind it was a rarely used stereo. To the right was a small writing desk, an end table, then the Barcalounger and an old hardwood sideboard. In the middle of the room, facing the fireplace, was a convertible sofa. Like the couch upon which Wakefield reclined, it was threadbare and styleless, but serviceable and covered over by a loose wool spread that Elizabeth had crocheted. Scattered about the walls were pictures John had collected of sailing ships, schooners and frigates. Hanging among the ships was a painted two-by-four, with the legend: "Now that I have your ATTENTION." She'd given it to him as a joke, but also hoped it would trip a circuit somewhere in the recesses of his mind that would cause the fog to lift; she dreamed that someday he would click off the television, sit up and clearly, unambiguously, initiate a conversation about something important or intimate. It never happened.

The room, the whole house, was in disarray, filled with newspapers—the Wakefields took both the morning and evening papers—stray scraps of paper, books, ashtrays acrid with old cigarette butts. For several years, Elizabeth hadn't had the energy to really clean the place; she'd been mystified by her constant exhaustion and occasional dizziness—she figured it was a function of age, along with her high blood pressure and arthritis—until the doctors diagnosed her as having myasthenia gravis, one of those new diseases that no one quite understood. It had something to do with a communications failure between her nervous system and her muscles; sometimes the electrical impulses just didn't get through. The result was that she had caught up to John in lassitude, just as he had caught up to her in age. They had become quite a pair.

She'd brought home pamphlets and reports about myasthenia for John to read, but he'd never made the effort. Which was not to say he wasn't concerned. He pampered her, attended to her every need, tried to protect her from the merest physical or emotional exertion—a cloying overreaction, she sometimes thought, as if he figured that by making an aggressive display of concern he might fend off actually having to understand her illness.

Sometimes she thought of leaving him. The monthly payments on the new room prevented her—as he'd expected—from kicking him out, but she did think about leaving. Maybe she'd spend some time with her sister in Dallas. If it came to that, she would be doing it for *his* good—to shock him off the couch and into the world again. Unfortunately, that scenario had become less likely since her illness was diagnosed. The very thought of all the exertion involved in such a move staggered her.

At times, she thought about their first date and the big deal he'd made about her "shield." It hadn't occurred to her then that his friendly, joking, buddy-buddy routine, the way he tended to latch on to people without attempting to know them or letting them know him, was a far more formidable barrier to intimacy than anything she ever did. Staring at him splayed across the couch, distant and unapproachable, she would sometimes want to scream, "Whoooa, boy, you wrote the book on shields!"

Occasionally, when he was watching a war movie, she would ask, "How come you like watching those darn things so much?"

There would be a long pause, as if he hadn't heard her. Then: "I dunno." And another long pause as he calculated—knowing his response hadn't been sufficient and not wanting to make her angry—the minimum he could get away with: "I like to see if they're realistic."

"And are they?"

"Yes and no."

She knew that he'd been to Vietnam, although she couldn't remember him actually telling her that. She knew there was a bullet lodged in his right arm, and various scars about his body. When she asked him about Vietnam, he would answer without really answering. His two favorite words were "yes" and "no," especially when used in tandem. Once, when she was out of town, he had gone to see *The Deer Hunter*, and walked out as soon as he saw Robert DeNiro standing next to a hooch wearing the camouflage fatigues that had been issued only to those in Recon. He didn't say why he'd walked out—in truth, he didn't know—and she, knowing the tension and evasion that would result if she asked, didn't pursue it.

There was one war movie Wakefield tended to think about more than others. He'd seen it on television and didn't remember the name or who was in it, but thought it probably was Pat O'Brien. It took place in Italy during World War II. O'Brien and his younger brother were in the same outfit, on patrol near enemy lines. The Germans, expecting them, were making noises as if they'd been hurt: "Help me . . . help me," and the dumb kid brother actually wanted to reveal their position. O'Brien told him to shut up, which triggered an ambush and the kid was blown away. After that, O'Brien did all sorts of heroic things, but kept hearing his brother's voice when he was on patrol. He couldn't shake it . . .

It was a ridiculous movie. Hollywood war. But it touched a nerve, triggered memories that Wakefield no longer allowed himself. He would not go so far as to consciously recall the sudden fusillade, and McIntyre falling . . . but the emotions, the sudden emptiness and anger, shook him to the bone and nailed him to the couch.

Elizabeth Wakefield would stare at her husband on the couch. Since the Little League debacle, he seemed to be diminishing before her eyes. He lay there, chin sagged down upon his chest, coughing occasionally—he smoked nearly three packs of cigarettes per day; when he awoke some mornings, it sounded as if he were going to die—eternally mired in the gunfights and car chases flickering before him; perhaps asleep, certainly not entirely awake. She wanted to grab him by the shoulders, shake him, bring him back from wherever it was he had disappeared. "Wake up!" she wanted to scream. "John, what in God's name is wrong with you?"

Later, she would kick herself for not putting two and two together.

Head to limp head, the sunk-eyed wounded scanned
Yesterday's *Mail*; the casualties (typed small)
And (large) Vast Booty from our Latest Haul.
Also, they read of Cheap Homes, not yet planned,
For, said the paper, When this war is done
The men's first instinct will be making homes.

—WILFRED OWEN

1

When Marilyn Anderson learned that Bill Taylor finally was coming home to Chicago from Vietnam in March 1968, she broke out in hives. It wasn't the first time her passion for him had proven embarrassingly physiological. Several months earlier, she had visited Bill's sister, Beverly, and was so excited just to be in his sister's house, talking about him as if she were one of the family, that she became sick to her stomach and had to rush to the bathroom. She had loved him beyond all reason since high school. She had been willing to do anything for him, and often did—at the Zanzibar Motel on Stony Island Avenue—even though she knew that he really loved Cathy Ruzic, and was interested in little more than sex from her. It didn't matter. The sex was terrific. And just as good were the times afterward when they would tell jokes and eat meatball heroes in that dingy, disinfected rendezvous.

Marilyn thought she knew Bill Taylor better than anyone she had ever dated. He was an open book, far less devious than most handsome boys (she even admired his cockeyed honesty about

Cathy), desperate for affection and approval, easily hurt and yet very manly, rather touching and entirely lovable.

He'd told her all about his childhood. It sounded like something out of *Oliver Twist*: his parents, drunken and grotesque; his mother, a barfly having an affair with a truck driver; his father, always working or drinking or politicking for the Democratic Party machine; their messy divorce, and Bill's subsequent banishment to military school in fifth grade; his curious emancipation a year later to the uncertain, upper-middle-class Irish precinct of South Shore, where he was neglected by his father and coddled by the devout and wealthy O'Brien family.

Marilyn sensed that Bill was badly in need of love and attention. She hoped he'd realize someday that Cathy Ruzic was too cold a fish to provide much comfort; it was more likely, though, that Cathy would tire of his demands—sexual and emotional—and send him packing. So Marilyn bided her time, writing him fervent letters overseas . . . and enjoyed a certain bittersweet satisfaction when she learned that Cathy *had* written the inevitable Dear John letter. She didn't like thinking of Bill brokenhearted and lonely in some rice paddy, but figured her big chance finally had come, and anxiously awaited his return.

When Marilyn learned that he had, indeed, arrived in town and there was to be a welcome-home party at Beverly's apartment in Pullman, she called him immediately and asked if she could come over.

"No," he said.

She went anyway.

All the Taylors were there: Bill's father, his grandmother and two maiden aunts, Beverly and her husband. The dining-room table was heaped with pasta—the Taylors were part Irish and part Italian, but the Italian half prevailed when it came to food—and everyone was eating. But where was Bill?

Asleep, she was told. She waited, not eating—how could she be expected to hold down food at such a moment?—and eventually he emerged groggily from the bedroom in his uniform. She threw her arms around him, and he seemed to stiffen; she noticed that he smelled funny, almost mildewed. He sat down in a corner and was very quiet while the relatives fluttered around him—except his father, dark, gruff and balding, immense and appearing to grow fatter by the moment, stuffing his face, indifferent as ever to his son. Billy had always been bubbly and gregarious, a compendium of the worst jokes ever told, so open with his feelings that at times Marilyn would feel as if she had to protect him from the cruelties so obviously swirling around him . . . but now, he sat there dully, his hand in front of his face, as if he were hiding.

She figured he was giving her the brush-off, but refused to concede: the next day she called to ask if he wanted to go to the Zanzibar Motel. He did. It was a cold, cloudy March afternoon; Bill was cold and cloudy too. Normally, he was insatiable, good for six or eight tussles an afternoon—he'd been a remarkable adolescent—but now he shut down after one indifferent performance. She asked if there was something the matter. He told her he'd come home with gonorrhea, had been treated for it when he visited his mother in Phoenix on the way to Chicago and was better now, but still feeling listless.

"Everyone else comes home with stereos," she tried to joke, "and you come home with *that.*"

He didn't laugh. She didn't mind the gonorrhea—she would have contracted it gladly, if she thought he loved her. But he was morose, distant, so unlike him. And, as the days passed, and she threw herself at him time and again, dragging him off to the Zanzibar, it didn't get better. Sometimes he wouldn't be interested in sex at all. One afternoon, she was scratching his back and noticed a scar. She gently ran her fingers over it. "Don't do that! Don't touch it!" he screamed.

"What is it?"

"Shrapnel," he said, then was quiet. He didn't say anything more about Vietnam during the weeks they spent together. Years later, she would begin to suspect that the war had had something to do with his odd behavior; at the time, she couldn't imagine a hero coming home any way but triumphantly. And he was still very much a hero to her, even though she was confused and—for the first time—somewhat frightened by him. She wondered if he still was mourning Cathy. She didn't know what to think.

Bill couldn't understand what was happening either. He didn't have strong feelings toward Marilyn—but then, *that* had never stopped him in the past. He wondered where his sex drive had gone. It certainly had been there in Okinawa, on his stopover after leaving Vietnam, much to his subsequent dismay. The gonorrhea had been painful, but not very embarrassing; it seemed as inevitable a consequence of Vietnam as jungle rot. His troubles with Marilyn were humiliating and inexplicable, though. He felt as if he'd been slipping downhill, slowly losing confidence and energy since he'd arrived in Chicago—all the more surprising because his thirty-day leave had started out so well, his visit to Phoenix an unexpected triumph.

He hadn't seen his mother in years. She had gone off to Arizona with her lover, Jimmy, about the same time that he joined the Marines. He was nervous about seeing her; in truth, he couldn't remember a single time that she'd shown him any affection as a child. But he was a man now, a war hero, and very proud of himself; maybe she would be proud of him too. He also had something to prove to Jimmy, who'd always disdained him. One of his clearest childhood memories was of a night—one of the rare nights—that he had stayed at their apartment and overheard Jimmy making fun of him while he pretended to be asleep on the couch. "Billy's nothing but a little pussy," Jimmy said, taunting Bill's mother. "He's a little sissy, a crybaby." It was all the more painful because Bill believed it was true.

After landing in Los Angeles, he flew to Phoenix and marched into their apartment complex, spiffy and solid in his dress greens, with a chestful of Purple Hearts—he had won three, for relatively minor wounds. Jimmy's reaction was everything Bill had hoped for: a big handshake, a clap on the back, a long stare at the medals. He even said, rather deferentially, "Billy, we're real proud of you." It was complete vindication, but Bill wondered where his mother was.

"She's over working a party at the country club," Jimmy said. "We can go see her if you want."

There was a luncheon at the club and, standing in the dining-room entrance, Bill could see his mother going from table to table with a pot of coffee. She was much the same as he remembered her, despite the unconvincingly demure waitress uniform. Pauline Taylor had never been very subtle—always the painted face, peroxided hair, fancy clothes, chain-smoking, heavy-drinking, not really an attractive woman, but alluring by tavern light. Her allure was beginning to fray now, with age and alcohol, her face hardening into pinched angularity, her hair more yellowed than blond. She'd never been a very warm person, or even vaguely motherly. Bill remembered a time he had gone shopping with his father and sister to buy her a birthday present. They settled on a dress, white with black stripes—not very fancy, perhaps, but a *nice* dress. He was very excited about it, couldn't wait for her reaction, certain she would love it. She unwrapped the box—she had a way of making it seem the present was something owed her, not a surprise—examined the dress and then threw it on the floor. "This," she said, "is a piece of crap." Bill convinced himself that her anger was directed at his father, that she couldn't possibly have known the present was from him and Beverly too. He always tried to think the best of her, and never gave up hope that someday she would show her love in a way he could understand.

And now, he saw the hostess telling his mother he was there. He saw her begin to shake, then plunk the coffee pot down on a table and turn to him, tears starting, and say, "Oh my God!" Everyone in the room was watching as she rushed toward him . . . and when they met, there was a standing ovation. It was pure Hollywood—the sort of scene Pauline played much more convincingly than real life. It didn't matter to Bill, though, that she might be playing to the crowd as much as to him. She was loving him, and that was enough.

The next few days were wonderful, except for the torture each time he went to the bathroom, and that began to ease after he visited a clinic downtown and was given penicillin. Meanwhile, Pauline and Jimmy were squiring him around town, introducing him to all their friends, parading him through their favorite taverns; they even went to church. He wore his uniform proudly—war protesters didn't seem to exist in Phoenix, and wouldn't have mattered if they had. He didn't care what people thought about the war. He'd never really considered the moral or political issues involved, and had no idea if the war was being won or lost—only that *he* had won. From the start, Vietnam had been nothing more to him than a personal challenge, and in combat he actually had experienced that most clichéd rite of passage: from boy to man under fire—at least, in all outward appearances. He and Jimmy talked about manly things, like fishing and Asian women. He told war stories, some of them true. People offered to buy him drinks; women made eyes at his uniform. He imagined himself John Wayne, home from the Big One . . . until he reached Chicago.

Years later, he would remember only bits and pieces of what happened there. He would remember Marilyn, sadly. He would remember the strange, deepening depression and his desire to get away. It had more to do with his family and his memories, he came to believe, than with the war. His pride remained, but his confidence ebbed. He was thrilled when his father invited him out drinking with the boys, but disappointed by the sodden reality of that excursion. "The boys" were the same old gang of Chicago ward heelers he'd found so repulsive as a child. His father had encouraged him to make connections, learn the ropes; these were important men, who could do him favors. But he found them trivial and obnoxious, either whispering or bellowing, passing wads of money from one to the other, conspiring to fix traffic tickets or arrange a city job for some friend and always—always—peddling tickets to the next political banquet. They brought back memories of all the nights Bill spent alone during the years when his parents were still nominally married, watching television in the little apartment in Burnside, while his father was out drinking with his cronies, and his mother sneaking around with Jimmy. His father was showing him off to the boys now, but it rankled, somehow, more than his mother's equally abrupt transformation.

In a way, he knew his father too well to forgive him. The expectations raised when his father rescued him from military school and subsequent disappointments suffered through that halfhearted attempt at parenthood were less spectacular than his mother's occasional explosions but, perhaps, easier to resent. His mother had never tried; his father had tried and failed. For several years, after Bill Sr. had moved him into the tiny room at the Westgate apartment hotel in South Shore, they had shared the same bed. Bill would seek refuge at the edge of the mattress, pillow over his head, trying to ignore his father's thunderous snoring when the old man would roll in each night at some ungodly hour, reeking of booze and obesity. Those trapped, exhausted hours were their most intimate times together.

For the most part, Bill Sr. left his son to his own devices. He rarely was home, even on weekends. He was either at work on the ore dock at Republic Steel, or at some patronage job, or in the taverns; after Pauline, he never allowed another woman into his life. He insisted that Bill join the football team at St. Philip Neri and bought him a pair of cleats so fancy that even the rich kids admired them, but rarely came to watch him play—was it lack of interest or embarrassment, Bill would later wonder, that prevented his dad from joining the platoon of trim, stylish fathers (doctors, lawyers, businessmen all) cheering on their sons from the sidelines?

Bill ate almost all his meals alone, at the Steinway drugstore on the corner of Seventy-first and Yates, across from the South Shore Country Club, where all the stylish dads played golf and Bill sometimes caddied; on Sundays, when the drugstore was closed, he would walk a mile down Seventy-first to a small sandwich shop. He would walk past the stately homes of his friends from the St. Philip Neri school, imagine them gathered around the table for Sunday dinner. He would sometimes, but not so often as to make himself a pest, spend Sundays with the O'Brien family; at times, he allowed himself to dream that they might someday adopt him.

He was confused and mystified by his father. The man had rescued him from military school and brought him to a fine neighborhood, where he'd meet the right kind of people—but why was he always so cold and resentful? There never was a kind word, never a gesture that might be interpreted as loving. Other people told him that his father bragged about how well Billy was getting on with the rich kids, how well he was doing on the football team, but he never heard it from the source. In fact, his father seemed to take a certain pleasure in putting him down, pulling the rug out from under his occasional triumphs. In the eighth grade, he had spent months selling subscriptions to the *New World*, the archdiocese newspaper. He set up a stand in front of St. Philip Neri on Sunday mornings, and went door to door as well. He sold more subscriptions than any other eighth-grader in the city, and won a full scholarship to Mendel Catholic High School—which wasn't as classy as St. Ignatius or Loyola, where most of his friends from South Shore were headed, but still eminently respectable. His father, though, was distinctly unimpressed. "So what?" Bill Sr. said, when he learned of the prize (and then bragged to everyone about how enterprising Billy was).

Later, when he decided to join the Marines—he wasn't much of a student, and never considered college—his father, who had seen action in World War II, said, "That's the stupidest fucking thing you've ever done." But, when Bill was in Vietnam, his father signed him up for the VFW and was there at the airport when he came home, very proud, shaking his hand and looking him straight in the eye, for once. Within days, and especially after their night out drinking with the boys, he became gruff and indifferent to Bill, impenetrable as ever.

He had three weeks in Chicago before returning to Camp Le-Jeune for his last year of service, and spent them in his grandmother's house on East Chicago Avenue. His aunts, Ruth and Mary Jane, lived with his grandmother; all too often during his childhood, they had been his substitute parents. And now he had been deposited with them again, with his father off working or politicking somewhere. Much too easily, he slid back into the old patterns, the old resentments. But it was different now. They were proud of him, doted on him, but he was unable to return their affection. One night, his aunts planned a surprise party for him. They told him to be sure to come home for a very special dinner . . . and he hadn't shown up at all. He went to Cathy's house, hoping to bring her to the dinner, wanting to be sure that the Dear John letter hadn't been a temporary aberration . . . and when he learned that it wasn't and, indeed, she was planning to be married, he had spent the rest of the evening driving about aimlessly, arriving home to find the guests had come and gone, and his aunts were angry and hurt.

He began to have nightmares about Vietnam. He would awaken with a start, sweat pouring, trembling, not remembering exactly what the dream was about, but knowing it had something to do with Bill Burgoon, his closest friend in Charlie Company, and his last big battle, just outside the Sandcastle, a reinforced bunker complex on the Vietnamese coast. Burgoon had joined the platoon just after Operation Cochise, and respected Taylor as an old salt. They had been ambushed on a night patrol north of the Sandcastle, and Taylor had gone for help. He returned with the rest of the platoon, but the fire was too intense to get back all the way. He wasn't sure now what was real and what was the dream, but he thought he could hear Burgoon calling him, begging for help. When they finally reached the trapped patrol, Burgoon was dead. Sometimes, watching television at his grandmother's house or at the Zanzibar Motel with Marilyn, he could hear Burgoon calling him.

The nightmares were exhausting. He felt listless and groggy during the day, as if he had the flu. They lasted only for about a week and then, just as his leave was coming to an end, they disappeared. *All* his dreams disappeared. It would be twelve years before he'd be able to recall another.

He would never remember saying goodbye to his father or Marilyn or anyone else. His uncle Matt and aunt Nancy drove him to the airport. On the way, they could see the west side of Chicago in flames. Martin Luther King had just been assassinated.

Marilyn Anderson joined the Marines soon after Bill returned to the service. About six months later, she bumped into him at Camp LeJeune. He had just arrived from a short hitch at Guantánamo Bay in Cuba and, once again, didn't seem very happy to see her. They made love once, listlessly, and she saw that it was going nowhere, and decided he was best forgotten.

2

Taylor spent the first month after he was discharged from the Marines hiding out in his sister Beverly's apartment. He wasn't frightened by the world outside, but he wasn't quite ready to enter it confidently either. He still aspired to middle-class stability—a wife, children (especially a son), a home in the suburbs. But now, back amidst the steel mills and railroad tracks, the dreary browns and grays of Pullman, those goals seemed impossibly remote; he had no idea where to begin, how to go about achieving them. In the service, he had fantasized that a job that required a tie and an attaché case would simply be waiting for him when he returned home; when it wasn't, he was more depressed than angry.

He was happy to be free of the Marines, but surprised to find that he felt naked without the uniform. Occasionally, women would drop by—friends of Beverly's—and some of them made advances, but he was afraid to respond. He was afraid that he would say or do the wrong thing . . . and particularly worried that he would disappoint them physically, as he had Marilyn Anderson.

Bill knew he couldn't spend the rest of his life sequestered in Beverly's apartment watching television; he was bored, lonely and, finally, desperate enough to chance a tentative foray into civilization. One of the women who'd shown some interest worked in a tavern called Partners No, where most of Beverly's friends seemed to congregate, and he decided to visit the place. He had grown used to the bellicose posturing in the military saloons that ringed Camp LeJeune, where horny Marines puffed and strutted, chasing after women who were hardly the flower of Southern maidenhood, but Partners No was nothing like that. It seemed at first a standard neighborhood tavern, but there was a benign zaniness to the place that often infected even those who had come there to drown their sorrows. The owner was an elderly woman named Grace Nelson. The patrons were motley and ecumenical—steelworkers, waitresses, clerks and salespeople by day; eccentrics by night, their eccentricities encouraged by Grace's son, Slicker, who sometimes presided over the bar, but more often could be found under it. Slicker was an ordained mail-order minister, who sometimes worked in clerical garb. He kept a box of musical contraptions beneath the bar—kazoos, tom-toms, plastic saxophones—and if an evening proved insufficiently stimulating, he would hand out the instruments and lead the patrons in appalling renditions of whatever struck his fancy.

Taylor's first night at Partners No was typically raucous. He took the only seat available at the bar, between an old woman and an older man with no teeth who looked up woozily from his drink and said, "Fuck you." Bill laughed, and offered to buy him a round. Grace was tending bar herself that night, and when she came to take his order, he said, "This place is really something."

"It's home, sweetie," she said.

And so it became, after a fashion. Within fifteen minutes, Grace had offered him a part-time job tending bar, and he'd accepted. She appreciated his steady stream of silly jokes—he was, he realized, telling them for the first time since he'd returned home—and he thought she was everything his mother should have been. Soon he took to calling her "Mom." They never argued. Grace knew that Bill was a most valuable asset—a bartender who was loyal, honest, sober, friendly with the patrons, and yet conveyed the distinct impression that he could defend himself, and her, if the need arose. At Partners No, the need arose several times a week and Bill usually was able to defuse troublesome situations without resorting to violence. He enjoyed the work, but had no illusions about it: tending bar wasn't likely to get him a home in the suburbs, nor was he likely to meet the woman of his dreams there. Tavern society was entertaining, but too reminiscent of the way his parents had wasted their lives. He had seen the way respectable people lived in South Shore, and that remained his goal.

Still, Partners No was about the only bright spot in his life after he returned from the Marines. His attempts to find real work were disheartening. He worked for a time as a switcher for the Rock Island Railroad, but left there for a better-paying job, driving a truck for a construction crew. When he was laid off there, it was nearly impossible to find anything promising—most employers figured he'd go back to construction work when the weather improved—and he was forced to take a job unloading trucks for Montgomery Ward. He was paid minimum wage for sweating all day in the brutal Chicago winter, which exhausted him and made him ill, so he quit.

By January 1971, he'd hit rock bottom. He was broke, unemployed and living alone in a tenement flat in East Pullman. He knew he was in bad shape when his Croatian landlady suggested he torch one of her other buildings for the insurance money, and he actually considered the possibility. The problem though, was that the building was occupied. "A colored family"—she shrugged—"animals."

"I don't care," he said. "I can't do that."

He tried filing for unemployment, but found he was ineligible because he had quit Montgomery Ward. He told the people at the unemployment office that he'd been looking for work, but couldn't find any, and they sent him to a public assistance office in downtown Chicago, on West Madison Street. He was shuffled from office to office there, eventually finding himself the only white male on a line of women applying for welfare. He spent most of the day waiting and finally was ushered into a cubicle. "You don't look like you need public assistance," said the caseworker, a black woman.

"What I don't need," he said, "is grief from you."

"Well, instead of hanging around here looking for a handout, you should go find yourself a job," the woman said.

Taylor, humiliated, left.

He tried calling the city's Jobs for Vets program, and was offered work shoveling coal at Sixty-third and Stony—the middle of the ghetto—which he refused. He was running out of money. His work at Partners No provided only enough for food. He began to hock his possessions—his television, his watch, everything salable except his coin collection. One evening, he was listening to the radio and heard, "If you have a problem, call Wanda Wells. She'll try to help."

He called and said, "I'm a Vietnam veteran with three Purple Hearts and I can't find work anywhere. I'm desperate. I've hocked everything I own. I need a job."

Wanda Wells went on the air with his plea, and a trucker from the northwest side called in to offer Bill a job—but it was all the way across town; he didn't have a car to make the commute, and wasn't willing to move from Pullman and his friends at Partners No, so he refused that too.

Finally, he was forced to do the one thing he'd hoped he would never have to do. He called his father and asked if it might be possible to get a job at Republic Steel.

"I *could* get you something," Bill Taylor, Sr., said. "It would pay about fifteen dollars an hour, but it's dirty, dangerous work."

"I don't care what kind of job it is," Bill said.

His father hesitated. "Look, I've worked there for thirty years and I never wanted any kid of mine to have to work in a steel mill ..."

Several days later, moping alone in his apartment, Taylor was startled by the doorbell. It was Eli Wagner, an insurance salesman who was an old friend of his father's. Years earlier, before he joined the Marines, Bill had bought a small life insurance policy from Eli, after much prodding from his father. Bill kept up the monthly payments, which were negligible, during his years in the service but had ignored the bills for the past eight months and figured the policy had lapsed. He wondered why Eli had chosen that particular time to visit him.

"I just wanted to stop by and let you know that your policy is due," Eli said.

"Eli, I can't even pay the rent," Bill said, and told him the story of the past few months.

"It sounds like you could use a job."

"No kidding."

"Well, did you ever think about selling life insurance? I could guarantee you a hundred thirty-five dollars per week for starters, plus all the commissions you can make. You could run it up to four hundred, five hundred a week if you're any good—*you're* the only limit," Eli said.

"Where do I sign?"

Eli just happened to be carrying a job application with him, and helped Bill to fill it out. He told Bill that he'd have to pass an insurance exam, but that wouldn't be much of a problem. Then: "Bill, what would it take to get you back on your feet? Two hundred? Three hundred? You're going to need a car. Do you own a suit?"

"No," Taylor said.

"Well, you've got that much money built up in your policy now. You could borrow it out, and get all the things you need."

"No kidding," Bill said, and realized that he'd better learn something about life insurance before he tried selling it.

Eli taught him. The company, Western and Southern Insurance, sold mostly to working-class people. The premiums could be paid by the week or the month. Part of Bill's job would be to keep what was called a debit book and collect premiums on an assigned route on Chicago's east side. The book value of his route was $114, which was his base pay; the $135 salary included a start-up bonus that would last for twelve weeks and eventually have to be repaid, either in new policies or in deductions from his base pay. His commission on new sales would be 60 percent of the premiums collected. If, for example, he sold a $10,000 whole life policy, the annual premium might be $1,430, and his share, $858 — or $16.50 added to his weekly paycheck. It sounded wonderful.

Eli said the sales pitch was fairly simple. He'd been using the exact same presentation for years. He would tell a few jokes (Bill figured that if telling jokes had anything to do with it, he'd be a millionaire in no time), try to ingratiate himself, try not to seem cold and formal (which was not easy for Eli, who was tall, gray-haired and rather stiff) and then begin: "Now, a lot of people don't understand insurance. So what I want to do is explain to you just exactly how it works. And how it works is — you take out a ten-thousand-dollar policy. This particular policy — you're paying and paying and you think you're not getting nothing out of it, right? But . . . *guess what*? In the second year of this policy, it starts building up money and paying dividends . . . just like the stock market! Now, say you have this policy for seventeen years. If you cash it in, you get all your money back. Every single penny. If you die along the way, your family gets the full ten thousand. So how are you going to lose? And then, if you decide to hold on to it for more than the seventeen years, you can actually *make* money. You can *triple* your money. And if you're making money, why cash it in? Because this is your savings plan. See, you're going to have twenty-five thousand dollars — *twenty-five thousand* — by the time you're sixty-five. If you wanted to save a little bit each month in the bank, all you'd get if you died in the first or second year would be the money you put in. With us, you get ten thousand dollars. So, how can you lose? You can't lose."

It sounded easy enough and very convincing when Eli did it, but Taylor soon learned a basic reality of the insurance business: People do not enjoy contemplating their own deaths. Eli had said the two key words were "savings" and "protection"; in the real world, that translated into delayed gratification and guilt. He felt uncomfortable with the hard sell, and was embarrassed approaching people he didn't know. When he was able to get someone to actually sit down and listen—rarely, at first—he would fumble defensively through his pitch. He met the people on his debit route and tried to get them to upgrade their policies, but most were struggling to make ends meet and thinking more seriously of canceling than adding to something they never saw and only remembered when he came around to take their money. He tried selling policies to some of the regulars at Partners No, where he continued to work. His standard opening line was: "You don't need some insurance, do you?" No one ever did.

Weeks passed, and not a single policy sold. His start-up bonus would be ending soon, and the company would reduce his salary to $98 per week. He thought back to junior high school, when he'd sold subscriptions to the diocesan newspaper. How had he done it? He remembered going door to door, just as he was now, but more successfully. He had a standard pitch then too. He'd start by asking the little old ladies, "Do you go to the show?"

Inevitably they did. "Well, this newspaper tells you which movies you can go to see and which are forbidden," he'd say. "You don't want to accidentally go into a show that's forbidden and get excommunicated, do you?"

And it worked. Fear sold. When he thought about it, it was not all that different from selling life insurance. He rushed downstairs, knocked on his old Croatian landlady's door and announced, very confidently: "I've got something very important to talk to you about—*insurance*!"

The woman, perhaps thinking that he finally was agreeing to torch her other building for the insurance money, told him to come in.

"Do you love your family?" he asked. Yes, she did. "Well, what happens if you *die*? They're going to have to pay for the funeral, right? Well, funerals don't come cheap these days . . . unless they bury you in some potter's field somewhere. You don't want that, do you?" She didn't. "And neither does your family. They love you and they'd never let you go like that. Unless you give them some protection, they're going to wind up thousands of dollars in hock for the funeral. You don't want that, do you? Of course you don't."

She bought a three-thousand-dollar policy.

Gradually, though, Bill realized that while fear sold policies, there was a more congenial way to get his message across. Instead of posing as the angel of death or a cool, efficient collection agent checking off names in a book, he could be a ray of sunshine in the lives of the hardworking people on his debit route. He could be a welcome respite from the drudgery of housework and the steel mill, telling jokes, gossiping over coffee, listening to their problems; he could become part of the family. And then, when Mrs. So-and-So said that her cousin's daughter was about to be married, he could find out the name of the happy couple. "You wouldn't mind if I called them," he'd say, "and gave them a little help planning the future?"

The fact was that he really enjoyed the work. He became a familiar figure on the dreary streets of shambling woodframe two-flats covered with tar-paper shingles of brown and gray. He was known in the taverns and the corner grocery stores; his clients welcomed his visits, never very happy to part with their money, but willing to trade cash for attention. He found that he truly believed in his product; he was providing a needed service. His favorite part of the job wasn't selling or collecting, but paying off.

There was one especially poor family, the Laskis, whom he visited frequently. Mr. Laski was a steelworker who was slowly losing his sight and finally had to quit work. The policy was supposed to pay triple cash value if there was loss of sight or limbs, but the wording said "total and irrevocable loss of sight," and Mr. Laski's blindness wasn't total. Bill wrote letters to the company, pleading Laski's case; even if there wasn't the legal requirement to pay off because of the technicality, there was a moral obligation (and it wouldn't look so good on the east side of Chicago if word got out that Western and Southern had stiffed the Laskis). At the same time, Mrs. Laski said they didn't have the money to continue paying their premiums and Bill began shelling out thirteen dollars per month to keep them current. It was four months before the company agreed to make the payment.

When Bill knocked on the Laskis' door, he found the family—they had a daughter—huddled around the kitchen table, eating a thin potato soup. "Hi, Mrs. Laski," he said, barely able to control his excitement.

"Oh, Bill," she said, "I'm sorry. We just don't have the money to pay you."

"Mrs. Laski," he said, "did you ever see the television program called 'The Millionaire'? It was about a very rich man who sent out one of his employees, a man named Michael Anthony, to give some unsuspecting person a check for a million dollars." Mrs. Laski obviously didn't know what he was talking about. "Well," he continued, "I feel a little bit like Michael Anthony now." He took the check from his pocket. "This isn't for a million, but I think it'll help."

She took the check for $6,327 and started to cry; then she invited him in to share their soup. Afterward, she began to tell all the neighbors about Bill Taylor, the insurance man, and what he'd done for them. Mrs. McPherson, down the block, bought a policy . . . and so the word spread. In little more than a year, he nearly quadrupled his debit book, from $114 per week to $425.

His future stretched before him in neatly spaced plateaus, provided by the Western and Southern Insurance Company. He had passed the $250,000 sales plateau in his first year, and received a not very attractive lapel pin from company headquarters in Cincinnati for his efforts. He was closing in on the $500,000 plateau, which would bring a $250 cash bonus—not exactly a windfall, but another indication that he was on his way to the top. After that came the Million Dollar Circle, and an expenses-paid trip to the company's annual convention. There was no doubt in his mind that he would get there eventually. He was beginning to think, too, about rising through the company ranks. He knew that if he kept on selling policies, he'd soon be in line to become an assistant manager, as Eli Wagner was; perhaps, someday, he could become a district manager . . . or even an executive at company headquarters.

His personal goals were equally clear—he had added a Cadillac to the wife, the children and the home in the suburbs—but the process of attaining them remained cloudy and mysterious (except for the Cadillac, which he hoped would come with the $500,000 plateau). Despite the confidence that came with success, his dealings with women continued to be frustrating. There had been inconsequential liaisons with several of the women who frequented Partners No; at times his physical performance was up to par, at other times he would grow frightened and fail. These uncertainties rendered him as clumsy with women as he'd been with his first insurance clients; his approach usually was the functional equivalent of "You don't need some insurance, do you?" For the most part, he let the women do the approaching . . . and none of those who showed interest bore much resemblance to his image of the woman who would preside over his suburban home. It was a problem too painful or complicated for him to spend much time analyzing; it was easier, and far more satisfying, to think about his progress in the insurance business.

He was doing just that one warm autumn evening in 1973 as he drove from the east side to Pullman, reviewing his debit book, thinking about new sales possibilities. He turned off the expressway at 115th Street and then, as he was turning onto St. Lawrence, he saw a CTA bus veer into the oncoming traffic, then slam into several parked cars in front of the old Pullman row houses. The cars were knocked onto the sidewalk and the front lawns. It seemed to happen in slow motion, like the shoot-outs in *The Wild Bunch*, one of his favorite movies. He saw a black kid hop out of the bus and start to run, and figured that there were people hurt and the kid was going for help.

Taylor jumped out of his car and saw the bus driver—a big,

heavy black man—slumped over, still in his seat, but with his head down by the coin box, unconscious. Moving quickly, Bill pulled him from behind the wheel and laid him out in the aisle. There was blood on his shirt. Bill tore it open, to get a better look at the wound. There was a small hole in his chest, not much larger than a pinprick. Maybe he got stuck by his CTA pin or a pencil when the bus slammed into the cars, Bill thought, trying to decide what to do next. He'd lost all track of the passengers, and couldn't hear the screams or the sirens. The driver didn't seem to be breathing. As Bill leaned over to start mouth-to-mouth resuscitation, a horrible sound rolled from the driver's throat: "cukchcukchcukch . . ."

Taylor had heard the sound before, in Vietnam. He remembered seeing a team of medics doing CPR on a grunt who'd stopped breathing. They'd actually brought him back to life. He slammed the driver in the chest, really hard. "C'mon," he said, pounding, "don't die . . . don't die."

Then someone was trying to pull him back. It was the police. A large crowd had gathered, staring at him. "And what the fuck do you think you're doing?" one of the cops said.

"I'm trying to save him. I'm doing CPR," he said, realizing the police probably thought he was mugging the driver.

"Forget it," said an officer, down by the body. "He's dead."

"It was the colored kid," someone said.

"The colored kid?" Taylor said; he was shaking. He was trying to keep his head straight, but that noise—the death rattle—had started his mind spinning. Suddenly, he was overcome by a very clear memory of the empty sloshing sound that Harvey's head had made the night he had gone down to retrieve the bodies after Operation Cochise. He shook his head to clear the image. "You mean," he asked, "this wasn't an accident?"

"What do you think *that* is?" one of the cops said, pointing to the small hole in the driver's chest. "That's a bullet hole."

"No!" Taylor said, astonished. It wasn't like any bullet hole he'd ever seen before; it was so tiny, almost delicate. In Vietnam, bullet holes had been gross, obvious, torn flesh and blood. He was thinking, once again, about Operation Cochise. He remembered the utter terror, being scrunched down in the corner of the paddy, the others screaming for him to go get help and the shame he'd felt, not going. He hadn't thought about it in years, and now the images were so entirely clear. "Hey," he said, simultaneously trying to remember the black kid and fend off those other memories, "I think I seen him running off the bus just as I got here."

"What's your name?" the cop asked.

"What's *your* name?" Taylor replied. "And your badge number . . . because I don't want my name associated with this." He was trying to seem authoritative—like a lawyer, someone who knew his rights—but he couldn't stop trembling. "I don't want that kid or any of his friends coming after me."

The cop was asking questions. Then another cop was asking questions. Bill concentrated hard on the answers, wanting to be precise and, at the same time, to keep his head together. He must have described the black kid half a dozen times before they were through with him. Whenever there was a pause, images skittered through his mind, but not as clearly as before: bits of memory, gone before he could grasp them. He was still shaking. When the police were done, a little Slovak lady from the neighborhood asked if he wanted to come into her house and clean up. "Here," she said, "give me your sweater."

There was blood on his sweater. There also was blood on his hands and, when he looked in the bathroom mirror, on his face. He splashed his face with soap and water, and rubbed hard. The blood was fresh and washed away easily; there had been times in the bush when he hadn't been able to wash for days. He took a deep breath and felt better.

The woman offered him a drink when he returned to the kitchen, then another. Her neighbors had come in and were sitting around the kitchen table, talking about the murder. The woman told them that Bill had been right in the middle of it, trying to help the driver. "A hero," she said. She patted him on the shoulder, and poured him another shot. He was feeling much better now; the trembling was gone and there were no more flashes, just a lingering uneasiness and that, too, soon began to dissipate. He remembered that he was supposed to have met John Cleek, his ex-brother-in-law, more than an hour earlier at a nearby tavern—that was why he'd come to Pullman in the first place—but the Slovak ladies were fussing over him as if he were a visiting celebrity, and he couldn't deny them the pleasure of hearing it all one more time. He was in his element, telling stories around the kitchen table, and they were rapt. "The hole," he said softly, dramatically, "was so tiny, I thought it was a pinprick . . ."

John Cleek had always seemed more an older brother to Bill than a brother-in-law. He was a large man, with a dark, slick pompadour and a goatee, who could have passed for a truck driver or a Beat poet; though actually the former, he had some of the sensitivity—if not the spirit—of the latter. There was a softness to him, an essential decency, that was sometimes mistaken for weakness in the casual brutality of the steel-mill taverns.

Bill had watched the marriage fall apart during his first months home from the Marines. Though he'd never admit it, his sympathies were more with John than his sister. He'd never quite forgiven Beverly all the evenings she'd abandoned him when they were kids, leaving him alone to watch television until the test patterns came on, while their parents slowly dissolved their marriage in separate watering holes. Bev's abandoning John seemed more of the same. His feelings toward his sister fluctuated between wary affection—there was always the hope that the Taylors might salvage some sort of family life—and residual anger. He tried his best to get along with John's successor, a layabout named Don Hutchins, simply because he was now part of the family. It wasn't easy, though; especially after Don sold him two used cars that turned out to be lemons.

He remained loyal to John Cleek throughout, despite Beverly's insistence that it was a betrayal. He admired John without reservation. Theirs was a simple, non-competitive camaraderie; when they were together, neither felt the need to pose. They were free to be silly or sentimental, to admit emotions and fears routinely scorned by their peers in the taverns and the mills, without fear of ridicule.

It was, in fact, a mission of elaborate silliness that John Cleek had in mind when he summoned Bill to the Step High tavern in Pullman that night of the bus accident.

After listening to Bill's story—which was becoming more dramatic with each retelling—John suggested they go to the east side to visit a barmaid he'd been courting. He had prepared a proclamation in her honor, the "Betsy Ross Award," which was a montage of patriotic symbols and pictures of cocktail glasses he had clipped from magazines and pasted on a sheet of cardboard, along with a text he'd spent hours chuckling over, honoring Barbara Nolan for her service to mom, apple pie and martinis with two olives. "You'll love her, Billy," he said, explaining that she worked in a tavern down by 106th Street on the east side, filled with old Serbs and Croats who, when soused, would grow nostalgic for the old country and run down America. "She throws it right back at them. You know, 'Go back where you come from if you don't like it here.' That sort of thing. And they love it." John figured she'd get a kick out of the proclamation.

Taylor, who had augmented the drinks the Slovak lady had given him with several more shots and beers, thought it was a stupendous idea. He loved Cleek's pranks, as John loved his.

"I told her all about you, Billy," John said proudly.

It was a dark, crowded little joint, smelling of stale beer and sweat. When they arrived around midnight, John approached the bar and introduced Bill expansively, with mock formality: "Barb, this is the famous Billy Taylor, of whom I have told you so much."

"Pleased," she said, "to meetcha."

"Howdly-doodly," Taylor said, straining to live up to his reputation.

Barbara Nolan's first impression was: This guy's a real squirrel. He was overweight in a marshmallowy sort of way; there was a soft, doe-like quality to his eyes, which was either kindness or weakness; he had an anemic, scraggly moustache, and no real sense of himself. "So, you're in the insurance business?" she said.

"I would've been a doctor, but I didn't have the patients."

"That's very funny," she said.

"Isn't it awful?" Taylor said, awash in titters. "Wait . . . wait: I would've been a sculptor, but I didn't want to be taken for granite.

"I didn't know if I wanted to be a cop or a fireman, but I finally decided on the ladder.

"I would've been an archaeologist, but I just didn't dig it."

"Hey, John," Barbara said. "You're right. This guy has a tremendous sense of humor."

There was a distinct possibility, Barbara Nolan thought, that he was gay. There were no sexual vibrations in his forced jollity. But then she'd thought the same of Cleek when she'd first met him and found out soon enough that he was decidedly heterosexual. John had been trying to put a move on her for months, but she wasn't interested. He was a nice guy, but something of a squirrel too, destined to live his life in the right-hand lane. If she was going to get mixed up with someone again, it was going to be a man with real prospects; someone who could keep her in a manner to which she hadn't been accustomed.

For his part, when he calmed down and considered her more carefully, Bill Taylor thought Barbara Nolan was unexceptional at best, and probably a little too snooty for her own good. She was good-looking in a tough sort of way: a bottle blonde, with penciled brown eyebrows over hooded, distant eyes, thin lips and a husky, sexy saloon voice—from smoking too many Kools, no doubt. Taylor disliked smokers; when his mother was drunk, she'd often blown smoke in his face to show her disdain.

But John liked her, so Bill decided to make the best of the evening, which, as it progressed, was becoming less difficult. The tavern was busy—between eleven and midnight the afternoon shift from U.S. Steel's South Works, Republic and the other mills drifted in, mixing with the malingerers from the day turn. Barbara worked the bar with effortless skill, pouring, cashing, making everyone feel at home. The gnarled, hulking old Serbs—it was an older crowd—would make clumsy, affectionate passes at her (mostly, it seemed, to hear her comebacks), and she'd fend them off with a husky "Ain't you got no manners?" or "You should be ashamed, an old slob like you, with a wife and twenty-six children . . ." Cleek was right: they did love her . . . and Bill could see that she loved the old guys too, in a way, which made her more attractive. When the crowd thinned out after one o'clock, John read the proclamation and Bill accompanied him by humming "The Battle Hymn of the Republic" in the background.

Barbara thought it was really sweet, but very squirrelly.

When she finished work at two, they went to an after-hours bar, smoking a joint along the way. Bill told her about the bus accident and she found herself thinking: Well, there's no harm to the guy . . . and maybe if he lost fifty pounds, he wouldn't be bad-looking.

When he finally arrived back at his apartment, Bill stumbled into the bathroom, looked in the mirror, took stock. It had been an amazing night. As he was taking off his clothes, he noticed flecks of dried blood still caked in his cuticles and went back to the bathroom to scrub them off. Drunk and exhausted as he was, he didn't want to go to sleep with blood on him.

3

"*Did you hear about the* two queer judges?" Bill Taylor asked. "They tried each other."

Barbara Nolan laughed. It was a Friday night early in the spring of 1974. She'd stopped with a friend for a quick drink at Partners No, and there was Bill Taylor. She hadn't seen him in months, not since the night he and John Cleek had presented her with the "Betsy Ross Award" at the old Serbian tavern.

He seemed as goofy, as inappropriately enthusiastic as ever. When she asked him how he was doing, he erupted: "Just great! *Fan*-tastic! Really good. How about you?" He was, she decided, still a squirrel . . . but he *had* changed, somehow.

"You lost weight?" she asked.

"Fifty pounds."

She remembered thinking the last time she'd seen him that he wouldn't be bad-looking if he lost fifty pounds, and she'd been right. He seemed more confident and prosperous too. He was wearing a nice suit, and his jokes were funnier.

He took off his jacket, loosened his tie and did about an hour of Polish jokes. Barbara and her friend were convulsed; he had a way of making even bad jokes seem funny. He continued on through his repertoire: doctor jokes, talking dogs, gays, blacks . . . she hadn't laughed so hard in years.

He asked if she wanted a lift home. She accepted, and was pleasantly surprised when he escorted her to a late-model Cadillac. "You must be doing pretty well," she said.

"I got promoted," he said. "I'm an assistant manager now. I got five salesmen working under me."

Not bad at all, she thought. He drove her home and kissed her good night. It was an interesting kiss: gentle, but not at all squirrelly—certainly not the clumsy, artless lunge she might have expected from him. He didn't grope at her; there was a shy tenderness to him. She was impressed.

"Hey," she said, "let's do it again soon."

They began to date—nothing serious, no heavy romance, just fun. This was frustrating to Bill. He was attracted to Barbara Nolan because she had the look of an easy woman—coarse, bawdy, casual—and yet he found he was frightened to make a move. His luck with women was growing worse; there had been several embarrassing episodes in bed in the past year. He couldn't figure it out; the more successful he became, the less successful he became. He thought it might, perhaps, be due to the constant tensions at work. He'd been promoted, all right, but over the objections of his district manager at Western and Southern Insurance, who'd had another man in mind for the job. Bill was convinced the manager had been out to get him from the start, looking for the merest excuse to bust him back to salesman. He did, indeed, have five men working for him—but, like most novice insurance salesmen, they weren't very dependable. They came and went, trying the business for a couple of months, then quitting when their start-up bonuses ran out. He often had to cover for them, collect their debit routes. He was working harder than ever, and not having nearly as much fun as he'd had his first years in the business. He'd earned enough money to buy his Cadillac (bayberry green, just slightly used), but the rest of his goals seemed a mirage that receded each time he advanced.

Barbara Nolan, meanwhile, found Bill's reluctance as winning as it was rare; it reinforced her feeling that he wasn't just another clunky steelworker, intending to put the grope on her and then—even worse—marry her and chain her to a stove with a dozen screaming kids and no money. She'd grown up with that, one of seven children in an all too typical working-class home on the south side. She considered her father a galoot, imperious and brutal; her mother endured his rages with humor and grace, a remarkable woman. When Barbara was nineteen, she married Dave Nolan and escaped the madhouse. He was a gorgeous man, stunning in his Navy uniform; they traveled the country together, from base to base, until he went off to Vietnam for a year on the *Coral Sea*. When he returned, she was four months pregnant, the result of a sodden, innocently ridiculous night with a homosexual friend of hers. Dave was very understanding; he wanted her to have the baby. He promised to love it as his own and, when Traci was born, he did. But Barbara couldn't forget he wasn't the real father. She treated him shabbily, especially after he went to work in the mills and she found herself living just the sort of life she'd wanted to escape. She ignored and abused him; he found solace in heroin, hanging out in Hammond, which seemed a center for steelworker junkies. Then she began to step out—there was an older man she met at the laundromat who had lots of money and was very generous—and eventually she moved from the house, taking a small apartment on the east side with her daughter.

There had been more than a few men since, but she carefully avoided entanglements. She tended bar, enjoyed her independence and resolved never to marry again—unless, of course, someone came along and offered her the Big Casino. She wanted not just money, but excitement; if husbands were cities, hers would be Las Vegas. She knew it wasn't likely that she'd hit the jackpot, especially on the east side of Chicago, but she was in no rush.

Bill Taylor certainly wasn't Las Vegas, but he was kind, funny, fairly prosperous and not at all brutish, a more than acceptable companion until the Big Casino came along. When her sister Karen was to be married that spring, Barbara asked Bill to come along as her date. The wedding was huge, several hundred people in the banquet hall of a social club in Burnside, and it turned out to be a rather memorable evening on two counts. First, there was Barbara's cousin Patsy, who made straight for Bill as soon as she saw him. "Aren't you Billy Taylor?" she asked, then: "Don't you *recognize* him, Barb? You two used to play together every day when you were kids."

Barbara searched her memory, and remembered a little boy who'd lived on Cottage Grove, then moved away, her first crush. "Did you live on Cottage Grove?" she asked, and Bill giggled affirmatively. He didn't seem to remember her at all, though.

"You're not going to believe this," Patsy said. "But I got a picture at home of the two of you playing together when you were about five years old."

It seemed, to Barbara, more than just a strange coincidence; it was *significant*, fateful.

The other notable event that evening was a fight Bill started, which in the end rivaled anything Barbara had ever seen on television. It happened late, just as the party was about to end. They were standing at the bar, and Bill nodded toward a rather thuggy-looking pair of wedding guests. "You see those two kids down there?" he said. "I don't like them."

"Why not?" Barbara laughed. He was pretty drunk.

"Just listen to them," he said. "They're making fun of everyone here."

It was true. They were loud and obnoxious, laughing at the way some of the older people were dancing. Then one of them began working his way down the bar toward the dance floor, jostling people, cursing them out. When he reached Bill, he stopped. "What the *fuck* are you staring at?" Bill said, and then decked the kid before he could answer. There was, for an instant, the same portentous silence as occurs in a game of musical chairs when the music is turned off, followed by bedlam. Soon everyone was fighting; chairs and bottles were flying. Barbara stood at the bar, watching as Bill flailed and grappled at the center of it all, wondering: Who *is* this guy? Then she saw her sister, the bride, slugged in the face by a young woman . . . and immediately, *she* was into it too, along with her aunt, punching and kicking her sister's assailant. When the police arrived, she escaped with Bill to Partners No.

She didn't see him for several weeks after that. She went to visit another of her sisters, in Pennsylvania, and found to her dismay that she was thinking about Bill Taylor more than seemed healthy. She couldn't figure him out. He was an innocent, one of the least guileful people she'd ever met . . . he seemed to have survived both Vietnam and a horrendous childhood without becoming at all cynical. She winced at his gushy enthusiasm—everything was always *fantastic*—and wondered if it could possibly be real. He had less sense of himself, less innate style, than any good-looking man she'd ever met. It was painfully obvious from the way he dressed: One day he'd wear a nice suit and look terrific; the next day he'd have on a chocolate-brown shirt with huge white polka dots, a brilliant white tie and a murky, burgundy-patterned double-knit jacket. He owned a purple suede leisure suit with a fringed jacket that was the single most preposterous garment she'd ever seen on a man. She realized she missed him.

Soon after she returned to Chicago, Barbara was invited by some married friends to spend a Saturday at Cedar Lake in Indiana. She wanted to invite Bill along, but couldn't find him and so went alone. It was a hot, humid, languid summer day; she passed the time on a blanket beneath a tree, playing cards with her friends, again thinking about Bill more than she wanted to admit . . . and then, there he was— dripping wet in his bathing suit, coming toward her. The coincidences, she thought, were beginning to pile up ominously. "Something was in the air that day," she'd later recall. "I was looking at him completely different than before. I was starting to have feelings for him."

She was reluctant to call these feelings *love*, even after he moved into her apartment several months later. She admired him, she was impressed by the way everyone seemed to like him. All her friends liked him. Even Traci—five years old by then, and a tough nut when it came to male visitors—thought he was terrific. She didn't feel an overwhelming physical attraction, but then she'd never been much for that sort of thing.

Bill's feelings toward her had been changing since the first time they'd made love (later, there would be some dispute as to when this event took place). At first, he went around bragging—to his sister, Beverly, among others—about what a hot ticket, what a wild woman Barbara Nolan was. Privately, he felt relieved that she'd been able to cure whatever had been ailing him. Over time, this relief ripened into gratitude and, finally, devotion of a sort. He began to share his dreams with her. He showed her a triple picture frame with photos of himself and his father in uniform and the third slot empty. "I'm saving that space for my son, when *he* joins the service."

A home in the suburbs and a son in the Marines were not exactly Barbara's idea of the good life, but she found herself succumbing to Bill's innocent enthusiasm for the ordinary; his dreams sounded very much like television commercials to her . . . but she was growing tired of having old Serbs slobbering over her. She wanted a solid, decent home for Traci, peace and quiet for herself. In the sense that *falling* in love implied a collapse, she was falling in love. Was it possible the Big Casino would be nothing more than an enormous, sun-splashed kitchen, sheets that were whiter than white and happy little neighbors who praised her coffee?

Of course, Bill hadn't yet mentioned marriage. But everyone could see that it was coming. His sister, Beverly, did. "Don't you see, Billy?" she wanted to say. "She's exactly like *Mom.* She's a bar-fly, a runner. She's everything you never wanted." But Beverly had neither the courage nor the heart to bust his bubble.

There were others, too, who were puzzled and somewhat disappointed by the courtship. Bill's old friends from South Shore, the O'Brien family, were among them. But if Bob O'Brien felt that way, he was too loyal a friend ever to admit it. He might correct Bill's grammar from time to time, but not his choice of women. He was determined to maintain their friendship, though he and Bill had little in common but their years together at St. Philip Neri. Bob had gone on to Notre Dame and then into the family's commodity trading business, which prospered beyond all expectations with the explosion of volume on the Chicago futures market in the early 1970s.

Bob O'Brien remained much as he'd been as a boy—serious, stolid and very religious. During the war, he'd written often to Bill, prayed for him and agonized over the killed and wounded lists in the newspapers each week, hoping not to find his friend's name. He felt guilty that Bill had been forced into the service, while he avoided it by going to college. When Bill returned home, Bob was relieved to find that he was still pretty much the same, though somewhat more profane and certainly less religious; quietly, he tried to convince Bill to return to the fold. He and his father also tried to give Bill a leg up when they could, without being too obvious about it. When Bill started out in insurance and needed a car, Bob had sold him an old Plymouth for a nominal sum; Bill was so grateful he insisted on giving Bob one of his Purple Hearts.

In the spring of 1975, Bob's father decided he was in a position to do Bill a real favor: He called him at the office and asked, "Bill, could you sell me a life insurance policy?"

"Sure, Mr. O'Brien," he said. "What would you like?"

"Well, I'll tell you what I need," Mr. O'Brien said, "but I'm not promising anything because there are three other companies bidding on it."

"Well, how much is it?"

"I'd like a three-hundred-thousand-dollar whole life policy," Mr. O'Brien said. "Can you do that?"

"Sure. Abso*lute*ly," Bill said, barely able to contain himself.

Taylor never would have presumed to initiate a discussion of life insurance with Mr. O'Brien; he had an acute sense of propriety when it came to such things. As an adolescent in South Shore, he'd always been careful not to test the limits of the O'Briens' generosity. There were times, Mrs. O'Brien would recall, when she'd invite Bill to stay for dinner and he would say no, thank you, and explain that he was expected at home, which she knew was hardly likely since "home" was the dingy apartment-hotel room he shared with his father.

Inevitably, someone would spot Bill eating alone at a lunch counter. Mrs. O'Brien admired Bill's pride and consideration.

He had been accepted by the other boys at St. Philip Neri, at first because he was a good athlete and later because they found him to be unpretentious and kind. It was a tenuous acceptance, though; a temporary guest membership in their lace-curtain circle. At times, he would find that certain boundaries did, indeed, exist—as when he asked Bob O'Brien's cousin Maureen Cox out to the movies and received a thunderous refusal from her father. He reacted to such affronts with resignation rather than bitterness. He felt lucky even to *know* such people as the O'Briens, and proud that they'd welcomed him into their house.

Final confirmation of his status came at the graduation dinner for his eighth-grade class. All the parents were there (except his, of course). Bob Monahan, the class president, read the customary list of awards—Most Likely to Succeed, Best Athlete—sprinkled with a few jokes (Most Likely to Join a Motorcycle Gang). Bill listened anxiously for his fate. It came near the end: Least Likely to Succeed.

He laughed, accepted his friends' mock condolences, was a good sport . . . but secretly accepted the judgment as accurate. He didn't see much of the South Shore crowd after that, except for Bob O'Brien; the others went on to elite private schools and colleges, he took his scholarship at Mendel Catholic and then joined the Marines. Later, though he often talked and dreamed of climbing the ladder to lace-curtain success, he would be daunted by the idea of selling insurance to the prosperous businessmen, doctors and lawyers his old acquaintances had become; he figured he simply wasn't in their league.

When he began to calculate the premium on the policy Mr. O'Brien had proposed, Bill realized once again that he was hanging out in the wrong neighborhood. Western and Southern was geared to selling $10,000 policies to steelworkers; his projections for a $300,000 policy were a good $10,000 higher than the prices quoted by the competition, companies far more accustomed to selling insurance to the business elite. If Bill wanted to compete, he would have to improvise. He called the home office in Cincinnati to see if something could be worked out to save the deal; he tried different formulas and combinations of policies, and eventually came up with a first-year premium of $14,000, which was still several thousand dollars higher than the competition. "We could lower the premium some more by taking out a loan against the value of the policy," he told Mr. O'Brien, who invited him to lunch at the Lamplighter Club to discuss the deal.

"Would you advise that, Bill?"

"No, sir, I wouldn't."

"Then let's do what you think best."

So it was done. Mr. O'Brien signed the application over lunch, and then endured physical examinations by two doctors (something the competition would never have required). Several weeks later, Bill delivered the policy and emerged with a check for $14,000. The city of Chicago looked entirely different to him then; he felt the equal of any of the businessmen walking along the street. He wanted to grab one and say, "Hey, I just made ten thousand dollars today. How much did *you* rake in?"

He took Barbara out to dinner that night and later, sitting in the Cadillac, asked her to marry him.

"Are you *nuts*?" she said.

"Well, we have this money now. We could have a nice wedding, then go on a cruise for our honeymoon," he said, trying to come up with something that might appeal to her. She had always insisted she never wanted to be married again.

"Look," she said, "instead of wasting all that money on a lousy cruise, why don't we use it for the down payment on a house?"

He was surprised and touched. The house was *his* dream, not hers. He figured it was Barbara's way of saying that she loved him.

She still wasn't completely sure. Some days she loved him; there were others, though, when she'd grow frightened and pull back — especially when he gushed about having lots of children. Looking for a house proved enervating, but at length they found a nice enough place in Chicago Heights, a modest suburb south of the city, near the Indiana border. It was a yellow brick split-level with the sun-splashed kitchen she'd expected and three bedrooms, as well as a near-finished basement, and a back porch enclosed by jalousie windows. It cost $33,000. Barbara liked the house; it would be a good place to raise Traci (whom Bill had insisted he adopt). But she was daunted by the prospect of suburban life, and by the presence of the third bedroom, which Bill promptly designated as the nursery.

Bill was suffering through some uncertainties too. He had wanted to be married in the Catholic Church. But Barbara was a divorced Protestant, and the priest said that while an annulment and special dispensation were possible, they would take time, possibly years. He was surprised and angered. The Church—which was, to him, the ultimate expression of the O'Brien family's moral and social code—seemed to be saying that he was doing something *wrong*. This made him uneasy, reinforcing doubts about Barbara that he refused to admit. The Church had in effect voted his marriage Least Likely to Succeed, or so he thought. He would proceed despite it, despite them.

So they were married in the Protestant church down the block from Partners No on May 10, 1975. Bob O'Brien, ever loyal, was best man. They rented the large basement room at Serpy's Lakeside Inn for the reception, supplied the liquor themselves and asked Barb's brothers to tend bar. It proved to be a quieter affair than the last wedding they'd attended, but there was one fistfight—Barb's brother Chuck decked her best friend's fiancé, sending him to the hospital. Bill's uncle Matt and his niece, Ronnie, also wound up in the hospital after they fell down a flight of stairs. None of the injuries was serious, though.

After a brief vacation in Wisconsin, the Taylors moved into their dream house. Within two months, Barbara was pregnant.

4

Bill Taylor cried when his son, William V. Taylor III, was born. He called his father from the hospital, and was so choked up he couldn't get the words out. His father was frantic: "Well, what is it? Boy or girl?"

"Boy."

"What's the matter? Something wrong with it?"

"No," he said. "Just crying. Happy."

He saw his son a few moments later, as they wheeled Barb from the delivery room. His first reaction was confusion: it looked like one of those shrunken heads, distorted, squished up. But then they put Bill in a hospital gown and handed him the baby . . . and, grinning like an idiot, he began to cry again. Barbara—who'd had a very rough delivery—watched the two of them together and thought: Well, thank God for that. He's got his son. I won't have to go through *this* shit again.

Bill cradled the baby proudly and, for an instant, remembered being trapped in the paddy during Operation Cochise, repeating to himself over and over that he was going to make it through, that he was going to have a son. I did it, he thought, staring at the child. I made it through.

He was twenty-nine years old. He had the job and the attaché case, the house in the suburbs, the wife (if not exactly the sultry but virginal All-American housekeeper of his fantasies), the son. Unfortunately, though, he had achieved all this in the mid-1970s, perilous times for domestic bliss. Even as he held the baby in his arms, he somehow knew that his success was liable to corrode like the dream house itself, where the tap water smelled like rotten eggs and was so coarse and putrescent that it ate away the enamel on the sinks and tubs. His predecessor had hoodwinked him, he learned too late, putting in new fixtures just before selling the house. The problem was community-wide, and not likely to be resolved soon; all his neighbors used bottled water. He tried to overlook this, furnishing the living room grandly, in ersatz French provincial style, then finishing off the basement with a bar, shag carpeting, rust-colored conversation-pit furniture modules, pictures of galleons and large, stern wood-like carvings of conquistadors made of plastic, a manly room where he could smoke his nightly joint and watch television in reassuring surroundings. But the thin reek of sulfuric decay, unobtrusive as it was when one became used to it, haunted the place.

Far more serious were his problems at work. He simply wasn't making it as an assistant manager; his salesmen weren't producing. There was constant pressure from his boss to step down. "Aw c'mon, Bill, you're not cutting it," he'd say. "You're giving me less volume than any of the other assistant managers."

He would argue, lamely, that he was concentrating on quality not quantity; the policies his men wrote stayed on the books. He fought to keep his job, worked like a demon, covered for his recalcitrant underlings, sometimes handled their debit routes himself. The tension wreaked havoc with his digestive system; he kept a bottle of Pepto-Bismol close at hand, swigging it regularly. A year earlier, about the time of his marriage, he'd suffered a spell of uncontrollable vomiting and spent a week in the hospital. The doctors said it was acute gastritis, probably caused by nerves. Still, he persisted, refusing to give up his dream of rising through the ranks.

Finally, Barbara said, "Look, if you spent all the time working for yourself that you spend covering for those turkeys who are supposedly working for you, we'd probably be millionaires."

He agreed to step down. He was given a debit route in the suburbs near his home, but it just wasn't the same—he felt less comfortable with his clients than he had on the old route. They were cooler, more insular, the children of the old Serbs and Poles he'd served so well on the east side. His jokes didn't go over in the suburbs—more a matter of uncertain delivery than bad material (the material had always been bad); his heart just wasn't in it. He slipped into an uncharacteristic despondency, sleeping late, dragging himself out the door, making a few calls, dragging himself home. He was reluctant to court new clients, especially the more affluent sorts he was likely to find in the suburbs. He started collecting his debit route monthly instead of weekly, allowing policies to lapse without much struggle, and his paychecks dwindled—from $500 as an assistant manager, to $400, to $300. He bottomed out at $112. There were weeks when Barbara would take his measly check to the bank and think: Well, I can't really complain. He didn't even *earn* this.

She was disgusted with him. He had lured her into this dim parody of a detergent commercial under false pretenses. He promised stability and prosperity; he hadn't delivered on either. Sometimes, when they were out with other people, she'd suddenly see him as she had that first night at the Serbian tavern—uncertain, squirrelly, something of a phony. He'd even regained the fifty pounds, and was looking decidedly blimpy. She cringed at the manic giggle, the hyperbolic enthusiasm over his nonexistent career: woe unto those who asked Bill Taylor, "How's it going?"

"Great! Just great! *Fan*-tastic!"

Dinners with the O'Briens were almost hallucinogenic: Bill, trying so hard to appear refined, his gush dammed to a trickle; Barbara, feeling like Belle Starr trapped at a meeting of the Anti-Saloon League, tempted to puncture the primness with a curt "C'mon, Bill, cut the shit." She imagined a mad dash for the rosary beads if she ever let fly; the house would have to be fumigated and sprinkled with holy water.

She wondered if he actually believed the nonsense he still spewed in public about his big future. She supposed he did; but then, reality was not Bill's strong suit. He seemed incapable of dealing with life as it was, preferring to float off into Perfect Family fantasies or lapse into equally unlikely, wildly histrionic rages when his expectations—of her, especially—were frustrated.

His expectations usually had to do with sex. He was insatiable, she thought; and his constant demands only served to dampen her interest, which never had been overwhelming. Over the years she traveled the well-worn route from "Not tonight, honey," to feigned headaches, to *actual* headaches whenever it became apparent he was looking for action.

"Why aren't you interested?" he'd ask.

"I don't know," she'd say. "It's just not there for me."

"Well, do you want to try something different?" he'd plead. "You name it. You want to swing from the chandelier? Do it on the pool table? In the backyard? Anything you want. If you want to go kinky, call me Mr. Kink."

The idea of calling him Mr. Kink was singularly unappetizing. The best she could offer, when she was in a good mood, was mild uninterest. And he would rage. He would storm and scream, accuse her of not loving him, of stepping out on him, of being gay, cold, spiteful—the accusations piling into heaps about as meaningful as piles of dirty laundry. He never was violent with her, but took out his frustrations on the dream house, slamming doors off their hinges, kicking and tossing furniture around, punching holes in the Sheetrock walls. She would be terrified when he did this—it reminded her of her father, of whom Bill was but a pale copy—but afterward, she would giggle at the banality of his accusations, and of her headaches too, the whole situation: Poor Bill. He'd wanted a happy television family—but instead of "Father Knows Best," he'd gotten "Peyton Place."

His parents came to dinner from time to time—separately, of course—and Bill would sulk, retreating to his basement lair as soon as the meal was done, leaving Barbara to entertain them. She didn't mind. The Taylors were people she could understand. She'd served hundreds of old guys like Bill Sr. at the Serbian tavern. He was quite ill now—cancer—and lonely, and trying to reach out to his son, so proud of all that Bill had accomplished but unable to express it. Barbara watched the two of them, mules both, fighting their last skirmish and was quietly angry with her husband for insisting on unconditional surrender. Bill Sr. died in July 1976, a few months after his grandson was born; Bill, relenting finally, visited his father often in the hospital, but never was able to pry from him the acknowledgment he'd always wanted. Recognition of a sort came only when the will was read: Bill Sr. left most of his money to his son, which helped the Taylors survive the era of $112 paychecks. Bill would have traded it all for a simple "I love you."

The situation with his mother was more dramatic. Pauline had wilted considerably, and was paying the price for her years of tavern hopping; she suffered from high blood pressure, heart disease and cirrhosis of the liver. She had returned from Arizona with her truck driver, who disappeared for weeks at a time now and abused her when he was home. Several years after Bill Sr. died, Pauline went to the hospital for a bypass operation. She recuperated alone in her grim apartment, the truck driver having taken up with a healthier woman. One day, though, she called Bill in tears and said, "He beat me. He came home and beat me."

Bill rushed to the apartment and found his mother groaning and

holding her side, a welt over her eye and bits of hamburger and on-
ions in her hair; a bag of White Castle hamburgers lay on the floor
nearby. "He pushed the hamburgers in my face," she said.

"Where is he?"

"In there," she said, pointing to the bedroom.

Bill carried his mother down to the car, then went back to the
apartment. He found the truck driver passed out on the bed, and
began shaking him, slapping him across the face, screaming, "You
like beating up defenseless women? Let's see how you like it when
you're defenseless . . ." He was punching him now, tears streaming.
There was blood. He stopped; Jimmy's face was a mess. Bill looked
at him and realized he'd been pummeling a pathetic old man, not the
young rake who'd stolen his mother away twenty-five years earlier.
He left then, and drove his mother home.

Pauline found a new apartment in Chicago Heights, not far
from Bill and Barbara's house. She visited them often, camping out
at the kitchen table with her daughter-in-law, gossiping over coffee
and cigarettes (despite her doctor's orders to avoid both), while Bill
sulked below. No matter how Pauline raved about the gallant way
her son had come to her rescue, he continued to keep his distance.
The sight of his wife and mother, his two neglectful barmaids, having a grand old time fouling the kitchen with smoke was more than
he could handle.

The incident with Jimmy caused Barbara to take her husband's
rages more seriously. There were all those stories in the newspapers
about Vietnam veterans going berserk, and she realized—for the
first time, really—that Bill was one of *them.* She'd never paid much
attention to his endless war stories. He could prattle on for hours
about gooks and grunts, Cochise, the Sandcastle, the DMZ, Phu
Bai, Steiner, Burgoon and the wonderful things the girls would do in
Bangkok, an appropriately named city if there ever was one—it was
all the same to her. She'd seen plenty of haunted, messed-up Vietnam
veterans in the taverns, and Bill didn't seem at all like them. He was
too jolly; he talked about his experiences too easily. The worst thing
that happened to him in Vietnam, she sometimes told friends, was
the Dear John letter he'd gotten from Cathy Ruzic.

Now, though, she wasn't so sure.

And when the first stories about Agent Orange began to appear on WBBM-TV in Chicago in March 1978, the joke about Cathy Ruzic's letter became very stale indeed.

Bill had been worried for years about the fatty tumors, some the size of golf balls, that disfigured his legs and had lately spread to his arms. He'd always suspected they had something to do with Vietnam, but Barb hadn't taken *that* very seriously either. The doctors said they were harmless, so why worry?

He'd first noticed the lumps at Camp LeJeune in 1969, about a year after he returned from the war. He ignored them, denied them, was frightened by them, and didn't do anything about them until late 1970, when he went to the Veterans Administration office on the south side to complain. He was out of work then, desperate for money and hoping to talk the government into paying him a disability. The VA wasn't very sympathetic. The doctor who examined him failed to see any connection between the lumps on his legs and Vietnam, and even if a connection existed, the lumps were hardly disabling.

Several years later, he finally gathered the courage to have two of them removed by his family doctor. There was nothing to worry about, he was assured; they weren't malignant, just fatty tumors—they looked like tiny cauliflowers—probably congenital. He remained unconvinced, though. He asked every relative he could find, and no one could remember anyone else in the family having them.

He'd never heard of Agent Orange, the code name for a mixture of the defoliants 2,4-D and 2,4,5-T that had been used extensively in Vietnam from 1961 to 1970. He also had never heard of dioxin, a chemical some scientists believe to be among the most poisonous extant, which Agent Orange contained in significant quantities. But at that time not many people had.

In 1977, a woman named Maude DeVictor, who worked in the Benefits Division of the Chicago VA, received a phone call from the wife of a Vietnam veteran. The woman said her husband was dying of cancer, which he believed was the result of exposure to Agent Orange. Several months later, the woman called again: her husband had died, and the VA had refused her claim for survivor's benefits. Curious, DeVictor began to ask other Vietnam veterans about their exposure to defoliants. She compiled statistics, and found that those veterans who had been exposed were more likely than other men their age to be suffering from a startling array of maladies—chloracne (a severe skin rash), chronic headaches, depression, gastritis and other digestive disorders, liver failure, lymphomas, impotence and various exotic forms of cancer. Their wives tended to have miscarriages and give birth to deformed children much more frequently than the norm.

DeVictor's superiors were not very interested in the information she compiled; in fact, they told her to stop wasting her time with the elaborate questionnaires she had devised. The official VA position was—and is—that while dioxin had been shown to have adverse effects on laboratory animals, it had not been *proven* harmful to humans. In a memo sent to its 172 hospitals and 58 regional offices on May 18, 1978, the VA acknowledged the growing concern among Vietnam veterans, but insisted: "the only chronic condition definitely associated with such exposure in humans is chloracne."

Part of the reason for the "growing concern" cited in the memo was that Maude DeVictor had gone public with her information, taking it to Bill Kurtis, a newsman at WBBM-TV, who used it as the basis for a documentary called "Agent Orange: The Deadly Fog," which was broadcast in March 1978 and was the first of a rash of reports in the media on the subject. Bill Taylor missed the documentary, but he saw a series of excerpts from it on the late news.

"Jesus Christ," he said, nestled in the basement, watching. "Jesus H. Christ."

"What?" Barbara asked.

"We drank water that smelled from that stuff all the time," he said. "The bomb craters were full of it. We filled our helmets with it, drank it, washed with it . . ."

He called the Chicago VA, and was asked to come in for a series of tests. He spent a day waiting on long lines for X rays, blood,

hearing and vision tests, a complete physical examination; he gave
urine, but balked when asked for sperm. At the end of the day, he
was ushered into a standard government-issue office where he was
interviewed by a doctor who was about forty-five years old and,
Taylor thought, rather sympathetic.

"What makes you think you were exposed to Agent Orange?"
the doctor asked.

Taylor told him about the times he'd been on patrol in the jungle
and suddenly the jungle stopped, and there would be a swatch of
land where everything had died . . . and then, just as abruptly, they'd
be back in the jungle again. He remembered one place in particular in the DMZ, an area called the Trace, where nothing lived. "It
smelled," he said, "like death. Not like napalm or explosives. You
know what death smells like? We'd fill our canteens in the bomb
craters, and cover the taste with Kool-Aid."

The doctor told him that it seemed likely he had been exposed
to Agent Orange. The trouble was, of course, there was no way of
knowing if he'd been *affected* by that exposure; his fatty tumors
could have been caused by any number of things. But the VA was
trying to learn more about dioxin, and the doctor said that Taylor would be a perfect candidate for one of their experiments. He
wanted to take a strip of fatty tissue from Taylor's midsection and
have it analyzed to see if it contained traces of the chemical.*

Taylor wasn't sure he wanted to have his stomach cut open in
the interests of science. He asked his family doctor, who advised
against it: "Say they open you up and find dioxin . . . so what?" he
told Bill. "The government is never going to admit a connection. It
could cost them billions to pay off all the claims."

---

* In its memo of May 18, 1978, the VA said: "All available data suggests
  that [dioxin] is not retained in tissues for prolonged periods of time."
  But at least one study—conducted by Dr. Michael Gross of the University of Nebraska—found traces of dioxin in the adipose tissue of ten of
  twenty Vietnam veterans.

He decided not to be a guinea pig. Occasionally thereafter, he would receive Agent Orange advisories from the VA, assuring him that research was continuing, files were being updated, that he was being placed on a mailing list "to receive Agent Orange informational material," that he hadn't been forgotten. Meanwhile, the tumors grew and spread. He had two removed from his arms, and more grew back; then growths appeared on his stomach for the first time. When people asked how he felt about the Agent Orange controversy, he would say he was "stunned, angry, *horrified.*"

All of which was true, but not the whole truth. He also felt a vague, somewhat embarrassing pride at having become a cause célèbre of sorts. For the first time in Taylor's experience, Vietnam veterans were being portrayed on television as something other than dupes or murderers; for the first time, they were being regarded with sympathy, instead of indifference or disdain. They were victims, entitled (as their opponents had been, ten years earlier) to all the dignity victimization seems to confer in the media. He saw the change in attitude—the interest, the concern, the *respect*—among his friends, and felt rather important as a result.

In truth, the notion that he might have been poisoned by his own government was too immense and abstract to be comprehended. The knowledge that his fatty tumors might have been caused by exposure to dioxin had surprisingly little effect on his life. He didn't become obsessed with herbicides, or moved to protest (as many other Vietnam veterans did, especially those with deformed children). Agent Orange took a back seat to his day-to-day dramas, the continuing deterioration of his marriage and his career. He fingered the growths, rubbed and scratched them constantly. But he didn't really *think* about them all that much. And when he did, the low-level anxiety was leavened by a touch of pride. They were battle scars.

The bathtub turned green from the bad water. Barbara stopped growing tomatoes and peppers in the garden; she let the house go.

Bill traded in the Cadillac for a van with a plush interior, like his basement room; he sold insurance intermittently. Pauline died of a stroke.

Barbara found occasional work as a bartender in a local banquet hall. She worked nights once or twice a week, made good money—fifteen dollars per hour—and enjoyed the independence both the work and the money gave her. Sometimes she'd go out for a drink after work with several of the other banquet-hall employees; inevitably, Bill would wait up for her. "Where were you?" he'd scream. "Screwing around?" She refused to honor this nonsense with a serious response. Sometimes she'd say, "I sure was, and it was the best piece of ass I've had all year." Or "Someone around here has to earn a living. *You* sure as hell aren't." Or she would just ignore him, and try to go to sleep. No matter how she handled it, the result was always the same: he would thrash about, put another hole in the Sheetrock, storm out of the house and go to a particularly sleazy Chicano bar in town, where he'd mastered the pinball machine. He'd come home at dawn, and sleep till noon; she didn't bother to wake him. She didn't care anymore if he earned a living or not. She had decided to leave. She got the name of a divorce lawyer from her sister, and called him.

And then she found out she was pregnant again.

"*Fan*-tastic," Bill said, as if the simple fact of her condition could wipe out all the bad blood between them.

"I'm getting an abortion," she told him. There was no way she was going to have another kid. Even if their marriage were working, she would have been against it; Traci and Billy kept her busy enough as it was. There was Agent Orange to worry about too. She didn't want to give birth to a freak.

"Barb, don't you see?" Bill said, at his sweetest. "It's a sign from God."

He had a point. Given their sex life, the fact that she was pregnant had to be the next thing to an immaculate conception. She reviewed the past month, and remembered succumbing only once. "Well," she said, "maybe God *is* trying to tell us something, if we only did it once and I got pregnant . . ."

Bill, as always, promised the moon. He'd get his career back on track, and try to control his temper. Things would be different, the way they used to be. And Barbara realized, very much to her surprise, that she wanted to believe him.

Kelly Marie Taylor was born on January 18, 1980, at Ingalls Hospital in Chicago Heights. Bill wasn't quite so ecstatic as when his son was born, but quickly surrendered to his daughter's considerable charms. Kelly was a perfectly formed little girl, with blond hair, immense brown eyes and an improbably husky voice; she was, from the start, a knockout. For all their troubles, Bill and Barbara had managed to produce two miraculous children; that *had* to count for something, he thought. The kids gave him hope that his problems with Barbara somehow would be resolved, though there was little other reason to think so. Indeed, after a few weeks of euphoria over the decision to have another child, they had slipped back into the old patterns. Barbara vowed never to be placed in so uncomfortable a position again, and had her tubes tied in the hospital after the delivery.

When he wasn't consumed by the doubts and fears that seemed a natural consequence of life with Barbara, Bill could be a wonderful father. He doted on all three of the kids (Traci was *his* daughter now; he loved her as he did the others), and tried to give them everything he'd missed as a child. He delighted in taking Billy to baseball games—the O'Briens had a box at Comiskey Park—and would shower him with hot dogs, ice cream and White Sox paraphernalia. He would take the family out to Sunday dinner and play the amiable patriarch, occasionally stealing a glance at Barbara, hoping to find her admiring him in the fullness of his beneficence. He savored such moments of stability, the pristine family times; the good times were *so* good. He never stopped hoping that someday Barbara would be so moved by the sight of him delicately wiping Kelly's chin at the Ground Round that she would explode in an uncontrollable *flood* of passion. And so it was all the more disappointing when, with the kids tucked in after a glowing day of patriarchy, Barbara would deny him his just reward, pleading exhaustion or a headache as always.

He persisted in the face of her indifference. He refused to contemplate the possibility of divorce. Once, in anger, he asked what she'd want from him if they were to separate, and was shocked when she rattled off a precise list of demands—a cash settlement (the figure specified), child-support payments, visiting rights, who would get what. He backed off immediately, stunned that it had gone so far with her; obviously, she'd given the subject a great deal of thought. He continued to believe that no matter how bad the marriage was, it had to be better for the kids than what he'd endured as a child. He would fight to make it work; all too often, though, that involved fighting Barbara. At times, his anger and desire for vengeance would get the better of him: If Barbara wouldn't give him what he needed, he'd get it elsewhere—there was an amenable waitress at Mr. V's, the restaurant where he often had lunch; there were others. He papered over his guilt with rationalizations. He wasn't hurting the kids, just getting what he needed.

Kelly's arrival at least led him to take his work more seriously. He finally gave up Western and Southern as a lost cause, and signed on with Allstate. He figured it had to be easier selling the practical products that were Allstate's specialty—auto, home, casualty insurance—than to go around reminding people they were going to die. Allstate, however, wanted its salesmen to push life insurance, not casualty, since it was the company's most profitable product. The rules were very strict: if quarterly whole life quotas weren't met, the salesman would be fired. Bill wasn't very pleased by this, but Allstate was offering him a guaranteed $1,500 per month, considerably more than his depleted Western and Southern debit route.

He started slowly with Allstate. He spent the last three months of 1979 in training, then was set loose on the street. He didn't meet his whole life quota during the first quarter, but not many new salesmen did. He did much better in the spring, working hard for the first time in years. The old confidence was back; Allstate was sending him little notes: "Keep up the good work!" and "Great week!" At the end of the second quarter, he was called to the regional office in Calumet City. He figured the manager, a woman, simply wanted to congratulate him on having done so well . . . but he allowed himself to hope that the company was *so* impressed that it was going to offer him a promotion. He told Barbara he'd meet her for lunch afterward to celebrate.

The regional manager got straight to the point. "Bill," she said, "we've got some bad news for you. You didn't make it."

"You're joking," he said. "I don't understand . . . Why am I getting all these great reports? It looks like I'm qualifying, and now I'm not?"

The regional manager told him that several of his policies hadn't cleared in time to count toward his quota; several others had lapsed. It was a close call, she said, and she regretted it—but rules were rules. He realized later that he might have fought to stay on; he might have offered to renegotiate the arrangement, accepted a lower monthly draw, begged for another quarter to prove himself. But he was too stunned to fight. He left the office weak-kneed, collapsed into the van and drove down the street in tears.

"So?" Barbara asked, when he picked her up.

"I got fired."

She rolled her eyes and said, "That figures." They were sitting in the van. Bill thought: No sympathy at all—*that* figures.

"So what are you going to do now?" she asked, with more than a trace of sarcasm.

Actually, he had an idea. It had come to him as he drove home from Calumet City. It was a long-standing dream, something he'd often talked about. "Barb," he said. "Don't you see? This is the time to start my own agency."

She almost laughed. More bullshit, she thought. The guy's a complete failure. He's living in a dream world.

For once, Barbara was wrong about one of Bill's dreams. Within two weeks, on July 11, 1980, the Taylor Insurance Company opened for business (its slogan, of course: "Taylor-Made Insurance"). He had moved quickly, adeptly, using contacts he'd made over the years. He found a brokerage house that was willing, for a commission, to handle any policy he'd write in the casualty area—auto, boat, motor-cycle, homeowner's insurance. His most important contact, though, was a man named Nate Silberberg, who ran an American United

Life agency. Nate was a luncheon regular at Mr. V's, and had tried
to recruit Bill several times in the past. "Nate, I'm starting my own
agency," Bill said over lunch, a few days after the Allstate debacle.
"Does your offer still stand?"

Nate assured him it did: a guaranteed $1,500 per month, and
Bill would be allowed to sell for other companies as long as he gave
AUL first crack at life, health, group health and pension plans. Sitting there with Nate, talking insurance, Bill began to realize how
little he knew about his chosen profession. "The thing is, Bill," Nate
said, "you tend to live at the same level as your customers. If you
want to live like a doctor, sell to doctors . . ." Nate spoke softly,
with a mild Austrian accent. He was an older man—in his fifties,
Bill guessed—and suave in a continental way. He said the trick was
to sell *love*, not fear or thrift (as Eli Wagner had taught him): "You
are taking out this policy because you love your wife and family."
He offered Bill "computer capabilities" and all the latest insurance
know-how, including a wonderful jargon that included terms like
"capital needs." Capital needs was the executive equivalent of the
question he'd asked his Croatian landlady when he sold his first policy: Who's going to pay for the funeral? Just *talking* to Nate gave
him confidence; he felt like a professional for the first time, and not a
glorified newsboy, collecting his route. Eventually, he would reward
Nate's faith by becoming one of his best salesmen.

"Bill, you could be the *very* best," Nate told him soon after their
arrangement began. "But you're going to have to resolve your family problems and put your whole mind to it."

"Bill, if you really want to do something about the situation between you and Barb," his uncle Matt said one day in the spring of
1981, after Bill had gone on another rampage, knocking out two sections of his wrought-iron fence, "you really should think about est."

Matt, who was his father's younger brother, had been talking
about est—Erhard Seminars Training—for years: how it saved his
marriage to Nancy, how it had made him a better businessman.
Bill had heard other testimonials too; est was something of a minor

contagion among insurance salesmen in the Chicago area. He knew that it involved being closeted with a large group of people in a hotel ballroom for endless hours over two weekends, not being allowed to go to the bathroom, having people yell at you . . . and then experiencing some sort of magical breakthrough. He knew that you had to pay $375 for the privilege of doing this. But he had no idea what it was. No one who had taken it seemed able to explain it in a way he could understand.

Matt had never tried to push Bill into est (though Nancy was rather more forceful about it). But now he suggested that Bill and Barbara attend a Guest Seminar with him and Nancy. "At this point," Bill said, "if someone told me a gun would ease the pain, I'd give it a try."

The marriage was over. Barbara had told him that. She had taken a job tending bar in a tavern owned by her uncle in Hegwisch, a Polish neighborhood on the east side, and was planning to move out of the house. She would buy a trailer and move into it with the kids as soon as Bill came up with a cash settlement. But he didn't have the money, and wasn't sure he wanted her to leave in any case. "Okay," she said, "I'll stay, then. It doesn't make any difference to me. But the marriage is over." She no longer wore her wedding ring.

Matt and Nancy had talked to Barbara about est too. She was interested, especially when she learned that one of the things they taught you was how to get rid of headaches. She had headaches all the time; she was afraid she was becoming an Excedrin junkie.

The Guest Seminar was held in the ballroom of one of the big hotels down on Michigan Avenue. Bill was impressed by the class of people in the room: doctors, lawyers, successful businessmen, college-educated people—the very people Nate Silberberg wanted him to have as clientele. There was a feeling of confidence in the room, a breathless enthusiasm, and deafening applause when a very attractive young woman—an assistant trainer—bounced up onto the stage and began to talk. She said that est—or "the training," as she called it—had been created by a man named Werner Erhard in 1971. Hundreds of thousands of people had taken it. Its purpose was "to transform your ability to experience living." At the same time, though, "you shouldn't take the training because you want to change. You're not going to *change*. You should take the training because you want to do something nice for yourself, to give yourself a gift." She went on like that. It was too abstract and confusing for Bill to understand exactly what she was talking about, but he was impressed all the same—est seemed to have a language all its own, ordinary words used in unfamiliar ways, comprehensible but mysterious. The verb "to get" was fraught with meaning. People in est didn't "understand" things, they *got* them; *getting it* was the climax of the training. Various est graduates in the audience talked about what had happened to them after they'd "gotten it"—wonderful things; only they didn't "talk," they *shared*; and when they finished sharing, the trainer would say, "I *get* what you are saying" or "I acknowledge that." The audience applauded wildly whenever anyone shared, even if it was something negative like "Why does it cost so much?" or "What does Werner do with all the money?" Bill felt as if he were stoned. The trainer, the sharers weren't saying anything very profound, they weren't offering any great insights into life, but he had the sense that *something* was happening in the room, just beyond his consciousness. He didn't *get it*—and that, apparently, was the point. When it was over, the est graduates circulated through the room, talking to the guests, cheerful and confident to the point of smugness. Bill wanted desperately to be one of them. He signed up for the training at once.

"Are you going to do it?" he asked Barbara.

"Yes," she said, "but I don't want to do it with you."

"Why not?"

"Because you'd ruin it for me."

Leave it to Barbara, he thought, to bring him down just when he was feeling good.

The est training is a precisely modulated series of mental exercises, meditations, relaxation techniques, pseudo-therapeutic harangues, brow-beatings and sensory deprivations calculated to produce, after sixty hours or so, a rough, middle American approximation of Eastern enlightenment. To create it, Werner Erhard—born Jack Rosenberg, a former salesman from Philadelphia—borrowed liberally from Scientology, gestalt therapy, Dale Carnegie, Zen and various of the other Eastern ephemera that washed up on the California coast in the late 1960s. It was an act of marketing genius, enlightenment neatly packaged for the masses with a price tag and a time limit. And if there was a diabolical quality to the boot camp atmosphere of the training and the deification of Werner Erhard, and no way to gauge whether the insight provided was lasting, damaging, positive or inconsequential, there could be no denying that a great many people—decent, unexceptional people, lost in the social chaos of the 1970s—believed that est "worked" for them. It had an especially powerful effect on those, like Bill Taylor, who'd had little experience with psychotherapy or Eastern religion.

Later, Bill would be very proud that he was the first person in his training to "get it." In fact, he got it before it was given.

The training took place in a banquet room at the Howard Johnson's Motor Inn near O'Hare International Airport. It began at eight-thirty on a Saturday morning. An assistant trainer spent what seemed to be hours explaining the rules and regulations to the 250 or so trainees who sat in straight rows before him. No smoking. No watches or timepieces. No use of alcohol or other drugs until the training is over next weekend (Bill would have to forgo his nightly joint). No one leaves the room until the trainer declares a break. Raise your hand if you want to share. Applaud when someone shares. If you have to vomit, an assistant will bring you a bag.

Finally, the trainer appeared. She was an older woman named Charlene, dressed casually, attractive in a matronly way, with reddish-brown hair. She told the trainees, very matter-of-factly, that they were "assholes." Their lives didn't work. They were trapped, tangled in "belief systems" of their own creation that prevented them from experiencing their lives. They were slaves to their minds, repetitive machines which prevented them from responding creatively to the events of their existence. Bill listened carefully to this; it made a lot of sense. He found himself thinking about his parents. He had created a "belief system" about them: that they were malicious people, intent on hurting him, purposely withholding their love. But they weren't. They were just who they were. *He* had turned them into ogres; he had chosen to experience them that way. He realized that he was crying, and raised his hand.

"Yes, Bill?" Charlene asked.

"One of my beliefs was that it was wrong for a man to cry in front of people. But I'm crying now, and it's no big deal."

The audience applauded. He allowed himself to cry harder. Charlene, who was about ten rows away, asked, "Where are you right now?"

He didn't understand what she meant.

"Just think," she said, moving up the aisle toward him. "Where *are* you right now?"

"Military school," he said. The words popped into his head. He didn't understand why.

"What's happening?"

"I'm all alone. They won't come to visit."

"Who won't come?"

"My father."

"Why not?"

"He doesn't love me."

"Where is he?"

"He's . . . working." Bill was having trouble getting the words out. He noticed that other people were crying too.

"How much does military school cost?"

"Three thousand dollars."

"Can you imagine your father having to come up with that money to put you through military school? He must have worked hard for that. Why would he do that?"

"Because he loved me?" It came out as a question, but only because the force of the realization was so overpowering: he had been guilty of the same stubbornness as his father. "I wasted thirty-five years of my life," he said, "and let my father and mother go to their graves without telling them I loved them."

"Thank you, Bill," Charlene said. The audience gave him an ovation.

Late in the second day of the training, he learned something else. It was during the Fear Process (a "process" is a set of mental exercises). Charlene told the trainees to sit facing one another and close their eyes. She gave them a long, elaborate set of instructions designed to relax them . . . and then suddenly she told them to scream. Immediately, Bill was back in Vietnam. He was at the Sandcastle, his friend Burgoon was trapped up front, and he was screaming. He was screaming because he couldn't move forward; Burgoon was dying and he was afraid to do anything about it. The image dissolved into Operation Cochise: the same screaming, the same frustration. Wayne Pilgreen was yelling at him, mocking him, telling him to go get help . . . and he couldn't move. He didn't have the guts to move; he would *die* if he moved. He was screaming out of frustration more than fear. He was ashamed of himself for not having the courage to help his friends. The shame, he realized, was a much stronger memory than the fear of dying. The shame was the worst thing he'd experienced in Vietnam—and he had created it himself, just as he'd created the image of his parents as ogres.

He went home buoyant that night, brimming with new insight. If his life was hell, he'd made it that way. And if he'd made it that way, he could unmake it. He would start with Barbara. He would appreciate her for who she was, instead of resenting her for not being the woman he wanted her to be. He would start by making a clean breast of things.

It was well past midnight when he arrived home. She was waiting up for him, anxious to hear how it had gone. "How was it?" she asked.

"*Fan*-tastic," he said. "I think I *got it.*"

"Already?"

"Barb," he said, almost giddy with rectitude. "I've got a confession to make. I've had affairs with other women, but that's because . . ."

And he lapsed into est talk, which sounded foreign and unconvincing to her. She was astonished—not so much by the fact that he'd had affairs, or that he was spilling the beans so . . . *confidently* now; she was mostly astonished by her own reaction. She had no reaction. The man who'd been accusing her for years of having affairs was now admitting that he'd been a hypocrite and, for all she cared, he might as well have been saying that he'd had spaghetti for dinner. It meant nothing. She could care less.

Bill was too excited to notice her reaction, much less "experience" it. He was, at that moment, more confident than he'd ever been in his life. He was absolutely positive that everything was going to work out just fine.

Why should you try to crush me?
Am I so Christ-like?

You beat against me,
Immense waves, filthy with refuse.
I am the last upright of a smashed breakwater
But you shall not crush me
Though you bury me in foaming slime
And hiss your hatred about me.

You break over me, cover me;
I shudder at the contact;
Yet I pierce through you
And stand up torn, dripping, shaken
But whole and fierce.

—RICHARD ALDINGTON

1

Judi Hall was in the bathroom still getting ready when her mother came in and announced: "He's here."

"What's he like?"

"He's the man you're going to marry," Mrs. Hall said.

"What?"

"Yeah, he is . . . I can just tell."

Judi Hall usually didn't place much faith in her mother's pronouncements, but she had spent the last year preparing herself to fall in love with Gary Cooper at first sight. His stepsister, Donna—a classmate at Calumet High—had shown Judi a picture and asked that she write to him in Vietnam. The picture was nice and his name—Gary Cooper—suggested a man who was quiet, sensitive, solid; Judi was happy to write. His replies were not memorable, but that didn't matter. She felt important doing it, touching part of the larger world, away—if only in spirit—from the smoke and grime and steel mills of northern Indiana. She was a sophomore in high school when it started in 1967, and was now a junior; he was twenty-one, a soldier wounded in action. He wrote to her from a hospital in the Philippines, and then from Vietnam. He was angry that he'd been sent back to the war, and couldn't wait to get home. She dreamed he would rescue her from the dull, brown-shingled little house, and from the squalid domestic battles that consumed her family. In a way, simply by writing, he already had.

Her older brother, Richard, knew Gary. They had been students together at Calumet High. Cooper's family was one of many in the area that shuttled back and forth between the steel mills and the South; he'd spent two years of high school at Calumet, and two in Tennessee. Richard remembered him vaguely, and mostly by reputation. "You're not getting involved with *that* guy," he said.

"Why not?"

"Why not?" Richard laughed and shook his head. "He's crazy, always getting into trouble. If there's a punch to be thrown, *that* sucker is going to throw it."

But Judi saw little evidence of that on their first date. They went to a drive-in movie with Donna and her boyfriend. Gary was quiet, polite and extremely shy. He was smaller than she had imagined, but dark and handsome as she'd hoped. He didn't play the rough, tough Marine, but spoke in a soft, graceful Southern accent. At the end, when he said good night on her doorstep and kissed her gently, she was charmed.

He saw her again the next day, and the day after. Her parents were out of town, and she decided to have a small party at home with her brother and his girlfriend. For all his talk, Richard seemed to get along very well with Gary. They drank beer and laughed and listened to music. By midnight, everyone was pretty drunk—especially

Gary, who could hardly stand. He followed her into the kitchen and said, "I love you and I want to get married."

Judi laughed. She put her hands on his shoulders and gave him a kiss. "Listen," she said, "when you sober up, you give me a call and we'll talk about it."

He called the next morning. "I'm sober," he said. "I love you and I want to get married."

"Okay," she said.

He reported to Camp LeJeune a few days later, but came home frequently on three-day passes. He bought her an engagement ring, and they decided to get married that summer. Actually, *he* decided; she was more reluctant than she wanted to admit. It was too much like a fairy tale—her mother's pronouncement in the bathroom, his proposal, her acceptance. It was so close to what she'd dreamed would happen that it made her light-headed; Gary was nicer than she'd had any right to expect, but she had been far more comfortable with her fantasies than she was with the reality of them. She wasn't sure that she wanted to leave home; she certainly didn't want to go off to a drab military base in North Carolina. As the days passed, she became more and more uncertain, terrified by the idea of marriage, of actually living with a man. She was afraid that it would turn out like her parents' marriage: her father so overwhelming and unpredictable, her mother trapped and acquiescent. She was very close to her mother and felt threatened by her father; she imagined that if she left home, something horrible would happen between the two of them.

She told Gary about her family. He seemed to understand—his own childhood hadn't been very happy—but he was a man, mysterious and formidable in his quiet way, and she was beginning to realize that she didn't know him very well. She found herself increasingly depressed, pulling back from him. In June, she refused to leave her bed one weekend when he came to visit. She told him she was ill, but he came to see her anyway.

"Gary," she blurted, "I'm not sure I want to get married."

"Okay," he said, teasing. "I'll hock the ring."

She wasn't sure what she'd expected him to say, but *that* certainly wasn't it. She took off the ring and threw it at him. "Here you go," she said. "Take your damn ring and get out of here."

His face reddened; she saw he was angry. "You'll never leave your mother," he said. She began to cry, and he softened. "Listen," he said, "we're getting married someday. Maybe not now, but someday. I know it."

Soon after that, the Marines sent Gary to Puerto Rico and she didn't see him for three months. With the pressure off, Judi's anxieties subsided. She decided that she really did love him, that she'd panicked and behaved foolishly. She wrote to him and asked that she be forgiven. When he returned from Puerto Rico that autumn, they set a new date for the wedding.

They were married in January 1969. It was a small civil ceremony, a double wedding with her brother, Richard, and his girlfriend. Judi arranged it so that her father would be at work and unable to attend. Her mother was there, and several friends. Neither Gary's mother nor his stepfather was invited; they opposed the marriage because Judi was a Catholic. He didn't seem to mind their absence—it was, he said, business as usual. After the ceremony, Gary and Judi honeymooned at the Crown Motel.

He wanted her to return with him to Camp LeJeune. It would only be for a month or two, he argued, they would go home as soon as he was discharged. It would be nice to have some time alone, away from their parents. But Judi refused to leave her mother; getting married was one thing, leaving home was another entirely.

Judi's parents lived around the corner from Gary's in an unincorporated section of Lake County, south of Interstate 80 and the city of Gary. The area had been woods and farmland until the 1950s, when trailer courts sprouted and tract houses were slapped together to accommodate the tide of hillbillies and Chicanos coming to work in the steel mills. There was an odd, transient feel to the place, a haphazard mingling of Appalachia and the Southwest plopped uncomfortably on the prairie. It had some of the impermanence but none of the excitement of a boom town. Many of the residents refused to consider it home, and longed—as Gary's stepfather, Thomas Brummitt, did—for the day when they'd be able to return South. There was a steady stream of people north and south on Interstate 65—people sick of the noise and bustle, and looking for some family cooking; people tired of the starvation wages down home, looking to make some good factory money. Everyone always seemed to have a curious relative from Kentucky or Tennessee sleeping on the living-room couch.

Gary's aunt Estelle—his mother's younger sister—and her husband, Wallace Chandler, had been the first of the clan to move north, in 1955. Gary's mother and Thomas Brummitt followed a year later. Wallace and Thomas and Judi Hall's father all worked at Inland Steel, the largest mill in the area, and Thomas found Gary a job there when he was discharged from the Marines in March 1969. Jobs were easy to find in those days. The late 1960s were boom times for the steel industry, and Inland was a small city on the shore of Lake Michigan, open around the clock, employing 24,000 people. Gary signed on as a general worker, but later was assigned to the crew of one of the fifty-five locomotives that pulled ore and coke and scrap iron from the docks to the furnaces over the 162 miles of railroad tracks that crisscrossed Inland's 1,900-acre site.

During the first month or so after he returned, Gary and Judi lived with her parents. It was, predictably, a disaster. There was constant tension between Gary and Judi's father, who considered him a usurper. Judi's mother would remember Gary as much different from the polite young man who'd first come calling. He was nervous, jittery, pacing the living room "like a caged animal," she would later say. Several times during that month, he had nightmares and his screaming awakened the whole house.

Judi still didn't want to leave home, but knew that Gary had to get out of there, and they soon found an inexpensive duplex apartment nearby. She moved into it tentatively, and never really completely—"home" was still her parents' house. She was constantly on the phone with her mother; they saw each other nearly every day. Gary wasn't too happy about that, but then, *his* mother was calling all the time too, asking him to run errands. She had multiple sclerosis, was steadily growing weaker, and could expect little help from a husband who seemed to Gary to be only intermittently attentive. Gary felt sorry for her and usually was willing to do her bidding. The mothers became an insufferable weight upon the marriage. They had an uncanny knack of calling every time Gary and Judi settled down to make love or watch television (a color set was their first major acquisition). The constant harassment was unnerving, but neither had the strength to make a stand.

Gary hated work in the mill. It wasn't much better than Vietnam, he said; the noise and heat were like an all-day fire fight. He talked about finding another job, maybe going to trade school, but never did anything about it. He seemed to come home angry every day, and would immediately launch into an inspection of the apartment, as if he were a drill sergeant. The ugly brown tile floors had to be waxed, the bed made just so. He would run his hand over the television and announce: *"There's dust!"* Judi, anxious not to displease him, tried to keep the house in good order, but with the ratty old furniture they'd collected from friends and family, it always seemed disorganized and incomplete — like the rest of their marriage.

The better Judi knew Gary, the more a stranger he seemed. His nightmares continued. He told her never to shake him when he was sleeping, and never to sneak up behind him. She wanted to know why, but he didn't like being asked about Vietnam. Sometimes, though, when he'd had a few beers, he would tell stories. He told her that once he'd seen a man's stomach blown open, and had been asked by a medic to urinate on the intestines to keep them moist. Much as she wanted to learn about his past, to know him better, such stories only served to increase the distance between them.

She dreaded fights. When Gary raised his voice, she'd fall apart. Sometimes, just *thinking* about his anger would give her the shakes and she'd wonder if it might not be better to leave him. She wanted to be honest, but couldn't bring herself to tell him how scared she was. In the beginning, they had vowed never to go to bed angry, even if it meant staying up all night to work out their problems. Judi soon found, though, that Gary wasn't much interested in talking about his feelings; his method for settling arguments was, at once, charming and frustrating and completely effective. He would take her by the shoulders and turn her toward the mirror. "Look at that," he'd say, and she'd grow angrier for a moment because she knew what was coming. "You see that man behind you?" he'd say, and she would already be melting, laughing despite herself. "That man *loves* you."

More often than not, their fights were about marijuana. She had been brought up to believe it was as bad as heroin, and nothing he could say would convince her otherwise. He told her that everyone in the Marines had smoked it—not in the field, but on the ship between operations. It wasn't so much the illegality that bothered her as the fact that it was another thing beyond her control, something that altered his personality in ways she couldn't predict. Sometimes he would just drift off, listening to the stereo (Janis Joplin was a favorite, especially the song "Mercedes-Benz"). At other times, he played the tough guy—the very thing he *hadn't* done in the beginning—ordering her around, setting down rules and regulations: "You will not leave this house when I'm at work without my permission."

She felt that her situation was precarious enough when he was straight; she had no idea at all who he was when he was stoned. She'd ask him to stop smoking the stuff, he'd yell at her and she'd crumple. He never became violent, but the potential was there. She told her mother what was happening; her mother told her father.

One day in August, Judi was cleaning the kitchen and banged her head on a cabinet. Later that day, she went to visit her parents and her father noticed the bruise. He was convinced that Gary had hit her; nothing she could say would dissuade him. She begged him not to cause any trouble, but she knew he would.

Several days later, Gary came home from work and began screaming as soon as he got in the door: "Why'd you sic your goddamn father on me?"

"What?"

"You know what I mean." She could tell then he'd been drinking and maybe smoking pot too. He was furious, more angry than she'd ever seen him. "You want to know what it's like to really get hit? You want to see what happens if I slug you?"

"Go ahead, big man," she screamed. "Hit me."

But he couldn't bring himself to do it; instead, he shoved her down on the bed. She jumped up, grabbed the telephone and locked herself in the bathroom. She wanted to call her mother, but he ripped out the cord. Then he was slamming against the bathroom door; the hinges cracked and the door fell on top of her. Gary stood there, breathing heavily, his anger spent. Embarrassed now, he lifted the door off her, then picked her up and turned her to face the mirror. "Look at that," he said.

Oh no, she thought, not this.

"You see that man there?"

"Yes," she said, trembling, wanting only to get out of there.

"He *loves* you."

"I know," she said, already planning her escape. She waited until he was asleep, then packed a bag and fled to her mother's house.

He came by the next day, but Judi's mother wouldn't let him in the door. Mrs. Hall already had called a lawyer; they were filing for divorce. Judi couldn't understand why her mother, so quick to hustle her into the marriage, was now so eager to get her out of it. Events were moving too quickly again; she wasn't sure she *wanted* to be hustled out of the marriage, but the question seemed out of her hands. When Gary rang the bell, Judi was told to stay in her room and she obeyed. Then she heard them shouting at each other, but couldn't make out what was being said. Later, she learned that her mother had called the police; they found Gary brooding in his car, in front of the elementary school down the street. They had apparently tried to search the car for drugs and there was a scuffle. He was arrested for disorderly conduct and resisting arrest, and was held overnight in the county jail at Crown Point.

He called his mother to bail him out the next morning, but she was indisposed as always and Thomas was either at work or lacked interest, so Gary was forced to call his aunt Estelle, who'd often come to his rescue in the past.

Estelle had always been as soft on Gary as she'd been hard on Gary's mother, her sister Lillian. Estelle and Lillian Woodward had grown up on a farm outside McKenzie, Tennessee. Their father was something of a celebrity in the area, a bootlegger who conducted his business from a wheelchair (like Gary's mother, he suffered from multiple sclerosis). Lillian was older and prettier—or so their mother often said—and Estelle was determined to make up for those disadvantages by being *better* than her sister. She was proper, obedient, a strict Baptist, something of a stick-in-the-mud for a bootlegger's daughter. But then, Fred Woodward expected propriety from his girls and was greatly offended when Lillian eloped with Thirby Cooper, one of the dozens of young sharps who came by the farm on payday for a pint or a quart. When Thirby and Lillian eventually divorced—a rare occurrence in Tennessee in 1950—Estelle considered it the inevitable punishment for their hasty and somewhat licentious betrothal. Lillian remained steadfastly unchastened, however, and soon married Thomas Brummitt, who seemed to Estelle every bit as fast and loose as Thirby Cooper; when Donna Fay Brummitt was born and it became clear that Thomas preferred her to his stepson, Estelle became Gary's unofficial defender. Even after she married Wallace Chandler (a proper Baptist wedding, of course), had children of her own, and both families moved north to the steel mills—they lived within a block of each other—she continued to provide a haven for Gary, always willing to take his side against the depredations of Thomas and Lillian, real and imagined.

Gary was aware of the lingering resentments between the sisters, and knew just how to massage Estelle. She was an eager audience for all the latest, distressing news from the Brummitt household, which he would divulge with the most convincing reluctance. When he came to visit, he also displayed an entirely unlikely degree of piety and allowed himself to be "saved" at a Baptist church service when he was twelve. She had disapproved of his marriage to Judi Hall, who was a Catholic; but when the young couple came to visit, Gary would always talk about how important Jesus was in his life (Judi barely able to control her giggles) and win her over. And now, hearing not only that the marriage was on the rocks but also that Thomas had refused to bail out the boy, Estelle immediately dispatched Wallace with a hundred dollars to the Crown Point jail.

Gary looked awful when the guards brought him out. He had a

black mark down the side of his face. The desk sergeant took Wallace's money, returned Gary's wallet and keys and launched into a stern lecture about the evils of marijuana. "Now wait just a goddamn minute," Gary exploded, and Wallace had to step in and drag his nephew out of there.

"I'm tired of people running over me," he told Wallace when they got outside. "I can't take no more abuse."

"Gary," said Wallace, a gentle and soft-spoken man, "that fellow in there had the argument won before it even started."

"He acted like I was an animal."

"It's true. He did," Wallace said. "But there wasn't anything to do about it. The battle was lost from the get-go."

"Wallace, you just don't understand," Gary said. "I'm *sick* of losing battles."

Within days after their breakup, Gary and Judi were seeing each other secretly again; he'd tap on her bedroom window, and she would sneak out the back door. Driving through the deserted stretches of Lake County beyond the subdivisions, stopping occasionally to make love or just talk, Judi found that she wasn't so frightened of him anymore. Somehow it was easier to love Gary when she wasn't living with him; out in the car, they didn't have to worry about their mothers calling . . . and she didn't have to worry about dusting the television. They talked about getting back together. She said she wasn't quite ready yet, but assured him she didn't really want a divorce either.

But she did nothing to stop it. A month later—eight months since their wedding, six months since they'd started living together—Judi found herself sitting in a courtroom next to her best friend, Janet Estrada, staring forlornly at Gary, who was all alone a few rows away. "You know," she said, "for two cents, I'd go over there and tell him, 'This is crazy. Let's forget about it.'"

Janet reached into her purse and pulled out two pennies. "Here you go," she said.

Judi went. She sat down next to Gary, touched his arm. "Honey, what are we doing here?" she asked. "Neither of us wants this."

"It's too late now," he said, more disgusted than angry. "We've gone too far."

He tapped on her window as usual that night, and they went out to a restaurant. She tried to pretend that nothing had changed, but something obviously had. He came around less frequently after that. She heard through friends that he was in bad shape, hanging out with the wrong sort of people. He didn't seem much different when he came to see her, though. He still played the patient suitor, willing to wait until she was ready to leave home (but convinced now she never would); she continued to hope they would someday remarry, but it was more a pleasant fantasy—as it always had been for her—than a serious possibility. She lived with her parents for several more years, wanting to break away, but lacking the fortitude. Finally, she joined the Air Force; it seemed the only way to guarantee her escape—dramatic, irrevocable and far more binding than a marriage. When Gary learned she was leaving, he stopped by with a present: a copy of "Someday We'll Be Together," by Diana Ross and the Supremes.

The rumors Judi had been hearing about Gary were true. Even before their marriage fell apart, he was spending a good deal of time at an old Calumet High hangout called the Corral, a classic drive-in which featured greasy hamburgers, garish neon, good-looking waitresses who came to your car and an open-air supermarket for all sorts of drugs. It was a time when new drugs seemed to sweep the steel belt every few months, augmenting the by then standard marijuana and Benzedrine; hallucinogens were the most recent arrival, and it was said that Gary was tripping on acid the night Judi's mother had him arrested.

One night an old friend named Rick Chandler, just returned from Vietnam, stopped in at the Corral. He had known Gary since they were kids, living on the same street in the scruffy town of Black Oak, which was lodged between the cities of Hammond and Gary. He remembered Cooper as something of a lovable rogue. The first time Chandler had ever seen him, Gary was standing on a street corner in his Little League uniform, taking donations from passing motorists. It was a typical Cooper scam—he was collecting the money for himself, not the league. They became close friends after that, which meant they played ball constantly (Gary was an excellent catcher in the Babe Ruth League) and had knock-down, drag-out fights at least once a week. Their last fight had been at a party just before both joined the Marines (and just after Gary had returned from his two years in Tennessee). Gary pulled a knife on Chandler for no apparent reason, except that he was drunk. Rick, who was much bigger and stronger, felt compelled to knock him silly—but, as always, there were no hard feelings.

Gary had never been the calmest person, but Chandler was shocked by his frenzied ravings at the Corral. He looked awful—emaciated, a mess—and was spewing venom at everyone and everything. He was bitter about the war, furious at the government, the military brass and the bosses at Inland Steel, as well as the draft dodgers, the peaceniks and anyone else who didn't have the guts to fight for what they believed; he was even more angry than that about the bust-up of his marriage. He had tried to go straight, start a family, but the *establishment* wouldn't let him. "So fuck it," he said. "Fuck them."

Many of Gary's words and ideas were new to Chandler. It was late 1969, and a major change had taken place in the steel mills. The style and rhetoric—if not the substance—of what was then known as the "counterculture" had trickled down to the working class. It had been a gradual development, too subtle to be noticed by the mass media; blue-collar workers were still caricatured as "hardhats," defiantly patriotic and filled with righteous indignation over the campus radicals' attack on middle-class values. There was a good deal of truth to the caricature—especially among the older workers like Thomas Brummitt. But the younger generation had been watching their more affluent peers cavorting on the nightly news, and the revolution seemed like a lot of fun. It promised sex, drugs, mayhem and good music.

Slowly, a distinctive blue-collar counterculture emerged; it was harsher, more anarchic and, in a way, more hedonistic than its better-known progenitor. There was none of the philosophical posturing, little of the youthful idealism. Herbert Marcuse and the Maharishi didn't dent the steel mills; if a Fonda was admired, it was not Jane (who was despised by even the antiwar veterans) but her brother Peter and his motorcycle. Steel workers didn't "experiment" with drugs, they *used* them; they weren't searching for illumination, just escape. They tended to favor the wilder fringes of rock music, disdaining the existential angst of Simon and Garfunkel for the less subtle pleasures of Led Zeppelin and Grand Funk Railroad. They grew their hair long (and left it that way, long after most of the campus radicals returned to the fold and discovered the twenty-five-dollar hairstyling parlor), and they began using some of the words they'd heard on television: the police became the "pigs," the factory bosses became the "establishment," and "party" became a verb as well as a noun. Their rage was diffuse; they weren't rebelling against their parents so much as the utter dreariness of factory life itself. Those who talked revolution, as Gary Cooper did, were mostly interested in tearing the old mess down. When Cooper would speed-rap in the Corral's parking lot about taking up the gun, his listeners were never quite sure whom he intended to "off" first, the establishment or the draft dodgers.

Still, Gary took his anger more seriously than most. He joined Vietnam Veterans Against the War. He followed the Chicago Conspiracy trial closely, and became enamored of Abbie Hoffman and Jerry Rubin, whose political philosophy—or lack of it—closely mirrored his own. Soon he was the Corral's resident yippie, sometimes reading passages aloud from Hoffman's work: "I like to experience pleasure, to have fun. I enjoy blowing people's minds. You know, walking up to somebody and saying, 'Would you hold this dollar bill while I go into that store and steal something?' The crazier, the better. I like being crazy, losing control. Just doing what pops into my mind."

One night at the Corral, Gary walked up to Fred Summers—a former athlete at Calumet High who'd gotten married and avoided the draft—and kicked him in the shin. Rick Chandler quickly stepped between Cooper and Summers (who could have destroyed

Gary, if he'd wanted). "What the hell did you do *that* for?" Chandler asked.

"I don't like waxy people," Gary said, and giggled.

Chandler never learned what made a person "waxy," but he figured it had something to do with smugness and not having been to Vietnam. Most of Gary's close friends were veterans; his closest friends were veterans who liked drugs. He was very tight with Eddie Frady, an ex-Marine who'd been busted from sergeant to private after he'd been caught smoking a joint on China Beach in Danang. Gary, Rick, Eddie and Jimmy Slevin, an Army veteran, usually would meet at the Corral after work, buy some drugs and go out for a drive, ingesting them along the way. Rick and Jimmy limited themselves to marijuana, acid and a little speed, but Gary and Eddie seemed willing to try anything.

Gary was always wrecked—either speeding, tripping, whacked out on downers, drunk, stoned or all of them at once—but he never failed to show up for work in the morning. Chandler had the feeling that Gary *needed* to work, much more so than the rest of them. The job was his guarantee of independence, his only source of funds; if he lost it, he couldn't fall back on his family, as the others could and often did. Rick remembered how Gary had agonized over money when they were kids. His father would send child-support payments, which would inevitably be side-tracked by Thomas and his mother. If he was lucky, he'd be given five dollars from the check, and immediately go out and buy clothes (for some reason, he'd always been obsessed about his appearance, needing to wear the latest styles, always changing his hair—in Tennessee, wanting to seem more All-American, he dyed it blond). Even though he was now playing the revolutionary outlaw doper, out of control like Abbie Hoffman, Rick figured that Gary would never go so far afield as to jeopardize that weekly paycheck. But at the same time, he seemed to be spinning farther and farther out, testing his limits.

Chandler reached his own limit late one night when they were parked out in front of the Beacon Lunch, next to the Corral, just drifting, letting the drugs wear off. Gary was floating on downers in the front seat, barely able to raise his head. Jimmy Slevin surveyed the car and said, "You know, I hate to admit it, but we're all hooked. We're going to be fucked up on drugs for the rest of our lives."

"*Wait* a minute," Rick said, bolting out of his daze. "That may be true for you guys, but not for me."

He knew that Jimmy was overstating the case, but was frightened all the same. He decided to pull back from that scene. He continued to see Gary occasionally, and each time he seemed worse—thinner, paler, weirder than ever. He heard that Gary and Eddie Frady had moved on to needle drugs, and didn't doubt it. One time, Gary said to him, "You just flat out quit, didn't you? How the hell'd you do it?"

"I don't know, Gary," Rick said. "I just got scared, I guess."

"Well, I admire you," Gary said, "but I don't think I could do it."

Gary began shooting heroin in 1970. Apparently, he figured that since he'd handled every other chemical thrown his way, there was no reason why he couldn't handle this one too. One day he and John Farrell, another of the Corral regulars, drove over to the black section of Gary and bought a ten-dollar button on the street. Farrell suggested they shoot up with a friend of his named Duke, who'd been a junkie for thirty years and knew what it was all about.

Duke had just finished a stretch in prison for writing bad checks, and was living in a trailer court nearby. He was a small, quiet, tightly wound man, with the craggy, emaciated look of a longtime user, his hair and skin both the color of sandpaper. He had to laugh when Farrell and Cooper came by, trying to be cool, but clearly excited. Gary began to go on about all the drugs he'd done in Vietnam, and Duke cut him short: "Then why would you want to put *this* stuff in your arm?" he said, cracking open the button—it was a red capsule—and examining the contents. It was salt and pepper, heroin cut with cocoa. "Shit, you ain't gonna get off with this. Why don't you forget about it and I'll give you a taste of something real."

Duke hadn't been back on the street long enough to be stingy about his supply; he was flush with freedom and feeling charitable, although he figured his charity probably would be wasted. He knew Farrell was a perennial amateur: tall, handsome, the son of a successful businessman, he was too flighty ever to settle into serious addiction. Cooper, on the other hand, was a payday Jones at best. Duke suspected that Gary was the type who'd always figure he was more hooked than he really was, too scared to get deep into the life, maybe someone who would talk more than he *did*. Neither was a stone junkie; after all those years, Duke figured he was an expert judge of such things.

And to a certain extent, he was right. For the next year or so, Gary dabbled in heroin, teetering on the edge of a habit. He would shoot up no more than two or three times a week; if he felt the urge coming on too strong, he'd switch to speed. He and Farrell would visit Duke from time to time. They turned him on to acid, which he considered interesting but gimmicky. Soon they were bringing Eddie Frady with them too.

Eddie was small and dark, as Gary was, more powerfully built but less animated. If Gary used drugs for stimulation as much as escape, Eddie was more interested in the latter. If Gary was angry about Vietnam, Eddie was remorseful. They would talk about the war often, especially after they began sharing an apartment in Hammond early in the summer of 1970. Gary tried to get Eddie to join Vietnam Veterans Against the War—"We were *taken*, man," he would say, "They *used* us"—but Eddie felt more displaced than rebellious. He wanted to forget the whole sordid business. He shot speed with Gary, but found the lightning-bolt rush brought him too much into the World. Heroin was more to his taste—the rush was warm, silvery, tiny finger-cymbals on tinsel strings spreading through his body. He became much more the classic junkie, living the street life, hustling for scores, dealing some, scamming, making up, nodding out, never thinking past the next rush.

One day Gary came home from work and said he'd been fired. He'd been high and accidentally derailed a locomotive. He didn't seem very upset by it—there were plenty of jobs around, and he soon found work at Youngstown Sheet and Tube; but he and Eddie were unable to make the rent for several weeks and they decided to move in with some friends who had a larger apartment nearby.

Eddie was never sure how many people actually lived in the apartment. They came and went. Jimmy Slevin was there when his marriage was going badly, John Farrell was there when the drugs were plentiful, there was a Mexican named Rudy and an Army vet named Larry, and several other more or less permanent residents. It was one continuous party, the stereo blasting hard rock, black light posters on the wall, people drifting in and out at all hours. The party seemed an organic entity with a life of its own; it lasted several months in their apartment, then moved elsewhere. Jimmy Slevin returned to his wife, Gary and Eddie to their parents, but they continued to meet at the Corral and follow the endless party from house to house through the steel belt.

If there was a spiritual center to northern Indiana's blue-collar counterculture, it had to be John Farrell. He was a dashing, outrageous figure, the unofficial social director of the endless party, the link between old-time junkies like Duke and the younger dopers, the angry veterans and the outlaw bikers, the hillbillies and the Mexicans. He came from a more affluent family than most, but never had any money and never worked. He was supported occasionally by a wife who was a nurse and not part of the scene, more frequently by a girlfriend who was a topless dancer, but mostly by his remarkable ability to cadge drugs, food, shelter and sometimes clothes from his friends. He didn't live anywhere for very long, but moved along with the party, entertaining the crowd with death-defying feats of needlework, willing to mainline anything liquid—whiskey, cold water and even adrenaline, which would leave him shaking uncontrollably for fifteen minutes. "Wow!" he'd say when finally becalmed. "That was far out. Anyone want a taste?"

Farrell had a motorcycle, and sometimes rode with a gang called Los Hombres. He was tight with the group's president, Jimmy Robinson, although Jimmy considered him too ethereal to ever be anything but a lone rider. Farrell and Robinson shared an apartment in Calumet City for a brief time, a liaison that produced two significant results. They sealed their friendship with identical tattoos—a Maltese cross with skull and bones—and Jimmy introduced Farrell to his sister, Barbara; Farrell, in turn, introduced Barbara to Gary Cooper.

Barbara Robinson was then nineteen years old, and a speed demon. She didn't consider herself very attractive, but rarely lacked for men. She had honey-colored hair which framed a round, pleasant face; she was loud, and blunt to the point of coarseness, which usually provided only temporary camouflage for her good mind and soft heart. Early in 1971, she spent a memorable three weeks with Farrell, his girl of the moment, speeding all the while. They ate very little during that time, made love twice and never slept for more than ten or fifteen minutes at a stretch. Barbara was brisk under the best of circumstances, and positively blinding when cranked: she talked a blue streak, jiggling her knee, pacing the floor, chewing gum furiously until she could barely move her mouth, chewing the inside of her lips until they bled. She and Farrell swirled along the party route, from Weird Harold's house, to Duke's trailer, to Armando Ramirez's place in Black Oak, where most of the action took place.

Armando was a railroad worker who'd lost his foot when a train ran over it. He'd received a generous cash settlement from the company, with which he bought the house, new furniture, a television, fancy stereo equipment, a pool table and numerous other accessories. One night Cooper was at the pool table with Teddy Valenzuela, attempting a game of eight ball; he disappeared into the bathroom between shots and then nodded out on the couch. Teddy, who wasn't in great shape himself, tried to rouse him with a cue ball. Teddy later maintained that he was aiming for an adjacent seat cushion, but the ball smacked Gary flush in the forehead. He didn't blink. Slowly, as blood began to ooze from the wound, the other partyers realized that Cooper had overdosed. There was a burst of activity: he was force-fed coffee, splashed with water, walked back and forth and eventually came around. Word of these events quickly reached Barbara and Farrell, who were sorry they'd missed all the excitement.

Barbara knew Cooper only by sight, but a few days after the cue ball incident, she was at Duke's trailer and Gary dropped by, looking to get high. Farrell came in soon after, having scored some heroin and cocaine for speedball. Barbara wasn't big on needle drugs, but speedball was always a kick: first the sugary cocaine rush, then the deep, rich heroin release. She never was able to find her own vein, so Farrell did her, and when the cocaine came on, she felt like talking to someone. She noticed the scar on Gary's forehead and said, "That must be where Teddy Valenzuela got you with the cue ball." Gary said it was. She reached up to touch it and asked, "Does it hurt?" He said no. Then the heroin came on, and they both nodded out.

She saw him several more times during the next week—at Armando's, at Weird Harold's—and he kept asking her to go out for a drive. "No no no," she would say, speeding too fast and hard (and for too long, by then) to think about being anyplace except where she was.

Then they all went to Chicago for a concert by Steppenwolf, a best-forgotten heavy-metal group, at a club called the Syndrome. Down in the basement, there were drug dealers posted every few feet in the shadows, offering tastes of acid. They went from one to the next, feigning interest—they didn't have enough money to buy—and sampling them all. By the time they went upstairs, it seemed as if there were a half dozen varieties of acid subdividing Barbara's brain into contending factions. There was a psychedelic light show, which didn't help. The music began, undifferentiated grindings and gnashings, chalk screeching across a blackboard. Farrell had disappeared. Barbara's heart was pounding, and her head spinning. She was beginning to lose control . . . and there was Gary, offering her Tuinals. Somehow he'd sensed that she needed to come down. She took a Tuinal, but it caught in her throat and she gagged. He went off, and came back with a drink to help her wash down another. She sat on his lap then, still wired and frightened, but calming.

After that, Barbara slept for three days. When she awakened, she was at Weird Harold's house and Farrell was gone—their three-week fling clearly over—and she found that she was thinking about Gary Cooper. She remembered that one of the girls at one of the parties had said that if she really wanted good sex, she should try Cooper. More important, though, was that every time she'd seen him during the past three weeks, he'd seemed truly kind.

Gary, meanwhile, was looking for her too. When he found her that night at Weird Harold's, it was clear to both that they'd been having similar thoughts. They made love, and then Gary took her on a triumphal tour of the other party outposts—Armando's, Duke's—as if to formally announce their union. Barbara was pleased and rather touched by the quaintness of the gesture, but she was having difficulty readjusting to the slowness of life without amphetamines. She suggested that they visit a friend of hers in Hammond, and score some speed. Gary agreed, and they spent the rest of the night driving about in his Nova, past the huge factory complexes, floodlit and noisy, fire roaring from the furnaces; they drove over and under and across the railroad tracks which seemed to bisect every street, clotted with coal cars, dragged by sluggish, enormous locomotives. She'd often felt lost and inconsequential against the massive industrial structures that enveloped their lives; now, though, Gary was there and listening avidly as she speed-rapped her past. Her parents had divorced when she was young, and she had bounced between them—neither was willing to care for her for very long—until one of her stepmothers (her father had married seven times) called the police on her, saying she was a runaway and a thief. She was made a ward of the court, and almost sent to reform school, but a friendly probation officer had stepped in and proposed a deal: if her father agreed to pay forty dollars per month, the court would send her to a nice Catholic boarding school in Kentucky. She remained there until she graduated from high school and wanted to stay longer, but the nuns said she had to go. So she returned to Hammond, and started hanging out with her brother's motorcycle gang. She had a quick, silly marriage to one of the members, which lasted eight months, and then she met Farrell. Her mother was in Iowa. Her father was in Hammond, but her latest stepmother didn't want to be bothered. She really had no place to go.

Gary said they had a lot in common. His parents had divorced. He'd also had a quick, awful marriage which lasted eight months. He wanted a family, stability, but had the sense that no one had ever really loved him. He'd slept on the couch most of his life, but now—finally—his mother and stepfather were living in a three-bedroom house and he had a room of his own, which she could live in too, if she liked.

As a greasy, yellow dawn was breaking over the steel mills, he suggested, "You want to come home and meet my mom?"

"Okay," she said.

As they neared the house, though, he seemed to grow nervous. "Act straight, now," he said. "You have to act straight."

"Gary, I'm speeding my brains out."

"Yeah, but act straight."

Thomas had already left for work, but Gary's mother was there and didn't seem to mind Barbara joining the family (Lillian always welcomed someone who might help with the chores). A deal was made: when Gary worked the night shift, Barbara could sleep in his room; when he worked the afternoon shift, she would sleep with his stepsister, Donna. Gary and Barbara agreed to these formalities, knowing they would be easy to breach, and that afternoon, in bed together, he said, "I love you."

"You're crazy," she said. "You don't even *know* me."

"Yes, I do," he said, "and I love you."

Barbara soon found the Brummitt house to be a strange, disorienting place: it seemed to her as if *everyone* there was on drugs, although it may have been they were simply overdosed with backwoods Tennessee lethargy. To a great extent, the tone was set by Gary's mother, who—whether because of illness or basic disposition—seemed fogbound much of the time. Several months earlier, Lillian had found syringes in Gary's car and mentioned it to the other family members, but not to him ("I thought that's what they were," Lillian later explained, "but I wasn't sure"); for whatever reasons, neither Thomas nor Lillian seemed overly concerned about what was happening to Gary. Thomas occasionally made a stab at seeming authoritative, but it was halfhearted at best. He would thunder, "Gary done moved a *woman* in the house," but Barbara soon realized that Thomas was incapable of doing anything about it. Consequently, she and Gary were able to do what they wanted without anyone ever seeming to notice. Sometimes the family would gather around the television in the evening, a placid domestic scene, Thomas and Lillian only mildly bemused by the fact that Gary and Barbara, tripping, were laughing hysterically at Cannon, the obese television detective.

The tension between Gary and Thomas was palpable, but sporadic. At times, much as they complained about each other, they seemed to share a grudging affection. They would split a bottle, and talk about hunting, fishing, football and Tennessee. At other times, their enmity seemed more a matter of family tradition than hard reality, an old habit neither was willing to break. Sometimes, though, and especially when Gary thought Thomas was mistreating his mother, their rivalry became primitive and furious. Several months after she moved in, Barbara saw Gary and Thomas go at it in earnest, and it was terrifying.

It was one of those days when everyone seemed to be getting on each other's nerves—Gary's mother aimlessly nagging about the household chores, Thomas morose and testy, Gary perhaps a little strung out on heroin (which, Barbara knew, he'd been using more and more frequently). Thomas and Lillian began to fight in the bedroom, there was the sound of a slap, and suddenly Gary charged in there and drop-kicked Thomas in the chest. It was a frighteningly effective move, the first time Barbara had seen evidence of Gary's Marine training; Thomas went down in a heap and Gary pounced on him. They scuffled, and Gary came up with Thomas in a choke hold. He sat down on the bed, almost casually, his right arm cradled around Thomas's neck. Then he began to add power to the hold, reinforcing it with his left arm, pulling back so hard that his knuckles were white; Thomas was struggling, kicking his feet, but getting nowhere. His face was turning blue. Barbara, frozen, figured that Gary was going to kill him and spend the rest of his life in prison. She began to scream, "Gary, Gary, you're *killing* him!" But Gary didn't seem to hear; his eyes were blank, and he was smiling slightly—he was *enjoying* it, she thought. She tried to stop him, pulling at his arms, screaming all the while. She began to work on his left hand, prying off the fingers, one by one, and finally—somehow—she was able to get Gary to let go. Thomas collapsed on the floor and stayed there for a few minutes, gasping, then got up and stormed out of the house.

Gary was very calm, as if nothing had happened. He'd recently bought a small black-and-white television set, and he began to check it out now, to see if it had been damaged in the scuffle. He switched from channel to channel, checking them all out.

"Hey, Gary," she said. "You realize you almost killed him?"

But he refused to talk about it.

2

Cooper didn't realize that he was addicted to heroin until he tried to stop using it in the spring of 1971. He was shooting up once a day by then—a modest habit as such things go, but a habit nonetheless. It had developed gradually, over a period of years, and he refused to believe he actually was hooked. He didn't *feel* particularly dependent; he had little in common with the anguished, palsied junkies who populated the police shows on television; he didn't spend every waking moment thinking about his next fix.

He was, in fact, far more concerned about the city of Gary's efforts to garnishee his salary at Youngstown Steel to pay for a collision he'd had with a taxi. His insurance had covered basic repairs, but the court also ordered him to pay $55 for each day the cab was out of service, a total of $785. When he learned the money would be taken from his salary, he said to Barbara, "The hell with them. Let's get out of here. We'll go to Tennessee."

They took an all-night bus from Chicago to Memphis, then another bus to McKenzie. Gary slept most of the way. But by the time they reached his grandmother's modest white farmhouse, he was—much to his surprise—as desperate and jittery as any junkie on television. His head hurt; he was nauseated, sweating and shivering. His nose ran and his eyes teared. Every joint in his body ached, as if they'd been lubricated with heroin and were now bone dry. Barbara told his grandmother that he had the flu.

Avis Woodward was a tiny sparrow of a hill-country woman who filled her wizened cheeks with chewing tobacco and delicately spat the juice into a small tin can she carried in her hand. She fluttered about, quite spry for her age, and enjoyed nagging Gary about the length of his hair and the fact that he and Barbara weren't married. She didn't seem to have the slightest inkling of the source of Gary's illness, though; heroin addiction was about as common in backwoods Tennessee as leprosy.

The agony lasted for nearly a week. He couldn't sleep or eat very much; he couldn't sit still. He'd scream at Barbara, then apologize and hang on for dear life. They took long walks through the soft woods and rolling hills, just to keep moving. They wrestled on the front lawn; they talked for hours and hours.

Gary remembered all the stories about his grandfather—Fred Woodward, the crippled bootlegger—that his aunt Estelle had told him. He found the old evergreen where Fred had kept his bankroll in a fruit jar, and the place where Fred spent afternoons in his wheelchair; he remembered climbing all over his grandfather, whom he called "Daddy-pap" (a nickname which soon caught on with the rest of the family), and playing with the chair, which he considered the most ingenious contraption ever invented.

Fred was in pretty bad shape by then, slurring his words, old and feeble and near death, but he still had his wits about him. Aunt Estelle often told about the time a tough sheriff new to the county, was vowing to clean it up. Bob Murray, Fred's supplier, had been out to the farm and warned him: "That damn fool is coming to put you out of business. You better hide the stuff."

"Well, Bob," Fred said, "you know what I'm going to do? I'm going to play crazier than hell." And when the sheriff arrived that night, Fred rolled out the front door, screamed, waved his arms, frothed at the mouth and then tried to set the porch on fire. Estelle watched as the sheriff and his men backed off and scattered to their cars, and said, "Daddy-pap, you are some actor."

"If I was a whole man," Fred said, "I would have stomped the hell out of them."

At least, that's the way Estelle told it.

Gary loved the old stories. He loved the idea that he was de-
scended from bootleggers on one side and Indians on the other (his
paternal grandmother had been a Cherokee); it was one of the few
things in his life that lived up to the mythic expectations inherent in
his name. He hated having to go through life as *Gary Cooper.* His
mother claimed that she hadn't named him after the movie star, but
that was little solace. She didn't have to live with the wisecracks that
attended every credit card purchase, every collect phone call: Where's
your limo? Where's your starlets? Aren't you supposed to be dead?
It was a constant embarrassment. At the same time, though, it was
something of an incentive—a strong, silent burden of a namesake to
be borne. The stoic perfection of his name was an ever-present reminder of his failure to live up to his own expectations. How could
Gary Cooper have allowed himself to become a junkie?

Being back in Tennessee, he couldn't help but remember a time
when he *had* lived up to his name—junior year at Gleason High,
when he had played on the school's undefeated football team. Gleason was the smallest high school in the state to field a varsity squad,
and Gary had been one of its smallest members. He was a 130-pound
pulling guard, tiny compared to most of his opponents, but more
determined. He was knocked unconscious in the second quarter
against South Fulton that year, but picked himself up and continued
on. The coach said, "Cooper, if we had eleven guys like you, I don't
know if we'd win every game, but we'd sure entertain the folks."

Each time he set himself at the line of scrimmage, the possibility
of complete success, of perfection, was there for the taking. When
he made a perfect block, even against a much larger man, aggressiveness was rewarded by the absence of pain. Of course, few blocks
were perfect . . . but there had been at least one, against Parsons
in the Rotary Bowl, the last game of the season. Gleason was losing. Coach Settlers had chewed them out at half time. "You're not
concentrating. I know they're bigger, but we're faster. Where's your
pride? You're playing scared . . ." Their first play from scrimmage
in the third quarter was a 23-quickie, a routine run between guard
and tackle, usually good for three of four yards. This time, though,
Cooper hit his man perfectly, the guy just crumpled, and Jimmy

Black darted past—sixty yards for the winning touchdown and an undefeated season. Nothing since had approached the complete satisfaction of that moment.

He was left feeling washed out and depressed by the ordeal of heroin withdrawal, but he decided to look up some of his old friends from the football team. He called Russell Byrd, who had played tackle next to him and was a good friend, and they spent a Sunday afternoon driving around in Russell's car, drinking beer and visiting former teammates. Russell was surprised by Gary's appearance— sallow, torpid, defeated. He bore little resemblance to the carefree, wisecracking Cooper whom Russell had known in high school; it was as if Gary had seen too much of the world. He seemed wilted, without ambition. They talked about Vietnam and Gary said, "If I had any guts, I'd go back to the Nam for a second trip. I'd take five thousand dollars and buy some goods and come home a millionaire."

It was idle Sunday-afternoon bravado, Russell thought, but the closest Gary had come to sounding like his old self.

Gary and Barbara had been staying with his grandmother for nearly a month when they learned that his father was coming to visit. Gary tried to be nonchalant about the news, but Barbara could tell that he was nervous. He told her, "I remember when I was a kid, my mother and Thomas would give me fifty cents to go to the movies, and I'd be real angry because I couldn't buy candy like the other kids. Then my dad would blow into town, give me five bucks for the movies, and I'd feel like he was trying to buy me off."

But Thirby Cooper didn't seem at all callous or manipulative to Barbara. He was a thick, sluggish, slow-talking man whose attempts to show affection toward his son were clumsy, but undeniably genuine. He offered to take Gary and Barbara to his home in Huntsville, Alabama, where he worked for NASA. Jobs were more plentiful there than in Tennessee, he said, and better-paying. Gary accepted warily; he seemed unnerved by his father's kindness.

They spent two rather constrained weeks at Thirby's house.

Gary and his father circled each other cautiously, the stiff formality never really eased. Gary made a few halfhearted attempts to find work, but eventually decided to return to Indiana—it was as if he were more comfortable with Thomas's antipathy than his father's love. Barbara didn't mind the decision; she had dreaded the prospect of spending the rest of her life a hillbilly.

One afternoon, she and Gary were in bed together at Thirby's house and he said, "You're pregnant, aren't you?"

"No, I'm not," she blurted before she knew what she was saying. The truth was, she wasn't sure. She hadn't menstruated in three months; but then, she'd gone nine months without her period when she'd been at the boarding school in Kentucky. The doctors had told her it was nerves, and she hoped against hope that it was the same thing now, although she guessed it wasn't.

"Yes, you are," he said.

"No, I'm not," she repeated, but not so firmly as the first time.

"That's all we need."

They went for a walk. She'd often wondered if it was love or need or just plain convenience that kept Gary hanging around. He'd said "I love you" too soon—the day that he brought her home to meet his mother—and too infrequently thereafter for her to be very sure. They'd been together for six months, and she'd grown to love him; their tenuous, contentious attempt at domesticity was the closest she'd come to having a real home in a long time. She was proud to be with someone so handsome, and constantly afraid she was going to lose him. A baby might be just the thing to scare him off; as they walked along, she was afraid that it already had.

"Look," he finally said, "we're going to take a bus back home and then it's over. You go your way, and I'll go mine. That's it."

"You son of a bitch," she screamed. "You don't have to marry me. I don't *want* you to fucking marry me. But you can't just go and make me pregnant, and then take no goddamn responsibility for it."

He didn't say anything. He didn't say much all the way home. He went back to live with his mother and Thomas; she moved in with her father temporarily.

But it wasn't over. Gary kept coming around to see her, obviously sorry for what he'd said, but too proud to come right out and apologize. Gradually, she realized that he needed her: for the first time in his life, he'd found someone who would love him without reservation. She still wasn't sure if he actually loved her, but she'd learned not to expect much from life and figured that anything he gave her would be better than nothing at all.

So their courtship resumed, though it seemed they had more troubles than ever. For one thing, Barbara decided to stop using drugs, at least until the baby was born, and Gary didn't like that. "I thought you were a party girl," he'd say, and then go off disgustedly on one of his weekend speed runs, or chip some heroin (which he'd started using again as soon as they returned north, certain that he could control it this time). For another, Barbara was beginning to balloon with child and felt fat, sluggish, ugly and more vulnerable than ever. And finally, the question of marriage remained unresolved; she wanted to be married, but didn't want to put any pressure on him. "You *don't* have to marry me," she told him at every opportunity. "You really don't."

But Gary was getting a lot of heat from his mother and aunt Estelle. "You've got to marry that girl and give that baby a name," Estelle said.

He dawdled, though. He decided to buy Barbara a dog. "She likes dogs," he told his mother.

"That's all she needs," Lillian said, "a dog *and* a baby. Forget the dog and do the right thing."

One night Barbara called Gary at his mother's house, and he wasn't there. She tried to find him along the endless-party route, but no one had seen him. She began to panic, wondering if he'd skipped out. She made more calls, and finally found him at his stepsister Donna's house. "Listen," he said, in the tone of voice that always meant bad news, "I'm gonna get a good job, and we're gonna get married."

"You don't have to do that."

"We're gonna get married," he said, and she thought: The least he could have said was "I want to."

He found a good job easily enough, in a training program for industrial welders at the Thrall Car Company. He finally would learn a skill; there was the promise of job security and solid paydays as soon as he graduated from the course. They found a decent if somewhat bizarre place to live, in a subdivision of Quonset huts, a remnant of the late 1940s, near his mother's house. They set a date to visit a justice of the peace, and Gary kept it—although he did bring along a shooting buddy from work named Leo, whom Barbara knew would mess up their day. Gary was neatly dressed, in a brown shirt and good slacks. She was wearing the one dress she could still squeeze into. As they waited outside the JP's office, she reminded him one last time: "We don't have to do this. I don't want you to marry me just because I'm pregnant. I don't want you to throw it in my face five years from now. We can just get up and walk right out of here if you want. I don't care. I just don't want you to hate me for this."

"We're getting married," he said, which still wasn't quite what she wanted to hear.

And so they were married. The date was December 23, 1971. As soon as the ceremony was over, Leo said, "Let's cop."

Gary said, "Good thinking."

Barbara thought: Oh shit.

They drove to Roselawn. While Barbara sat in the car, Gary and Leo scored some heroin in a tavern. They shot it up in the car, and nodded out. Barbara drove them to her father's house, where her stepmother had arranged a reception.

"Don't do it," Barbara had told her, suspecting that her stepmother mostly was celebrating her departure. But the woman insisted and—Barbara had to admit—she arranged a nice little affair, with a wedding cake and a bottle of champagne, broiled chicken and sloppy joes. Gary's folks weren't there: Thomas was off in Tennessee and Lillian immobile. But then, Gary wasn't quite there either. He was lost in space, and no one seemed to notice except her brother, Jimmy, who had been that route more than a few times himself and was jealous that his new brother-in-law hadn't seen fit to share. The stepmother, oblivious, insisted on pushing food at Gary, which was a mistake. He couldn't hold much food in his stomach when he was smacked, but was too polite to turn her down . . . and Barbara could see him growing paler, rather green in fact. When it came time to cut the cake, there were the usual photographs.

"Now you feed him a piece, Barb," someone said.

She did. He gagged, put a hand over his mouth and ran for the bathroom. Later, Barbara would remember the moment with a wistful smile.

There was no honeymoon. Three months later she gave birth to a son, whom they named Craig.

The next few years were relatively quiet. The endless party dispersed; couples paired off, were married, had babies. The partygoers moved into trailer courts and garden apartments, saving their money for down payments on modest homes, which they eventually furnished with Early American and Mediterranean living-room suites, Formica dinettes and twenty-five-inch color television sets in imposing wood cabinets. They covered their walls with dime-store art (galleons and conquistadors were popular, replacing the water mills and covered bridges favored by their parents), and improbably benign photographs of their children. Some hung crucifixes; others—including Gary and Barbara—purchased a remarkably ubiquitous piece of erotic statuary: a man and a woman naked, caressing, his hands on her behind, her arms around his neck, seeming to pull him down toward her—it was something their parents never would have countenanced, one of the few artifacts that distinguished their homes from the ones in which they'd been raised. Long hair and marijuana were other remnants of the blue-collar counterculture to survive the 1960s, along with an abundant cynicism about management, the unions, the government—any and all forms of authority. For the rest, though, they became surprisingly like their parents, at least in outward appearance. The men watched "Monday Night Football," talked about hunting and fishing and listened to country music, which began to express their frustrations and fantasies more accurately than hard rock. The women haunted the shopping malls, smoked long cigarettes and played Bingo at the church. Such things were by no means universal, of course, merely pervasive; and beneath the tranquil surface there were stirrings—especially among the women—of profound changes to come. Still, the early 1970s were in general a deceptively calm period for Gary and Barbara's friends, a breather between the turmoil of the 1960s and the economic upheaval that soon would ambush their dreams and challenge their most basic assumptions.

In the Cooper household, Barbara quietly assumed control. She handled the money and paid all the bills. She wasn't domineering—she knew better than to push Gary—but she established the restraints that provided whatever stability there was, which wasn't much. Gary was basically rebellious, threatening divorce almost from the start. He would scream, pound the table, pull the "C'mere, bitch" routine—especially when his friends were around—but there was a tacit understanding that these displays were not to be taken seriously. Once performed, they were forgotten and Gary would return to his favorite outpost, on the couch in front of the television, or go to sleep.

Vietnam hardly was mentioned during those years. Once or twice he told her stories—how it always seemed wet there, how everyone had crotch rot down to his knees, how frightened he was to return to the field after he was wounded at Operation Cochise. But he no longer had nightmares, and Barbara sensed no strong undercurrents of anger or remorse—although she'd later suspect they were there throughout: Why else would he bother to go to Chicago and endure the pain of having his Marine Corps bulldog tattoo remade into an eagle? All she noticed at the time was that his interest in Vietnam Veterans Against the War waned and he stopped reading Abbie Hoffman.

If Gary was more subdued than he'd been, he was not quite ready to settle into propriety either. He remained tight with his old shooting buddies—Farrell, Duke, Eddie Frady and the rest—and much of the money that might have gone into the trappings of middle-class respectability—a house, some furniture—went instead to drugs. He was careful not to get strung out on heroin again, though; if he felt himself slipping toward addiction, he would shoot some speed and try to race past it. Still, there were more than a few times when he'd be sick for two or three days, recovering from a payday fix.

Barbara learned how to read Gary. As soon as he'd walk in the door, she could tell if he'd been using drugs and, if so, what kind. If he was speeding, his pupils would be dilated and he'd head straight for the bathroom and primp, combing and recombing his hair, trimming his moustache, sometimes even shaving it off, changing his clothes again and again. When he smoked marijuana, his eyes would be watery and he'd head straight for the refrigerator. When he smoked hashish, his eyes would be heavy and he'd head for the couch. When he was drunk, he'd be angry, domineering and insulting—he was a lousy drunk. When he shot heroin, though, he'd head straight for her; junk made him warm and kind and wonderful, the best of all possible Garys.

That was a problem. Obviously, she had mixed feelings. More than once she'd had to scrape him off a couch or a floor, slap him around, splash him with water, walk him back and forth across the floor, wondering if this time he'd really gone and done it. At the same time, though, Gary was never so loving as when he was smacked; heroin made him the husband she'd hoped he'd be . . . and so she didn't complain.

After several years at Thrall Car, he found a much better paying job at the Union Tank Company, welding railroad cars. At first, Barbara was hopeful that they'd now be able to save some money, and live decently for a change; but Gary soon found a four-star connection at work, highest quality and very dependable. His resistance crumpled and he was quickly back to where he'd been before they left for Tennessee—shooting up once a day, strung out.

Once again, there was the charade of Gary pretending not to be addicted and Barbara pretending not to notice. Usually, he was very discreet, copping and shooting away from home; one day, though, she came home from the store and found Gary and some of his shooting buddies in her living room, with their spoons, needles, rubber tubing and glassy eyes; it seemed a flagrant escalation, and she was angry. She thought Gary had understood their tacit agreement.

Craig was to be protected from that sort of scene. But Gary didn't seem to be the slightest bit embarrassed; in fact, he was showing off. "Hey," he said, "maybe we ought to check out that methadone program over in Gary. Then we can stay high all the time."

"*You* don't need that," Barbara said bitterly. "You're *cool.*"

About a month or so later, though, Gary approached her quietly. "Hey, Barb," he said, "I think I better check out that methadone program."

It was the first time she'd really seen him frightened. He didn't like being strung out on the job; it was dangerous, working on massive tank cars which were suspended by cables in midair—if he screwed up, there could be a serious accident.

"You wouldn't be ashamed of me," he said, "going to that place?"

"Gary," she said, "I'll never be ashamed of you."

3

GARY COMMUNITY MENTAL HEALTH SERVICES
PSYCHO-SOCIAL HISTORY

Name: *Gary W. Cooper*

Date: *August 23, 1976*

The earliest thing I remember is: *my dad came to visit.*

My father is: *just a word—no feelings one way or the other.*

My mother is: *a pain.*

I was most influenced by: *my father.*

My family thinks I am: *Parents: drug problems. Wife and kid: a breadwinner.*

I wish my father: *would have been closer to me.*

I wish my mother: *would have been closer to my father.*

The worst thing about my childhood was: *my stepparents.*

The best thing about my childhood was: *growing up.*

The three words that best describe my family are: *no love, no understanding, feeling of obligation.*

The three words that best describe me are: *hard worker, love my family, happy.*

Someday I'd like to give my family: *a drug-free life.*

I left/would leave home because: *I felt discriminated against by my stepparents.*

When my family and I had fun we: *used to go on picnics.*

I never tell my parents: *that I use drugs.*

My family helped me: *finish high school.*

The methadone clinic was located where it was needed, in the very worst section of Gary. It was a low-slung cinder-block bunker, a tentative outpost of social-work bureaucracy in the midst of urban cataclysm, surrounded by abandoned buildings and vacant lots carpeted with shattered glass; surrounded too—besieged, in fact—by a loopy clutter of winos and junkies hoping to buy, sell or beg some action, drawn there by the scent of uncertain willpower that suffused the place. Merely parking his car on the street beside the clinic was, for Gary Cooper, a humiliation; there could be no illusions here about what he was. But the junkies attempting cloudy transactions on the sidewalk strengthened his resolve. He *had* to get himself clean before Craig was old enough to know.

Inside, the clinic was divided by a long green-tile corridor. On the left there was a waiting room with plastic chairs, ashtrays brimming with cigarette butts, end tables covered with half-empty Styrofoam coffee cups, tattered magazines and government pamphlets on health and nutrition; usually there were several sleepers or nodders, black inevitably, lounging about haphazardly, like rag dolls discarded by a thoughtless child. Down the hall on the left, there was a meeting room—group therapy for junkies. Cooper never talked in group therapy; Barbara, who insisted she come with him, never stopped talking. At their very first session, she'd gotten into a fight with a black junkie—the Coopers were the only whites there—who said to Gary, "It's different for you, man. It's a lot easier being a junkie when you're white."

"Bullshit," Barbara roared. "A junkie is a junkie."

The group leader asked Gary what he thought about that. Gary shrugged and smiled.

The methadone was dispensed from behind a dutch door down the hall on the right. There were daily urine checks, and a book to sign. An attendant would measure out Gary's dose—40 milligrams—into a paper cup, then mix it with orangeade to cut the drug's bitter taste.

In the beginning, the new addiction had an unsettling effect on his system. He often was nauseated, especially when he tried to sip a beer, and—for several weeks—impotent, which frightened him. He threatened to quit the program, but Barbara said, "Hey, don't worry about it. Your body is going through a change is all."

Often, in those first weeks, she would catch him staring at his arms in the mirror. "They're clearing up," he'd say, "ain't they, Barb?"

For the next four years, their lives were ruled by methadone. It was a constant source of embarrassment for Gary, a constant reminder of his weakness. It was, at the same time, the glue that bound their marriage, a shared secret, a reassuring limitation on his wanderings, a ball and chain. It prevented them from taking vacations out of town, or even weekend camping trips. He insisted that no one know about his daily visits to the clinic. Sometimes, in winter, he would drive through snow and ice to get there. He worked the afternoon shift at Union Tank—from three to eleven—and he would drive to Gary just after noon, receive his dose, then come home for dinner and go to work. He knew that sooner or later he would have to detoxify, but he also knew that methadone was a much more difficult addiction than heroin; detoxification would take months to complete, and he was afraid he wouldn't make it.

"When I get off," he would say to Barbara, "I don't know if I'll be able to handle staying off."

"It takes willpower," she would say, "like a diet."

"Well, maybe I'll just quit going around with the guys."

"You can't quit going around with the guys you work with."

As a test of his resolve, Gary dropped by his friend Leo's house—a virtual shooting gallery—and found several of his buddies making up. "He began to preach at them about how evil junk was,"

Barbara would recall, "and then he flushed their stuff down the toilet. They were really pissed at him, but I was kind of proud."

Despite the bravado, Gary was anxious to prove to his friends at work that, though straight, he hadn't become a straight arrow—too anxious, as it happened. His job at Union Tank was the best he'd ever had. The pay was good and the overtime plentiful. It also was easy to goof off; there weren't enough supervisors on the afternoon shift to keep an eye on everyone. When the workload was light, slackers could vault the fence that ringed the factory and visit one of the local taverns, then come back and punch out at quitting time. The truly brazen would wait several more hours before clocking out and collect overtime. All of Cooper's friends did this occasionally; few had much loyalty to the heat and noise and danger of the factory. Gary, though, vaulted the fence more often and less successfully than most. In four years at Union Tank, he was warned three times for leaving work early. Finally, in the summer of 1978, he was caught filing a phony overtime claim and fired on the spot. He asked his friend Carl Turner, president of the Boilermakers' local at the plant, to challenge the firing. "Okay, Gary," Turner said, "but they got you cold. They know people have been sneaking out, and they want to make you an example. If I was you, I'd start looking for work."

Once again, work wasn't difficult to find. Within weeks, Cooper landed a job welding freight cars at the Pullman Standard Company in Hammond. He moved his family to a yellow brick duplex near the factory. It was a modest but comfortable place, with a living room, dining room and kitchen downstairs, bedrooms upstairs and a backyard perfect for barbecuing, or tossing a football with Craig.

Over the years, Gary had become much more of a father to his son. They spent weekends together glued to the television, especially during football season, and made bets on the games. When Craig was old enough to join Little League, Gary helped coach the team. He and Barbara tried not to fight when Craig was around; they had a tacit agreement that their son was going to have the idyllic childhood they'd been denied. They went overboard buying gifts for him each Christmas; at Halloween, Gary would figure out an appropriate costume for Craig and take him trick-or-treating. He also supervised Craig's schoolwork. "You've *got* to get good grades and go to college," he'd say. "I don't want you working in no mill like your old man, eating smoke and getting weld burns."

As he began to take his domestic responsibilities more seriously, Gary also decided that it was time to stop screwing around on the job. He worked hard and well at Pullman, steered clear of the druggies in the plant and made friends with several younger workers who were decent, clean-living family types. It seemed to Barbara that Gary finally was getting a grip on his life. The only thing left for him to do was kick methadone.

In February 1979, Gary told Louise Irby, a counselor at the methadone clinic, that he was ready to begin detoxification.

Lou Irby was a middle-aged black woman, a former addict who encouraged Cooper to take the big step, but warned him: "Detox isn't going to do you much good unless you start figuring out what made you an addict in the first place."

He wasn't very cooperative. In fact, according to Lou Irby's notes, it was a month before Cooper was able to establish eye contact with her at their weekly counseling sessions; even then he refused to discuss anything personal, and limited their talks to the intricacies of detoxification. "You can't pay attention to every little discomfort," she told him. "You might wake up some days with a crick in your back or your knee, and think it's detox—and then you'll say to yourself, 'I've got to get something to take an edge off this.' But it might just be a crick in your back—you know, *reality* . . . and getting used to reality is the toughest thing about detox. It's not like going cold turkey. It'll be gradual. The doctor might cut your dose one week, then keep it at that level for a month. Sometimes he might even bring it back up a little, if he decides he's been cutting you back too fast."

According to clinic records, the doctors reduced Cooper's daily methadone dose by 2.5 milligrams every two weeks from February to July 1979, at which time he was stabilized at 10 milligrams per day. In June, he told Lou Irby that he was having trouble sleeping and was feeling depressed.

"That's not uncommon," she said. "Maybe you should talk to the doctor about bringing you back up a bit."

"No way," he said. "I want to get this goddamn thing over with."

That summer, Barbara noticed that Gary was eating more and gaining weight rapidly. Worse, he was in a foul mood, always touchy, nervous, pacing. Hardly a day went by when he didn't talk about divorce. "You can do better than me," he'd say. "Why don't you just leave and find some guy who isn't so fucked up?"

"C'mon, Gary . . ."

"You're just staying for the paycheck."

"Fuck you."

"Fuck *you*."

When she asked him how he was doing, he'd either ignore her or tell her to be quiet. "Maybe you should get an increase from the doctor," she'd say.

"Fuck you. If you don't like living with me, *leave.*"

Months passed, and he remained irritable. His methadone dose continued stable at 10 milligrams. In October, Barbara learned that her mother was dying of cancer in Davenport, Iowa; for the next month, she divided her time between Hammond and the hospital, alternately neglecting Gary and her mother—they were *both* invalids, she realized—which made no one very happy. When Barbara was away, Gary tended to get very drunk, trying to find some way to smooth out the rough edges. One night he called her in Iowa and said, "Don't come home. It's over. I want a divorce." She told him to cool it, sober up. He called an hour later. "I really mean it. Don't come home." He called her four more times that night and then, in the morning: "Hey, Barb, when are you coming home?"

When Barbara's mother died in early November, Gary had to produce an obituary notice in order to get several days' rations of methadone so he could attend the funeral. "I can't take this shit no more," he said. "It's like getting a note from the doctor in kindergarten. It's like I'm a fucking baby. I'm sick of this shit."

"He's driving me nuts," Barbara told Lou Irby. "I can't take him like this. Can't you get him to take an increase?"

"No. That's his decision," Lou said. "Look, he's been seeing the world through drugs for a long time. No aches, no pain, no rough edges. He's in pain now, not because of the addiction, but because he's seeing reality without a crutch, without anything to relieve it. And believe me, after you've been an addict, reality isn't very pretty."

Reality gave no quarter in Hammond. It left platoons of men scarred and empty in the taverns that ringed the steel mills like turrets on a prison; it left them angry and frustrated as their wages rose and prices rose faster; it left them paralyzed with fear as the steel industry began to implode in the late 1970s. Wisconsin Steel in East Chicago closed; the local Ford assembly plant closed; U.S. Steel's massive South Works on the east side of Chicago became a ghost town, with only a skeleton crew kept on for appearance' sake; layoffs began at Republic Steel, Youngstown, even Inland. The bars were filled with anxious men talking about Texas, where work was supposedly plentiful. A small domestic revolution was taking place: their wives were being forced to find jobs—at minimum wage, usually, in fast-food outlets, convenience stores and non-union shops. More and more, it was the former steelworkers who were staying home, taking care of the kids, doing the housework, watching the soaps. Traditional concepts of manliness were taking a beating in the steel belt; depression and unease were epidemic.

At Pullman, though, there was plenty of work. The freight-car business was booming, an unlikely bonanza that had little to do with the law of supply and demand. Freight cars, it seemed, had been "discovered" as a tax shelter. In 1978, the year Cooper was hired, orders suddenly doubled (from 67,000 to 126,000 nationally). "For a time there, every doctor and dentist in the country seemed to own a piece of a freight car," said a Wall Street analyst who specialized in Pullman's corporate performance. "Inevitably, this created a glut and the bottom dropped out of the market." The boom lasted two years. Early in 1980, with orders evaporating, Pullman decided to close its Hammond works when the current contracts were fulfilled.

Management pushed workers to produce more, faster (though not necessarily better), in order to close the plant as quickly as possible.

Gary Cooper knew only that he was working harder and bringing home more money than ever before. He had volunteered for an especially messy and difficult job—repairing defective hitches (the clasps that secured truck bodies to flatbed freight cars). The hours were long—some days, from five in the morning until five at night—and the work exhausting, but the pay was incredible: one week he brought home a $780 paycheck. He was so proud that he kept the stub in his wallet for weeks after and showed it to all his friends.

In December 1979, though, the first rumors of layoffs began to float through Pullman's freight-car division. Cooper knew that, with only a year's seniority, he would be one of the first to go.

Also in December, Cooper began the last phase of his detoxification. Early in the month, he was dropped from 10 milligrams daily to 7.5. At about the same time, Barbara's stepfather, still mourning his wife's death, decided to move in with them in Hammond. He was an unobtrusive sort, but his presence—and the resulting lack of privacy—unnerved Gary. He was drinking heavily, flying off the handle more often, driving Barbara crazy.

One evening in mid-December, Gary was drunk and decided he wanted to make love. Barbara, exhausted, wasn't interested.

"Well, if you don't want to," he said, "there's a girl I know who'll do anything I want."

"Go to her then," she said. "Leave me alone."

They were shouting at each other, and finally he said, "If you don't shut up, I'm gonna smack you."

"No, you ain't," Barbara said. In eight years of marriage, he'd never hit her. "You're too chicken, you ain't man enough to do it."

He slapped her then, and she grabbed his hair. They were upstairs, in the hall, and at first it seemed more ridiculous than dire to her. He had grabbed her hair, and the two of them were grappling in the hall, screaming, refusing to let go of each other's hair. They swung into Craig's room—he was downstairs, watching television—and somehow she managed to shove Gary down onto Craig's bed (he was very drunk). She leaned over him, still pulling his hair, but slowly sliding backwards, her feet slipping on the floor. As she went down, he came up. His eyes, which were very nearly black, had grown blacker still—blank in a way, as if they were empty holes drilled deep into his skull. She'd seen that look once before, when he'd almost killed Thomas Brummitt, and she knew she was in trouble. He pinned her to the floor and punched her in the face—he was beating her as if she were a man. She scratched back at him, and he grabbed her by the neck, slamming her head against the floor, slowly increasing the pressure on her throat. "You're *killing* me," she managed to gasp.

And he let go. He stood up, kicked her in the ribs and disappeared into their bedroom. Barbara went to the bathroom and saw that her left eye was closing; the side of her face was throbbing. She wet a washcloth, went downstairs and put it over her face. Craig looked at her, but said nothing. Then she heard Gary coming down the stairs toward her. As she bolted up, he kicked the leg of her chair and walked out. He returned several hours later, but said nothing.

The next morning, after Craig went off to school, they talked. They sat at the kitchen table, drinking coffee, her face swollen and discolored. "I told you from the start," she said, "that there were only two things that could make me leave you: if you hit me, or if you were going out on me. So last night you hit me, and you've never admitted it, but I'm sure you've been screwing around on me too."

"I'm not gonna lie," he said. "Yeah."

She began to cry. She asked for details. He said he'd done it three or four times, and only when he was drunk. "So if you want to leave, leave," he said. "But don't come back. I'll ask you one time not to go, but I won't ask you again."

"You think that little of me?"

"I don't want you to go, but I ain't gonna beg you to stay. I'll make it through, one way or the other." He softened then. "You know, when I was hitting you last night, it wasn't you I was hitting."

"Who was it?"

He didn't say anything.

"I know you're under a lot of pressure," she offered, but the conversation was over.

Barbara told her friends that she'd gotten the black eye in an automobile accident. She punished Gary by cutting off her long blond hair and getting a permanent. She called Lou Irby, and told her the truth.

Lou suggested to Gary that it might be a good idea to continue their weekly session even after he finished detox. "Maybe two or three times a month," she said. "Just to be sure you're okay."

"Yeah, sure," he said, "I may do that." And she knew then that he wouldn't.

On January 2, 1980, Cooper's dose was reduced to 5 milligrams per day.

On January 28, it was reduced to 2.5.

On February 4, it was reduced to 2.5 every other day.

On March 3, his detoxification was complete.

On May 14, he was laid off at Pullman.

It was the day before Barbara's birthday. He came home at 11 a.m. and started packing. "What the hell are *you* doing home?" she asked.

"Going camping, me and some of the guys," he said. "We all just got laid off."

"You son of a bitch, what about my birthday?" she asked, not really angry. She understood he needed to get out of town.

Actually, Cooper wasn't very worried about the layoff. He'd never had trouble finding work in the past; he'd never gone more than a week or two without a job. Gradually, though, it became apparent that this time would be different: there was no work to be had in the Calumet region, not even for an experienced welder. The summer slid past. Barbara had to take a job at a local mail-order house, running an envelope addresser on the afternoon shift for minimum wage, while Gary stayed home and played with Craig. "I hate this," he said to her. "I don't like my wife to work."

"You'll work soon enough," she said. "I'll be only too happy to sit on my butt and let you support me. Enjoy yourself while you can."

In other years, when July curled into August and summer decayed languorously in the steel towns along the Lake Michigan shore, Cooper would work himself into a frenzy of anticipation over the upcoming football season. He would haunt the local drug-stores, flipping through the annual guides and forecasts . . . giddy with visions of the elegant Cowboys, beefy Steelers, perfect spirals, open-field tackles, "Monday Night Football." He knew the National Football League cold—statistics, draft picks, strategies—and friends who'd watch the games with him would be amazed by his ability to understand the minutiae. "The left guard wasn't out fast enough on that one, the linebacker was *his* responsibility," he might drawl . . . which would, in turn, evoke an admiring "Jeez, Coop, you know more than Howard Cosell."

This year, though, even the prospect of football season didn't help much. He was bored and dispirited. The idea of *Gary Cooper* babysitting while his wife brought home the bacon was hard to swallow. He was as temperamental as he'd been during the worst moments of detox; Barbara found herself thinking often about the way his eyes had looked the night he beat her. She was afraid he would lose control again. One afternoon, they were caught in a traffic jam on Indianapolis Avenue, near their home. A car was stalled in the left-hand lane at the corner of 163rd Street, where they normally turned left . . . and Gary went berserk. As they squeezed past the stopped car, he railed at the driver: "Whatsa matter with you, you stupid *fucker*, you're holding up half the cars in Hammond, you asshole. Get a move on!"

"What do you want me to do?" the guy replied. "It won't go."

"I'M GONNA COME BACK HERE AND BLOW YOUR FUCKING HEAD OFF, YOU SORRY MOTHERFUCKER," Gary screamed, now holding up traffic himself.

"C'mon, Gary," Barbara said, trying not to provoke him further. There was no telling where this might be headed now.

"If you're still here when I get back," he said, shaking a finger at the man, "your ass has had it." They made the left turn . . . and Barbara believed—it was strange, thinking this—that Gary was screwy enough to get his gun and go back there. When they arrived home, she raced upstairs and hid his little .22-caliber peashooter, then ran back down, huffing; but his mood had passed and she felt a bit foolish. It had only been a stalled car.

They spent a good deal of time with family that summer, barbecuing with Gary's stepsister, Donna, and her husband, or with Barbara's brother, Jimmy, and his wife. Everyone was a little crazy with all the layoffs going around, and there was a feeling abroad that it was best to stay close to people you knew. Even then, quiet evenings had a way of turning into melees. One night they were barbecuing with Donna and her husband, smoking some marijuana, drinking piña coladas and good-and-plentys (a concoction named after the candy, consisting of twin shots of Kahlúa and ouzo), when Barbara's brother, Jimmy, burst in, very drunk and looking for trouble. Lacking anything better, he resurrected their oldest and silliest argument: who'd had it worse when they were kids. Usually the topic was good for a solid hour of screaming, but Barbara was tired of all the recent tension and screaming; she wanted no part of Jimmy . . . but he was very persistent. "C'mon, Jimmy, let it go. Leave me alone," she'd say, and move away from him, but he just trailed after her. Finally, she went into the kitchen and Jimmy followed her there; cornered, she lit into him—from out in the yard it sounded like the sharp, ravenous growling of two pit bulls mauling each other. Gary came to the rescue, forcefully stepped between them and told Jimmy, "Lay off my wife and get the fuck outta here."

She loved it. She wished he'd strut his stuff in her defense more often; usually, it was at her expense.

They weren't on the outs with Jimmy for long. They were all too close for any long-term disagreements or, for that matter, any long-term reconciliations. Jimmy and Gary, especially, had a quicksilver friendship that was always intense and never predictable. Both tried to present themselves as tough guys—Jimmy never let it be forgotten that he'd once been president of Los Hombres motorcycle gang—but they were growing older, and the posturing seemed increasingly childish. Jimmy was more flamboyant, with his long, kinky brown hair and his leather vests, but also more accessible—always talking, as if by talking he could outmaneuver his fear. Gary looked more conventional, with his short black hair and neatly trimmed moustache, but less likely to speak his mind and ultimately more explosive. Sometimes he would get angry at Jimmy for running his mouth—especially when Jimmy ran his mouth about Vietnam (he'd been in the Navy) and didn't quite get his stories straight; at other times, Barbara would walk in on them and they'd be talking about the war or their childhoods, and both would have tears coursing down their cheeks.

One night in late summer, Gary did something that both Barbara and Jimmy would later agree was not only exceedingly strange but also ominous. They were at Jimmy's house. Barbara and Jimmy's wife, Nancy, were in the living room, the kids were watching television and the men were in the kitchen, carrying on their usual doleful drunken ruminations.

"It's like we was cattle," Jimmy said. "You're just a number in the herd. If you drop, you drop. It's just a number they don't count anymore."

"Nobody gives a shit," Gary agreed.

"You get laid off, and they forget all about you," said Jimmy, who hadn't been laid off—he worked in the maintenance department at the Glidden paint factory—but, as with Vietnam, could imagine himself in Gary's shoes a little too easily.

"It's the establishment," Cooper said. "The whole system. Everything is stacked against you."

"It's all impersonal."

"It's like the war," Cooper said. "They wouldn't let us go in there and whip them little suckers. They were too busy raking it in." Then: "Hey, *Barb.*"

"Yeah?" she said, belligerently. She knew what was coming. Gary was going to start bossing her around. Ever since he'd been laid off he'd had the need, especially when drunk, to prove he was still in control. She wasn't sure what it was going to be this time, but she didn't want to hear it and told him so. "I don't want no grief from you," she said. "In fact, I'm leaving. Piss on this."

She went home. The phone started ringing as soon as she walked in the door. It was Gary. He told her—he didn't *ask*—to go over to Calumet City and get some beer.

"Get it your own self," she said.

"Can't. Jimmy's car is busted. His battery is dead."

"Get a jump," she said, and hung up. Then she thought: I'm here all alone and those guys are over there partying . . . I might as well get the beer.

Meanwhile, Gary and Jimmy had re-established themselves at the kitchen table and Gary was talking about Vietnam. It seemed to Jimmy that the war had been on Gary's mind quite a bit lately. He hadn't seen Gary so deep into it since the time they'd gone to see *Apocalypse Now* and Gary provided a running commentary, much to the dismay of the other patrons in the theater. During the scene where the helicopters assaulted a village, he'd been really excited. "Wow, look at that! . . . Beautiful! . . . That's what we did! . . . Man, look at those choppers!" Afterward, he said, "I've got to take Craig to see that movie so he'll know what his daddy did in the war."

That was an exception, though; Gary had never talked much about the war until he was laid off. Now, everything seemed to lead him back to it. That night, he launched into an elaborate description of the battle Charlie Company had had in the DMZ, where Sergeant Malloy had been killed. He told Jimmy all about Malloy, and how he'd died.

Then he stood up from the kitchen table. "I'm gonna try Barb again," he said. But there was no answer when he called, and he grabbed Jimmy. "Let's go over there. She's not answering on purpose. She *knows* it's me, goddamn her."

Jimmy had a feeling that Gary was building up to something drastic, but he didn't care. They had a neighbor help jump the battery on Jimmy's car and, as they drove off, Gary started in on Vietnam again, more emotional now, angry. He talked about the doctors who'd treated him on the hospital ship after Operation Cochise, and how they'd let his leg get infected (he didn't tell Jimmy that he'd splashed dirty water in the wound just after he'd been shot). Nobody gave a shit, he said. He was just a grunt. When the infection cleared, they just packed him up and sent him off to the boonies again.

He drifted back from Vietnam to Barbara, cursing her out. Then he was quiet, and Jimmy sensed the wheels turning. When they reached the apartment, Gary dashed upstairs. He came back down with a shotgun and a buck knife, and cut the telephone wire.

"What'd you do that for?" Jimmy asked.

"No lines of communication," Cooper said. "No one's getting in here." Then, with perfect calm: "Hey, want a beer?"

"Okay," Jimmy said, frightened. He'd never seen Gary quite so wired before, not even when they'd shot speed together in the old days.

They sat there—Cooper now drinking shots with his beer—and he began to talk about the ambush, the day he was shot . . . and suddenly he was *demonstrating* it. He grabbed the shotgun and crouched down in the plants Barbara kept along the back windowsill. They were bushy, leafy plants, almost a curtain of foliage. Jimmy could see that Gary wasn't fooling around; he seemed to be getting deeper and deeper into it. He wasn't exactly *back* there—he was still talking about the gooks in the tree line, the trapped squad, the heavy fire—but he wasn't exactly in Hammond either. He didn't point the gun out the window, but he was crouching, ready, his finger at the trigger . . .

"Hey, Gary," Jimmy said, with some trepidation, hoping to break the spell. "Lemme see the gun."

"Yeah, okay," Cooper said, standing abruptly; whatever had been happening was over now. Jimmy took the gun and saw that it was loaded.

When Barbara returned home several hours later, she found the two of them on the floor, silly drunk, trying to piece the telephone wire back together.

4

For the first time in memory, the air was clear over northern Indiana; there was no smoke coming from the mills. In the past, there had been column after column of "help wanted" ads for welders and assorted factory hands in the local newspapers; now the ads had dwindled and the papers were filled with stories predicting the end of basic industry—autos, steel, heavy equipment—in America. Stores were closing all over Gary and Hammond. Even some of the *bars* were closing. On weekday afternoons, carloads of men could be seen driving around aimlessly, sharing pints and six-packs, instead of spending their money in the taverns. Gary Cooper whiled away a good many such afternoons that autumn. He spent the mornings looking for work.

He drove his friends crazy talking about work, asking if they'd heard anything new, complaining about the economy, the politicians, the *system*, but most of all about himself: "If I hadn't've gotten fired at Union Tank, I'd be working today. They're still pulling *overtime* over there."

He answered every ad in the paper. He went through the phone book, calling every factory in the region. He talked about going to Texas. He made regular pilgrimages to Inland Steel, figuring that any mill that employed nearly 20,000 people must have *something* available from time to time. Once he stood in line at Inland for an entire day, waiting for a job application. When he finally reached the employment office, he was told the applications that day were only for college students looking for summer work. Too proud to admit he didn't qualify, Gary told them he was a student at Calumet College.

He and Glen Peters, a young friend from Pullman, often went on scouting expeditions, driving from factory to factory. "Well, the sun's gonna rise in the morning," Gary would say in the face of each new disappointment. "It's got to get better, because it can't get no worse."

But as autumn passed and winter came, Peters noticed a change in Cooper. He seemed to be giving up. One morning in December, they drove to a factory where they'd heard there was work. There wasn't, as usual, and Gary said, "You got any money? Let's go buy a pint."

"Hey, Coop, it's nine in the morning."

Barbara also had noticed that Gary was starting to drink as

soon as he got up each day. He always seemed to have a half-pint of vodka stuffed in his back pocket. She tried to limit his drinking by pouring some of the vodka off into another bottle when he wasn't looking, or by mixing the drinks herself and making them weak, but he wasn't easily fooled. He was getting fatter; he looked pasty and bloated. She suggested he go to the family doctor for diet pills, but Gary's blood pressure was high and the doctor refused to prescribe them. He suggested that Gary might lose some weight if he stopped drinking, which he did for a week and a half.

Doctors were not the only source for diet pills. As the weeks passed, Gary began to spend more time with his old shooting buddies. He didn't have the money for heroin, but Preludins—a brand name for the appetite suppressant phenmetrazine—were cheap, plentiful and sweeping the steel belt as hallucinogens had fifteen years earlier; when cooked and mainlined, they provided a speed-like rush. In December, he went a step further: he pawned the small color television he'd bought Barbara, and scored some heroin.

Barbara didn't like losing the television, but she wasn't very worried that Gary was about to get strung out again. There simply wasn't the money for it. She figured—correctly—that the heroin episode was a one-shot deal and, in truth, was almost happy he'd done it: his life was so miserable that he needed to get away from it for a day or two.

Apparently, though, Gary was more concerned about backsliding than his wife. Just before Christmas, he made a flushed, glassy-eyed appearance at the methadone clinic. Lou Irby realized that he was drunk and asked, "What brings *you* back here, stranger?"

"Just came by to say hi," he said. "I love you people." And then he hugged Lou Irby, the first time he'd ever shown her any affection.

"Okay, Gary," she said. "Why are you really here?"

"I've been chipping," he said. "I don't want to get strung out again."

"Chipping's not all you been doing," Lou said. "You've been drinking too. That's a worse addiction than heroin."

"I'm really down."

She suggested they resume their weekly counseling sessions. He filled out a form and agreed to come back the next day. She never saw him again.

Christmas was terrible. There wasn't enough money to buy Craig the usual truckload of presents, only a few odds and ends. Gary and Barbara didn't buy presents for each other, or for the other members of the family. Barbara had never seen him so depressed.

There was, however, some hope just after the holidays. Barbara's brother had a friend, Charlie Marshall, who worked at Calumet Industries, and he'd heard that they were about to hire some welders. Gary contacted Marshall, who put in a good word with his supervisor. The supervisor told Gary to fill out another application (he already had one on file at Calumet, as he did at every other factory in the area) and said, "You'll be hearing from us in a couple of days."

The days passed, and no word. A week passed, and Gary stopped getting dressed in the morning. He lay on the couch in his pajamas all day. Craig would come home from school and ask, "Are you sick? Why aren't you dressed?" And Gary would just laugh.

On January 20, the headline in the Hammond *Times* was:

SAFE!

After more than a year of confinement, the fifty-two Americans held hostage in Iran finally had been set free. Below that story on the front page, there was another headline almost as big:

PULLMAN CLOSES FREIGHT DIVISION

It wasn't much of a surprise. Gary had come to believe the plant never would reopen—but, all the same, it was depressing to see it in black and white. "Well, that's that," he said to Barbara.

On January 21, Gary and Barbara drove over to the Inland Steel complex in Indiana Harbor. Thomas Brummitt, who still worked at Inland, had called Gary to say that he'd seen an item in the company newspaper that said the employment office would be giving out job applications on January 21–23. There was no promise of work; the company merely wanted to update its file.

Word about the applications spread quickly through the area. The Hammond *Times* ran a little story about it; several local radio stations got it wrong, and said that Inland would be giving out *jobs.* A line began to form outside the factory on the evening of January 20. By the time the employment office opened at eight-thirty the next morning, a very large crowd had gathered—estimates ranged from 5,000 to 10,000 people. Cars were parked for miles down Cline Avenue, leading to the factory. People were pushing and shoving for places in line; some were climbing the chain link fence; the crowd spilled into the street and blocked traffic. Just after eight-thirty, security guards emerged from the employment office with stacks of job applications, the crowd surged forward, the applications went flying and there was a scramble for them. People were trampled in the rush; about a dozen were injured. Ambulances were called to the scene.

As Gary and Barbara approached Inland and saw the cars lining the road, she said, "I wonder what's going on." Then she realized what it was and said, "Oh shit, I can't believe it."

He laughed softly. "You didn't know how bad it was, did you?" He turned the car around and went home.

Two days later, Gary called his father in Alabama. "Something better turn up quick," he said. "I only got about three or four weeks of unemployment left. I'm thinking of hitching a ride down to Dallas, and looking for work there."

"That sounds like a good idea," Thirby Cooper said. "You need a little pocket money for the trip?"

"No, I'm fine," Gary said abruptly. Then: "Say, Dad, you been watching this stuff about the hostages? You see all this stuff they been getting? Lifetime passes to the ball park and all? I don't get it.

They were just doing their jobs. They didn't see any action. They didn't get shot at. But they're getting treated like *heroes* . . . I just don't get it."

The hostages were all over the television that weekend. On Sunday, the day of the Super Bowl—traditionally, a very important day for Gary—the hostages returned to America, arriving at a small air base in upstate New York. Thousands of cheering people had tied yellow ribbons around the trees lining the route to the hotel at West Point, where the hostages were reunited with their families.

Throughout the football game, there were updates on the return of the hostages, the cheering crowds, the flags and ribbons and marching bands. The Superdome in New Orleans was draped with a huge yellow ribbon; at half time, as the band played "Tie a Yellow Ribbon 'Round the Old Oak Tree," the hostages were said to be enjoying a steak-and-lobster feast. It was a day of national celebration; some commentators compared it to the euphoria at the end of World War II.

And that was just the beginning. For the next several days, as Gary Cooper sat watching in his pajamas, the hostages were greeted at the White House, interviewed on television, showered with gifts and paraded through the main streets of their hometowns. One night, Barbara came home from work at one in the morning and they were *still* on television, Gary watching impassively. Jesus Christ, she thought. Here's a guy with two Purple Hearts, busting his tail to find a lousy job . . . and having to watch all that. It's just not fair.

On Wednesday, January 28, Gary spent the afternoon driving around with his old friend Armando Ramirez. They bought a six-pack, smoked a joint and took Gary's 12-gauge shotgun out to the woods for some target practice. Gary had a box of deer slugs and, when they were done shooting, there were only about four or five left.

That evening, Gary decided to call Charlie Marshall and find out if there was any news about the welding job at Calumet Industries. "Haven't you been called?" Marshall asked. "I heard they hired two welders, and I was sure you was one of them."

On Thursday, January 29, Gary visited Dave Reczek, another friend from Pullman, who was earning some money by doing brake jobs for his friends. As Dave worked on Barbara's ancient Pinto, Gary talked about the hostages: "Those guys are gonna get a hundred dollars a day for the rest of their lives—and they were just secretaries, just clerks doing their jobs. You know what I got when I came home from the Nam? Bullshit. Nothing. It really pisses me off."

When Dave finished, Gary asked, "What do I owe you?"

"Nothing, man," Reczek said, knowing Gary's financial problems. He wanted to *offer* the guy some money.

"No, what do I owe you?"

"Okay, five bucks."

"Fine, I'll tell Barbara it cost me twelve dollars and go out and have one last bash."

Dave thought it was a curious thing for Gary to say, but didn't ask him what he meant.

On Friday, January 30, Barbara Cooper left for work in midafternoon. Gary called his stepsister, Donna, and asked if she could score him some Preludins. She said she'd see what she could do. At about 5 p.m., Gary decided to visit Charlie Marshall. Even though Charlie lived just down the street, he drove the Pinto there and left Craig at home watching television.

As it happened, Charlie had some good news about the job at Calumet Industries. "I talked to the boss," he told Gary. "He said they're going to be hiring more welders and your chances of getting on are real good."

Another worker from Calumet, Merle Stuart, was there and the three of them sat in Charlie's living room, drinking whiskey and talking. Gary dominated the conversation, going on about the hostages and Vietnam. "I was just a babe in the woods when I got out of high school," he said. "I had no idea what I was getting myself into."

Later, his desperation turned aggressive. He and Merle had a punching contest, walloping each other in the chest to see who'd flinch; Merle was an amateur boxer, and Cooper got the worst of it. By eight o'clock, all three of them were very drunk. Gary stumbled over a glass coffee table and shattered it. Marshall's wife said that enough was enough, and asked him to leave. He fell down the front steps, bruising his forehead and mouth.

At about eight-twenty that evening, Don Gray heard a ruckus outside his apartment. He went to the window and saw his next-door neighbor, Gary Cooper, rolling around on the ground; he was bloody and appeared to have been beaten. Gray rushed out and asked, "Gary, are you okay?"

"Who are you?" Gary said.

"Don, your neighbor," he said. Ron Hilliman, another neighbor, joined them. Gary didn't recognize him either. Don left Gary with Ron, and went inside to call Barbara at work. He told her that if she didn't get home fast and do something about Gary, he was going to call the police. When he got off the phone, he noticed that Gary was up and trying to break into his own apartment. He smashed the front-door window, then went around to the rear and attacked the kitchen door with a garbage can.

As it happened, both doors were unlocked.

Several hours earlier, Barbara Cooper had had a premonition. She had a sharp, queasy pain in her stomach and *knew* that something was wrong with Gary. She tried to call home during her dinner break, but the line was busy. About an hour later, Don Gray called. The message was garbled; she couldn't understand what was happening. Gary had been in a fight, and was busting up the apartment. Where was Craig? "You better get home fast," Don Gray said.

When she arrived home, the apartment seemed to be empty. There was glass on the floor—a broken window, a shattered mirror. The phone was off the hook.

"*Craig?*"

"Upstairs, Mom."

"You all right?"

"Uh-huh."

Gary was upstairs too. He was sprawled on the bed with a welt over his right eye, a swollen lip and blood trickling from his ear.

"Honey, what *happened*?"

He didn't say. He wanted to make love. "C'mon, Barb, lay down here with me."

"In a minute," she said. She went to Craig and told him to get dressed and go over to the Grays' house, then she returned to the bedroom and lay down with her husband.

An hour later, Gary seemed to be asleep. She decided to get Craig. She also was worried—panicked, really—about the Pinto, which Gary said he'd left over at Charlie Marshall's house. It had been her mother's car. She was afraid Gary had wrecked it. At that moment, it seemed very important to her that she retrieve the car and make sure it was all right.

"Where you going?" he asked as she slipped out of bed.

She told him.

"Don't leave me. Don't go. Lay down with me."

She told him she'd be right back, then started down the stairs and heard a crash. He'd fallen in the bathroom. "Barb?" She went back upstairs. He'd hurt his back, and she rubbed it for him. "I love you," he said. "I love you." And then he put his head in her lap and began to cry.

He stopped crying after a while, curled up in the bed and seemed to go to sleep again. Barbara went to pick up Craig and get the car.

At about ten-thirty, just after Barbara had left with Craig, Don Gray heard a knock on his door. It was Cooper, with a shotgun. "Where's Barb?" he asked.

"She just left."

"Where's Barb?" he asked again in exactly the same way, as if he didn't remember asking it the first time.

"Gary, she just left . . ."

Cooper raised the shotgun, pointed it down the street and fired it twice. He then broke it open, and reloaded. Gray slammed the door, went inside and called the police.

Barbara was rounding the corner in the Pinto when she saw Gary, shirtless in the January night, standing on the porch with the gun. He ducked back inside.

Two police cars roared down the street in front of the apartment. She could hear more sirens around back. "Let me talk to him," she pleaded with the officer who seemed to be in charge. "I'm his wife."

She walked calmly down the path to the front door, up the two steps onto the landing. She could see him through the broken window, crouched inside with the gun. "Tell him to put his gun down and come out," the officer in charge said.

"Honey, the cops want you to put down your gun."

He didn't seem to understand. He was crouched—his back straight, his knees slightly bent—amidst the hanging plants, the leaves tickling his nose, his eyes wide and glarey, two hands on the shotgun, one on the barrel, the other on the trigger.

"Didja see that, Barb?"

"What?"

He didn't say. He moved his head slowly, back and forth, scanning a blank wall. She remembered Jimmy's story about the night that Gary had cut the telephone wire.

"Didja see that, Barb?"

"*What?*"

The lights from the street threw wild nighttime shadows against the walls. Leaves became palm fronds, strips of light were elephant grass, police lights arced through the courtyard like flares.

"Tell him," the officer said, "that if he don't come out, we're gonna start shooting."

Shooting?

"Hey, wait a minute!" she screamed, running from the door to the police, one of whom was saying to another, "Pete, you got that shotgun in the car?"

"No, hey no, please don't hurt him," she begged, grabbing one of the cops. "He's just drunk and crazy. He flipped out. He thinks he's back in Nam. *Please*, don't hurt him."

She saw the police start, and turned to see Gary standing in the doorway. He seemed to be dangling the gun nonchalantly, and she figured he was coming out to give himself up. But there was an explosion. He had fired at two officers crouched to the left of the landing. The police said, "Oh *shit*," and scattered. Gary ducked back inside.

Barbara ran after the police, still begging, "Please, don't hurt him . . . please, don't hurt him," but they weren't listening. More police cars screeched into the street in front of the apartment and into the parking lot behind. She ran to the neighbors. She didn't want to see it, but she heard the bullets whanging and echoing, and the glass shattering, and then she heard it stop.

Officers Monte Miller and Bud Carney were crouched to the left of the landing when Cooper came out the front door and fired at them. Miller felt his face burning, and figured Cooper was firing buckshot. "Am I bleeding?" he asked Carney when Cooper had ducked back inside.

"No," Carney said.

"It must have been the powder," he said. "Jesus."

There was firing now from the rear of the apartment building. Carney went around back to help out. Miller used his walkie-talkie to inform his superiors that he was going to approach the front door. He moved slowly to the landing and then, leaning to his right, looked through the picture window. He could see Cooper backing away from the kitchen door, toward the dining room. He was in a crouch, holding the shotgun in front of him, ready—it seemed to Miller—to blow away anyone who came through the back door. He was framed in the doorway, silhouetted perfectly in the light from the backyard . . .

Miller fired once, and Cooper went down.

"I'm *hit*," he screamed.

Miller crashed through the front door, and approached cautiously. Cooper was on his back, groaning, but still holding the shotgun. "Don't shoot," he said. "I'm hit . . . I'm hit."

Miller took the shotgun from him and put it on the dining-room table. More officers came in, and they stood over him in a circle. Cooper stared up at them, not saying anything. There wasn't much blood. The bullet had entered his right side, severed his spinal cord, passed through his left lung and lodged in his arm.

They heard an ambulance. Monte Miller looked up and saw the ambulance driver coming through the door. When he looked back down, Cooper was dead.

Outside, Barbara was begging the police to allow her inside. She waited for what seemed an hour, then an officer came out and said, "Mrs. Cooper, your husband has expired."

Later, in the dark emptiness of the early morning, she wondered if she might have had a few more minutes with him. She hoped that he'd died instantly, but if he hadn't . . . at least, she could have been there to say goodbye. Later, she would be angry with the police—why hadn't they waited? why hadn't they used tear gas?—but in the first numb hours afterward, she just wanted to see him alive again, just for a moment.

Alone, no longer crying, she had an odd thought: At least he wouldn't have to stand on line anymore, waiting for job applications, waiting for the telephone to ring, waiting for his unemployment to run out, thinking about getting high again, always fighting that temptation, inevitably succumbing. Maybe—and she was horrified to realize that she was thinking this—maybe he was better off.

ENTER THE DRAGON

I mean I'd like to be able to think there's a way out of this thing. That you can just somehow or other fight your way out of it . . . It would be great if this thing . . . you know, the war, the state of things in the world—I wish it were one big dragon . . . If it were one big dragon I'd just do what I could do. You know, if it ate me up well okay . . . it's a simple solution . . . sort of a do or die thing. But it's never that way.

—A VIETNAM VETERAN, QUOTED BY
ROBERT JAY LIFTON IN *HOME FROM THE WAR*

1

Gary Cooper's death was news, but not big news. It was consigned to the inside pages of newspapers across the country—"Viet Vet Goes Berserk over Hostage Welcome"—a curious footnote to the larger story, a brief shadow flickering across the glow of the first truly national celebration of heroism since John Glenn's ticker-tape parade in 1962.

There were other such shadows. On the day Cooper died, a paraplegic Vietnam veteran named Ron Kovic—the author of a powerful postwar autobiography called *Born on the Fourth of July*—held a press conference in Los Angeles to complain about all the parades and hoopla of the past few weeks. The former hostages had been merely captives, he said, not heroes . . . unlike the 55,000 Americans who had died in Vietnam and their millions of comrades who had returned home to be reviled and ignored.

The next day, three hundred Vietnam veterans and their families staged a two-mile march in Indianapolis to protest the "Hostage

Welcome." Another group of veterans in Evansville, Indiana, held a press conference to deliver the same message.

There were other such protests and press conferences, followed by television programs and news stories airing the veterans' grievances. The return of the fifty-two American hostages from Teheran was proving a catalyst. There was a growing sense among the small group of people who had devoted their lives to the problems of Vietnam veterans that a corner was being turned: for the first time, significant numbers of veterans were speaking up, gathering together, expressing pride in their accomplishments and sacrifices, and anger over the treatment they'd received. There also was a sense that the country might—finally—be willing to examine the consequences of its first defeat in a foreign war, to acknowledge finally the special problems of those who had fought and lost, and welcome them back into the fold.

It had been a long haul. As early as 1969, Senator Alan Cranston of California had held congressional hearings on the readjustment problems of returning veterans; after days of emotional testimony, Cranston proposed that the government sponsor a network of storefront counseling centers specifically for Vietnam veterans. There wasn't much interest in the program. The military insisted the rate of battle-related mental disorders was much lower in Vietnam than in previous wars, the result of more sophisticated psychiatric treatment. The established veterans groups—the American Legion, the Veterans of Foreign Wars—were decidedly cool as well. The Vietnam Veterans Against the War (VVAW) lobbied for the program, but was dismissed as a radical splinter group; most Vietnam veterans seemed determined to fade back into society and forget about the whole business. Cranston's proposal languished.

In 1970, VVAW began holding "rap groups" in New York for returning veterans, supervised by therapists. "In the group raps," one of the therapists, Professor Chaim Shatan, wrote in 1971, "certain commonly shared concerns have emerged. Since they do not fit any standard diagnostic label, we refer to them loosely as the post-Vietnam syndrome."

Another VVAW group leader, Dr. Robert Jay Lifton, described the rap sessions in depth in *Home from the War*, published in 1973.

The psychiatric establishment scorned the idea that there might be such a thing as the post-Vietnam syndrome. Lifton and Shatan were seen as antiwar radicals, troublemakers. Their diagnosis—the amorphous commingling of anxiety, alienation, depression, rage and blunted emotions—wasn't very precise. If such a thing existed, why hadn't it shown up in other wars? Why hadn't it been spotted before?

The answer was: it had been. In a paper published late in 1973, Drs. Timothy Van Putten and Warden H. Emory speculated that the post-Vietnam syndrome was another version of the "traumatic neuroses" diagnosed in World War I soldiers, concentration camp victims and survivors of natural disasters. In fact, in 1952 the first edition of the American Psychiatric Association's *Diagnostic and Statistical Manual* (DSM-I) had acknowledged the existence of traumatic neuroses as a distinct affliction. The diagnosis was dropped from the revised *Diagnostic and Statistical Manual* (DSM-II) in 1968. "It would appear," Drs. Van Putten and Emory concluded, "that much that has been learned about traumatic neurosis in World Wars I and II has been forgotten and needs to be relearned."

But the psychiatric establishment—like most other Americans in the mid-1970s, including the veterans themselves—seemed more intent on forgetting than relearning. The Veterans Administration continued to attribute the complaints of Vietnam veterans to "long-standing characterological difficulties and to unresolved family and marital problems," instead of a delayed reaction to the stress of combat.*

---

* The VA's unwillingness to acknowledge post-Vietnam syndrome led some of the psychologists working with Vietnam veterans to overreact in the opposite direction; that is, to deny that "long-standing characterological difficulties" had anything at all to do with the depressed, hostile behavior of many veterans.

In 1975, several mental health professionals organized the Vietnam Veterans Working Group. Their purpose was to convince the American Psychiatric Association to restore traumatic neurosis to the next edition of its diagnostic manual. They began to collect case histories of post-Vietnam syndrome from around the country.

Such histories were not hard to find. A young professor at Cleveland State University named John P. Wilson conducted interviews with sixty returned veterans on campus and found a persistent pattern of the same sorts of problems encountered earlier by Shatan, Lifton and the others. "I had been a conscientious objector during the war," Wilson said, "and I began to notice that friends of mine who had gone to Vietnam were coming back . . . *different.* There was something so compelling and sad about the men I interviewed; I just became obsessed by it. I'd go to parties and start talking about Vietnam and wouldn't be able to stop. But people didn't want to hear about it. They wanted to forget about the war. I tried to get funding for a larger study. I wrote proposals, and every one was turned down. I approached the veterans organizations; they weren't interested either. Finally, the Disabled American Veterans gave me $45,000 to begin what became the Forgotten Warrior Project."

Wilson's study was published in 1978, and the Disabled American Veterans responded by opening "Outreach Centers" for Vietnam veterans in several cities (one of them opened in Erie, Pennsylvania, and was staffed by Dale Szuminski's old Marine buddy Don Rogers). Also in 1978, the Vietnam Veterans Working Group finally convinced the American Psychiatric Association to include post-Vietnam syndrome—it was now called *post-traumatic stress disorder*—in its revised diagnostic manual (DSM-III), to be published in 1980.

There were changes, too, at the Veterans Administration, where Max Cleland—a Vietnam veteran who was a triple amputee—had taken charge. Cleland had testified at Alan Cranston's first hearings on post-Vietnam syndrome in 1969, and now he began to lobby for passage of Cranston's Vet Center bill . . . which had been introduced and approved in the Senate four times in the past decade, only to be ignored by the House of Representatives. "It wasn't that there was opposition in the House," said Bill Brew of Cranston's staff. "If you're looking for a villain, you won't find one . . . but you won't find any heroes either. The bill needed an advocate, and no one in the House was willing to play that role. The sad truth is, for most of the 1970s, Vietnam veterans weren't sufficiently organized to convince anyone the role needed playing."

In March 1979, Jimmy Carter held a conference on Vietnam veterans at the White House and announced his support for the Vet Center program. Cranston's bill finally was passed by the House two months later. By early 1980, government-sponsored storefront Vet Centers were opening in cities across the country. At about the same time, the Veterans Administration announced that it now accepted post-traumatic stress disorder as a service-related ailment.

The government had acted, but the vast majority of Vietnam veterans remained in hibernation. In a way, the Vet Centers only served to reinforce the public image: service in Vietnam had come to be regarded as an affliction, certainly nothing to be proud of. The media concentrated on the horror stories. Vietnam veterans went berserk with abysmal regularity on prime-time television. It seemed the country was not yet willing to acknowledge that it was possible to have served honorably in a lost cause.

It remained for the veterans themselves to change that. Bobby Muller, a paraplegic former Marine lieutenant, had been trying since 1978—without much success—to build an organization like the American Legion for Vietnam veterans. "But everything changed for our group—Vietnam Veterans of America—when the hostages came home," Muller would recall. "That's what broke us loose as an organization. I remember sitting in our office the day of the ticker-tape parade in New York for the hostages . . . and suddenly the phone started ringing off the hook. People wanted to join up, help out, give money. Guys started coming out of the woodwork. Part of it was that the public had been given the *emotional opportunity* to deal with Vietnam for the first time: they were waving flags, singing 'God Bless America.' It was okay to be patriotic again. But it was also that the guys—the veterans—finally woke up and began to demand the respect and attention they'd been denied."

There was a surge of interest in the Vet Centers, where, according to *Time* magazine, "business . . . dramatically increased" after the hostages came home. "The vets' anger," *Time* reported, "has a new force. It contains a certain aggressive pride, almost for the first time."

It was during this time of reawakened pride and anger that I first called Bill Taylor, John Steiner, Dale Szuminski, John Wakefield and the others.

2

In the beginning, I labored under the standard journalistic delusion that I might insinuate myself into the lives of Cooper's buddies without changing them. I would visit their homes, they would tell me their stories and life would go on as before. The author would remain unseen, an objective observer.

That conceit was shattered when I visited John and Elizabeth Wakefield on Sunday evening, September 13, 1981.

I had called a week earlier. Unlike the other members of the 2nd Platoon, who had been excited, curious, eager to tell stories and ask questions, Wakefield was subdued, distant, tentative.

"How'd you get my number?" he asked.

"John Steiner remembered you. He said he was in your squad, and that you were one of the guys who really knew how to handle themselves out there. Do you remember him?"

"Uh . . . yup."

"Do you remember Operation Cochise?"

"Uh-huh."

"Well, listen, I'm planning to visit Bill Taylor in Chicago next week and Indianapolis is along the way," I said. "Would you mind if I stopped by? Would that be okay?"

"I guess so."

The Wakefields lived in a small white frame house on a cul-de-sac near the Indianapolis Speedway, indistinguishable from the others in the neighborhood except for a sign, hand-written in Magic Marker on a shingle, warning salesmen and peddlers to keep away.

John answered the door. He looked a mess, unshaven, wearing an old undershirt; his eyes were bleary and distant behind a new pair of trifocals. He offered me a Pepsi, then led me into the chaotic clutter of the new room, where Elizabeth was sitting in the Barcalounger, crocheting and trying to ignore the football game on television. She looked up at me, said a cool hello and then asked, "Why are you doing this?"

As I began to explain, John sat down and lit a cigarette. His hands were shaking.

"I'll be honest with you," he said quietly. "I'm leery about going back and reliving this thing. I think the thing that scares me most is that I've never dealt with it yet. I've never forced myself to deal with it. Maybe that's right, maybe it's wrong."

"I *knew* there was something he was holding back," Elizabeth said, her skepticism dissolving—it seemed to me—with surprising speed. "I could kick myself for not figuring out it was Vietnam. My feeling is, he should talk about it. That's the only way you ever get over these things."

"I'm scared of it," Wakefield said. "Hell, I'm not scared—I'm terrified. I haven't slept very good since you called. I've been withdrawn, which is just totally opposite from me."

"I'm sorry," I said. "I feel rotten about this."

"Don't," he said. "You're not the only cause of it. Something strange happened at work a few weeks ago. We build the engines for helicopters. I do quality control. And a few weeks ago, they brought in this guy—a North Vietnamese helicopter pilot who defected— and it was all I could do just to be around the guy. I mean, he was the right age. He might have been trying to kill me . . . so I was upset about that too. Then you called. I asked my neighbor what to do and he said the same thing I was thinking: that it's probably a story that needs to be told. Anyway, I think I want to talk about it—but I want to do it with someone who was there. So I was thinking, would it be all right if I go to Chicago with you and see Taylor?"

"We can do it any way you feel most comfortable," I said. "If you don't want to do it at all, that's fine too."

While Wakefield packed a bag, I called Taylor—whom I'd visited once before—and told him we were coming. "Wakefield's coming too?" he asked, ebullient as ever. "*Fan*-tastic! I'll wait up for you."

As we were leaving, Elizabeth kissed me on the cheek and said, "Take care of him."

Take *care* of him? Well, yes; she had a point. Having barged into his life and opened this can of worms, there was no way I could continue to pretend that I was merely an objective observer. There was no way of knowing what might happen when he started reliving Vietnam (visions of Cooper-like headlines came to mind). I was frightened by the responsibility, and resolved to nudge him in the direction of his local Vet Center. But there was another feeling as well. As we headed out on the highway north, there was also the excitement—we both felt it—that comes with any adventure into unknown, perhaps dangerous, territory.

We arrived in Chicago after midnight. Taylor was waiting at the door. He and Wakefield stopped, stared—it was obvious, in that first split second, that they didn't recognize each other—and then they hugged. "Hey, brother," Wakefield said.

Taylor had tears in his eyes. "God!" he said. "You look completely different! You put on weight."

"You did too," Wakefield said. "But I'd know you anywhere. You've still got that same loud voice."

"You had a moustache, didn't you?" Taylor asked. "A big handlebar job?"

"Shaved it off," Wakefield said.

We went down to Taylor's basement den and spent the next four hours talking, mostly about Operation Cochise. They drew maps of the battlefield. Taylor brought out old snapshots of the platoon. Wakefield was restrained throughout, very factual, unemotional . . . except for a brief moment when, after several hours, Taylor asked, "Hey, Wake, did you go down with us that night to get the bodies?"

"You went back to get the bodies?" Wakefield said, startled. His hands were shaking again.

"We didn't want to go out," Taylor said. "We were all upset."

"I can't imagine where I was," Wakefield said. "I can't place myself that night. The last thing I remember was in the afternoon. Lieutenant Francis told me Whitey was hit, and I was supposed to take over the squad. Whitey and I were pretty tight . . . and so I'm *sure* I would've gone out there that night to get him."

"It was really dark out there," Taylor said, talking past Wakefield, deep in his own memories. "I figured the gooks had booby-trapped the bodies. They could've killed us . . . but they'd pulled out. I brought Harvey in."

"I pulled foxhole duty with Harve all the time. God, I remember him running across that damn paddy," Wakefield said. "The only thing I can figure . . . well, I've blocked it. I can't remember a thing after Francis said Whitey was hit . . . see, this is the first time I've ever talked about this stuff, or even *thought* about it. I went through a bad time after I came home. Booze and drugs. I went through the Synanon program, you ever hear of it? I was pretty well spaced . . . but this is *strange*, not being able to remember."

Taylor went up to bed at about five o'clock. Wakefield and I stretched out in sleeping bags on the basement couches. I asked him how he was doing.

"Pretty good, still a little nervous," he said. "I'm detaching myself. It's as if I was up here, looking down at my body, which is doing the talking. I'm making it talk, but I'm distanced from it."

I was up with a start—a nightmare, about Operation Cochise—three hours later. Wakefield was smoking a cigarette, staring at the ceiling.

"How'd you sleep?" I asked.

"I didn't," he said. "I went into combat repose—it's a trick they taught us in recon school. It's a way to relax totally by controlling your breathing, but still be aware of everything around you. You can even hear a snake crawl."

"No kidding."

"A snake," he said, "can be tremendously loud."

Taylor had an early appointment; Wakefield and I went out for breakfast and he continued to talk about Vietnam, especially the time he spent in Force Reconnaissance. He spoke softly, matter-of-factly, about weapons and tactics and operations. At one point, he mentioned that his closest friend in Force Recon—Robert McIntyre—had been killed.

"What happened?" I asked.

"There are some things I can't talk about yet," he said. "There are some other things I'll *never* talk about."

When Taylor arrived home that afternoon, we resumed the conversation around the kitchen table, drinking coffee. As we talked, it became clear that although Bill Taylor had been more successful by most traditional measures since the war, he deferred to Wakefield when it came to Vietnam. Their old battlefield relationship slowly re-established itself. Wakefield was the old salt—he seemed quite confident now, even arrogant at times; and Taylor, the green new guy. "Truthfully, Wake," Bill finally asked, "what kind of Marine was I?"

"You were pretty good out in the field," Wakefield allowed. "It wouldn't have bothered me to stand a hole watch with you . . . but you were also pretty noisy. The thing I remember best is that when we were in a defensive position, dug in or something, I could always hear you. No matter where you were on the platoon line, I could hear you."

"I was under the impression," Taylor said, "that I was a tremendous soldier."

"Well, you were good," Wakefield said. "You weren't bad."

"You know, there's something about that old squad—now that we're bringing this out in the open—but I never got acknowledgment until after Cochise," Taylor said. "On Okinawa, I felt . . ."

"You were a tag-along," Wakefield said. "Everybody would be going out on the town and someone would say, 'Okay, Taylor, you can come too.' If I remember, you were tight with . . ."

"*Nobody!*" Taylor exploded. "I had this feeling of inferiority. Nobody ever looked up to me. No one noticed. No acknowledgment. That's what I got from my mother and father too. That's why I *joined* the service. On Okinawa, the old guys were really clannish. They looked down on me. I was just an eighteen-year-old punk."

"You were full of piss and vinegar," Wakefield said, "and I'm not so sure about the vinegar."

"What sort of Marine was Cooper?" I asked.

"Everyone thought he had a pretty good head on his shoulders," Wakefield said. "A lot of the younger guys looked up to him."

"Do you remember when he offered the fruitcake to that mama-san?" Taylor asked. "Was he kidding or did he really want to screw her?"

"He was dead serious," Wakefield said. "She had black betel-nut teeth. She looked like she was sixty, but she was probably more like forty-five . . . but that was Cooper."

They continued on, going through the roster of old friends—Steiner, Szuminski, Wayne Pilgreen, Dave Muller, Sergeant Jones, Sergeant Malloy. Barbara Taylor stood off to the side for a while, listening; Bill's children bounced in and out. They talked on through dinner, and into the evening. Wakefield had been talking nonstop for nearly a day now, except for three hours of combat repose and an hour's break that morning. He was planning to take a late-night bus back to Indianapolis.

"Bill, while we were in Nam," he asked, toward the end, "did you ever realize that what we were doing had absolutely no use?"

"I realized at some point that there was no way we could win that war. We didn't know who the hell we were fighting, and I had no idea why we were fighting."

"You know what?" Wakefield said. "I don't even care why we were over there. It was a job. We were told to do it and we went out there and tried."

"I'm glad I *didn't* know," Taylor said. "When I finally learned the history—about the French and Dien Bien Phu—I was pissed. I don't know if I could have survived over there if I'd known all that."

I drove Wakefield to a bus station in downtown Chicago about an hour later. "How're you doing?" I asked.

"Okay. Not bad . . . in fact, I'm feeling pretty good."

"You know," I said, "now that you've started talking and thinking about it again, you might not be able to just go home and turn it off."

"I know," he said.

"If you want to keep talking about it with guys who were there, you might consider going to a Vet Center," I said, still uneasy playing social worker. "I'm sure they have one in Indianapolis."

"I'll think it over," he said.

When I stopped in Indianapolis on my way home from Chicago a week later, the Wakefields seemed very happy, relieved and unduly grateful.

"You saved our marriage," Elizabeth said. "John had been plastered to that darn couch for so long, watching television, I didn't think he'd ever get off it. But he's been so different since he got home from Chicago—much more open. I feel like we've been *talking* for the first time in years."

"You know," John said, "when I got off that bus from Chicago, I took a taxi home . . . and it was almost like coming home from the war for the first time. After all the talking we did in Chicago, I almost feel like you were over there with us."

This was all very flattering, of course, but not entirely convincing. Elizabeth's relief was understandable; but John seemed to be acting out a role he had seen on television. He said he realized his struggle was only beginning, that he had just scratched the surface when it came to understanding what the war had done to him, that he probably would go to the Vet Center and try to find out more. He said all the right things. But he said them dispassionately, analytically, as if he were talking about someone else.

Wakefield visited the Indianapolis Vet Center the following week, and soon became a regular there. Within a month, he joined a closed rap group that met each Thursday night. All of the others in the group had seen heavy action in Vietnam—two had lost legs, a third had been severely injured—but John quickly established himself as the old salt, the unofficial group leader. Dan Lonnquist, the Vet Center's director, was very happy to have him there. Lonnquist also had served in the Marines, but hadn't seen much action. "My approach to a group," Lonnquist said, "is the less involved in it I am, the better. With someone like John there, that isn't hard. He has a lot of insight. He's really sensitive to what's going on inside himself and the other people." Still, Lonnquist had to admit that for all his sensitivity and insight, John had managed to do a lot of talking without revealing very much of himself.

He did this rather cleverly, embracing the notion of post-traumatic stress disorder. He assumed that it was the source of all his problems since the war. Having neatly packaged his troubles into a syndrome, he could hold it at arm's length, examine it, make pronouncements upon it. It became a convenience, the psychological equivalent of fast food. His ailment had a name. He was, as he had suspected all along, a victim. Thus reassured, he could offer elaborate, official rationales for his behavior.

He said he'd been subconsciously reliving Vietnam at work. "My job at Allison's—quality control—is like being on patrol. I'm looking for flaws, just as I used to look for flaws in the jungle when I walked point."

He said the same was true of his years as a coach in Little League. "I'd be back in Vietnam. Wrong was dead. Losing was dead . . . and I didn't want to die. My anger became uncontrollable. I was angry at the upper echelons, the people who ran the league—they were like the military brass. When I argued with them, it was like a contact skirmish. When I'd go to watch the other teams play, that was like a recon patrol—you'd look for weaknesses, flaws, ways to beat them."

He said, "I battered my wife emotionally. And she is the external control of my internal rage. In a battering situation—this is purely clinical now—where he is battering and she is being battered, he does it because he doesn't want to look inside himself to see what the mess is. Therefore he uses his external control to express anger and rage. Without this external control, it can turn into a very dangerous, very violent situation. I'm not doing that anymore. My external control has changed. I'm venting my anger in group, at the Vet Center."

Although Wakefield could sound very convincing—or, perhaps, convinced—during these recitations, there were occasional hints that he wasn't buying his own line. Once, late at night, he admitted: "A lot of times, I'm manufacturing feelings. Fear, anxiety—what I *should* be feeling. The truth is, I don't feel much of anything. I don't feel any remorse about the things that happened in Vietnam."

John's sudden transformation was greeted with a certain amount of skepticism by his family—this Vet Center business, his parents believed, was just another case of Johnny being Johnny, another extravagant emotional reaction. He had spent his life latching on to things, becoming totally involved and then dropping them: the Catholic Youth Organization, the Marines, Synanon, Little League and now the Vet Center. They'd never forgotten what the man at Synanon had said: Johnny was a compulsive liar. He'd never complained about Vietnam before, but now, suddenly, fifteen years later, he was blaming the war for all his problems. He pressured them to visit the Vet Center, and they did—three times. Once John and Elizabeth were there too, and the discussion centered on all the things the Wakefields had done wrong when Johnny was a boy; Vietnam was hardly mentioned. Johnny even brought up the old football incident from junior high school, when they'd allowed Steve to go out for football a year earlier than John had been. What did that have to do with Vietnam?

"These are repressed feelings," they were told, "and it's important for John to bring them out."

Repressed feelings! John had been complaining about that business with Steve ever since it happened. "My feeling is," Dorothy Wakefield said, "that the best thing is to bury the past and get on with your life."

Wakefield was frustrated by his parents' inability to understand; in fact, he seemed far more troubled by his grievances against them than by the business supposedly at hand—his experiences in Vietnam and his life since. As his parents predicted, he was beginning to repeat the pattern he'd established in Little League and elsewhere; he was becoming something of a busybody at the Vet Center, offering gratuitous advice on the structure, duration and frequency of group meetings . . . and this officiousness soon led to trouble.

It began when some of the veterans' wives formed a group of their own that also met on Thursday nights at the Vet Center. As the weeks passed and the women became more willing to air their grievances, there were domestic troubles in several households. The men were furious; they were convinced the women's group was ganging up on them. Wakefield was a leader of the insurgents, demanding a combined meeting of the two groups even though Elizabeth—who preferred her therapy private—wasn't one of the wives involved. The meeting was a success (with Wakefield apparently playing a very active role in smoothing out the differences), and it was decided that the groups would meet together every three weeks thereafter. At the next combined meeting, though, several people proposed that only couples be allowed to attend. Wakefield believed this was subtly directed at him; they were trying to kick him out. He argued for an hour, then walked out of the meeting. He was so upset, he would later tell Lonnquist, that he drove to a friend's house and retrieved a small-caliber revolver he'd left there years earlier for safekeeping. He felt threatened, he said; he wanted protection. He carried the gun in the glove compartment of his car for a week, but returned it when he learned that Lonnquist and his new group leader—Ken Martin— had taken his side in the dispute.

Vindication bolstered Wakefield; his attachment to the Vet Center deepened. He was beginning to see himself as a paraprofessional, an expert on the problems of Vietnam veterans. His demeanor in group was regal, almost condescending. He always sat in a corner facing the door, more erect in his chair than the rest, above them. And if the group chose not to take advantage of his expertise, there were others out there who would, no doubt, be more receptive to his ministrations . . . his old platoon, for example.

Bill Taylor and John Steiner were organizing a reunion to be held at Taylor's house on the weekend of January 15–17, 1982. Wakefield was intent on using the occasion to proselytize the others; he planned to distribute literature and invite a speaker from a

Chicago-area Vet Center. He seemed to see the reunion as a marathon group therapy session rather than a celebration.

At about this time, Wakefield had a dream. It was the first dream that he could recall since returning from the war: He was addressing a joint session of the Indiana legislature on the problems of Vietnam veterans.

3

When Wakefield arrived at the reunion, he walked down the stairs to Taylor's basement, trailed by Elizabeth, into a thick cloud of marijuana smoke. All conversation stopped. He stood at the base of the stairs for a moment, smiling nervously. No one recognized him.

"Who are you?" asked Mel Sands, who hadn't been recognized either when he first walked in.

"Who are *you*?" Wakefield responded.

There was an awkward silence. Neither seemed willing to make the next move.

"Do you want to know who you are?" I asked, reaching for John Steiner's photo album and flipping to a picture of the two of them chatting together in Vietnam. I showed them the photo. "That's who you are."

"Noooo," Sands said, looking at the picture. "You're not him."

"Yes, I am," Wakefield said.

"Wakefield?" John Steiner said. "It's got to be Wakefield."

"Jesus Christ, Wakefield, what *happened* to you?" asked Robert Smith. "You seem so . . . *old.*"

"Well, we're all getting on," Wakefield said, and then introduced Elizabeth, who felt decidedly out of place. John hadn't wanted her to come, but she'd insisted . . . and now she sensed what they were all thinking: What was Wakefield doing married to this *grandmother*?

Smith couldn't stop laughing. He sat down on a couch holding his stomach, tears rolling. "I don't know who any of these people *are*," he said. "I know who they *were*, but they're someone different now."

According to the newspapers, it was the coldest weekend of the century in Chicago. The temperature held below zero throughout; the wind-chill factor hovered at about fifty below. It snowed and snowed.

"Whose idea was this anyway?" Dale Szuminski asked. "Why couldn't we have had it in Florida?"

Szuminski was disappointed that Wayne Pilgreen hadn't been able to come. Pilgreen worked for the utility company in Alabama, and an ice storm had knocked out electric service across the state; he was working double shifts. Szuminski hadn't seen or spoken with Pilgreen since Operation Cochise, when Wayne had saved his life by guiding him out of the paddy. "He was the guy I really wanted to see," Szuminski said. "But what the hell, it's a party."

And so it was, much to Wakefield's dismay. No one seemed interested in a serious discussion of post-traumatic stress disorder, try as he might to get one started. He began almost immediately, as soon as the shock and embarrassment of his arrival died down. Steiner approached, shook his hand and asked, "So, Wakefield, how're you doing?"

"A lot better," he said solemnly, "since I got some help."

"Oh," Steiner said, not knowing where to take it from there. He was beginning to wonder why he'd been so anxious to have this reunion. He and Taylor had done most of the work, calling the others, making preparations. The response to their phone calls had not been overwhelming. Dave Muller was the only one who actually said no—he wanted no part of a reunion—but many of the others had sounded tentative; as the weekend approached, only seven were definitely coming. It hardly mattered, though. Both Taylor and Steiner were so excited by the *idea* of a reunion that neither had given much thought to the event itself. Taylor's house had been chosen for its central location; Steiner had set the unlikely date (it coincided with an unpaid two-week furlough that Fish and Wildlife Service budget cuts had imposed on the refuge staff).

Steiner hadn't considered what might actually *happen* when they were all together again until that morning, on the plane from San Francisco—and then he realized that he was worried. What would they think of him now? What if they turned out to be a bunch of jerks? He sensed that he was placing in jeopardy the only good memories he had of Vietnam; he wasn't so sure anymore that he wanted the pristine myth of their camaraderie muddied by reality.

He'd been looking forward to seeing Smith, one of his closest friends. He remembered an innocent farm boy from upstate New York, small, quiet, sensitive, obviously frightened but never cowardly in the field—they'd had a lot in common. The Robert Smith who'd arrived from Houston that afternoon was a stranger, though. After the war, he'd left the family farm to become an underwater welder on offshore oil rigs. It was dangerous work, and it had hardened him—more than the war had, it seemed. He was colder, louder, more aggressive now; he and Szuminski—whom Steiner hadn't known very well—were the most fervent partyers.

Steiner looked around the room, hoping to make contact with something other than feigned joviality. He recognized the pose. It was the way they used to come back from R & R, before reality set in.

He remembered not having much to talk about with Mel Sands when they'd bumped into each other at Camp Pendleton in 1968, and so he wasn't expecting much now—but it was sad, nonetheless, to see Mel (whom he'd admired so much over there) in his current state: unemployed, separated from his wife, adrift and alone. Smith had been recognizable, but Sands even *looked* completely different. His hair, which had been straight and blond in Vietnam, was now brown and curly; he had a thick, bushy beard and wore eyeglasses. Sands had come from northern Michigan, lured by the prospect of seeing his closest buddy in Vietnam, Burt Wilson, for the first time since the war; Wilson would be flying in from North Carolina the next day with his wife, Cathy.

Taylor, Steiner thought, was still Taylor, still trying too hard to be one of the guys. Bill hadn't been around much that day. He'd been off selling insurance, calling the local media to tell them about the reunion, making last-minute arrangements for a banquet the following night, securing a videotape camera from a friend to record the festivities. Steiner sensed an edge of desperation in all this. He sensed, too, that there were problems between Taylor and his wife; if Bill was still trying too hard to be one of the guys, it was nothing compared to the effort he was making to impress Barbara, who seemed entirely immune to it.

And Wakefield. Steiner liked Wakefield, but after all the months of couples counseling and group therapy, the last thing he wanted was to discuss more group therapy with Wakefield.

Smith was right. They'd been intimate once, but they were strangers now . . . and their former intimacy made the estrangement all the more awkward. The others might pretend that time and distance didn't matter, that the foxhole bond still prevailed, but Steiner felt trapped in the defensive perimeter that had been re-created in Taylor's basement; the blizzard outside seemed as vast and claustrophobic as the jungle. He kept to the edge of the party, looking for a safe place . . . and then Sands, of all people, pulled him right into the middle of it.

"Hey, Steiner," he said, "you can tell us the truth now. Did you really shoot Hollins in the leg?"

Everyone laughed. Steiner froze. "It was an accidental discharge," he said. "The medic agreed."

"Aww c'mon, Steiner," Smith jumped in, "everyone *knew* you did it."

"That Hollins certainly was one crazy son of a bitch," Sands said.

"He wasn't crazy," Steiner said. "He did what he did for a reason. He wanted to go home. Remember how we used to douse ourselves with bug juice and roll down our sleeves at night so the mosquitoes wouldn't get at us?"

"It didn't help much," Taylor said.

"Yeah, well, Hollins would roll up his sleeves at night and just sit there as the mosquitoes feasted on him. I couldn't believe it. He'd be sitting there watching this tribe of mosquitoes feasting on his arm. He wanted to get malaria. There were times in fire fights he would wave his hand in the air, trying to get shot."

"So, Steiner," Smith pressed, "you did it for him?"

"You guys . . ."

"C'mon, Steiner."

"Okay, okay."

The others laughed and cheered. Steiner's admission seemed to break the ice, and then Szuminski had one of his own: "How many people in this room," he asked, "never fell asleep on watch?"

"I did," Taylor said.

So had everyone else, except Wakefield.

"I remember the lieutenant would come around and say, 'Szuminski!' and I'd say, 'Yessir, right here! I'm up!' The son of a bitch always seemed to catch me just as I was dozing off. But, man, you just couldn't help it. I was *tired* . . . humping that damn radio through the boonies all day, and then they expect you to stay up half the night."

For a moment, the party coalesced around the quietly startling realization that the war was *over*: these things were safe to talk about now. Steiner no longer could be court-martialed for shooting Hollins; falling asleep on watch was no longer a matter of life and death. The sense of relief was palpable, as if everyone had exhaled in unison. Gradually, the conversation fragmented; smaller groups formed, more intimate misdemeanors, and some felonies, were divulged. In a corner, Mel Sands told Steiner and me about the time he and Gary Cooper had kicked the Vietnamese prisoners out of the medevac helicopter after Operation Cochise. "I looked at Coop, and it was clear that he and I were thinking the same thing," Sands said, teeth clenched, trembling with rage . . . or perhaps excitement. "Coop just picked up his big boot and went *wham*, and sent that little sucker flying."

"You actually did that?" Steiner asked.

"Yup."

Steiner, appalled, said nothing.

Wakefield understood what was happening in the room, but was unimpressed. The truths being told were distant and safe (he was, in fact, disgusted by the admissions of amateurism). Nobody wanted to talk about the things that really mattered; nobody wanted to talk about the curse they'd all been under since they'd come home. Elizabeth was exhausted from the long day, and disappointed too that serious conversation seemed an unlikely prospect. He decided to take her back to the motel.

The party continued most of the night. Taylor ordered pizza, which—to everyone's amazement—was delivered after midnight, in the midst of the blizzard. Taylor's den was warm and cozy, and softly lit. There was music, an oldies station playing songs from the 1960s. Joints and scrapbooks were passed from one to the next. Motel rooms had been reserved, but there was little interest in braving the cold. At some point, it was decided to call Wayne Pilgreen in Alabama. Szuminski was the first to get on the line; I listened in on the upstairs extension.

"Hey, man," Szuminski said, "why ain't you here?"

"It's crazy down here, Ski. The whole state's a sheet of ice. I'll make the next one, though," Pilgreen said. "Y'know, I tried to call you a few months back. Klein gave me your number, but your wife answered and said you were asleep."

"That was Sandy," Szuminski said. "She was blocking all my calls. Didn't want me stepping out."

"So," Pilgreen said, "how come you never sent me that vodka screwdriver mix you promised?"

"When did I promise that?"

"When we pulled you out of that paddy."

"Yeah, well, I really had my wits about me at that point."

"You sure took your sweet time getting out."

"I took the scenic route," Szuminski said. "Hey, Pilgreen . . ."

"Yeah?"

"About that day . . ."

"No sweat, Ski."

Robert Smith was the only one of those present who hadn't been in the field for Operation Cochise; a severe skin rash had confined him to sick bay on the USS *Okinawa*. He took pictures of the others being loaded onto landing boats, going off to battle; when they returned two weeks later, he was stunned by the carnage and wrote a long letter to his parents describing what his surviving buddies had told him about it. More than any of the others, Smith had been determined to record his thirteen months in Vietnam as precisely as possible. He took hundreds of photographs, including the picture of Sergeant Malloy that was prominently displayed in each of the scrapbooks piled upon Bill Taylor's coffee table. When he wrote home, he would include detailed—and honest—descriptions of battles (most of the others kept their letters upbeat and innocuous). After the war, he carefully sorted the letters by month, and kept them in neat packets secured by rubber bands.

And now, Smith resumed his role as unofficial platoon historian, a position of no small authority under the circumstances. He was the guardian of the past; as the scrapbooks circulated, he was the final arbiter of disagreements that arose—whether a certain photograph had been taken at Danang or Phu Bai, whether the guy weighted down by bandoliers was Gilbert or Green. When the videotape equipment arrived on Saturday afternoon, Smith took charge of it, orchestrating the action, arranging the room so that everyone would be on camera when Burt Wilson and his wife finally arrived toward evening.

Wilson had been universally respected in Vietnam, and it wasn't hard to see why. He moved and spoke with a quiet, self-assured grace; he never seemed to take a false step. Like Sands, he was a construction worker—but work was much easier to find in North Carolina than in Michigan. He appeared serenely prosperous, dressed in brightly colored sports clothes, as if he'd just stopped in from a round of golf. His wife, Cathy, also was attractive and graceful, but still jittery after an icy flight from Greensboro and already dreading the trip home.

Though he was the last to arrive, Wilson moved effortlessly into the flow of the party. Smith had been teasing Mel Sands throughout, and now Wilson subtly readjusted the pecking order, putting Smith—who'd had less seniority in Vietnam—in his place, kidding him about the weight he'd put on. Sands joined in, gaining a measure of revenge. He pinched Smith's cheek and said, "Hey, Bob, you're growing tits!"

Smith did not yield his position easily, though. At the banquet that evening, he was the first to rise and propose a toast. "To all the guys who can't be with us tonight," he said, "the ones who are alive, and those who are gone from us . . ."

"They'll always be alive in our memories," Taylor added.

"Amen," said Sands. "Bottoms up."

The dinner was held in the back room of a coffee shop owned by one of Taylor's clients. There was a banner on the wall: "Welcome Vietnam Veterans." A reporter and photographer from the local Chicago Heights newspaper added to the relative formality of the occasion, as did the presence of Barbara Cooper.

The men introduced themselves to Barbara, then kept their distance. The reporter asked her some questions about Gary, dead now for almost a year, and then went off to interview the others. She sat alone at the head of the table, watching them all, thinking about how much Gary would have enjoyed himself here. She could imagine him, beer in hand, over in the corner with Sands and Wilson; she could just about *see* him there, engrossed, drawling away about gooks and ambushes. For a moment, she felt as if she had him back; there was the odd sense that these guys were *family*.

"You know, you and I have something in common," Elizabeth Wakefield ventured, interrupting her reverie.

"What?"

"We both married one of *them*."

"Yeah." Barbara laughed. "Never again!"

At the other end of the table, Wakefield was talking to Szuminski about Operation Cochise. "I never made it up to the front paddy," he said. "We were back in that gully, giving cover fire. I was there with Whitey, but then Whitey went up front with Lieutenant Francis to help get you guys out."

Szuminski said he'd seen White get killed. "He was coming out to get me. He flipped over the back wall and bought it right there. That was the end, I thought. When White got wasted, I figured there was no way I was going to get out of there alive."

"Whitey and I were pretty tight," Wakefield said softly.

"I guess," Szuminski said, "that was the most important day of my life."

"Not for me," Wakefield said.

"What was yours?"

"It was the day I stopped running, and decided to get some help."

"Hey, Smith," Szuminski said. "I think we should start drinking earlier tomorrow. I can't seem to get a buzz on."

Several of the veterans had mentioned Operation Cochise to the reporter from the Chicago Heights newspaper. He asked Steiner about it. "I don't like talking about it," Steiner said. "I change the subject if I get the chance."

"Hey, Steiner," Smith said, "why don't you tell the reporter about the time you shot Hollins in the leg?"

Smith, somewhat at a loss when the reporter asked *him* about Operation Cochise, decided to substitute an appropriate bit of melodrama from another battle: "One guy was wounded real bad. I carried him as far back as I could. It was hot, real hot . . ."

Wakefield told the reporter that his life had been saved by going to the Vet Center.

Taylor told the reporter his life had been saved by est. He recommended it for any veteran suffering from post-traumatic stress disorder.

Barbara Cooper said, "I look at all these guys and I think about what a great time Gary would be having here with them . . . But then, if Gary hadn't died, this wouldn't be happening. I'm glad *something* good came out of all that pain."

Mel Sands stayed close to Burt Wilson. "You got work down there in Carolina?" Sands asked. "There ain't much up my way."

"We do okay," Wilson said. "You ought to come down and check it out."

"I just may do that."

"This is slowing down," Szuminski observed when the meal—soup, salad, thick slabs of roast beef, baked potatoes and ice cream—was done. "I'm still stone sober. If something doesn't happen soon, I'm gonna fall asleep."

Smith stood and proposed his toast.

Taylor was next: "I'd like to propose a toast to Gus, who gave us the back room."

"I'd like to propose a toast," said Mel Sands, "to everyone having a happy life."

Later that night, the party resumed in Taylor's basement. Smith produced several trays of slides, as did Taylor and Steiner. Taylor set up a screen; again, Smith presided, proud of his slides, which were excellent.

"There's Wilson, asleep."

"He must have been on watch," Szuminski said.

"Who's that?"

"It's Walsted . . . I can tell by the way he wore his helmet."

"Hey, remember the way Sheoships always kept his chin strap buckled? That was weird."

"Isn't that a pretty picture? Just an old gook standing on a hill with the sun going down."

"Who's the guy squatting in the front there?"

"Is that Gilbert?"

"No, Gilbert had redder hair."

"It's White," Wakefield muttered, angry that no one else had recognized him.

"There's *Gary*," Barbara gasped. "He looks so young."

"Ol' Coop was a hell of a Marine," Sands offered.

"Look at that. Everything's all burned up. They must have napalmed that place."

"It's the DMZ," Steiner said. "They used defoliants."

"Agent Orange," Taylor added.

"What's that?"

"It's a foxhole . . . look down the row, it's a defensive perimeter," Smith said. "Jesus, would you look where they put us! Out in an open field, surrounded by jungle. The gooks could just sit back there and pick us off. How stupid can you get? No wonder we . . ." He caught himself in midsentence. "No wonder we came back like we did."

It was the closest any of them came to admitting that they had lost.

Wakefield found that he was enormously relieved when the reunion finally ended after breakfast on Sunday, and so were most of the others. There were long, awkward silences by then, punctuated by the retelling of stories already told, a good deal of forced laughter and premature remembrances of events that had taken place only hours earlier; the weekend already was becoming legend.

It was no longer snowing, but the wind blew showers of icy pinpricks and the roads were glacial. Elizabeth Wakefield was nervous about driving conditions, and had John call the Indiana Highway Patrol; they were the first to leave. Then Taylor drove Steiner, Smith and the Wilsons to the airport; Mel Sands headed home to Michigan. Szuminski was the last to go, collaring each of the others as they left, pleading with them to stay for one last drink. Finally, in late afternoon, he gave up the fight and departed with two six-packs and a jar of whiskey to sustain him on the drive back to Erie.

That night, Taylor and I sat in the basement trying to digest the weekend. There was one bottle of vodka left, and we polished it off. "It went by so fast," he said. "I don't know what happened."

The basement seemed terribly quiet and empty, too quickly cleared of all the debris. We were exhausted, and somewhat disappointed. The reunion hadn't lived up to expectations. It had been forty-eight hours of undifferentiated drinking and getting stoned, cracking wise and looking at old photographs, more an endurance test than a catharsis. The camaraderie remained pleasantly superficial and safe throughout, a pale imitation of what they'd once shared . . . and that, no doubt, was the main source of disappointment. Once, they had depended on each other for their lives, and each—in his way—had been hoping to retrieve a piece of that. It was impossible, of course.

But if the camaraderie was irretrievable, something else had been gained. The simple hand-lettered sign at the coffee shop— "Welcome Vietnam Veterans"—had struck home: They had gathered together openly, proudly; their picture, arms linked, would appear on the front page of the Chicago Heights newspaper that week. A corner had been turned. Their service no longer was a potential embarrassment, something to be kept secret. There was a measure of pride and relief mixed with the disappointment as they headed home.

4

Later, Bill Taylor admitted he was in agony throughout the reunion. He felt as if his marriage were a cliff, and he was hanging from it by his fingernails. All weekend, he watched Barbara not watching him. She looked especially good on Saturday in her cream blazer, silky blouse and dark slacks, her hair piled up and falling in sexy blond ringlets over her ears and down her neck. More than any of the other women there, she seemed one of the guys, matching them drink for drink. She didn't say much, but listened closely, appreciatively, to their stories. He'd hoped the reunion would make some difference, that she'd realize he'd once been part of something important, that he'd been a hero. But nothing changed.

It was another hope destroyed, like est. He'd been certain life would be different when she took the training. Then she took it—in early September—and came home flushed, excited.

"Did you get it?" he asked.

"Yeah," she said. "It was the most profound experience of my life."

"What came up for you?"

"None of your business," she said. "It's private. I think it's wrong for you to talk about it as much as you do."

They both remained deeply, if separately, involved in est, taking post-graduate workshops and volunteering to assist at various functions. One time, Bill was asked to guard the door to a hotel ballroom while the training was in progress. Someone was playing a piano down the hall. He worried that the trainees would be disturbed by the music. He wanted to tell the piano player to stop, but he'd been ordered explicitly not to leave the door. Then he remembered his *intention*—the powerful, almost mystical force of pure will he'd learned about in the "What's So" seminar. He concentrated on the piano, *intended* it to stop . . . and it stopped.

But his intention did him no good with Barb. Try as he might, he could not intend that they be happy together again. It turned out that she had an intention too, and it was running in the opposite direction.

At the time of the reunion, he was attending a workshop called "The Conditions of Life." It was a series of ten weekly seminars, held on Wednesday nights. Each seminar lasted three and a half hours. It was important to be punctual; if you were a minute late, you had to explain to everyone just precisely *why* you'd been late. Invariably, this would become a public humiliation. In the end, it was always the same: you were responsible, you had *chosen* to be late. Bill had been late to a seminar only once, and he vowed never again. The idea that he might just *skip* a meeting seemed beyond the realm of possibility. But on Wednesday evening the week after the reunion, he found himself rooted to the kitchen table, unable to move. Barbara was out playing Bingo with her mother. The kids were downstairs watching television. He was alone, thinking about his marriage. His thoughts were startling, clear and perfectly formed, without any of the usual false hopes and background noise. The marriage, he realized, was over. He went to the bedroom and packed his bags.

Traci asked what he was doing.

"I'm leaving, honey," he said. "It doesn't mean I don't love you, just that your mom and I aren't getting along. I'll still come and see you."

When Barbara came home later, Traci told her what had happened. "He left," she said. "He said it was all over."

"Good," Barbara said. "But I think he'll be back."

He came back two days later. He said he was staying with his friend Mike. "Good," Barbara said. He dropped by two days after that. He didn't try to move back in, but he couldn't seem to stay away either. He was confused, his thinking muddled; he couldn't sustain the moment of clarity he'd achieved at the kitchen table that Wednesday night. He didn't want the marriage to be over, and so he kept coming back, hoping that Barbara would ask him to stay.

Just then, Barbara was taking the "What's So" seminar, and strange things were coming up for her. She realized that she had been disloyal to every man she'd ever been with. She hadn't been unfaithful to Bill—indeed, *he* was the one who'd been stepping out on her—but she wondered if she hadn't forced him out the door. She hated his yelling and bluster, but wasn't *she* partly responsible for the frustration that caused it? She realized that she had never tried very hard to love him.

And so, when Bill asked rather pathetically if she would celebrate his birthday with him, she agreed. It was a Saturday in February. She wanted to buy him some presents, but the banks were closed and she didn't have any money. She remembered that he still kept his business checkbook in the desk on the back porch—it was one of his excuses for coming back so frequently—and she thought that maybe she could borrow a check from there to pay for the presents. He had warned her many times about using the business checks for personal things, but this was special and she figured he wouldn't mind.

He arrived late Saturday afternoon. She gave him the presents—
dress shirts, a pair of jeans, socks and sexy underwear. He wondered
if there was a message in the underwear.

"Listen," she said, "I was up late tending bar last night and I'm
tired. Why don't we go upstairs and lay down for a while before we
go out?"

"Fine with me," he said, convinced now that there *had* been a
message in the underwear. "I'm tired too."

Upstairs in bed, she told him about using the business check to
pay for the presents.

"You *what*?"

"It was for you, Bill."

"You had no fucking business going into that checkbook. I've
told you a thousand times."

She rolled away from him. He stormed out.

He returned about an hour later. He had gone to pick up Traci
at the roller rink. Barbara went downstairs to the kitchen. He was
standing with his back to her. "So," she said, "you want to go out
or what?"

He wheeled and smacked her in the face. She bounced against
the sink, then came after him. They grappled against the refrigerator, slipping, sliding, scattering Billy's school drawings that had been
taped there. Billy was in the middle of it, screaming, "What are you
doing, Daddy? What are you doing?"

Barbara was thinking about Vietnam veterans going berserk.
It was the first time he'd ever struck her, and now he was scream-
ing, "You *like* it . . . you like it when I hit you, don't you, bitch?
Don't you? Don't you?" Later, she thought this was pretty silly and
laughed, remembering it. Bill wasn't very convincing as a berserk
Vietnam veteran.

As it happened, Bill *was* thinking about the war. He was thinking about the Doors song "The End," which had been popular toward the end of his tour. He was singing it in his mind while she
tried to get up the stairs and he pulled her back down.

At some point in the grappling, she realized he wasn't going to
kill her. He was losing steam. Finally, he let go of her and left.

"Well, that's that," she said. She called a cousin who'd been contemplating divorce and knew about a lawyer.

On Tuesday night, she went to the "What's So" seminar, and more strange things came up for her. The seminar leader talked about the games people played in order to be able to say, "I didn't do anything wrong." Bill had hit her. She hadn't done anything wrong. She had always said it would be all over if he hit her, and so it was. She remembered him screaming, "You *like* it!" It had been ridiculous, but was he right? Had she gotten satisfaction out of the fact that he'd finally done the one thing that would irrevocably break the marriage? Had she created the situation—not just by using the business check (she hadn't done anything wrong there)—but by fending him off for all those years? Poor Bill, she thought, always trying so hard. Images of Bill floated through her mind. She was surprised that the images were pleasant ones.

On Wednesday morning, she went to see the lawyer. He had an office in the neighboring town of Lansing. It was a typical office, filled with law books. He seemed a typical lawyer too. Later, she'd be unable to remember what he looked like.

"What do you have?" the lawyer asked.

"We don't have anything."

"You have a house."

"We have a house," she agreed.

She felt as if she were stoned. She sat there for an hour, drifting off as the lawyer talked about things like cash settlements, alimony payments, custody. She'd had all these things worked out in her mind for years, but she couldn't seem to remember any of them. The lawyer kept saying, "Excuse me . . . about the alimony . . ."

"Oh yeah, what about it?"

"How much do you need to live?"

And then she would drift off again, saying something to the lawyer, but not really thinking about what she was saying. She couldn't remember from one minute to the next what was being decided there. Finally, he said it was time to sign the papers.

"What papers?"

"To put things in motion."

He buzzed his secretary. "Hold it," she said.

"You want some time to think about it?"

Her head was swimming. "I guess so," she said.

Later, she called Bill at Nate Silberberg's insurance office. "Bill, I got to speak to you," she said. "I'm coming over right now."

She parked the van in the alley next to Nate's office. She went in to get him and said, "Let's talk out in the van."

"Okay," he said.

They went out to the van and she said, "Bill, I did something . . . I went to see a lawyer."

"What!"

She could see he was getting angry. "Wait a minute, let me finish," she said. "I went to see this lawyer and we talked for about an hour, and then he gave me papers to sign . . . and I just couldn't do it. I don't know why. I just kept thinking about all the games I've been playing since we got married. I guess I really care about you after all."

Bill was crying. "This is what I've been praying for," he said. "I didn't think this day would ever come. We'll be happy together, you'll see. We'll be one big happy family. I'll work really hard. Everything is going to be great, just *great*."

Barbara realized she had gone too far. She hadn't really thought about getting back *together* again; she'd just wanted to tell him that she couldn't sign the papers. And then she thought: Uh-oh, here I go again. I'm playing games with him.

"Well," she said softly, "let's not make any big plans or anything. Let's just try it one day at a time."

"Oh sure," he said. "Absolutely. One day at a time."

He leaned over and kissed her then. She kissed him back. She's *kissing* me, he thought, unable to remember the last time she had done that. He began to laugh, his stomach jiggling the very same way it had the night she'd met him in the Serbian tavern.

She wondered: What have I done now?

Their marriage would never be very stable. There were good times and bad, separations and reconciliations, even a brief divorce. Bill lived alone in an apartment for a few months, then moved back into the house. They didn't remarry, but continued living together in near-marriage, Barbara never quite able to move beyond near-love, Bill hanging on by his fingernails.

He found that he could live with that. Gradually, he learned to do it Barbara's way, one day at a time; his expectations diminished, he turned his attention to other things.

When the story about the reunion appeared in the Chicago Heights newspaper, Bill began to receive phone calls from other Vietnam veterans. The Rotary Club asked him to give a speech. He became active in veterans' affairs, joining the Military Order of the Purple Heart, a fraternal organization limited to those who had been wounded in combat. He rose through the ranks, and became senior vice-commander of the Chicago Heights post.

In 1983, he went to Washington as the Purple Heart's representative at the Veterans Day memorial service in Arlington National Cemetery. It was a great honor; he carried a flag in the color guard. He wore the organization's official uniform: purple Eisenhower jacket, light purple slacks, purple cap.

After the ceremonies, still in uniform, he visited the Vietnam Memorial on the Capitol Mall. He had been planning to do this for some time, intending to search the black marble wedge for the names of his friends who'd died. At a Vet Center back in Chicago, there had been a book listing the 57,000 names and their location on the monument; he jotted down the appropriate panel and line numbers in his checkbook.

It was a cold, rainy day. He was awed by the enormous, sullen dignity of the monument; it seemed to acknowledge the sacrifices made without glorifying them. It was a perfect reflection of his feelings about Vietnam.

He approached the monument from the west, and looked in his checkbook. As it happened, the first name he'd be searching for, the one closest to where he was standing, was the one he least wanted to see: Billy Joe Taylor, Panel 49 West, Line 1.

Billy Joe Taylor: a black from Mississippi who'd arrived several months after Operation Cochise. The irony of having two Bill Taylors in one unit, one white and one black, hadn't been lost on the other grunts; there had been jokes. The two Taylors weren't close friends, but there was a quiet understanding between them: neither wanted anything bad to happen to *any* Bill Taylor in Vietnam. They looked out for each other.

Bill found Panel 49 West, Line 1. He saw the name, *his* name . . . and then he saw Billy Joe Taylor lying in the dirt after a mortar barrage, faceless. He began to cry.

He was enveloped by arms; three Vietnam veterans in khaki uniforms were comforting him. He felt silly in his gaudy purple uniform.

"The same thing happened to us," one of them said. "What did it for you?"

"I remembered seeing him dead . . . I have this list," he said, showing them his checkbook. "But these are only the names I remember. There were others . . . that's what really gets me about this place. There were others, and I can't remember their names."

5

Wakefield was disappointed by the reunion, but he recovered quickly. For the first time since the war, he had an ambition, a personal goal. He wanted to help other Vietnam veterans. He was beginning to think about going to college to get the training in psychology he'd need to become a counselor like Dan Lonnquist or a group facilitator like Ken Martin.

He was a star at the Vet Center, one of the most eloquent veterans there. Lonnquist invited him to various public functions—college seminars, the opening of other Vet Centers—to explain the problems of Vietnam veterans. He would talk about how hard he'd run from reality when he'd first come home, the alcohol and drug abuse, the occasional violence, the way he'd shut out Elizabeth. He talked about these things coolly, analytically—that was what made him so attractive a speaker. He was an antidote to the public perception of Vietnam veterans as half crazed and violent. Dan Lonnquist considered him a valuable resource.

When I visited Wakefield again that March, he was very proud of all that he'd accomplished. Our interviews had become lectures; his life was a case history—but the components of that history kept shifting slightly. When the differences between his parents' version of the events of his life and his own were pointed out, he would quickly back away from stories he'd told previously with a great deal of conviction. His parents were probably right, he would say; his faulty memory was a consequence of post-traumatic stress disorder. The dream he'd had about addressing the Indiana legislature was beginning to seem appropriate: like a good politician, he had the ability to speak with authority and yet be quite elusive.

Wakefield wanted me to see what a group was like, but his Thursday meetings at the Vet Center were closed to outsiders. "There's a new American Legion post in town," he said. "It's specifically for Vietnam veterans. They hold open groups on Monday nights, and maybe we'll go over there."

The post was a ramshackle former roadhouse. The roof leaked and the heating system had seen better days; when the furnace turned on, it did so with a bang that startled several of the dozen veterans who had gathered there for the group. They sat in a circle of folding chairs, smoking and drinking coffee. One was a woman, a former nurse who had seen too many mangled bodies in field hospitals. Several others were attending their first group; they were quiet, reluctant to speak. The facilitator was not a professional, but a local construction worker named John Smalley. He did his job well, reassuring the newcomers that they weren't required to say anything. "I know you're probably nervous," he said. "But you can be sure, the rest of us were nervous our first times too. The thing to remember is that we're all brothers—and sisters," he said, nodding toward the nurse. "No one here is going to call you a war criminal or a baby-killer. Each of us has horror stories of his own. Now, who wants to start?"

"I've been having the dream again," a solid, tough-looking man said abruptly.

"What's the dream, Jim?" the facilitator asked.

"The truck blowing up. The bodies . . . It was my fault."

"Was this something that really happened, or just a dream?"

"Yeah, it happened," Jim said. His job in Vietnam had been to inspect roads for mines. He was very good at it, he said, but one time he made a mistake. "I don't know how I missed that damn mine. I'm sure I covered that ground." He'd seen the truck explode, the men die. "John Wayne wouldn't have missed that mine."

"Fuck John Wayne," said a huge man wearing coveralls, devouring a hero sandwich.

As Jim continued, the circle appeared to grow smaller. Most of the others leaned forward, elbows on their knees, listening closely and with obvious sympathy. They seemed flattered that Jim had honored them with his trust, and were anxious to reassure him that it hadn't been misplaced. They did this through small, almost imperceptible smiles and murmurs of encouragement. It was hard to believe that many of these people had known each other for less than an hour.

Jim went on to talk about the rage he began to experience after leaving Vietnam. He told a particularly harrowing story about a barroom brawl he'd been part of while stationed in Germany. He had seized a man's arm with both his hands, and snapped it across the edge of the bar.

Wakefield had been leaning back in his seat, legs crossed, smoking a Benson and Hedges, listening with what appeared to be cool detachment. Now he leaned forward and asked, "How did you feel when you did that?"

"Pretty damn good."

"Yeah, I know," Wakefield said. "I had some moments like that too when I came home."

The others turned to him, expecting amplification. But he had nothing more to say, and attention returned to Jim. The group continued for another two hours, Wakefield aloof, occasionally interjecting impartial, almost formal questions and comments. Even the facilitator seemed more a part of the action, at one point speaking emotionally about the anger he'd felt upon returning from Vietnam.

When it was over, Wakefield said that he'd been very nervous. "There were times my hand was shaking so bad I couldn't pick up my coffee cup."

"Do you feel that way in your closed group?" I asked.

"Not so much," he said. "I think just being in an American Legion hall shook me up."

Apparently, though, Wakefield's performances in his regular group were much the same. Later, Dan Lonnquist would say that the other vets were growing impatient with John's attempts to be an unofficial facilitator. They were beginning to challenge him, much as the group leaders at Synanon had ten years earlier. The pressure was gentler, more loving now . . . but the stakes were higher too. The time was approaching when Wakefield would be forced to make a choice—to start talking, or flee as he had in the past, as his parents predicted he would.

In April, Wakefield visited me in New York. I had told him that Steiner was coming for a weekend. "Do you mind if I join you?" he asked. "I'm kind of curious about how you live, and I haven't been to New York in a long time."

That Sunday night, the three of us sat around the dining-room table, drinking beer and picking at the newspaper. Steiner began to talk about the story Mel Sands had told at the reunion about tossing the Vietnamese prisoners out of the helicopter after Operation Cochise. "I'd heard things like that happened," Steiner said. "But I just can't believe it."

"Worse things than that," Wakefield said.

"But that's murder!" Steiner said. "There's no excuse, no earthly reason for that. It's like when we used to go through villes, I could never understand why some of the guys would beat up the old people. We were real tough guys, weren't we? Winning hearts and minds! Beating up defenseless old people . . ."

"It was a war," Wakefield said. "Some of those old people weren't so defenseless. There are good reasons for using terror tactics." And then he launched into an elaborate defense of the use of unexpected force against civilians in unfriendly territory. Steiner, disgusted, tuned out; he picked up a section of the newspaper and pretended not to be listening. Wakefield pretended not to notice.

It was the only time all weekend that they talked about Vietnam.

Wakefield returned to Indianapolis on Monday, and went to his regular group meeting on Thursday. The session began, as it sometimes did, with a film. This time, it was a curious, disturbing little film called *Good Morning, Vietnam*. It was standard combat footage for the most part—helicopter assaults, patrols, fire fights, medics tending the wounded, medevacs, grunts sitting about dazed and exhausted, eating C rations; interspersed, though, were shots of a lone soldier on patrol through a forest. The soldier was fully outfitted with camouflage fatigues, a pack, an M-16. But he had longish hair, tied in a bandanna, and the forest seemed more American than Asian. It wasn't very realistic, Wakefield decided. He wondered if, perhaps, that was the point—maybe this guy was a Vietnam veteran back home. Toward the end of the film, the soldier stepped gingerly across a small stream. He crouched on the far side, studying the terrain, listening, watching. He began to move again, through a swamp. There was the sound of cannon fire. He moved slowly through the swamp, every step measured carefully—Wakefield remembered the feeling, the heightened senses, the bracing sharpness of each perception. Then the soldier had to take a slightly larger step, moving out of the swamp onto higher ground. As he planted his foot, a shot was fired and the soldier fell dead. The camera pulled back from a close-up of the dead soldier, to a wider shot of the soldier in the field, to an aerial shot of the field, and wider still—the field was part of an island, the island was in the Potomac River.

So it *had* been some sort of metaphor, but Wakefield wasn't thinking about that. He was thinking about McIntyre.

"What did you think about the movie, John?" someone asked.

"Well, I was trying to figure out what sort of mistake the guy made to get himself killed."

"Mistake? Why would there have to be a mistake?"

"Well, I always thought that the guys who got themselves killed were the ones who made mistakes."

And then he told them about how McIntyre had moved too quickly—or done *something* wrong—and gotten himself killed on the patrol in North Vietnam.

Later that night, he said to Elizabeth, "Y'know, a funny thing happened when I was telling them about Mac. I told them that I'd never been sorry about his death, just angry that he made a mistake—even if I could never figure out what the mistake was. Then I remembered that after Mac died, they kept his bunk empty for about six weeks. Finally, they brought in a new guy . . . and I went off by myself and cried. I completely forgot all about that. But I *did* cry."

As he said this, tears came to his eyes, then trickled sideways out his crow's-feet and down the sides of his face. Elizabeth remembered a conversation we'd had about Operation Cochise. We'd been trying to figure out why John couldn't remember a thing that happened after White was shot. Maybe he had cried then too.

That Sunday, Elizabeth left on a long-planned trip to visit her sister in Texas. She would be gone for a week. Wakefield wasn't feeling very well. He was tired and feverish; he figured he was coming down with the flu.

On Monday night, he took some NyQuil and assumed his usual position on the couch in the new room, watching television on his back. At about midnight, the phone rang. The caller's voice was familiar, but he wasn't quite sure who it was.

"We know you've been talking," the caller said. "We've listened to Klein's tapes. We know who's in your group . . ."

Wakefield leaped from the couch. He made sure all the doors were locked, then got out his old hunting rifle and shotgun. He scanned the street in front of the house, saw nothing. He went from window to window the rest of the night, waiting for them to come after him.

At first light, he made a dash from the house to the car. He drove to the Vet Center, and positioned himself in a corner of the parking lot. The Vet Center was an abandoned bank building located next to an elevated highway. He watched the morning traffic on the highway carefully. A sniper, he figured, could stop there feigning a breakdown and pick him off very easily.

After several hours, Dan Lonnquist and Ken Martin arrived for work. Wakefield collared them and said, "I've got to talk to you."

He positioned himself in Lonnquist's office so that no one could come up behind him. He had a clear view of the door, and could monitor the highway through the window. This would be a harder shot, he figured, but not impossible for a pro.

"Why do you think," Lonnquist asked, "the government doesn't want you to talk?"

He told them that his first year in Vietnam—the year he spent with Force Recon, operating in North Vietnam—was supposed to have been secret. Officially, his unit was still based at Camp Le-Jeune. His letters home were routed through there. From time to time, members of his unit would be flown individually back to the States so they could spend weekends at home, to maintain the illusion. He told them about some of the operations he'd been on, the interrogations, the torture, the murder and mutilation.

Lonnquist and Martin were skeptical, to say the least—although they didn't say so at the time. The operations, horrible though they were, sounded plausible. They had heard of similar operations, and Wakefield described these with a certainty and detail that were convincing. The secrecy of the mission was somewhat less plausible—why would the government go to all that trouble?—and the phone call was most troubling of all. If any other veteran had come in with that story, Lonnquist would have dismissed it immediately as a stress-related delusion, but Wakefield had seemed so solid, so rational. Lonnquist wasn't sure how to proceed. He suggested that perhaps Wakefield should tell the group about what had happened.

"No," he said. "If I do, someone innocent might get hurt."

The meeting ended without resolution. Wakefield returned home wondering if Lonnquist and Martin were part of a conspiracy against him. Somehow, the caller had known all about his group . . . and the book too. Later that day, Wakefield called me—ostensibly to say thanks for the weekend he'd spent in New York, but hoping I'd tell him my house had been robbed, the tapes stolen.

"Is everything okay there?" he asked.

"Sure, fine," I said. "Why do you ask?"

"No special reason, just asking."

"Is everything okay with you?"

"Well, Elizabeth's with her sister in Texas this week. Guess I'm feeling a little lonely."

Somehow he made it through the rest of the week. When Elizabeth called, he didn't say anything. He went to work as usual, and to group on Thursday—but he didn't say anything about the phone call. He watched the other members of the group closely, looking for spies.

Elizabeth Wakefield had been loyal to her husband through the worst of times. She defended him when he made a fool of himself in Little League (the umpires *were* incompetent, she'd insist, the league hierarchy *was* arrayed against him). She took his side the time he was fired by Allison's, and enjoyed his vindication when he was rehired. She defended John against his family when he became a janitor; she believed that his parents had never understood him. She was proud of him for having joined the closed group at the Vet Center (although she did want him to take the next step and go into individual therapy)—and if he tended to be almost pompous at times about the progress he'd made, well, that was just the natural pride that came from facing his problems squarely.

She had trouble accepting his story about the phone call, though.

Her first reaction, when she arrived home and he told her, was not to question him too closely about it. He was obviously a mess, and she didn't want to make the situation worse. As it was, he was acting in a way that was downright frightening—introverted, jumpy, checking the windows; she imagined it was the way he'd been in Vietnam.

When John left for work on Monday, she called Dan Lonnquist to see if he knew anything more about what was going on. Lonnquist told her about the strange meeting in his office, and the story John had told. "What do you think?" she asked.

"I don't know," he said. "Do you think it's possible the phone call was something John dreamed . . . or imagined?"

"I haven't the vaguest idea," she said.

She hung up the phone, and thought about it for a moment. Then she called Lonnquist back. "Yes," she said, "I think it's *very* possible that it may have been a dream."

She told Lonnquist that John hadn't dreamed—at least, he hadn't remembered his dreams—until a few months earlier; it was still something new for him. He'd been on the couch watching television, and he often dozed off when he did that. He had taken Ny-Quil, which sometimes made him feel logy and strange. And the message, the threat that something bad might happen if he continued to talk—that was something he'd been scared about from the start. So much had been happening in recent weeks: the trip to New York, telling the group about McIntyre, the constrained trickle of tears that night—she wondered if the phone call wasn't a message from his subconscious.

"It's something I've thought about," Lonnquist agreed. "The tricky thing is how to present all this to John."

Elizabeth suggested that the three of them meet at the Vet Center.

"He might feel that we're ganging up on him," Lonnquist said.

"He probably will," Elizabeth said. But there didn't appear to be any alternatives.

They met two nights later. Lonnquist got straight to the point: "John, did you ever consider the possibility that your phone call might have been a nightmare?"

Wakefield looked at the two of them, and knew that they were both convinced that he had dreamed the whole thing up. He knew, too, that they'd been conspiring behind his back. He felt angry, betrayed . . . and somewhat embarrassed—because it *was* possible that the phone call had been a dream. As Dan laid out the dream scenario for him, he could see the logic of it.

If it was a dream, it was the first he'd ever had that could have been real. Addressing the Indiana legislature obviously had been a dream, as had another one he'd had recently—he was backing his car around a corner. When he awakened both times, it was clear that he'd been dreaming. Was it possible that he had dreamed he was on the couch watching television and the phone rang when he was actually *on* the couch?

"Maybe," Elizabeth suggested, "the dream was triggered by a phone ringing on television while you were asleep."

"It's possible," he said. He wasn't going to give them the satisfaction of agreeing with their scenario immediately. The truth was, he still wasn't sure.

Once again, Dan suggested that John tell his group about what he'd been going through. "Well, I can't tomorrow night," Wakefield said. "The men and women are meeting together. I don't want to bring it up then."

"What about next time?"

"I'll think about it."

As it happened, Ken Martin didn't give him much choice. He started the next group meeting by asking, "John, isn't there something you want to talk about?"

"Well . . . I suppose so," he said. "A couple of weeks ago, I got this phone call. It *may* have been a phone call . . . or it might have been a flashback, or a dream—I don't know . . ."

He told them the story. Then he told them about his first tour in Vietnam. He told it slowly, with difficulty at times. When he faltered, they nudged him along with questions. Eventually, it all came out. He'd been afraid that they might react as Steiner had to the story about Sands and Cooper in the helicopter. He was afraid they might be disgusted by him. They weren't, though. They accepted what he had to say. They even accepted his unwillingness to believe the phone call had been a nightmare. When it was over, they gathered around him, hugged him, slapped him on the back.

It was all somewhat disappointing.

Two days later, I arrived in Indianapolis for what was supposed to be my last series of interviews with Wakefield. Elizabeth answered the door and said, "John's in bad shape. He's been going through a tough time, and so you'll have to forgive him in advance—he's saying he doesn't want to be part of the book anymore."

"Why not?"

"I'll let him tell you that. He asked me if he should be part of the book, and I said yes. I think he'll come around and pull out of this. But you should be prepared . . . he's out on the back patio."

The back patio was a bare, gray patch of concrete off the new room. Wakefield was sagged in a chaise longue, shirt off. There was hazy sunshine, and the steady roar of racing cars doing time trials at the nearby Speedway.

"You haven't had anyone break into your house or anything?" he asked.

"What?"

"Break into your house?"

"No, why?"

He told me about the phone call, and some of what had happened since. "I talked quite a bit about my first tour in group on Thursday," he said. "And part of what's been happening to me since then is the lack of sorrow about some of the things I did. I felt bad about them, but I wasn't sorry. I didn't feel any sorrow . . . and that's been kind of messing up my head. I told the group about some of the more memorable torture scenes . . . and I'd always assumed it would be an absolution-type thing: I would say it, get it over with, that would be the end of it . . . but it wasn't. Now I have to examine in my head why it didn't feel the way it was supposed to."

"It only happens that way in the movies," I said.

"I guess."

"So why do you want to stop being part of the book?"

"I don't know," he said, tears trickling out the corners of his eyes. "I'm just really messed up right now. I'm not sure of anything. You can use what I've told you so far, but I don't want to do any more . . . and nothing about the phone call."

"That's pretty hard," I said, "if this is going to be a book about how you came home from Vietnam. What would you do if you were me?"

"Probably blow up."

"I'm not going to do that, John."

He reached out and grabbed my hand. I hugged him.

"I've got to think about all this," he said. "There's this place I go . . . a hill. I just sit there and think sometimes. I want to go there now."

When he left, Elizabeth told me more about what had happened during the past two weeks and then she said, "Don't go yet. Wait until he comes back from his hill. I think it's important to know that even if the book is through, you're still a friend. I think it's real important that he sees you're not angry with him."

"I'm not," I lied. "I just hope he gets it all straightened out."

I sat down on Wakefield's couch and tried to watch a baseball game. Was it possible that he was upset about more than just the numbness, the lack of sorrow over what he'd done in Vietnam? He had held on to those secrets so tightly . . . and yet, so noisily. He never stopped talking about them, reminding people—me, the counselors at the Vet Center, his group—that he had them, and they couldn't be revealed. They set him apart from the others at the Vet Center. They made him feel important, different, dangerous, unique. "They involve things that might be considered war crimes," he'd once said. He had done things so horrible—whatever they were (I'd never asked, figuring he'd tell me if he was ready)—that even the battle-hardened veterans in his group would be disgusted. But they hadn't been disgusted. They'd accepted his stories, as if they were nothing out of the ordinary—as if *he* were nothing out of the ordinary. "I was surprised by their reaction, or lack of one," he would later say. "Maybe the things I did weren't as horrible as I thought."

And now, the secrets divulged and the melodrama over, there was nothing to buffer him from the thwarted, frustrating reality of his life since the war.

When he returned home two hours later, John thanked me for sticking around to say goodbye. "I'm still pretty confused, though," he said, "and real embarrassed about this."

Elizabeth called me in New York several days later. "I think John's ready to talk to you now," she said.

I called him that night. "I'm sorry I caused you to make that trip for nothing," he said. "I feel real bad about that . . . I guess this whole thing is a lot harder than I thought it would be. Anyway, if you can afford another trip out here, I'd like to make it up to you. I'm ready to talk about it now—most of it, at least. There are still some things I did over there that I don't want to make public."

We had a barbecue at Dan Lonnquist's house. We talked about the phone call—John now called it a nightmare—and the events that followed. John appeared to have regained much of his old pride. He had been through a crisis, he said, but such things were to be expected.

About a month later, he quit his closed group at the Vet Center. "I think I've taken this about as far as it can go," he told Lonnquist and Ken Martin.

They had their doubts about that, but Martin said, "He'll be back."

And so he was, a year later. He was thinking now about starting individual therapy, he said. His progress continued in fits and starts.

There were depressions, crises, recoveries and months in between spent lying on the couch in the new room watching television as if nothing had changed. There were times when Elizabeth was convinced that he was back to square one, as impenetrable as ever. There were times she feared for the marriage. But he always managed to gather himself together, and take the next step.

6

Szuminski loved the reunion. It was the best party he'd been to in years. When he returned to Erie, it was all he could talk about. He invented nicknames for the other guys—Wakefield was the Old-timer, Steiner was Smokey the Bear. He would tell his friends George and Teka Choklas stories about the weekend over and over again. They enjoyed listening—Szuminski was always entertaining—but it was sad too. The reunion seemed about the only good thing that had happened to Dale lately; everything else was falling apart.

The divorce proceedings with Sandy were a protracted nightmare. She was still living in their house; Dale was staying with George's brother, Bucky. Sandy was willing to give him the house—she wanted out of Erie—but at a price. For a time, Szuminski was reluctant to negotiate: he didn't care about the house, he wanted Sandy. His attitude changed, though, when Sandy began to hint that maybe if the divorce were out of the way, she'd give him another chance. Everyone thought Dale was crazy to believe her. In all the years Szuminski had stumbled half smashed through the streets of Erie, no one had ever taken him for a fool; on the contrary, his cunning was legend. But now, for the first time, it seemed Szuminski was being snookered. "She's got him wrapped around her little finger," said one friend. "I never thought I'd see Dale get taken for a ride."

He was still Rent-A-Party, still pulling into random driveways at odd hours with six-packs under his arm. But often, late at night, friends would notice that Dale had broken off from the party and was in the kitchen on the phone with Sandy, sweet-talking her, pleading with her, negotiating for a second chance. He grasped at straws: Sandy said maybe—*maybe*—when the divorce was final, she might think about getting back together, but only if they went away to someplace like California, away from his drinking buddies. Szuminski's friends told him not to be a fool, she was just stringing him along, but Dale would insist: "Why would she do that? What's in it for her? We're getting divorced."

On a Friday night several weeks after the reunion, Bucky's house burned down. Bucky said it was probably a short circuit, but most people assumed that Dale had had something to do with it, even though he was out drinking at the time. After the fire, he bounced from house to house, a nomad in Erie. His friends had never seen him so low; he was drinking hard, but not very well.

The settlement with Sandy was negotiated in February. He agreed to pay her $18,000 over ninety days, $5,000 of it immediately, in return for the house. The divorce became final on March 1, and Sandy returned home to Columbus, Ohio.

He tried to call her. She said she was living with her old friend Pam Smith, but he never seemed able to reach her there. When they connected, it was because Sandy called him. She called frequently and allowed herself to be wooed, but refused to make any commitments. He agreed to move to California and look for a post office job there. He said he'd do anything she wanted, if only she'd come back . . . and, to everyone's amazement, she did for a time. She spent a week with him in Erie in late March, then left abruptly. She hated Erie, she said, she had no friends there. She was frightened too—she loved him, but wasn't sure she wanted to risk getting hurt again. She returned to Columbus.

Again, he had difficulty reaching her there. Again, she called him. She was confused and uncertain, she said. Part of her wanted to try it again, and part of her wanted to go to California alone and start a new life. She had relatives in San Jose, and was thinking about moving there.

"Is there anything I could do to make you trust me?" he said.

Sandy said that paying her the rest of the cash settlement would go a long way toward rebuilding trust.

Szuminski raised the money, borrowing much of it from his reluctant parents. He sent it off to Sandy in early May.

"Did you get the money?" he asked when she called again. "Can we get back together again now?"

"Let's wait until the check clears," she said.

When she called again, the check had cleared. "Dale, I don't know if I can go ahead and do it," she said. "I've got a job here now, a good job. I'm going to take a test to be a stockbroker. I don't know if I want to drop everything and then get hurt again . . . I'm sorry."

Szuminski's friends figured that Sandy had taken him to the cleaner's. Dale still couldn't believe it, though. "If she was only stringing me along for the money," he'd say, "why does she keep on calling me? Why does she promise just about every week that she's going to come up for the weekend?"

Why doesn't she ever come? his friends would reply.

Szuminski did some detective work. When Sandy stayed with him that week in March, she'd made some very expensive phone calls to Columbus; several were an hour, two hours long—all to the same number. He decided to trace the number, and found that it was registered to a Mr. Carl Herbert.

"Who is this guy Carl Herbert?" he asked the next time she called.

"It's a girlfriend of mine," she said. "Judy. Carl's her husband."

"I never heard of this Judy before," he said. "If you're seeing another guy, fine. I can understand that . . . as long as we keep talking, trying to get back together."

"Well, we're never going to get back together if you accuse me of being a liar," she said.

In early June, Szuminski and I drove from Erie to Columbus. I wanted to meet Dave Horn and some of Dale's other old friends. Szuminski had his own agenda—he wanted to make one last attempt to see Sandy. As soon as we reached Dave Horn's house, he called

Pam Smith. "She's not here, Dale," Pam said. "Anyway, I don't think she wants to talk to you."

"Where's she at?"

"I can't tell you."

Dave Horn seemed the very picture of middle-class respectability. He jogged, was moving up the ladder at the carpet store and owned a Chrysler Imperial; his wife hugged Szuminski when we arrived, but eyed him warily. At my request, Dave played his old boot camp record, "The Making of a Marine." He and Dale reminisced about the parties they'd had when they came home from the war; they talked about the time Horn drove his Corvette through the hardware-store window. "That was the end of partying for me," Dave said.

Szuminski grew antsy. "Hey, Davey," he said, "let's show Joe some of our old haunts."

Horn was reluctant. He had work the next day. Szuminski was insistent, though, and we piled into Horn's car. "I can't stay out long," Dave said, "just a few beers."

It turned out to be a few pitchers of beer, but that wasn't nearly enough for Szuminski. "Time to go," Horn said.

"You're quittin' on me?" Dale said. "I can't believe it, Davey. It's not even midnight."

"I've got to be home by midnight."

"Curfew, huh?"

Horn ignored the needle, but when Szuminski went to the bathroom he said, "I never thought I'd say this, but I'm beginning to feel sorry for Dale."

***

Late that night, after everyone had gone to sleep, Szuminski made a phone call. A man answered. Szuminski said nothing. The man said, "Who is it? . . . Hey, Sandy, is that you?" Szuminski hung up. He sat in the darkness smoking, drinking a beer. He dialed the number again, and pretended to be Pam's husband.

"Hey, Chuck," the man said, "how're you doing?"

"I'm trying to get ahold of Sandy," Dale said. "Dale called—he's looking for her. You know where she is?"

"No," the man said. "I haven't seen her either."

Szuminski was morose on the ride home. The phone call had been inconclusive. She wasn't living with the guy; maybe she was just dating him.

"I've got to get her out of my mind," he said. "If she'd only stop calling, promising me she's coming on Friday. Then she don't come . . . She always used to accuse me of lying to her. 'Don't lie to me,' she'd say. To her, a lie was saying that I was going over to George and Teka's for a couple of beers and then staying for five or six. Well, that's nothing compared to what she's doing now."

He talked most of the way home, reviewing the history of his life with Sandy, looking for clues. "I think about George and Teka with a new baby and all," he said. "It's real nice. They've got a home, and security . . . and I think that for the first time in my life I'm ready for that. All these opportunities to settle down hit you when you're not ready, and then when you *are* ready, the opportunities are gone. There was never any doubt in my mind that everything was going to work with Sandy—until now. I was dead sure. We were going to grow old together . . . When we got together in Columbus four years ago—the time we were going to try to make a life in Florida—I waited for three weeks at Davey Horn's house for her to settle up and leave. She was hemming and hawing around, not telling the guy she'd been married to that she was going to Florida with me . . . same thing she's doing to me now. She's telling me the exact same thing she told *him* four years ago. I bet there's some other guy waiting, just like I did, for her to make up her mind."

He stared at the trees and fields for a time. It was a cloudy day with occasional spatters of rain. "Sometimes," he said, "driving along like this, I see a tree line . . . and it could almost be a tree line back there, in Nam. It's something you feel for just a second, you get all tensed up . . . and then you realize it's just some trees, nothing to get worried about."

Then he said, "I think about all the things I did since the war, the things I did to women—Linda, Jeannie, Sandy. All the games I played on them . . . and she's doing the same thing to me now. I'm finally ready to settle down, and it seems like everything I did bad in my life is coming back on me."

"Payback is a motherfucker?" I suggested.

"Yeah," he said. "We used to say that, didn't we?"

In the months that followed, Sandy and I had several long and emotional telephone conversations. She had gotten her revenge, but it didn't feel very good. She was convinced that it never would work with Dale—he had promised so many times that he would change, and never had—but she couldn't get him out of her mind either. She found that she wasn't very interested in other men. One night on the phone, she remembered the beautiful letters he had written her from the drunk tank at St. Vincent's Hospital. Several days later, I received a packet of the letters in the mail and we talked again. How could he have written such beautiful letters and not mean them? "I think he did mean them on some level," she said. "It wasn't *all* a con job. I wish I could believe that it was something definite—like the war— that makes Dale the way he is. Sometimes I do believe that, but then I think—Dale is Dale. Everyone says he was the same person *before* he went to Vietnam. But people can change, can't they? I can't stop myself from thinking that someday we'll get together again, but the truth is: I don't believe we will."

Later she would say that our phone conversations had been a turning point, an opportunity to think aloud about Dale and get past her anger. She began to miss him then.

She called him when she passed her stockbroker's exam. He sounded different—nothing she could put her finger on, but different. She called him again, and realized what had changed. He wasn't promising the world and sweet-talking her as much; he didn't sound as if he were trying to pull a con job. He talked more about himself, his feelings. There was nothing specific she could point to, no one single moment when she began to trust him again, but she did. She agreed to see him.

The courtship progressed slowly . . . weekends in Columbus, weekends in Erie. She didn't make the mistake of trying to limit his drinking again, and was amazed to find that she didn't have to. He still drank, but not as much. She never had to drag him home at the end of an evening. More important, she never had the sense that he was being elusive, trying to put something over on her. It seemed that he had put his magic in mothballs; there would be no more fantastic escapes.

In September 1983, she agreed to live with him again in Erie.

"We're doing fine," she told me several months later. "I think it's actually working. He's really open with me; we talk all the time. He doesn't drink a fraction of what he used to. He doesn't spend nights out with the guys anymore. We spend most of our time at home."

"I don't know what it is," Dale said. "I don't feel like I've changed, but I guess I have. Maybe I'm just getting older."

He could remember only one time in the past few months that he'd gone out drinking without Sandy—Marine Corps Birthday. "I don't know why that day is so important to me," he said, "but it is. I rounded up some of the guys—Joey Bruno, Don Rogers—and we had a couple of beers."

He was home by midnight.

7

An odd thing happened to John Steiner on the second night of the reunion. Back at the motel, he lay on his bed unable to sleep. There was a sudden, anxious, distant but intense feeling of déjà vu . . . and then he slipped into a semiconscious numbness, staring at the ceiling. When the attack passed—he had no idea how long it had lasted—he sat in the bathroom, trying to figure out what he had just experienced.

"It's the first time I had one of those spells since high school," he told me a month later, on our way to Chico State University in his pickup truck.

"Your mother says you always had those spells at the same time—a couple of weeks before your report card was due," I said.

"No kidding," he said. "I didn't know that."

"They never told you?"

"No. The only thing I knew was that it was some kind of petit mal epilepsy. It went away when I joined the Marines, and I never thought about it again."

"Apparently it wasn't epilepsy," I said. "Your mother said the doctors could never find anything physically wrong. They asked her to keep track of when you had the spells, and it turned out you only had them just before report-card time."

He was stunned. We pulled off the highway for a cup of coffee.

"Well, I guess it makes sense," he finally said. "I was always really scared about report cards. I knew I wasn't going to live up to their expectations."

"Why do you think you had one at the reunion?"

"Beats me," he said. "Maybe I was afraid I wasn't living up to the guys' expectations. Everyone was kind of slipping into the way we talked and acted back then. I guess I was afraid they'd figure out I wasn't a rough, tough Marine anymore."

"But weren't you afraid of the same thing in Vietnam?"

"I guess," he said. "But I never had any spells there. You want to know something funny? I almost had one yesterday on the ship. I felt that old déjà vu feeling, but then nothing happened . . . although I did feel pretty weird being there."

The day before, we had taken a tour of the USS *Okinawa*, which had steamed into San Francisco on its last cruise before being retired from the fleet. Steiner had heard on the radio that the ship would be open to the public, and we visited it with his parents and Eve.

One of the first things we saw, on the hangar deck, was a large wooden plaque listing the operations launched from the ship during the war in Vietnam. Most of the *Okinawa*'s current crew had been toddlers when those operations had taken place. Was it possible that they looked at the plaque with the same awe—and envy—that we'd felt looking at World War II memorials? The operations had romantic and aggressive-sounding names that belied their futility—Buffalo, Bearclaw (Cochise had been next but was, oddly, missing from the list), Beacon Guide, Medina . . . Steiner had known men who'd been killed or wounded on each of them.

The lower decks were closed to the public, but John found a friendly sailor who agreed to let us pass.

"I was a Marine stationed on this ship in 1967," he said.

"Did you see action?" the sailor asked.

"Yep."

John's parents and Eve waited on deck while we went below. As we walked through the bowels of the ship, John remembered all sorts of things—little things like the green tiles in the stairwells ("I remember those!" he blurted) and the acrid, sweaty locker-room smell in the troop quarters. He lingered in the cafeteria, where he'd been served the only hot meals he'd eaten during his first tour. In the troop quarters, he sat on what had once been his bunk and remembered Wakefield dancing around the night before they'd left on Operation Cochise, asking everyone, "Are you coming to the *happening* tomorrow?"

We passed through the sick bay. "Hey," he said, "I just remembered something. I was in here just after Operation Cochise. I had an infected foot or something. I remember sitting cross-legged on a top bunk with Hollins, who was also sitting cross-legged. We were facing each other, talking about the operation and how awful it had been. I don't remember anything specific we said, but we both had the same feeling . . . that the war was useless, crazy. I don't think either of us *said* it, but we both knew."

Back on the hangar deck, we went out to the fantail. Steiner said he'd spent a lot of time there. "It was our hangout," he said. "We'd sit here cleaning our equipment, talking, watching the ocean. It's funny, looking out there now and seeing Sausalito instead of the coast of Vietnam."

The memories were mostly pleasant; he'd always felt safe on the *Okinawa*. But as we walked through the ship, he'd been battling off the familiar anxious feeling that usually preceded one of his spells. The queasiness dissipated as soon as we returned to shore. Later, he would be at a loss to explain why he'd been frightened.

Steiner had proposed that he be hypnotized in order to remember Operation Cochise better. I told him it wasn't necessary, but he insisted that it was something he really wanted to do. He investigated several hypnotherapists and selected a man named Jesse Miller, who lived in the Berkeley Hills.

We visited Miller twice in late February 1982. The first was a preparatory session, to see if Steiner was reasonably stable and receptive to hypnosis. He was; in fact, we both were. It was a wonderful sensation, light, diaphanous, tingly; not at all like the ominous you-are-growing-sleepy trances we had seen in the movies. Miller did not wave any pocket watches or metronomes in our faces, he merely began to speak softly, rhythmically. The trance rolled in like fog; the room seemed to become softer, fuzzier; the armchairs we sat in became deeper and more comfortable.

"Wow," Steiner said later. "That was really neat . . . and really *weird*. I couldn't tell when I was hypnotized and when I wasn't."

A mild euphoria seemed to linger through the evening; but there were also several doubts—in my mind at least—about the wisdom of the enterprise. Steiner had been through a rough time in recent months—the accusation that he was "cold, insensitive and militaristic" at work, the problems communicating with Eve, the constant prodding in couples counseling and group therapy, the strange reappearance of his "spells," the reunion, the dozens of hours we had spent together discussing his past. Many of his most basic assumptions had been called into question, and I suspected that despite his denials he was beginning to wonder about the war's impact on him as well. Perhaps combat had affected him more than he'd realized. I had a feeling that his desire to be hypnotized was part of his quiet search for answers. At the beginning of the first session, Miller had asked, "Why do you want to relive something so unpleasant as the war?"

"I just want to help out Joe," Steiner maintained.

"Don't do it just for me," I repeated. "It isn't necessary."

"Well," he said, "I guess *I'm* kind of curious too."

Jesse Miller was forty-two years old, nationally recognized in his field, and had been practicing hypnotherapy for ten years. He was a charming man, given to casual clothes and the aggressive informality that seems the special province of transplanted New Yorkers in California. His home was light and airy, filled with comfortable furniture, modern art and soft classical music.

The den where Jesse Miller performed his magic was unlike the rest of the house—small, dark, mysterious . . . and filled with bizarre objects that were, in a way, an ironic commentary on his patients' fantasies about hypnosis. There was a crystal ball, a pocket watch, red and white roses, a lamp with mica chips floating and glittering within . . . and dragons everywhere. The walls were covered with paintings of dragons, some playful, some ominous; several of the paintings were done by children. There were tiny joke-shop statues of dragons, and an elaborate modern sculpture of baby dragons hatching from a nest of eggs.

"Why all the dragons?" Steiner asked at the beginning of the second session.

"Good question," Miller said. "People often come to me with certain expectations. They expect me to be a white knight who'll slay their dragons. But that's not realistic. Dragons are a fact of life. We all have them. There are always dragons rumbling around in the basement." Almost imperceptibly, Miller began his work. "What we did last time . . . and what we did together . . . was to have the op-por-tun-ity . . . for you to know me . . . and for you to disco-ver . . . what it might be like . . . to let yourself relax . . . in an easy chair . . . in a strange house . . . to do a different kind of work . . . than you normally do . . . and you can count backwards . . . from two hundred and six . . . and as you are counting . . . you can choose to listen to me . . . or not listen to me. It really doesn't make a difference . . . I'll keep talking . . . and you can relax . . ."

"I can feel it," Steiner said.

"You can feel it . . . and you're *good* at it . . . I don't know . . . what kind of car you *drive* . . . but mine has a dial . . . that measures RPMs . . . and your mind is like a motor . . . and you can rev yourself up . . . but you don't have to go beyond the red line . . . As we're talking today . . . if you feel you're approaching the red line . . . your eyes will open if they're closed . . . and if they're open you can stand up and walk about . . . and anything that happens . . . you'll find you'll be able to forget just as fast . . . because there are things you might find for Joe . . . that you won't need for yourself . . . Forgetting is a natural . . . normal . . . completely regular experience . . . Everyone forgets . . .

"Now you have a good feeling . . . about yourself . . . in your work at the refuge . . . and I want you to get that back . . . the good feeling that you have . . . as a teacher . . . with a group, perhaps . . . and where did you *learrrrn* . . . how to *obserrrve* like that . . . so you could *descriiibe* . . . the grasses . . . and the water . . . and the life . . ."

An odd thing was happening. Steiner found that he could *feel* Vietnam, he even remembered smells long forgotten. For the next hour, he talked about the heat, the leeches, the way his clothes would rot after several weeks in the field, the enormous relief he'd feel when they returned to the ship. Finally, Miller asked, "What do you remember about Operation Cochise?"

"I remember making contact that day. It was real hot and I was real tired, and I remember thinking: Oh shit," Steiner said.

"When you say—*making contact*—what do you mean?"

"When they got ambushed."

"When who got ambushed?"

"The squad."

"Now, I don't *know* . . . much *about* it," Miller's voice—it seemed disembodied—resumed the rhythmic pattern. "So why don't you *tell* me . . . from the beginning . . ."

"Well," Steiner said, "everybody was stretched out in formation, and we were moving forward. And . . . and then . . ." Steiner's chest tightened; he was breathing faster. "Uhhhhm . . . I'm trying to remember if I heard the fire start . . . I must have, but I can't remember . . . But I remember saying, 'We're in contact up ahead.'"

"Up forward there was contact? And someone said that to you?"

"I was stopped at the time. We weren't moving forward. I was standing there . . . and then they made contact, and I got down . . . and we waited for a hell of a long time. I was wondering what was going on . . . I was worried, really worried . . . about what was going to happen. If they were in contact, we were going to have to go forward."

"What kind of thoughts go through a person's mind"—the thin, soft voice pierced the tingling—"while you're lying there?"

"I could imagine the people up front."

"You knew the members of your outfit who were up there?"

"They said it was White's squad . . . and we waited and waited and waited and waited, and didn't know what was going on."

"You were by yourself . . . or someone next to you?"

"I was by myself."

"In the shade? In the sun?"

"In the sun . . . it was all open. It was on a hill, not an abrupt hill, but a gently rolling area . . . and I couldn't see what was up ahead."

"The hill was blocking you?"

"No . . . I don't know. I don't know why I couldn't see. Nobody knew what was going on . . . and I was really worried . . . and really tired."

"Worried about what was going to happen to you?"

"And everybody. I knew people were dead. I knew people were wounded."

"How did you know that?"

"I just knew it. I knew they'd never be able to bring a helicopter in, and there were people lying there in agony, scared to death . . . I just knew that."

"Had you seen that before?"

"It was standard stuff."

"So you knew what to expect. You'd seen people shot?"

"Yeah."

"You'd seen people dead?"

"Yeah."

"And you knew what was up front?"

"Yeah." Steiner's throat had tightened. He tried to remember what had happened next, but he couldn't. He *knew* what happened next, but he couldn't remember it, couldn't say it. He couldn't get himself down off that hill and into the valley.

"I've got to take a leak," he said, sitting up abruptly. "That doesn't break the spell?"

"Not a bit."

". . . You remember a million different times and circumstances . . . and you remember the *day* . . . that you heard the *shooting* . . . and you remember being on that *hill* . . . and not knowing what was *happening* . . . and you remember being *worried* . . . and it must be very *frightening* for an eighteen-year-old boy . . ."

"Nineteen."

"Nineteen-year-old boy . . . to be thinking that this might be it."

"I didn't think that," Steiner said stubbornly.

"You never thought you might be killed?"

"Not that day . . . I felt safe the whole day," Steiner said, wondering how that could possibly be true.

"What were you doing that made you feel that way?"

"I was fighting," Steiner said, realizing that it sounded a little ridiculous. "But I was down low."

"On the hill?"

Steiner thought about the hill, and the fear started coming again. He could feel the hill. "I was scared . . . and worried. Scared, scared, scared . . . and worried. Really scared."

"Really scared . . . and you feel that way now?"

"Well, I do . . ." he started, then pulled back. "But not like I did then."

"John, you should never have to feel as scared as you were then."

"I was really scared."

Jesse Miller could sense the fear, and was somewhat frightened by it himself. He could feel Steiner struggling to hold it back. His heart went out to the small, almost delicate man sitting there, clenched tight—it was hard to imagine Steiner as a soldier. "There is no reason for you to ever have to feel that scared again . . . so frightened of the unknown that was just past the hill." Miller decided reluctantly to press on. "Well . . . you were just there, lying in the sun, being scared and worried . . . When did you know to do something, to move?"

"I was there for the longest time, and knowing that I had to go forward eventually . . . and wondering when . . . I remember observing the tree line where the ambushers were hiding and firing into it . . . before we moved up."

"So you did eventually move up?"

"Yeah, I just . . ." Steiner cleared his throat. "I remember feeling panicked."

"You couldn't see them?"

"No . . . no . . . It was just a terrible feeling. I wasn't crying, but I felt terrible. I felt scared. Worried as hell. I knew I was going to move forward."

"And you didn't want to?"

"I didn't but I did . . . I knew I had to do it."

"You had to? You were going to do your duty . . . and you were scared."

"Shitless. I was scared shitless. I was thinking, Here we go again . . . and why did it have to happen now? Everything was going so well. It was a nice day. We were just moving along. Why now? Why now and why *me*? It was a beautiful day, beautiful, everything was . . ."

"So this was an unexpected event?"

"We didn't expect to get hit. In fact, we expected not to get hit. I counted on it."

"How did you count on it?"

"I just knew. This may sound weird, but I *knew* . . . if I could plan on us having a good day, the chances were we wouldn't make contact."

"That's a very positive perspective," Miller said, "and it kind of makes sense. When something is so awful and terrifying, if you can wish it away, it may make it go away." Miller had a fleeting image of a child marching along with a group of John Wayne types. He was awed by Steiner's strength. "And how does a nineteen-year-old Marine, with all these tough guys who enlisted, experience feeling so frightened and so worried?"

"I acted unfrightened," Steiner said, "as cool and calm as I could get."

"And what about the other people, were they cool and collected too?"

"Yeah ... wait. Muller was crying. But that was later ... a lot later."

"So you were waiting for something to happen, and you heard the noise ... and you were on the hill."

"I can't remember hearing the noise now."

"Close your eyes ... sit back ... take a deep breath ... that's right ... just let your mind wander the way it will ..." Steiner cleared his throat. "Let it keep going ..." Steiner cleared his throat again. "Comfortable ... an easy chair ... you can enjoy that ..."

But no, he couldn't go down the hill.

Miller tried several more times to get Steiner into the battle, but he simply would not go. He was able to talk about going back down into the valley that night to retrieve the bodies, but he refused to remember the experience of battle itself. Finally, Miller asked him what happened the next day.

"It was sunny," Steiner said. "It wasn't too hot then. Early morning. It was nice and sunny. It wasn't such a thick tree line. There were breaks in it, and we walked through the breaks. I don't know who was the first one through. The point guy must have been scared ... I was quite a ways back."

"And you walked through?"

"We walked through the tree line."

"What happened?"

"I looked around, trying to see where they'd been ..."

"Were there signs?"

"Oh yeah, there were flies all over . . . and the odor of blood. Real heavy, moist odor . . . and there were pieces of bandages—our bandages—around. They had gotten them out of our packs . . . There was blood everywhere, just everywhere."

"Was there blood on you?"

"Yeah, there was blood all over the sides of my pants. There was blood everywhere, there was blood everywhere, there was blood and pieces of bandages and bandages . . ."

"Had all the bodies been removed by now?"

"Oh yeah, they'd been removed hours before. They were gone. We went up there in a single file . . . and I remember looking around. The trees were all blown apart. There were splinters of trees everywhere, just ragged stumps, splintery, ragged black stumps . . . and branches, clumps of branches off of trees that were still there."

"Do you remember what your thoughts were, seeing all of this?"

"A couple. I was pissed. I was sad . . ."

And then, suddenly, Steiner exploded in tears with a ferocious vehemence that was truly horrifying. He let out a deep wail, and his body shuddered. He struggled against the tears, trying to pull himself together, but they exploded from him again . . . and then again. Miller and I glanced at each other. For a moment, I was afraid that John wouldn't be able to pull himself together, that he had simply shattered from the force of the eruption. I realized that I was crying too . . . and then he stopped.

"Are you okay?" Miller asked.

"Yeah, well, I guess I was pretty sad," Steiner said. "Could I have a glass of water or something?"

"Would you like something stronger?"

"A shot of bourbon would be very good."

Miller went to the kitchen, and Steiner to the bathroom. When they returned, Miller said, "You know, John, it's very different reading about a war in a newspaper and hearing you describe it . . . Sometimes it's tough being tough—that cry might have been fifteen years in the coming."

"Hmmm," Steiner said.

"You're just a normal human being," Miller continued, "and

you've been through some of the most unbelievable stress that could be . . . and you had to see some of the most awful, inhuman, disgusting . . ."

"And that was only one day," Steiner said. "You know, I wonder if any of the North Vietnamese are in hypnosis, reliving the same battle . . ."

That was something he'd realized while he was crying. The North Vietnamese had been through the same ordeal. Worse, maybe. He'd been crying for them too.

We went to lunch, and had another drink. Then we went to a park and Steiner played with his dog, Snoopy. He stood in the middle of a field and threw a rubber ball high in the air; the dog would catch it in flight, and return it to him.

"I have a terrible headache," he said.

He took a nap. When he awoke, the headache was gone and Steiner was Steiner again. "Please don't tell Eve what happened," he said. "I'll tell her myself, later."

"Do you want me to write about this?" I asked.

"Sure," he said, "why not?"

———

"Is he going to be okay?" I asked Jesse Miller the next day.

"I think so," he said. "He's a pretty strong fellow. He's had to be *very* strong to control those emotions the way he has, and still have the energy to live a normal, valuable, creative life."

———

It was a brilliant day, blue and clear with a light breeze, a perfect Saturday. Steiner stood outside the refuge, waiting to begin his regular weekend morning nature walk. He was wearing a khaki Fish and Wildlife Service shirt, neatly pressed and starched, and brown denim jeans. "Doesn't look like anyone's coming," he said. "Usually I get a pretty good crowd on Saturdays . . . Oh well, if no one comes, we'll walk it ourselves."

Just then, two women and a boy appeared and asked where they could find the nature walk.

"This is it," Steiner said. "Let's go."

The women were in their mid-thirties, and fairly slouchy. One had her hair done up in curlers, covered by a scarf; the other was bleached blond, and wore sunglasses. The boy was blond, about ten years old, with random teeth and a runny nose.

Steiner led them down a narrow path from the refuge, along the spine of a scraggly hill. He stopped abruptly and whispered, "Hey, look, you see that?"

"What?" asked the boy.

"The butterfly, see what it's doing?"

"Just sitting there," the boy said, not very interested.

"It's *basking*," Steiner said. "You know why it does that? Because it has to warm up in order to function. It just basks in the sun. That's why you rarely see butterflies flying around in the morning, and never on cold days. It has to reach what's called a *threshold* temperature before it has the strength to fly. Now, that one is called an anise butterfly. I'll show you why . . . c'mon over here."

The women followed Steiner to a weed-like plant. The boy, already bored, moseyed on ahead. John took several leaves from the plant and spindled them in his hand. "Smell that," he said.

"Licorice," said one woman.

"Fennel," Steiner said. "They get anise from it, and licorice from anise. The anise butterflies usually lay their eggs on fennel."

Steiner moved on to where the boy had stopped; as he approached, the boy wiped his nose and spun away. "Hey, wait a minute!" Steiner said. "This is a great plant here, just a *super* plant . . . It's called the Indian soap plant. I'll show you why." He crouched down and pulled out the plant by its roots, then slipped a white bulb-like core from the skin. "Feel this," he said. The boy kept his distance. Steiner handed the bulb to one of the women. "Feels pretty slippery, doesn't it? Well, they say the Indians used to use it as soap—and it does contain an emulsifier."

"Is it a flowering plant?" the blond woman asked.

"You bet," Steiner said. "It's a lily . . . and it flowers only at night, a beautiful white lily."

He continued down the hill and around a bend, bouncing along as usual to cover his limp. The boy ran on ahead. Steiner yelled after him, "Hey, look up on the rocks, on the side of the hill."

The boy stopped and looked. There were lizards all over the place. "See what they're doing?" Steiner said. "It looks like they're doing push-ups, doesn't it?"

The boy picked up a handful of rocks and started throwing them at the lizards. The blond woman yelled at him, "Cool it, for Christ's sake!" The boy walked away, kicking a pebble.

"Why *do* they do that?" the woman in curlers asked.

"Well, those are western fence lizards and it's believed the males do that as a kind of aggressive posture, protecting their turf."

"Does it have anything to do with mating?"

"Probably," Steiner said.

The women laughed. "Typical men," said the blonde. "They're not much different from a lot of guys I know."

Steiner led them down to the water's edge and onto a catwalk that spanned the salt marsh. The boy skipped ahead, dragging a stick along the picket side rail. "Most people think a salt marsh is pretty boring and ugly," Steiner said, "but it's just a *factory* of life."

The women peered over the rail at a channel through the marsh. The water seemed to be moving in opposite directions at once; the channel was clear in the middle and cloudy with silt at the edges. "Why is the water moving in two different directions?" the woman in curlers asked.

"It's not," he said. "It just looks that way. The tide is going out, but the breeze is coming in and riffling the surface. You know, if you picked up two handfuls of mud down there, you'd be holding about sixty thousand living organisms in your hands. The cordgrass out here is submerged about twenty-three hours per day, and it grows faster than just about anything on earth except a coral reef. It grows and it dies, and it decays and produces protein . . . lots and lots of protein. It's not hard to see why this is probably where life began . . ."

"What's this?" the boy interrupted. He was holding a small brown clump of congealed something or other in his hand.

"Yeccch," said the blonde. "Drop it!"

"No, wait," Steiner said, taking it from the boy and breaking it apart. "This is very interesting. It's an owl pellet. We've got lots of owls out here, and they eat mice. This is all the stuff an owl can't digest—the hair, the bones and so on. They cough these things up in a ball. Now, look, this little thing is a bone from a mouse's forearm. Do you know the names of the bones in the forearm?"

"The radius?"

"Hey, *very* good. How'd you know that?"

"We learned it in school."

"Well, you're right. The radius is in the forearm. But this isn't a radius. What's another bone in the forearm?"

"The ulna?"

"Right!" Steiner said triumphantly—he had the boy's full attention now—and giggling. He held up the toothpick of a bone. "This," he declared, "is the ulna of a mouse!"

"What's that shack down by the water?" the boy asked.

"The shack?" Steiner said. He took the boy by the hand. "That is a really neat shack. C'mon, I'll show you . . ."

ACKNOWLEDGMENTS

I would like to thank Barbara Cooper, John and Elizabeth Wakefield, Dale and Sandy Szuminski, Bill and Barbara Taylor, John Steiner and Eve Holguin for allowing me to intrude upon their lives for weeks at a time, sleep on their couches, eat their food and pester them with innumerable late-night phone calls. They suffered my prying with patience and dignity; I hope I haven't betrayed their trust.

Also to be thanked are the Cooper, Wakefield, Szuminski, Taylor and Steiner families and friends—parents, brothers and sisters, aunts and uncles, former spouses and drinking buddies—the staff of the Indianapolis Vet Center, Jesse Miller . . . and the other members of the platoon who cooperated in the writing of this book: Wayne Pilgreen, Mel Sands, Burt Wilson, Richard Vanderwalker, Ed Kalwara, Charles Drust, Thomas Clark, Dave Muller, Leon Sheoships, Theodore Kochmaruk, Gerald F. Reczek, Martin Rangel and Brett Eugene Stinney.

Bobby Muller and John P. Wilson helped me to understand post-traumatic stress disorder, as did Drs. John Lipkin, Arthur Blank, John Talbott, Herbert Hendin and Paul Singer. Bill Brew of the Senate Veterans Affairs Committee helped with the legislative history, and Dr. Paul Kaunitz was a continual source of support, advice and the latest clippings from the psychiatric journals.

Terry McDonnell, David Rosenthal and Jann Wenner of *Rolling Stone*—and Bob Gottlieb, Martha Kaplan and Chuck Elliott of Knopf—once again indulged my penchant for the obscure.

Finally, I'd like to thank Victoria Kaunitz for tolerating my extended absences—and, occasionally, my presences—during the past three years with extraordinary patience and good grace. The war came home for her too.

ACKNOWLEDGMENTS

PERMISSIONS ACKNOWLEDGMENTS

Grateful acknowledgment is made to the following for permission to reprint previously published material.

ATV Music Group: Lyrics from "You Never Give Me Your Money" by John Lennon and Paul McCartney, © 1969 Northern Songs Limited. All rights for the United States and Mexico controlled by Maclen Music, Inc., c/o ATV Music Corp. Used by permission. All Rights Reserved.

Basic Books, Inc.: Excerpts from *Home From the War* by Robert Jay Lifton. Copyright © 1974 by Robert Jay Lifton. Reprinted by permission of the publisher.

Chatto and Windus Ltd and the Literary Estate of Wilfred Owen: Excerpts from "Smile, Smile Smile" and "Insensibility," in Wilfred Owen: *The Collected Poems of Wilfred Owen,* Copyright © 1963 by Chatto and Windus Ltd. Reprinted by permission of the author's Literary Estate, Chatto and Windus, and New Directions Publishing Corp.

Rosica Colin Ltd: Excerpts from *Cooper* by Richard Aldington, © Madame Catherine Guillaume.

Peer International Corporation: An excerpt from the lyrics to "Everyday" by Norman Petty and Charles Hardin, Copyright © 1957 Peer International Corporation. All Rights Reserved. Used by Permission.

Viking Penguin Inc.: Excerpts from "Does It Matter?" and "Repressions of War Experience," in *Collected Poems* by Siegfried Sassoon, Copyright 1918 by E. P. Dutton & Co., Copyright 1946 by Siegfried Sassoon.

Reprinted by permission of Viking Penguin Inc. All rights reserved. Rights outside of the U.S. administered by the Estate of Siegfried Sassoon. Reprinted by permission of George Sassoon.

Warner Bros. Music: An excerpt from the lyrics to "Blowin' in the Wind" by Bob Dylan, © 1962 Warner Bros., Inc. All Rights Reserved. Used by Permission.

ABOUT THE AUTHOR

Joe Klein is an award-winning journalist and the author of seven books, including the #1 bestseller *Primary Colors* and most recently, *Charlie Mike*. His weekly *Time* column, In the Arena, covers U.S. politics, elections, and foreign policy and has won two National Headliner Awards for best magazine column. Previously, he served as Washington correspondent for *The New Yorker* and as a political columnist for *Newsweek*. Klein is a member of the Council on Foreign Relations and a former Guggenheim fellow.